黒鷺死体宅配便
the KUROSAGI corpse delivery service

story
EIJI OTSUKA

art
HOUSUI YAMAZAKI

original cover design
BUNPEI YORIFUJI

translation
TOSHIFUMI YOSHIDA

editor and english adaptation
CARL GUSTAV HORN

lettering and touch-up
IHL

DARK
HORSE
MANGA

contents

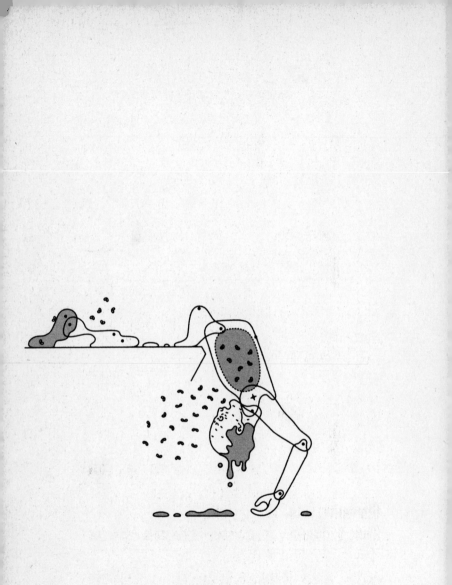

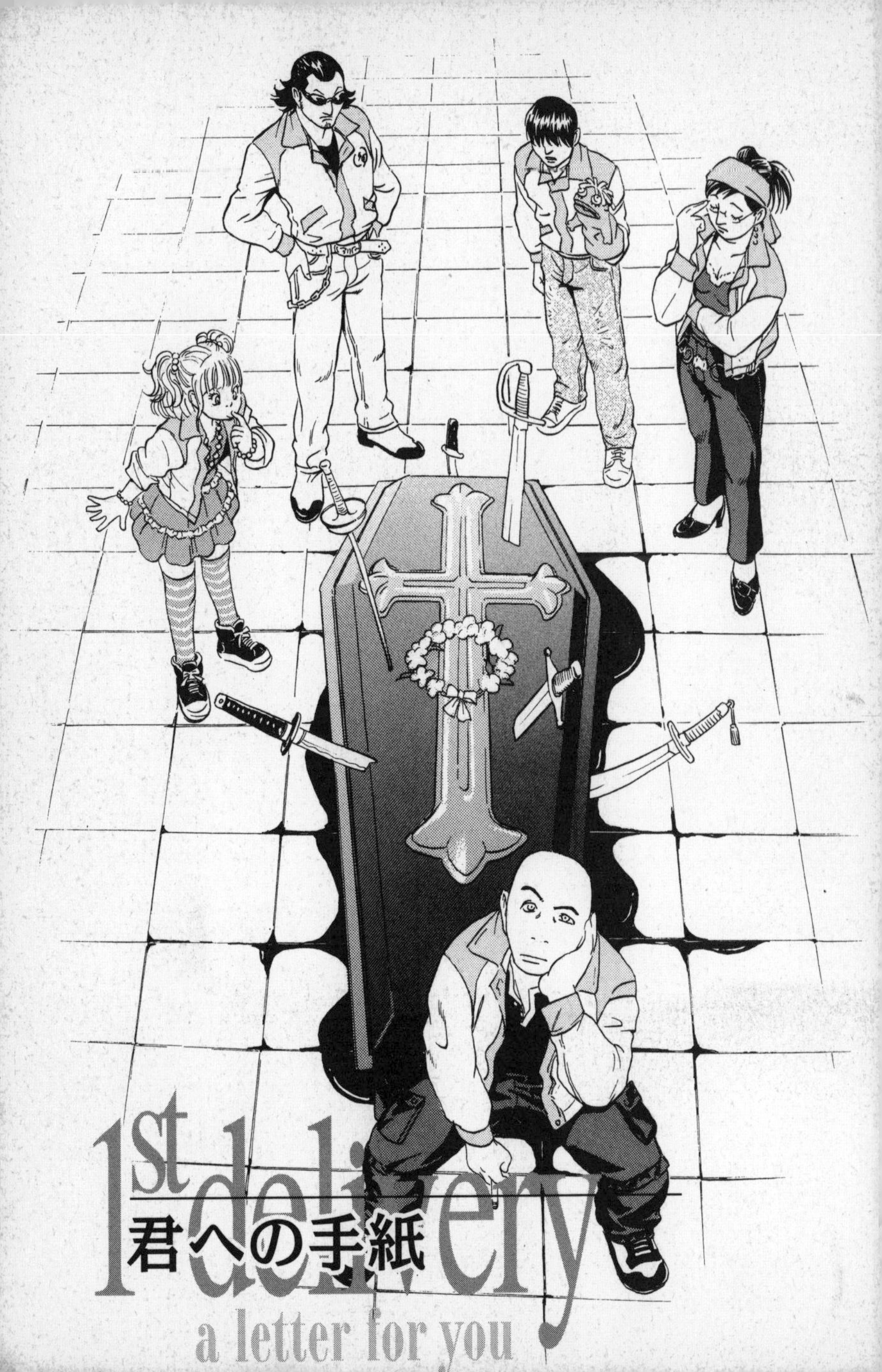

1st delivery
君への手紙
a letter for you

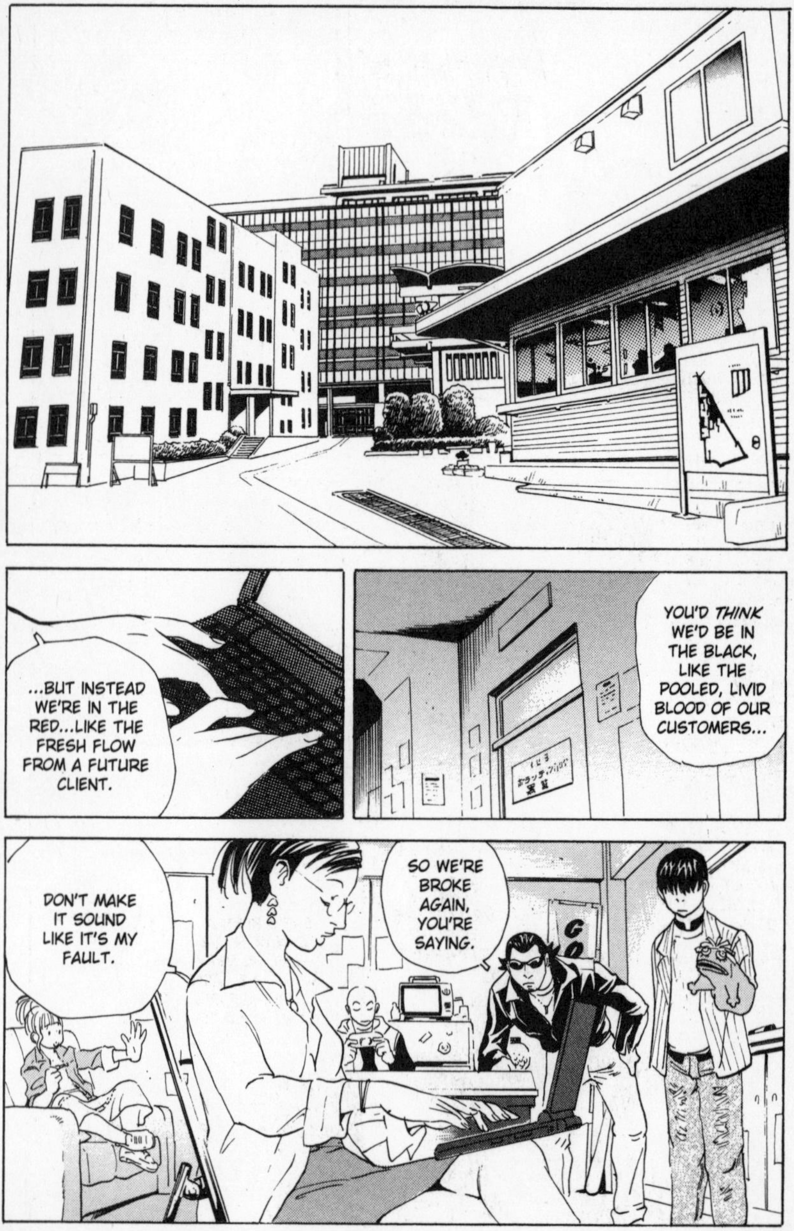
YOU'D *THINK* WE'D BE IN THE BLACK, LIKE THE POOLED, LIVID BLOOD OF OUR CUSTOMERS...
...BUT INSTEAD WE'RE IN THE RED...LIKE THE FRESH FLOW FROM A FUTURE CLIENT.
SO WE'RE BROKE AGAIN, YOU'RE SAYING.
DON'T MAKE IT SOUND LIKE IT'S MY FAULT.

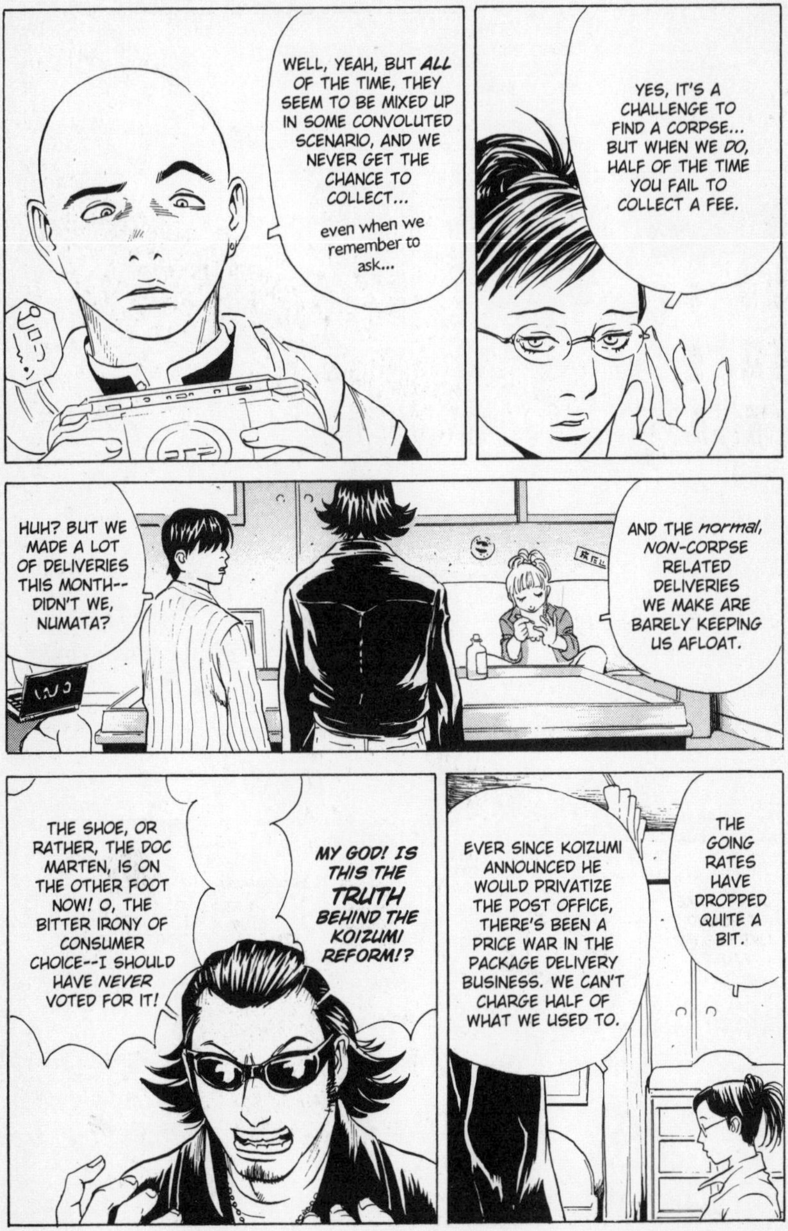
YES, IT'S A CHALLENGE TO FIND A CORPSE... BUT WHEN WE *DO*, HALF OF THE TIME YOU FAIL TO COLLECT A FEE.
WELL, YEAH, BUT *ALL* OF THE TIME, THEY SEEM TO BE MIXED UP IN SOME CONVOLUTED SCENARIO, AND WE NEVER GET THE CHANCE TO COLLECT...
even when we remember to ask...
AND THE *normal*, *NON*-CORPSE RELATED DELIVERIES WE MAKE ARE BARELY KEEPING US AFLOAT.
HUH? BUT WE MADE A LOT OF DELIVERIES THIS MONTH--DIDN'T WE, NUMATA?
THE GOING RATES HAVE DROPPED QUITE A BIT.
EVER SINCE KOIZUMI ANNOUNCED HE WOULD PRIVATIZE THE POST OFFICE, THERE'S BEEN A PRICE WAR IN THE PACKAGE DELIVERY BUSINESS. WE CAN'T CHARGE HALF OF WHAT WE USED TO.
*MY GOD! IS THIS THE **TRUTH** BEHIND THE KOIZUMI REFORM!?*
THE SHOE, OR RATHER, THE DOC MARTEN, IS ON THE OTHER FOOT NOW! O, THE BITTER IRONY OF CONSUMER CHOICE--I SHOULD HAVE *NEVER* VOTED FOR IT!

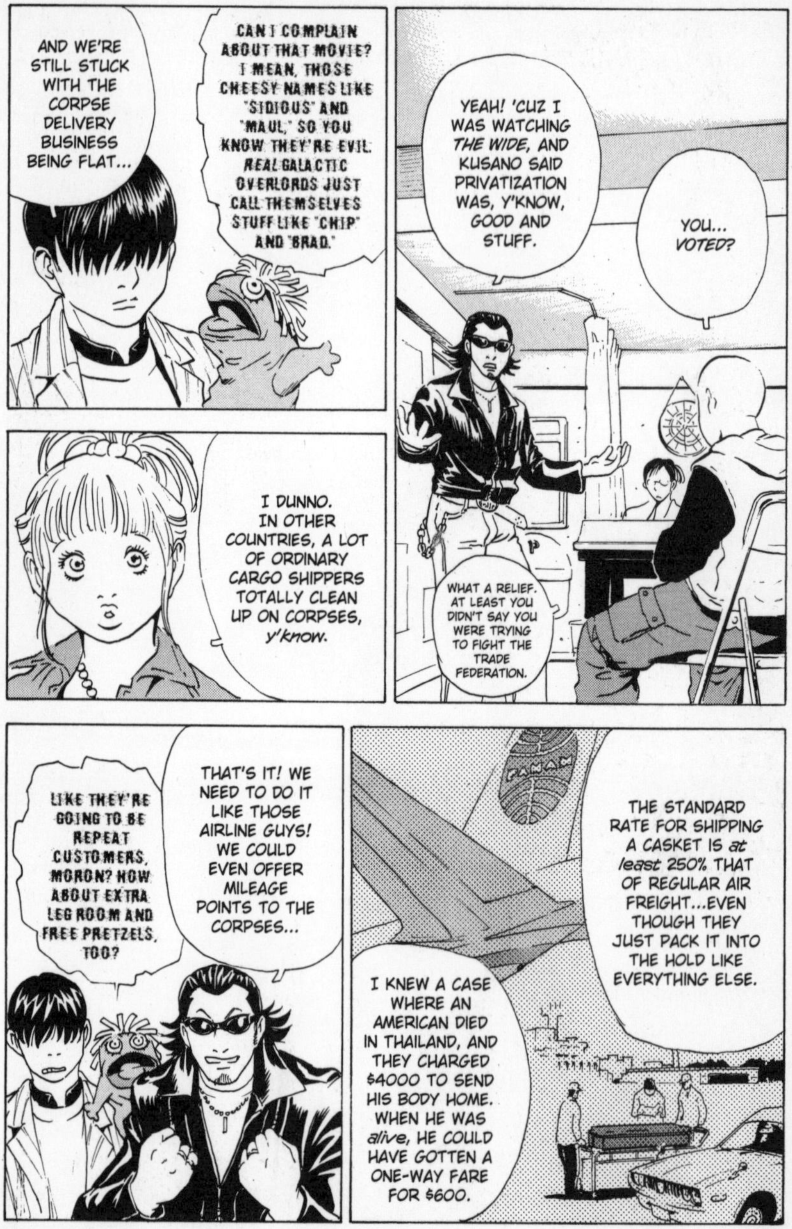
YOU... VOTED?
YEAH! 'CUZ I WAS WATCHING THE WIDE, AND KUSANO SAID PRIVATIZATION WAS, Y'KNOW, GOOD AND STUFF.
WHAT A RELIEF. AT LEAST YOU DIDN'T SAY YOU WERE TRYING TO FIGHT THE TRADE FEDERATION.
CAN I COMPLAIN ABOUT THAT MOVIE? I MEAN, THOSE CHEESY NAMES LIKE "SIDIOUS" AND "MAUL," SO YOU KNOW THEY'RE EVIL. REAL GALACTIC OVERLORDS JUST CALL THEMSELVES STUFF LIKE "CHIP" AND "BRAD."
AND WE'RE STILL STUCK WITH THE CORPSE DELIVERY BUSINESS BEING FLAT...
I DUNNO. IN OTHER COUNTRIES, A LOT OF ORDINARY CARGO SHIPPERS TOTALLY CLEAN UP ON CORPSES, y'know.
THE STANDARD RATE FOR SHIPPING A CASKET IS at least 250% THAT OF REGULAR AIR FREIGHT...EVEN THOUGH THEY JUST PACK IT INTO THE HOLD LIKE EVERYTHING ELSE.
I KNEW A CASE WHERE AN AMERICAN DIED IN THAILAND, AND THEY CHARGED $4000 TO SEND HIS BODY HOME. WHEN HE WAS alive, HE COULD HAVE GOTTEN A ONE-WAY FARE FOR $600.
THAT'S IT! WE NEED TO DO IT LIKE THOSE AIRLINE GUYS! WE COULD EVEN OFFER MILEAGE POINTS TO THE CORPSES...
LIKE THEY'RE GOING TO BE REPEAT CUSTOMERS, MORON? HOW ABOUT EXTRA LEG ROOM AND FREE PRETZELS, TOO?

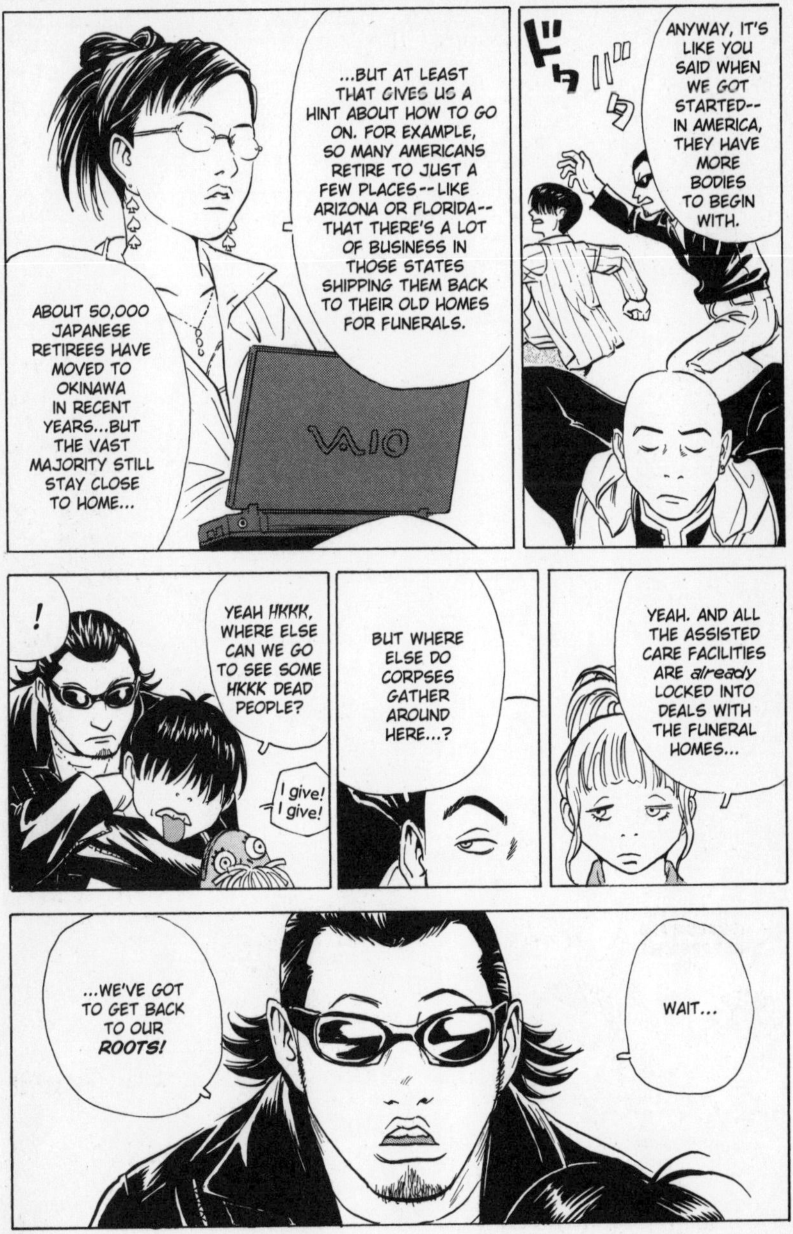
ANYWAY, IT'S LIKE YOU SAID WHEN WE GOT STARTED-- IN AMERICA, THEY HAVE MORE BODIES TO BEGIN WITH.
ドタバタ
...BUT AT LEAST THAT GIVES US A HINT ABOUT HOW TO GO ON. FOR EXAMPLE, SO MANY AMERICANS RETIRE TO JUST A FEW PLACES--LIKE ARIZONA OR FLORIDA--THAT THERE'S A LOT OF BUSINESS IN THOSE STATES SHIPPING THEM BACK TO THEIR OLD HOMES FOR FUNERALS.
ABOUT 50,000 JAPANESE RETIREES HAVE MOVED TO OKINAWA IN RECENT YEARS...BUT THE VAST MAJORITY STILL STAY CLOSE TO HOME...
VAIO
YEAH. AND ALL THE ASSISTED CARE FACILITIES ARE *already* LOCKED INTO DEALS WITH THE FUNERAL HOMES...
BUT WHERE ELSE DO CORPSES GATHER AROUND HERE...?
YEAH HKKK, WHERE ELSE CAN WE GO TO SEE SOME HKKK DEAD PEOPLE?
!
I give! I give!
WAIT...
...WE'VE GOT TO GET BACK TO OUR *ROOTS!*

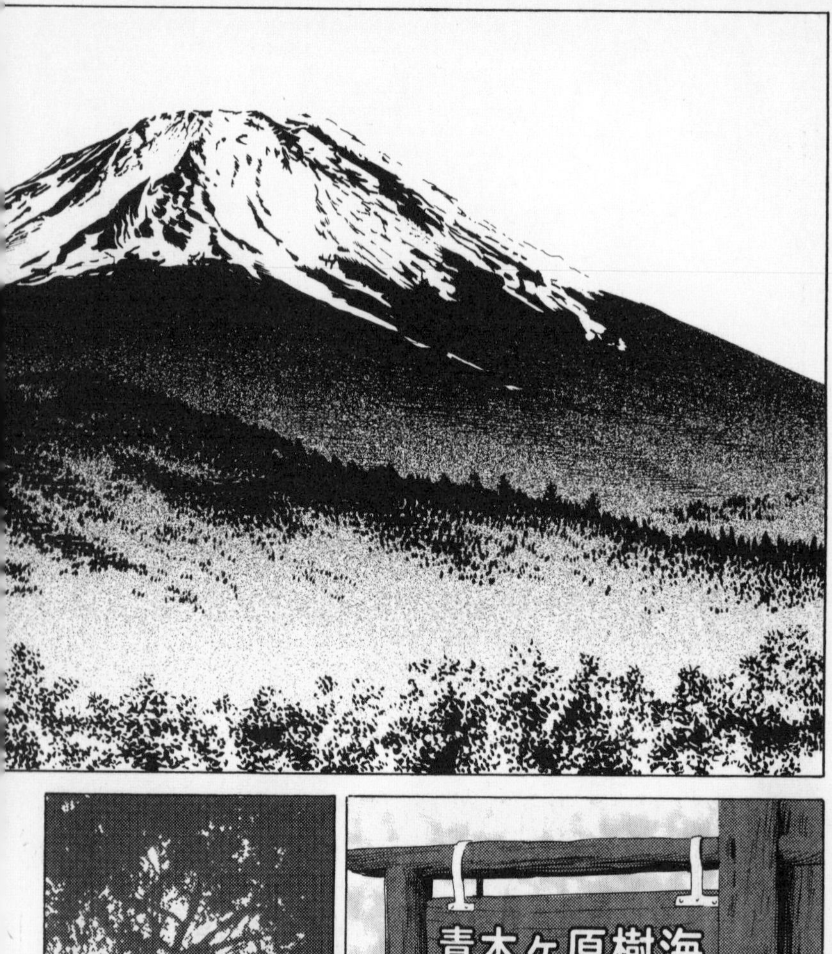

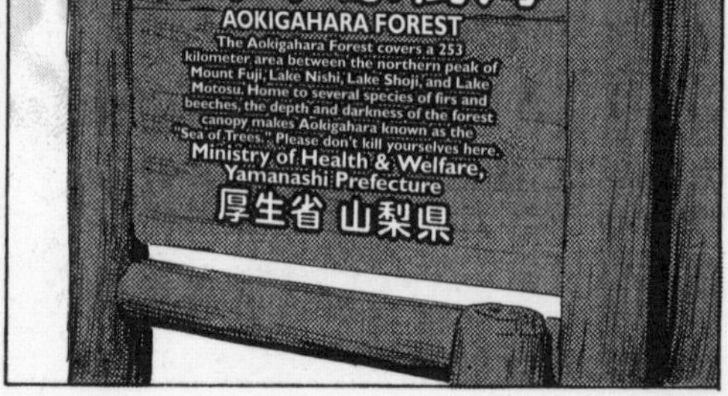
青木ヶ原樹海
AOKIGAHARA FOREST
The Aokigahara Forest covers a 253 kilometer area between the northern peak of Mount Fuji, Lake Nishi, Lake Shoji, and Lake Motosu. Home to several species of firs and beeches, the depth and darkness of the forest canopy makes Aokigahara known as the "Sea of Trees." Please don't kill yourselves here.
Ministry of Health & Welfare, Yamanashi Prefecture
厚生省 山梨県

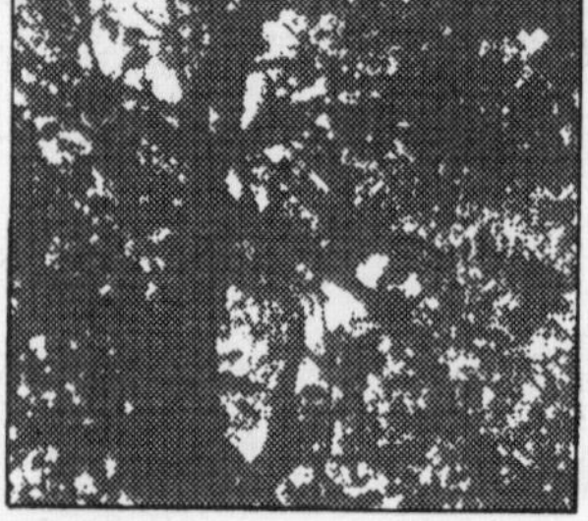

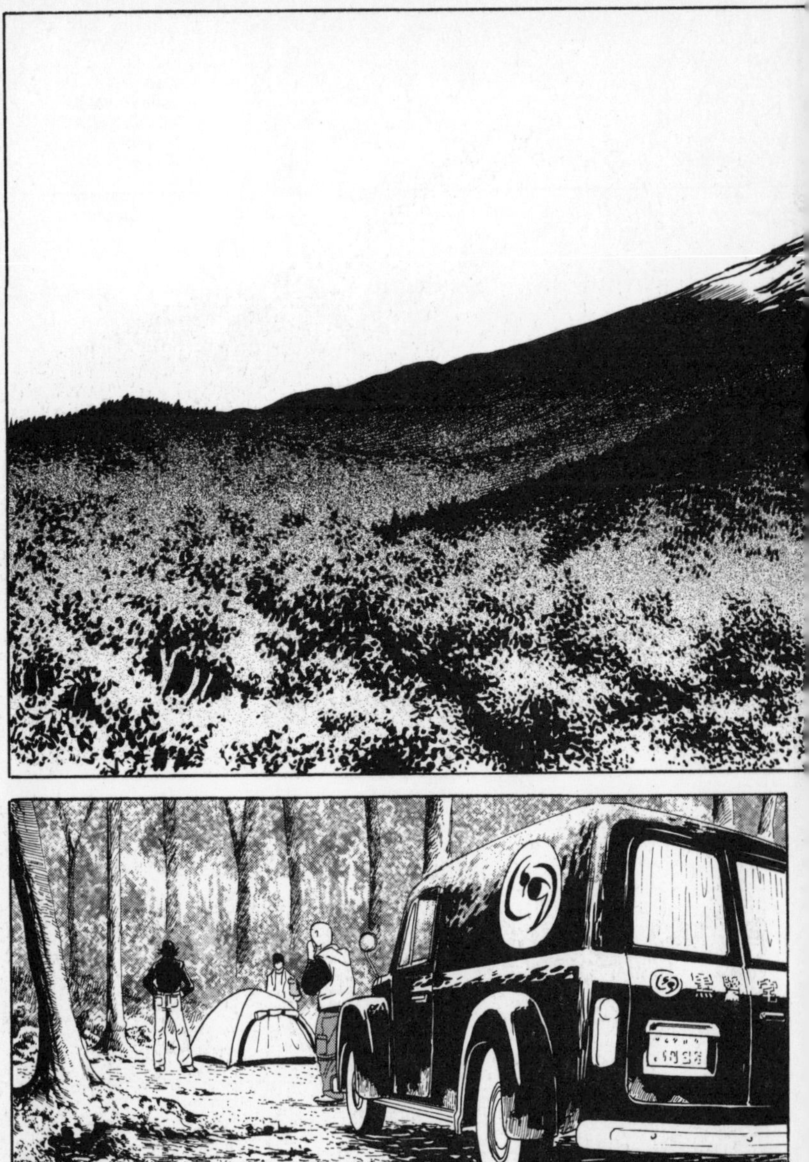

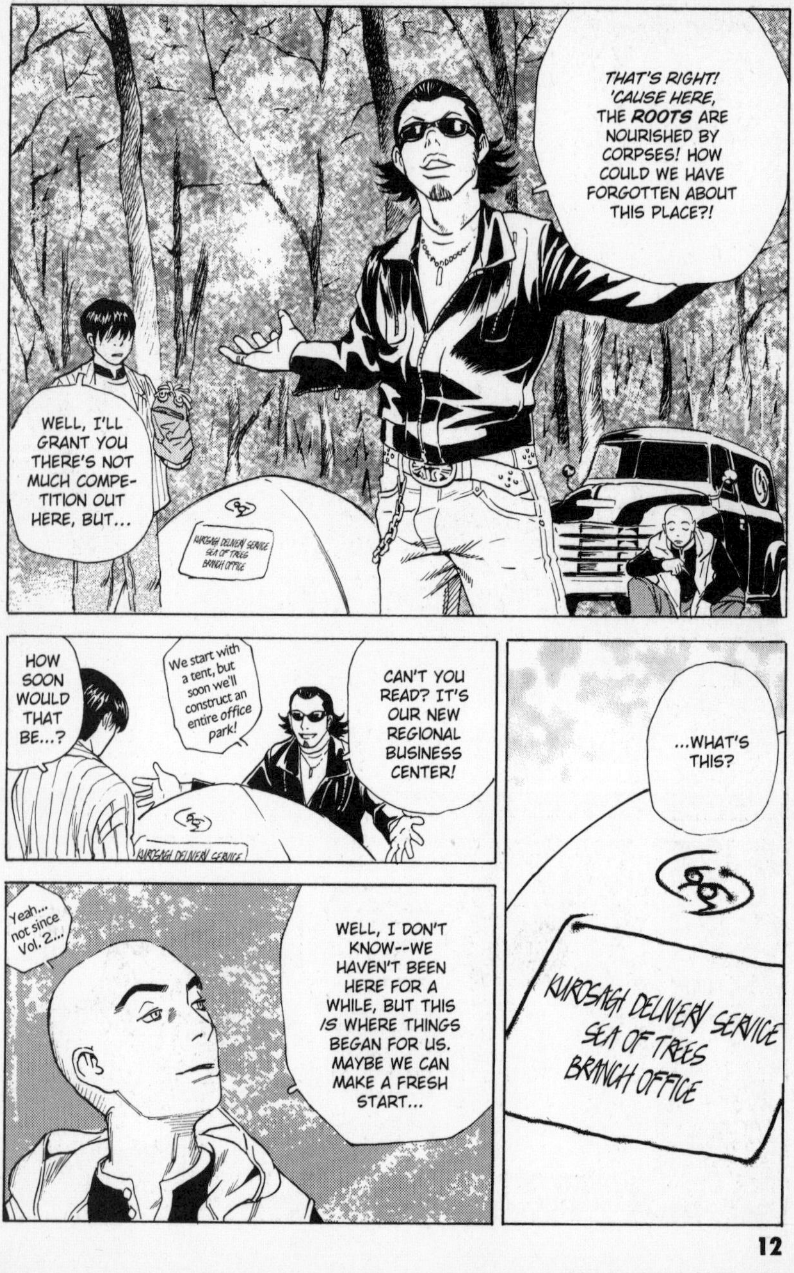
THAT'S RIGHT! 'CAUSE HERE, THE ROOTS ARE NOURISHED BY CORPSES! HOW COULD WE HAVE FORGOTTEN ABOUT THIS PLACE?!
WELL, I'LL GRANT YOU THERE'S NOT MUCH COMPE-TITION OUT HERE, BUT...
KUROSAGI DELIVERY SERVICE SEA OF TREES BRANCH OFFICE
...WHAT'S THIS?
KUROSAGI DELIVERY SERVICE SEA OF TREES BRANCH OFFICE
CAN'T YOU READ? IT'S OUR NEW REGIONAL BUSINESS CENTER!
We start with a tent, but soon we'll construct an entire office park!
HOW SOON WOULD THAT BE...?
KUROSAGI DELIVERY SERVICE
WELL, I DON'T KNOW--WE HAVEN'T BEEN HERE FOR A WHILE, BUT THIS IS WHERE THINGS BEGAN FOR US. MAYBE WE CAN MAKE A FRESH START...
Yeah... not since Vol. 2...

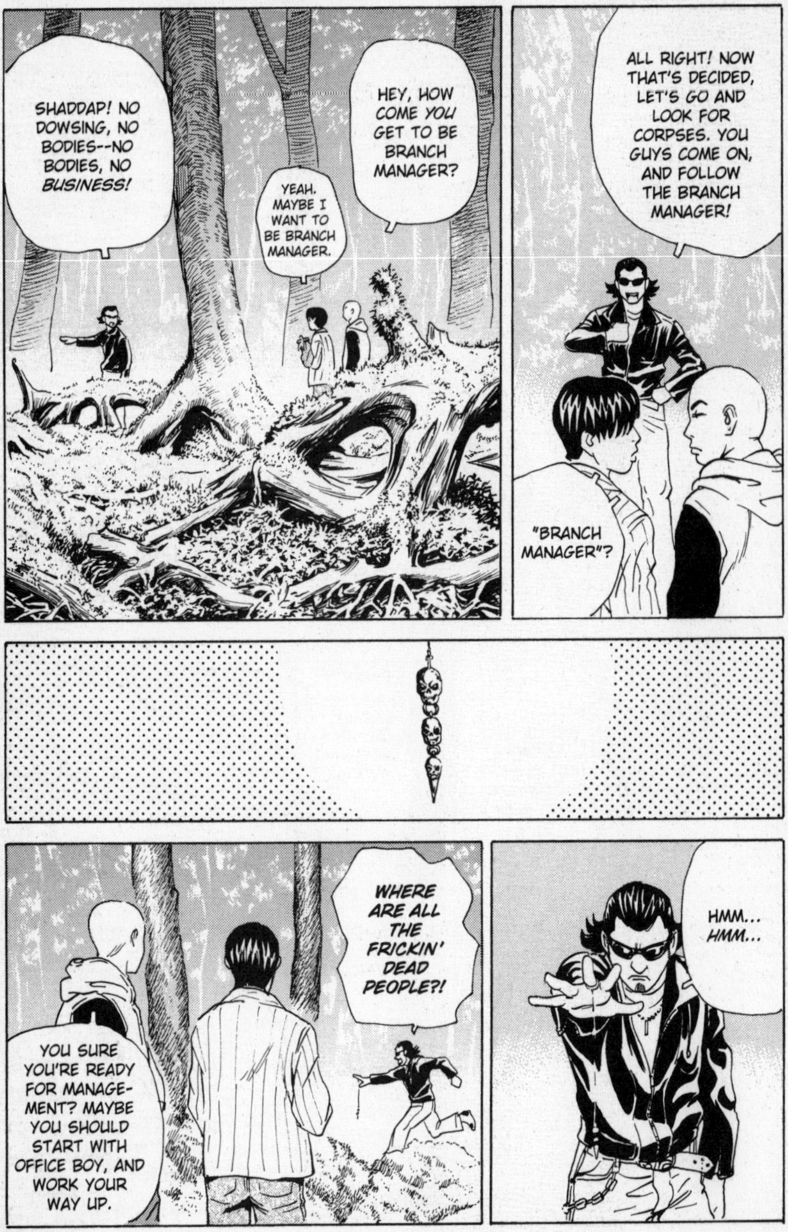
ALL RIGHT! NOW THAT'S DECIDED, LET'S GO AND LOOK FOR CORPSES. YOU GUYS COME ON, AND FOLLOW THE BRANCH MANAGER!
"BRANCH MANAGER"?
HEY, HOW COME *YOU* GET TO BE BRANCH MANAGER?
YEAH. MAYBE I WANT TO BE BRANCH MANAGER.
SHADDAP! NO DOWSING, NO BODIES--NO BODIES, NO *BUSINESS!*
HMM... *HMM...*
WHERE ARE ALL THE FRICKIN' DEAD PEOPLE?!
YOU SURE YOU'RE READY FOR MANAGEMENT? MAYBE YOU SHOULD START WITH OFFICE BOY, AND WORK YOUR WAY UP.

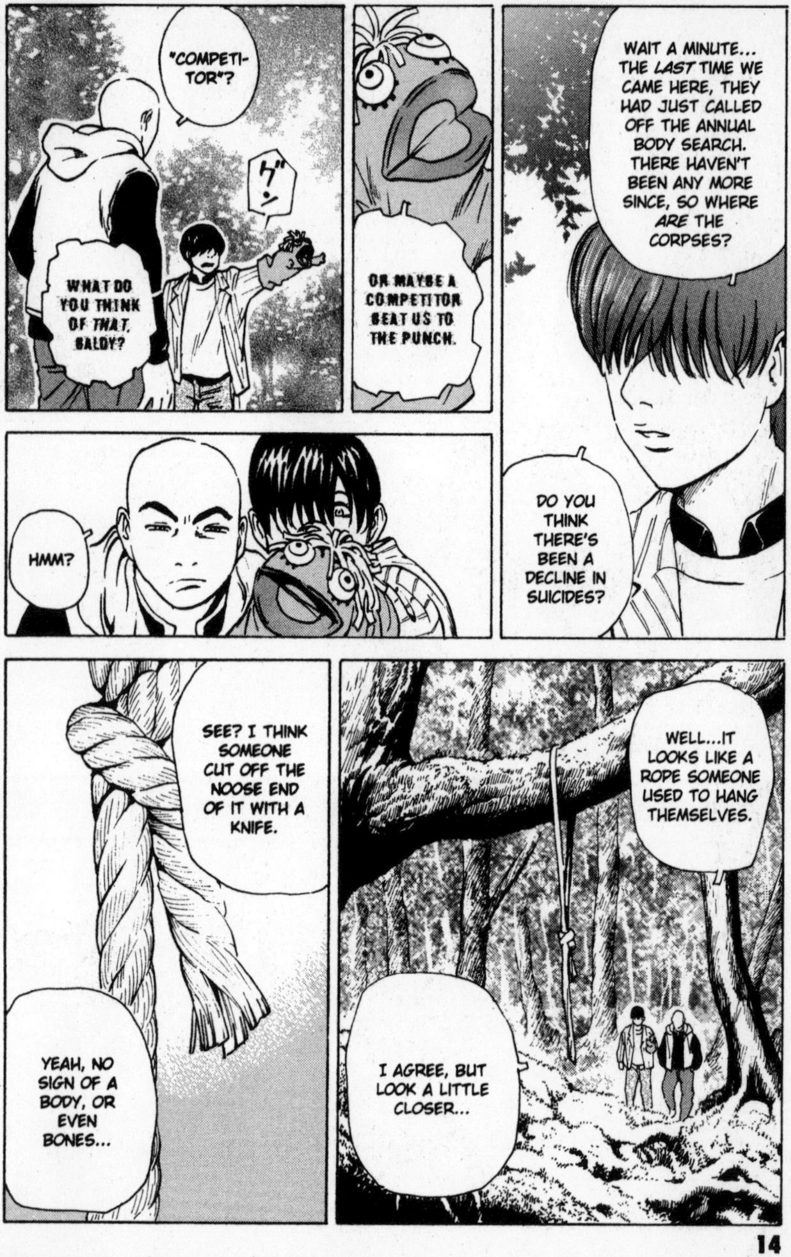
WAIT A MINUTE... THE *LAST* TIME WE CAME HERE, THEY HAD JUST CALLED OFF THE ANNUAL BODY SEARCH. THERE HAVEN'T BEEN ANY MORE SINCE, SO WHERE *ARE* THE CORPSES?
DO YOU THINK THERE'S BEEN A DECLINE IN SUICIDES?
OR MAYBE A COMPETITOR BEAT US TO THE PUNCH.
"COMPETI-TOR"?
ゲン
WHAT DO YOU THINK OF *THAT,* BALDY?
HMM?
WELL...IT LOOKS LIKE A ROPE SOMEONE USED TO HANG THEMSELVES.
I AGREE, BUT LOOK A LITTLE CLOSER...
SEE? I THINK SOMEONE CUT OFF THE NOOSE END OF IT WITH A KNIFE.
YEAH, NO SIGN OF A BODY, OR EVEN BONES...

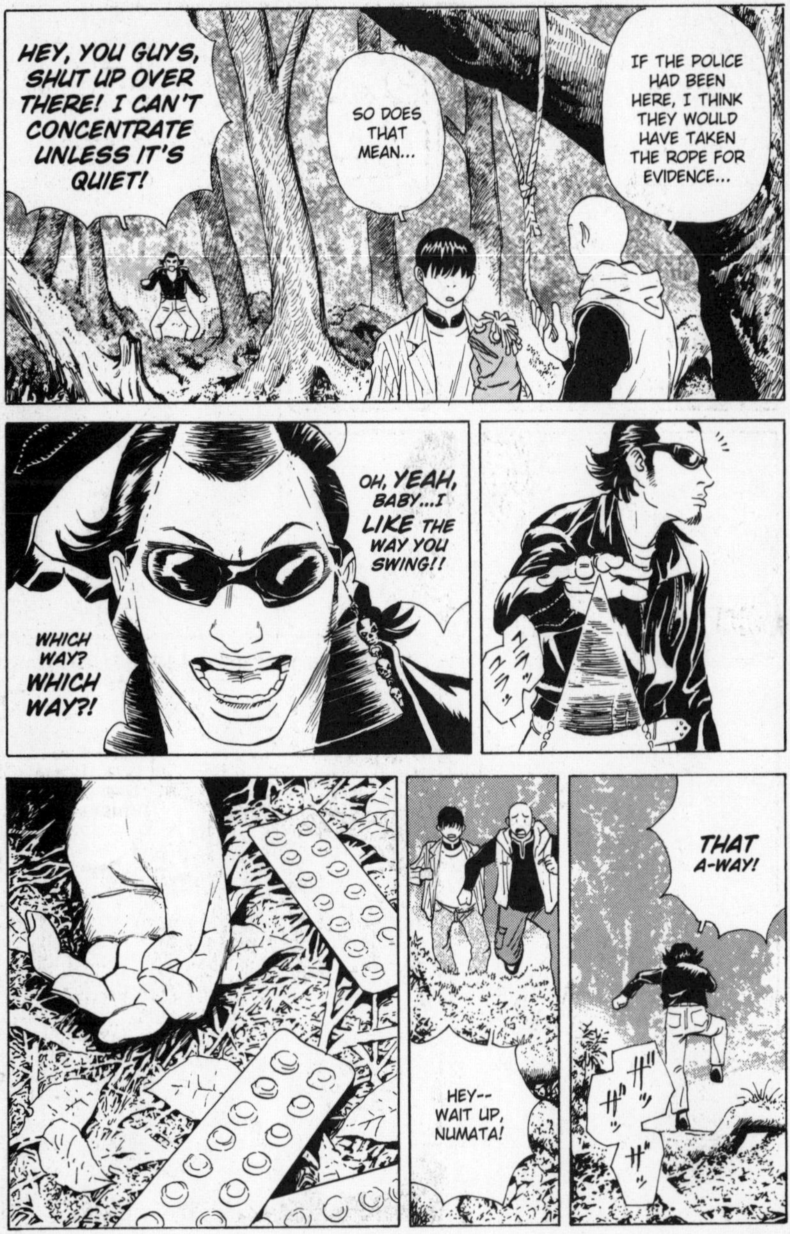
IF THE POLICE HAD BEEN HERE, I THINK THEY WOULD HAVE TAKEN THE ROPE FOR EVIDENCE...
SO DOES THAT MEAN...
HEY, YOU GUYS, SHUT UP OVER THERE! I CAN'T CONCENTRATE UNLESS IT'S QUIET!
OH, YEAH, BABY...I LIKE THE WAY YOU SWING!!
WHICH WAY? WHICH WAY?!
THAT A-WAY!
HEY-- WAIT UP, NUMATA!

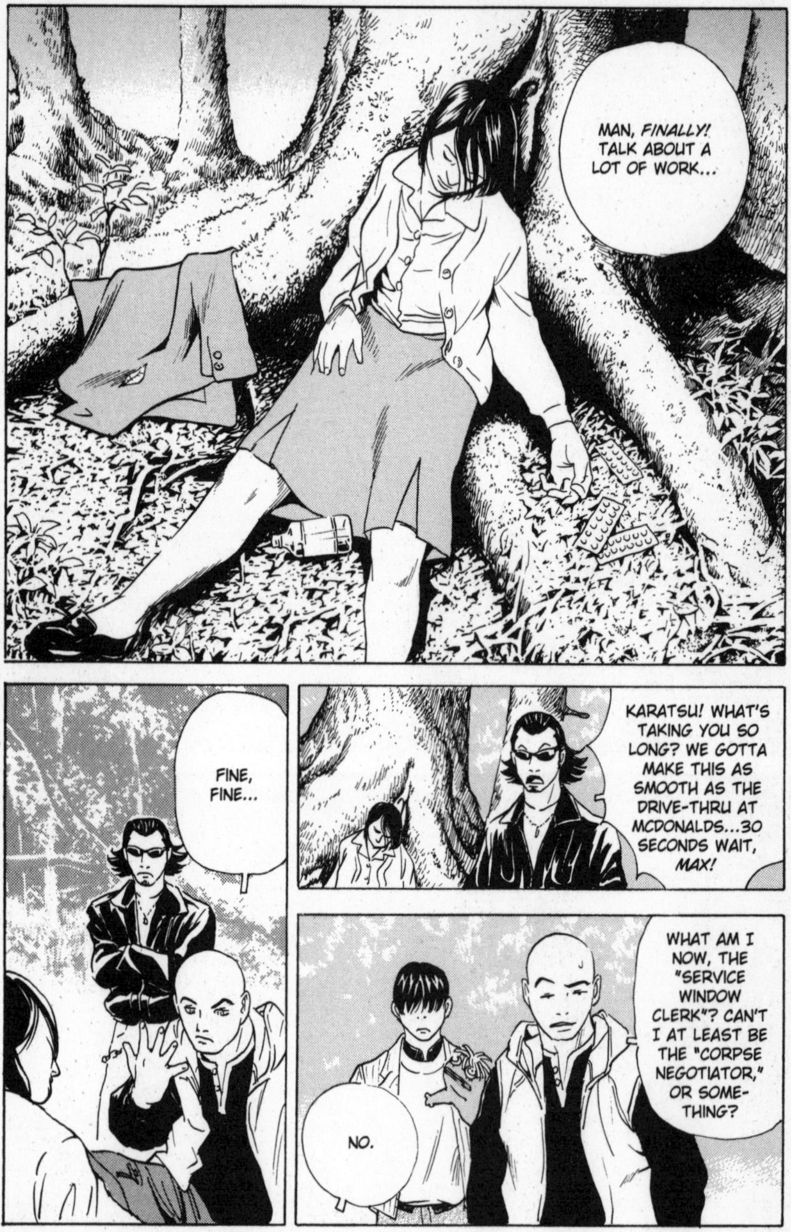
MAN, *FINALLY!* TALK ABOUT A LOT OF WORK...
KARATSU! WHAT'S TAKING YOU SO LONG? WE GOTTA MAKE THIS AS SMOOTH AS THE DRIVE-THRU AT MCDONALDS...30 SECONDS WAIT, *MAX!*
WHAT AM I NOW, THE "SERVICE WINDOW CLERK"? CAN'T I AT LEAST BE THE "CORPSE NEGOTIATOR," OR SOME-THING?
NO.
FINE, FINE...

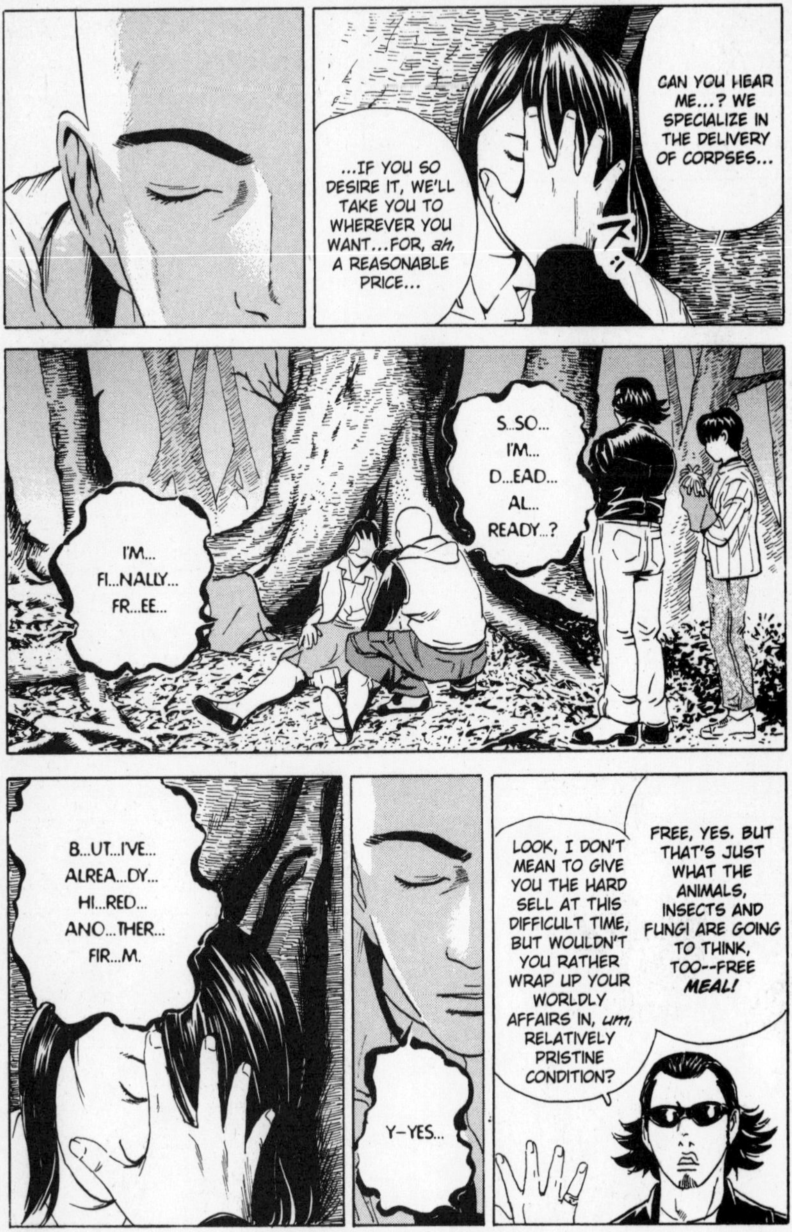
CAN YOU HEAR ME...? WE SPECIALIZE IN THE DELIVERY OF CORPSES...
...IF YOU SO DESIRE IT, WE'LL TAKE YOU TO WHEREVER YOU WANT...FOR, *ah,* A REASONABLE PRICE...
S...SO... I'M... D...EAD... AL... READY...?
I'M... FI...NALLY... FR...EE...
FREE, YES. BUT THAT'S JUST WHAT THE ANIMALS, INSECTS AND FUNGI ARE GOING TO THINK, TOO--FREE ***MEAL!***
LOOK, I DON'T MEAN TO GIVE YOU THE HARD SELL AT THIS DIFFICULT TIME, BUT WOULDN'T YOU RATHER WRAP UP YOUR WORLDLY AFFAIRS IN, *um,* RELATIVELY PRISTINE CONDITION?
Y-YES...
B...UT...I'VE... ALREA...DY... HI...RED... ANO...THER... FIR...M.

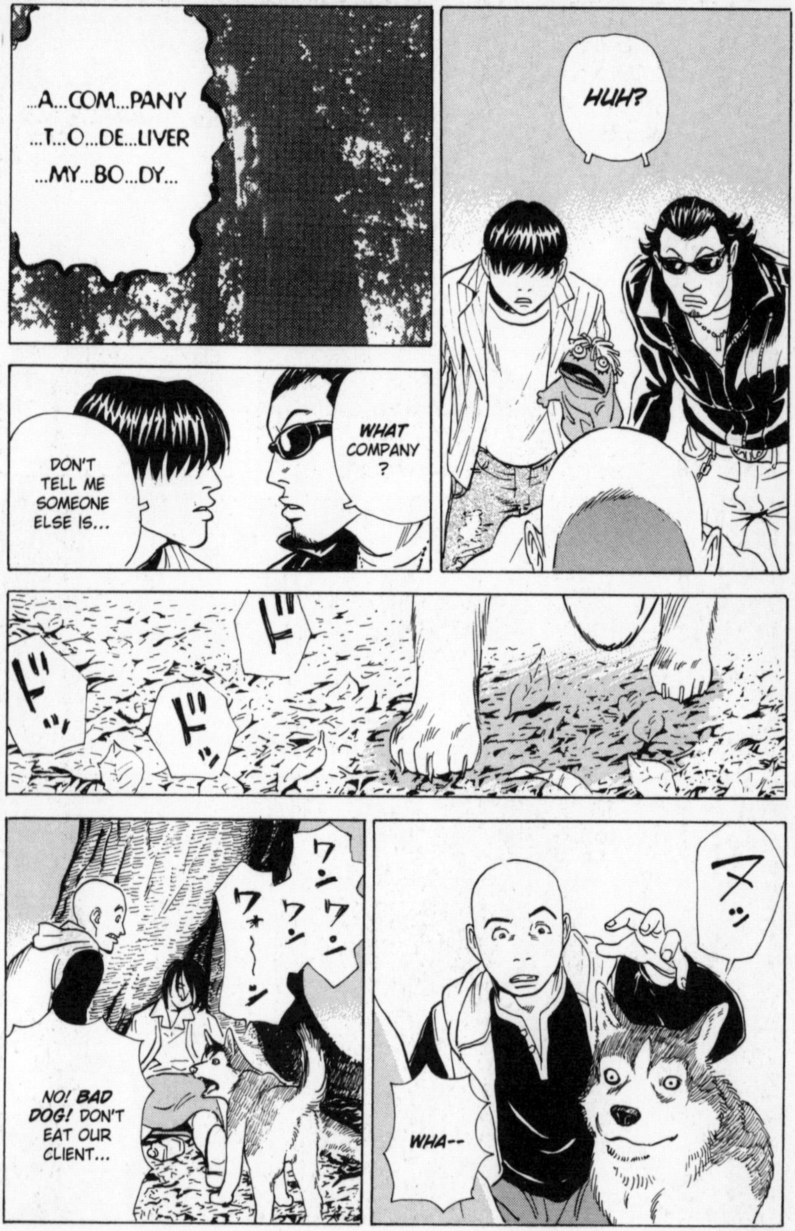
HUH?
...A...COM...PANY ...T...O...DE...LIVER ...MY...BO...DY...
WHAT COMPANY ?
DON'T TELL ME SOMEONE ELSE IS...
ド
ドッ
ドッ
ヌッ
WHA--
ワンワン ワン ワォ～～ン
NO! BAD DOG! DON'T EAT OUR CLIENT...

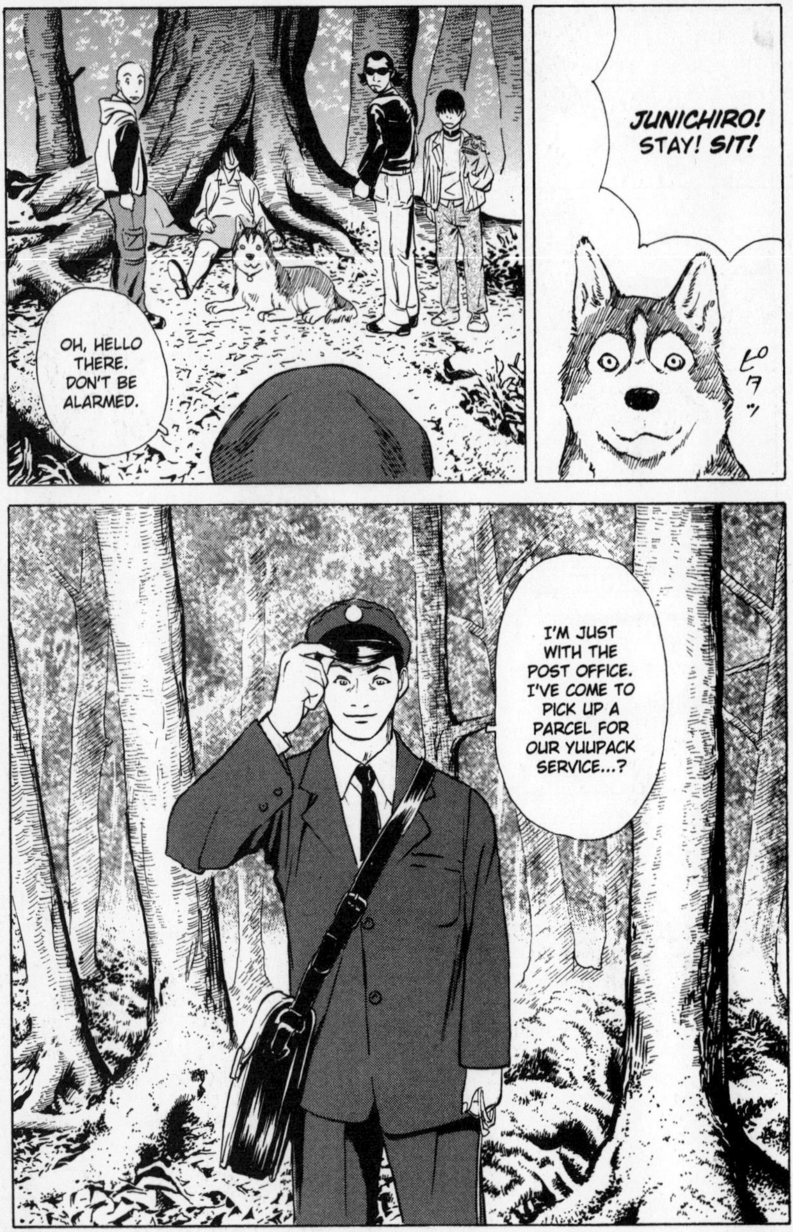
JUNICHIRO! STAY! SIT!
ピクッ
OH, HELLO THERE. DON'T BE ALARMED.
I'M JUST WITH THE POST OFFICE. I'VE COME TO PICK UP A PARCEL FOR OUR YUUPACK SERVICE...?

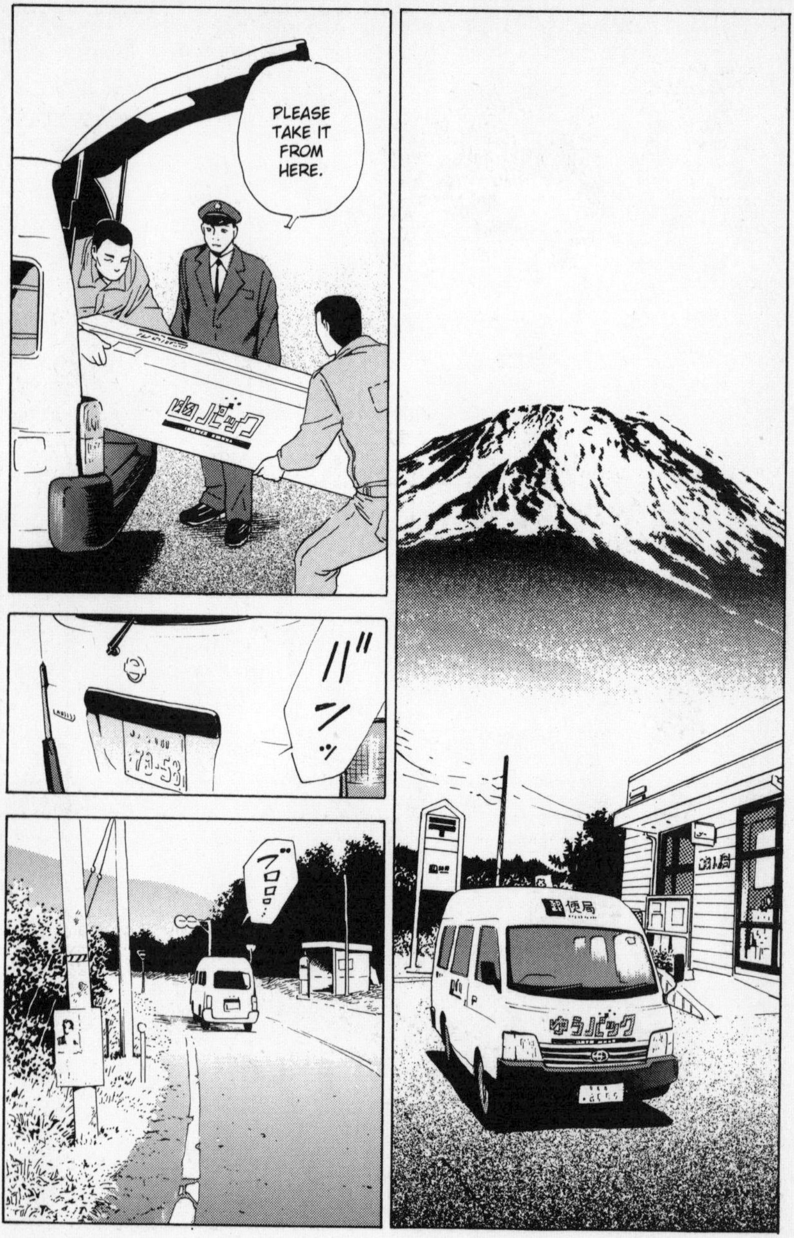
PLEASE TAKE IT FROM HERE.
バンッ
ブロロロ…

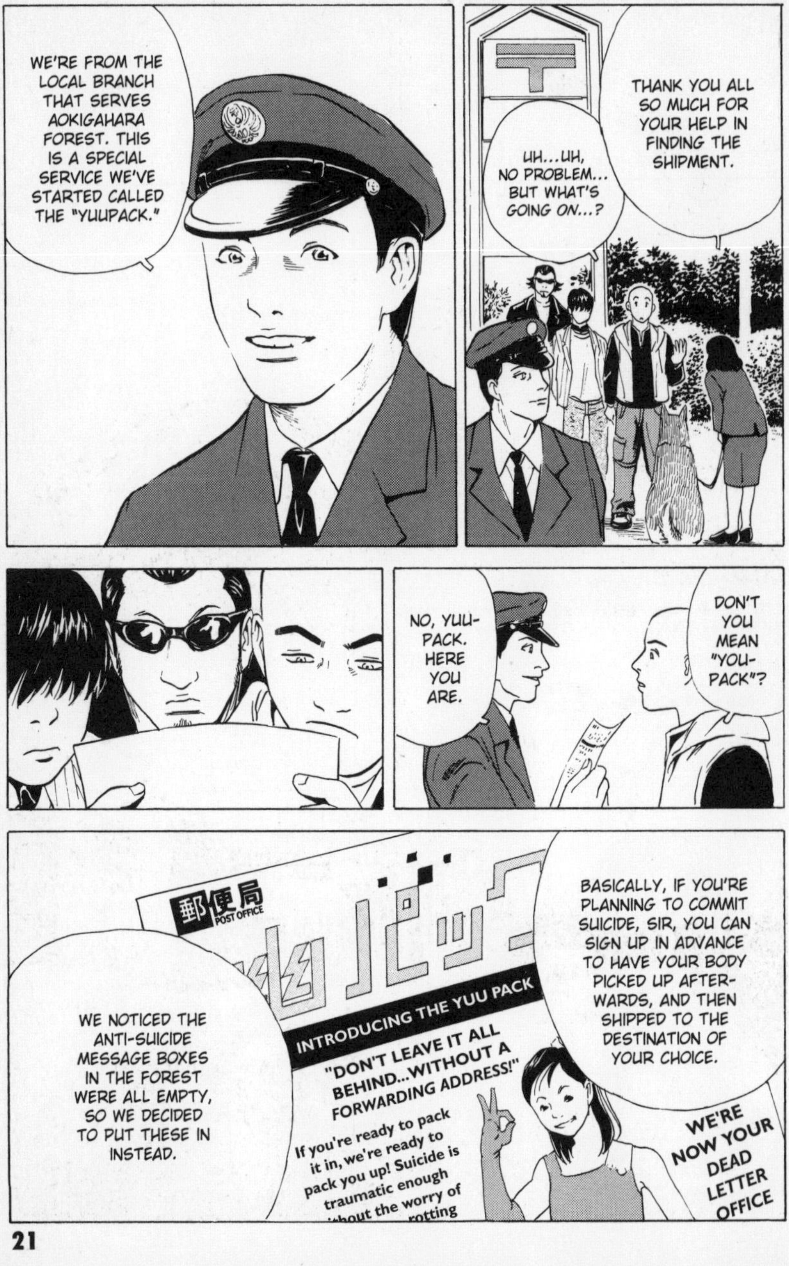
THANK YOU ALL SO MUCH FOR YOUR HELP IN FINDING THE SHIPMENT.
UH...UH, NO PROBLEM... BUT WHAT'S GOING ON...?
WE'RE FROM THE LOCAL BRANCH THAT SERVES AOKIGAHARA FOREST. THIS IS A SPECIAL SERVICE WE'VE STARTED CALLED THE "YUUPACK."
DON'T YOU MEAN "YOU-PACK"?
NO, YUU-PACK. HERE YOU ARE.
BASICALLY, IF YOU'RE PLANNING TO COMMIT SUICIDE, SIR, YOU CAN SIGN UP IN ADVANCE TO HAVE YOUR BODY PICKED UP AFTER-WARDS, AND THEN SHIPPED TO THE DESTINATION OF YOUR CHOICE.
郵便局 POST OFFICE
INTRODUCING THE YUU PACK
"DON'T LEAVE IT ALL BEHIND...WITHOUT A FORWARDING ADDRESS!"
If you're ready to pack it in, we're ready to pack you up! Suicide is traumatic enough
WE'RE NOW YOUR DEAD LETTER OFFICE
WE NOTICED THE ANTI-SUICIDE MESSAGE BOXES IN THE FOREST WERE ALL EMPTY, SO WE DECIDED TO PUT THESE IN INSTEAD.

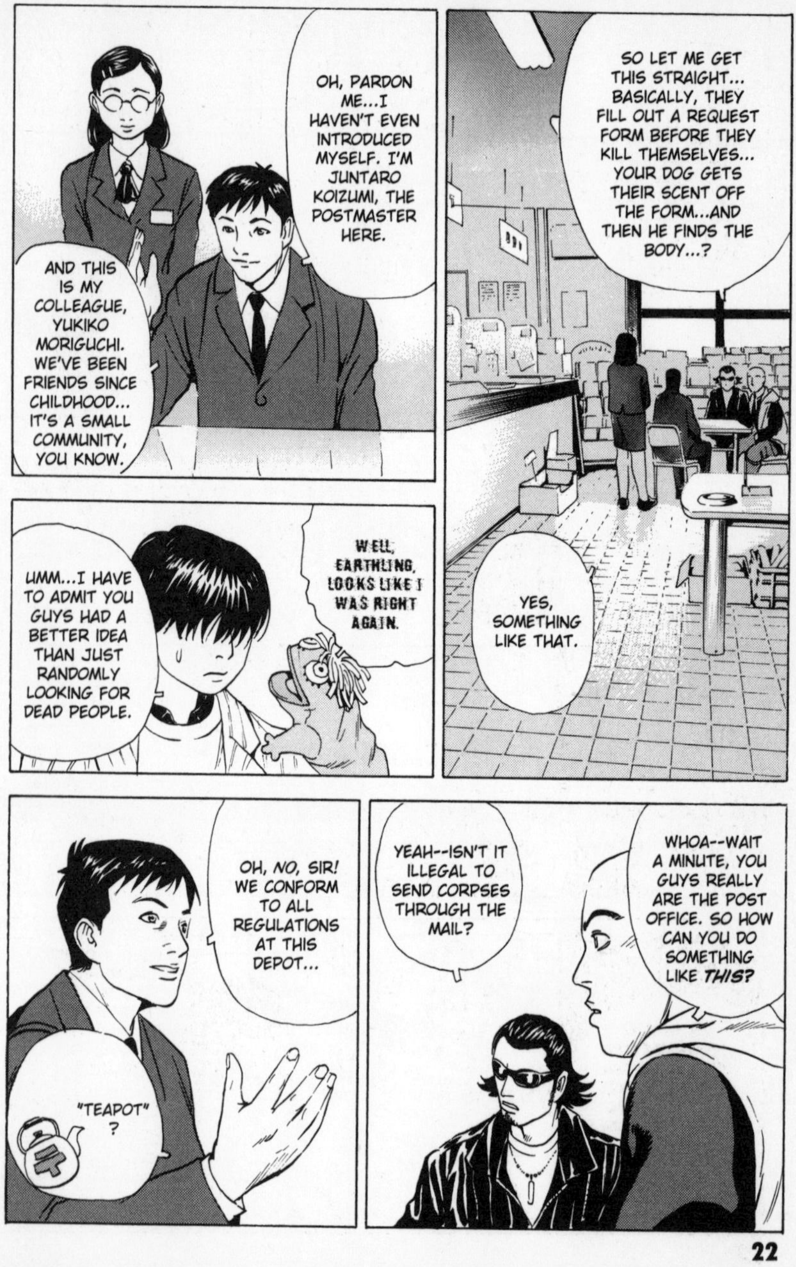
SO LET ME GET THIS STRAIGHT... BASICALLY, THEY FILL OUT A REQUEST FORM BEFORE THEY KILL THEMSELVES... YOUR DOG GETS THEIR SCENT OFF THE FORM...AND THEN HE FINDS THE BODY...?
YES, SOMETHING LIKE THAT.
OH, PARDON ME...I HAVEN'T EVEN INTRODUCED MYSELF. I'M JUNTARO KOIZUMI, THE POSTMASTER HERE.
AND THIS IS MY COLLEAGUE, YUKIKO MORIGUCHI. WE'VE BEEN FRIENDS SINCE CHILDHOOD... IT'S A SMALL COMMUNITY, YOU KNOW.
WELL, EARTHLING, LOOKS LIKE I WAS RIGHT AGAIN.
UMM...I HAVE TO ADMIT YOU GUYS HAD A BETTER IDEA THAN JUST RANDOMLY LOOKING FOR DEAD PEOPLE.
WHOA--WAIT A MINUTE, YOU GUYS REALLY ARE THE POST OFFICE. SO HOW CAN YOU DO SOMETHING LIKE *THIS?*
YEAH--ISN'T IT ILLEGAL TO SEND CORPSES THROUGH THE MAIL?
OH, *NO*, SIR! WE CONFORM TO ALL REGULATIONS AT THIS DEPOT...
"TEAPOT" ?

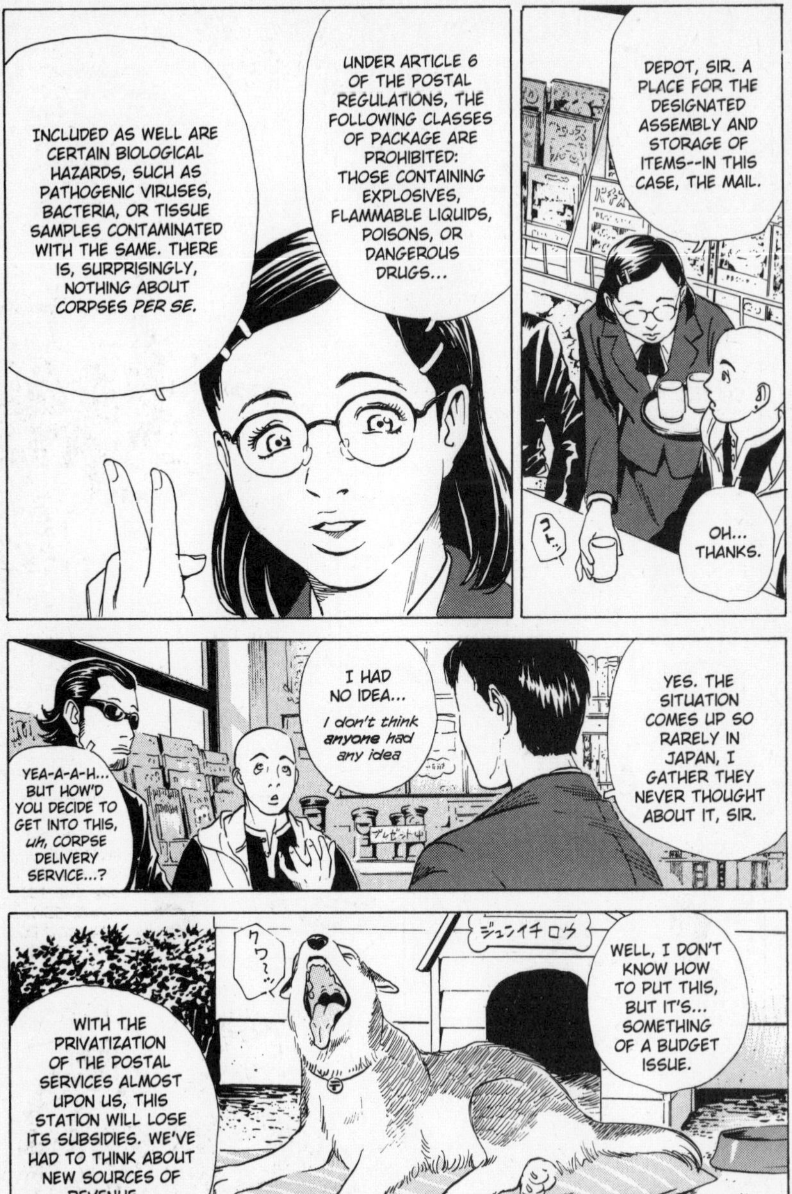
DEPOT, SIR. A PLACE FOR THE DESIGNATED ASSEMBLY AND STORAGE OF ITEMS--IN THIS CASE, THE MAIL.
コトッ
OH... THANKS.
UNDER ARTICLE 6 OF THE POSTAL REGULATIONS, THE FOLLOWING CLASSES OF PACKAGE ARE PROHIBITED: THOSE CONTAINING EXPLOSIVES, FLAMMABLE LIQUIDS, POISONS, OR DANGEROUS DRUGS...
INCLUDED AS WELL ARE CERTAIN BIOLOGICAL HAZARDS, SUCH AS PATHOGENIC VIRUSES, BACTERIA, OR TISSUE SAMPLES CONTAMINATED WITH THE SAME. THERE IS, SURPRISINGLY, NOTHING ABOUT CORPSES *PER SE.*
YES. THE SITUATION COMES UP SO RARELY IN JAPAN, I GATHER THEY NEVER THOUGHT ABOUT IT, SIR.
I HAD NO IDEA...
*I don't think **anyone** had any idea*
プレゼント中
YEA-A-A-H... BUT HOW'D YOU DECIDE TO GET INTO THIS, *uh,* CORPSE DELIVERY SERVICE...?
WELL, I DON'T KNOW HOW TO PUT THIS, BUT IT'S... SOMETHING OF A BUDGET ISSUE.
ジュンイチロウ
クワ〜ッ
WITH THE PRIVATIZATION OF THE POSTAL SERVICES ALMOST UPON US, THIS STATION WILL LOSE ITS SUBSIDIES. WE'VE HAD TO THINK ABOUT NEW SOURCES OF REVENUE...

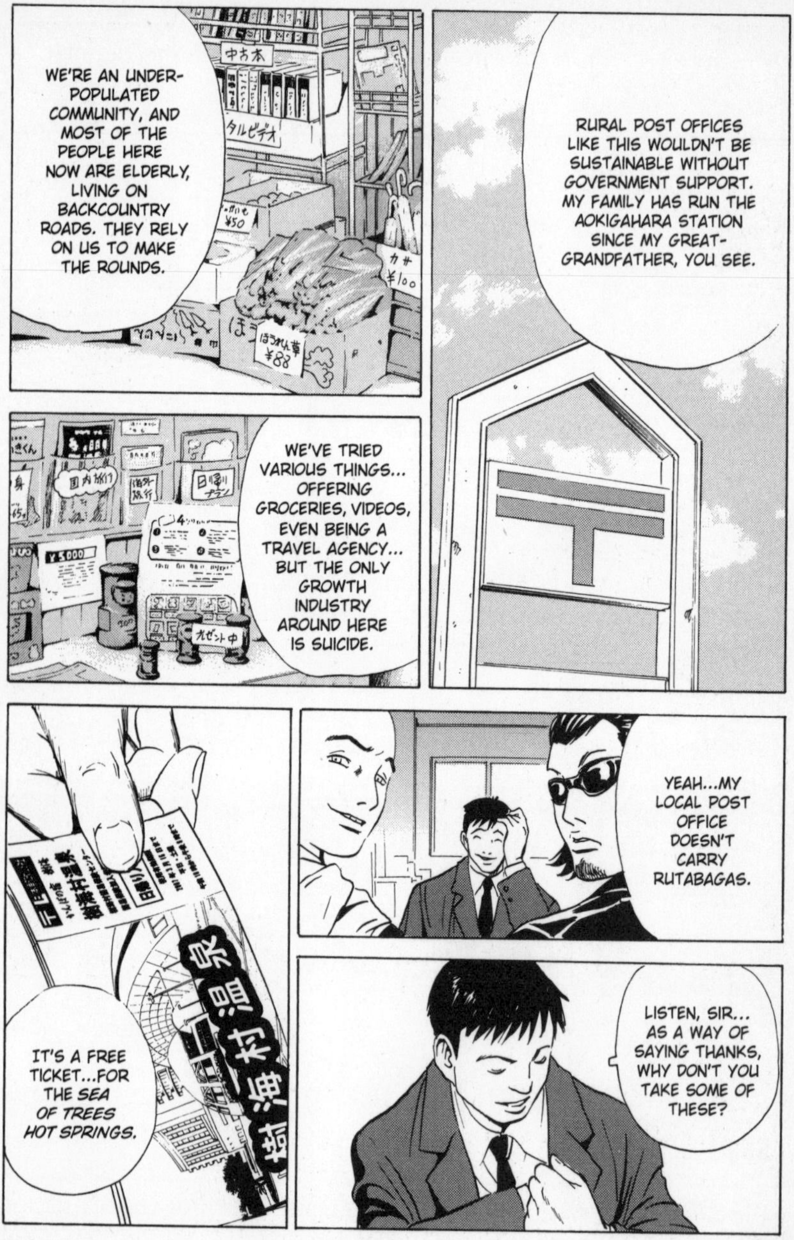
RURAL POST OFFICES LIKE THIS WOULDN'T BE SUSTAINABLE WITHOUT GOVERNMENT SUPPORT. MY FAMILY HAS RUN THE AOKIGAHARA STATION SINCE MY GREAT-GRANDFATHER, YOU SEE.
WE'RE AN UNDER-POPULATED COMMUNITY, AND MOST OF THE PEOPLE HERE NOW ARE ELDERLY, LIVING ON BACKCOUNTRY ROADS. THEY RELY ON US TO MAKE THE ROUNDS.
WE'VE TRIED VARIOUS THINGS... OFFERING GROCERIES, VIDEOS, EVEN BEING A TRAVEL AGENCY... BUT THE ONLY GROWTH INDUSTRY AROUND HERE IS SUICIDE.
YEAH...MY LOCAL POST OFFICE DOESN'T CARRY RUTABAGAS.
LISTEN, SIR... AS A WAY OF SAYING THANKS, WHY DON'T YOU TAKE SOME OF THESE?
IT'S A FREE TICKET...FOR THE SEA OF TREES HOT SPRINGS.

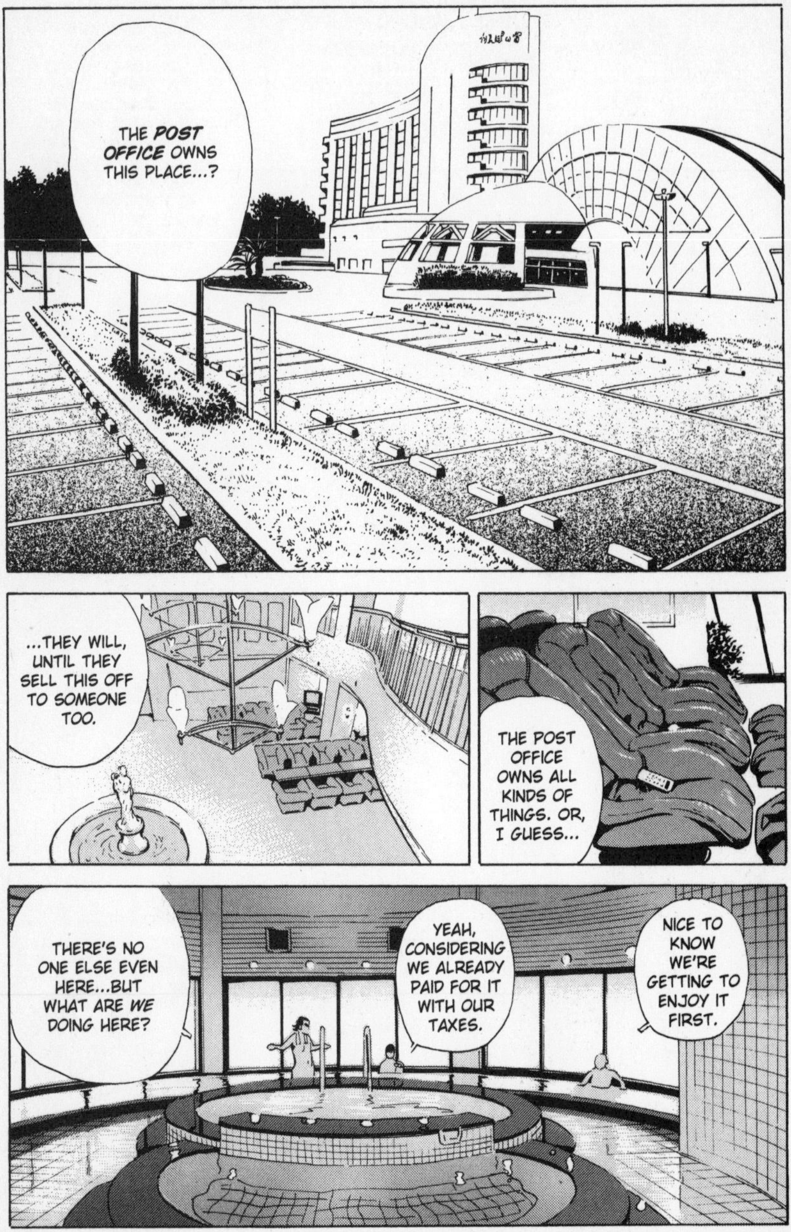
THE *POST OFFICE* OWNS THIS PLACE...?
THE POST OFFICE OWNS ALL KINDS OF THINGS. OR, I GUESS...
...THEY WILL, UNTIL THEY SELL THIS OFF TO SOMEONE TOO.
NICE TO KNOW WE'RE GETTING TO ENJOY IT FIRST.
YEAH, CONSIDERING WE ALREADY PAID FOR IT WITH OUR TAXES.
THERE'S NO ONE ELSE EVEN HERE...BUT WHAT ARE *WE* DOING HERE?

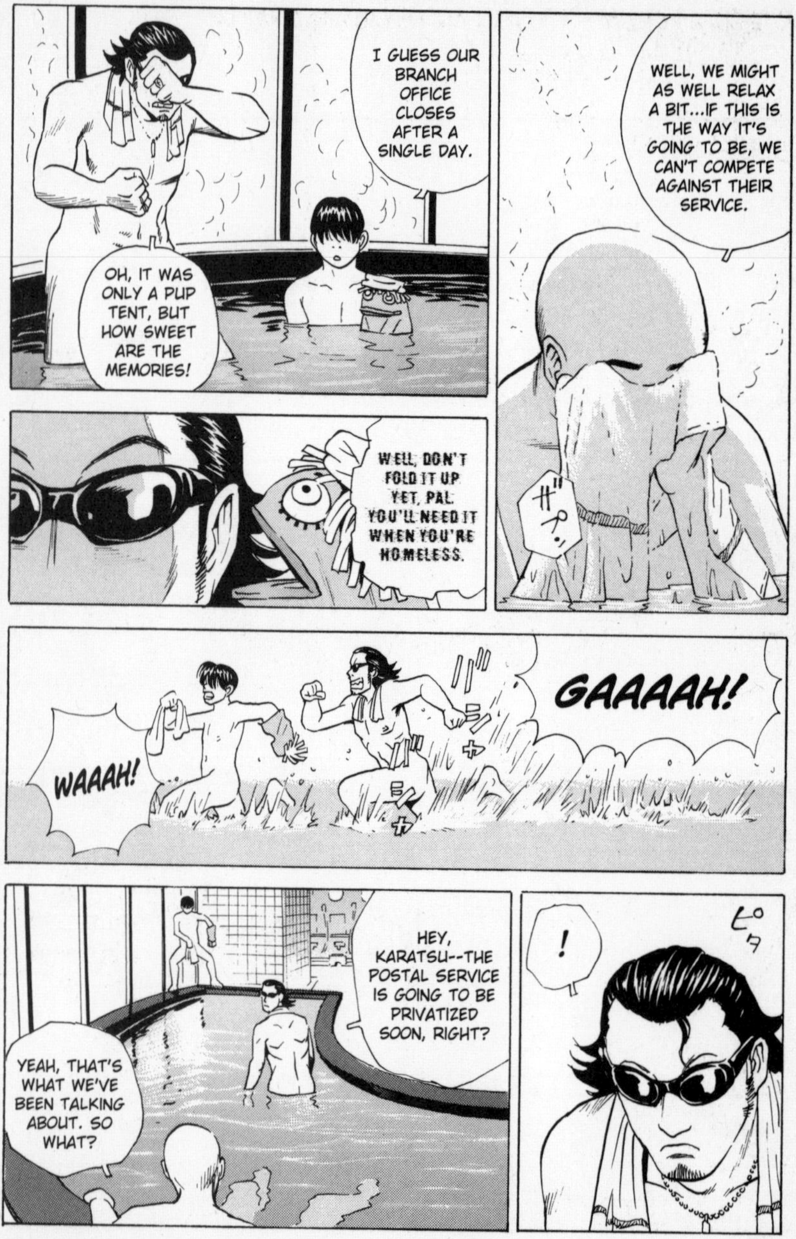
WELL, WE MIGHT AS WELL RELAX A BIT...IF THIS IS THE WAY IT'S GOING TO BE, WE CAN'T COMPETE AGAINST THEIR SERVICE.
I GUESS OUR BRANCH OFFICE CLOSES AFTER A SINGLE DAY.
OH, IT WAS ONLY A PUP TENT, BUT HOW SWEET ARE THE MEMORIES!
WELL, DON'T FOLD IT UP YET, PAL. YOU'LL NEED IT WHEN YOU'RE HOMELESS.
GAAAAH!
WAAAH!
!
HEY, KARATSU--THE POSTAL SERVICE IS GOING TO BE PRIVATIZED SOON, RIGHT?
YEAH, THAT'S WHAT WE'VE BEEN TALKING ABOUT. SO WHAT?

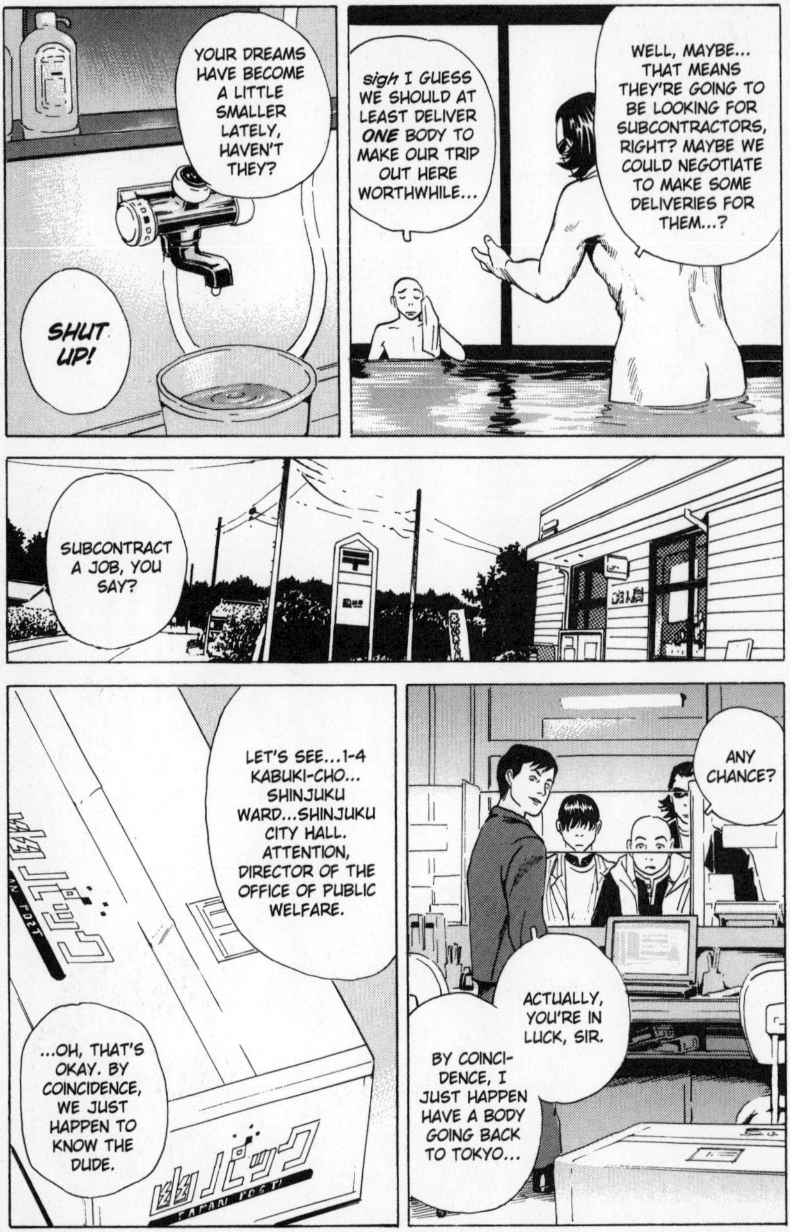
WELL, MAYBE... THAT MEANS THEY'RE GOING TO BE LOOKING FOR SUBCONTRACTORS, RIGHT? MAYBE WE COULD NEGOTIATE TO MAKE SOME DELIVERIES FOR THEM...?
sigh I GUESS WE SHOULD AT LEAST DELIVER ***ONE*** BODY TO MAKE OUR TRIP OUT HERE WORTHWHILE...
YOUR DREAMS HAVE BECOME A LITTLE SMALLER LATELY, HAVEN'T THEY?
SHUT UP!
SUBCONTRACT A JOB, YOU SAY?
ANY CHANCE?
ACTUALLY, YOU'RE IN LUCK, SIR.
BY COINCIDENCE, I JUST HAPPEN HAVE A BODY GOING BACK TO TOKYO...
LET'S SEE...1-4 KABUKI-CHO... SHINJUKU WARD...SHINJUKU CITY HALL. ATTENTION, DIRECTOR OF THE OFFICE OF PUBLIC WELFARE.
...OH, THAT'S OKAY. BY COINCIDENCE, WE JUST HAPPEN TO KNOW THE DUDE.

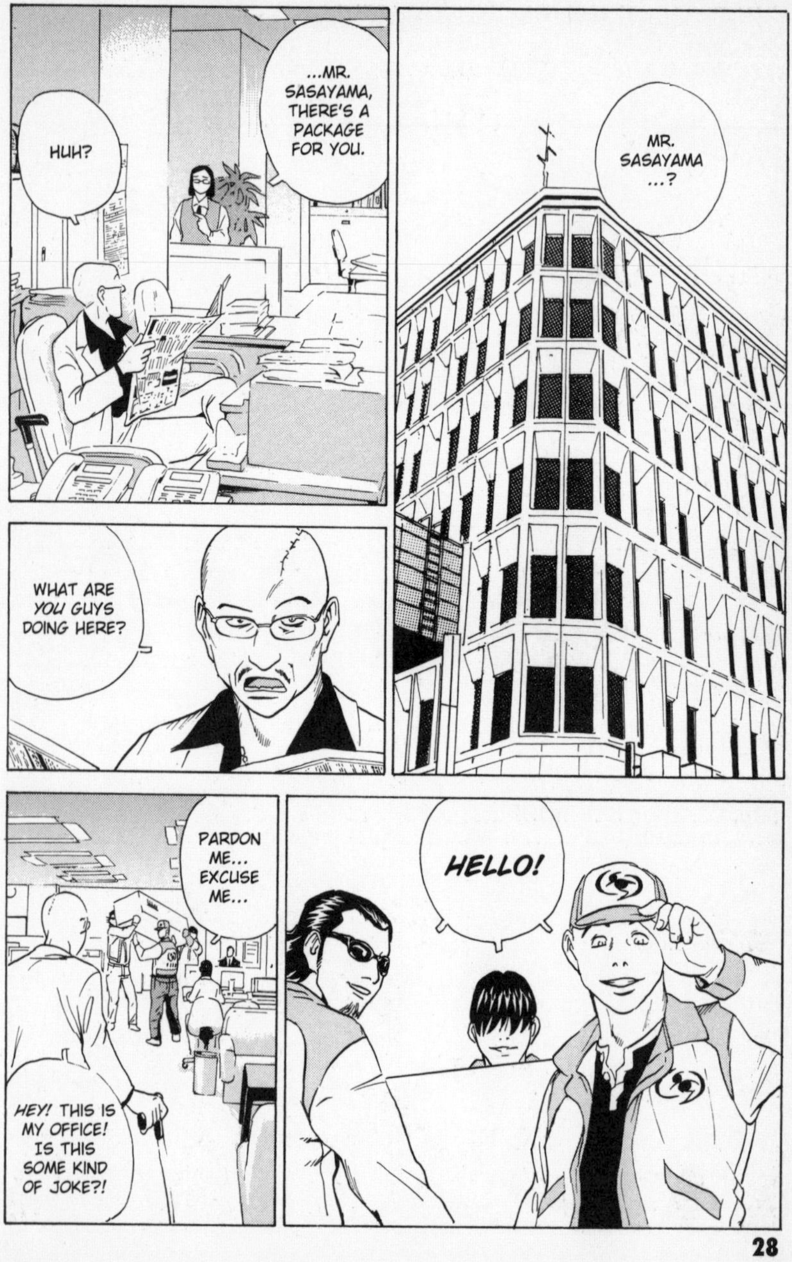
MR. SASAYAMA ...?
...MR. SASAYAMA, THERE'S A PACKAGE FOR YOU.
HUH?
WHAT ARE *YOU* GUYS DOING HERE?
HELLO!
PARDON ME... EXCUSE ME...
HEY! THIS IS MY OFFICE! IS THIS SOME KIND OF JOKE?!

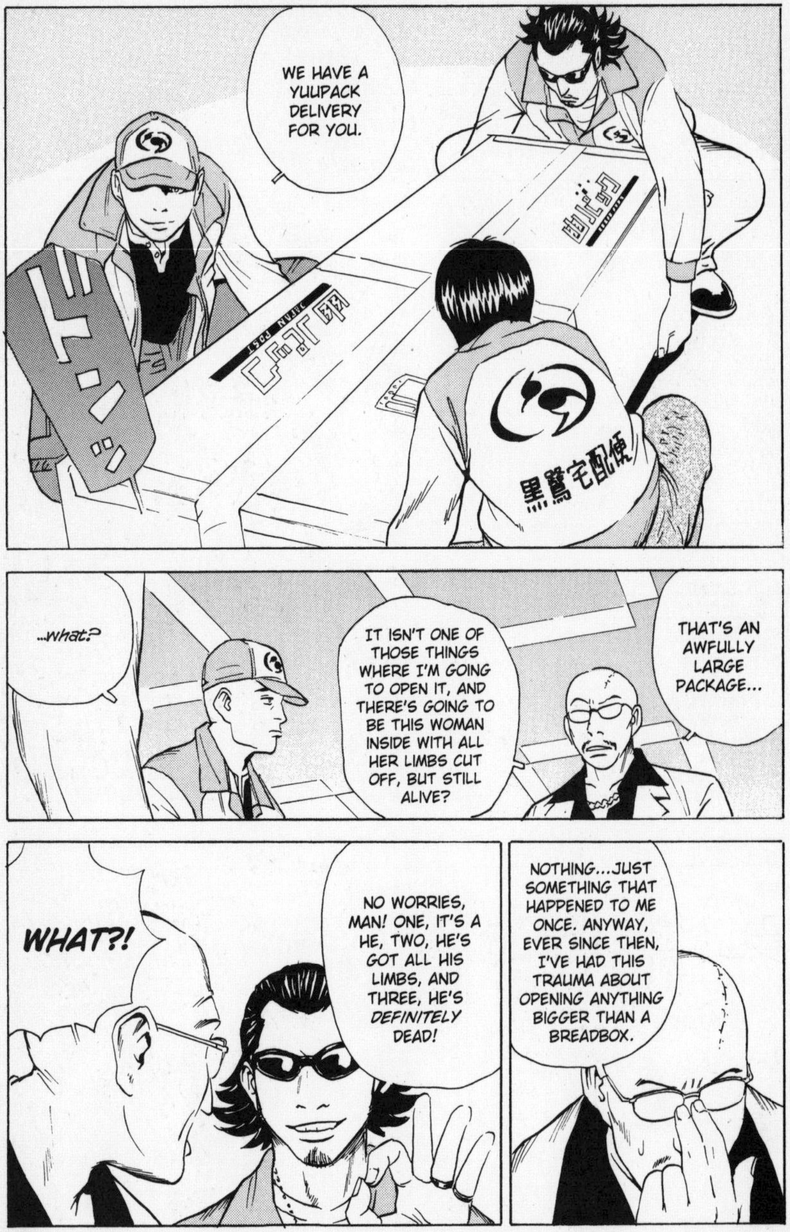
WE HAVE A YUUPACK DELIVERY FOR YOU.
黒鷺宅配便
THAT'S AN AWFULLY LARGE PACKAGE...
IT ISN'T ONE OF THOSE THINGS WHERE I'M GOING TO OPEN IT, AND THERE'S GOING TO BE THIS WOMAN INSIDE WITH ALL HER LIMBS CUT OFF, BUT STILL ALIVE?
...what?
NOTHING...JUST SOMETHING THAT HAPPENED TO ME ONCE. ANYWAY, EVER SINCE THEN, I'VE HAD THIS TRAUMA ABOUT OPENING ANYTHING BIGGER THAN A BREADBOX.
NO WORRIES, MAN! ONE, IT'S A HE, TWO, HE'S GOT ALL HIS LIMBS, AND THREE, HE'S *DEFINITELY* DEAD!
WHAT?!

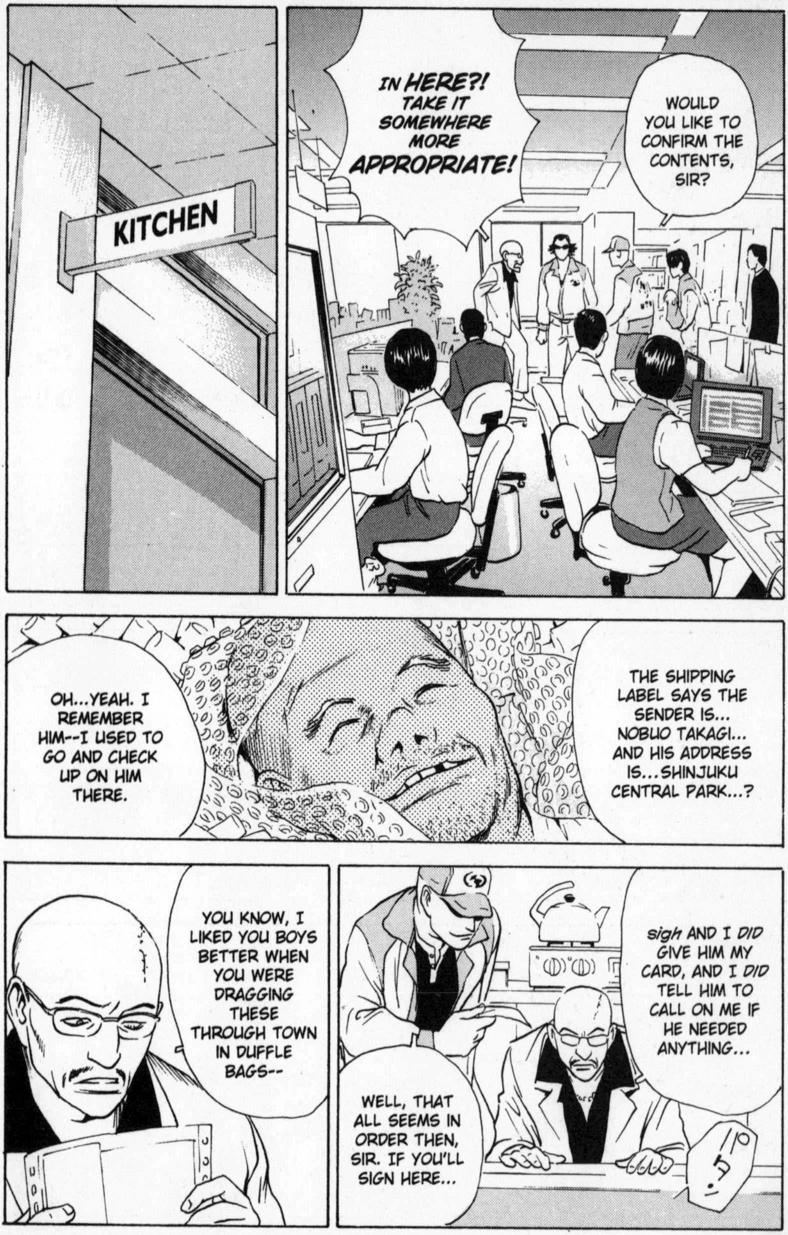
WOULD YOU LIKE TO CONFIRM THE CONTENTS, SIR?
IN HERE?! TAKE IT SOMEWHERE MORE APPROPRIATE!
KITCHEN
THE SHIPPING LABEL SAYS THE SENDER IS... NOBUO TAKAGI... AND HIS ADDRESS IS...SHINJUKU CENTRAL PARK...?
OH...YEAH. I REMEMBER HIM--I USED TO GO AND CHECK UP ON HIM THERE.
sigh AND I *DID* GIVE HIM MY CARD, AND I *DID* TELL HIM TO CALL ON ME IF HE NEEDED ANYTHING...
WELL, THAT ALL SEEMS IN ORDER THEN, SIR. IF YOU'LL SIGN HERE...
YOU KNOW, I LIKED YOU BOYS BETTER WHEN YOU WERE DRAGGING THESE THROUGH TOWN IN DUFFLE BAGS--

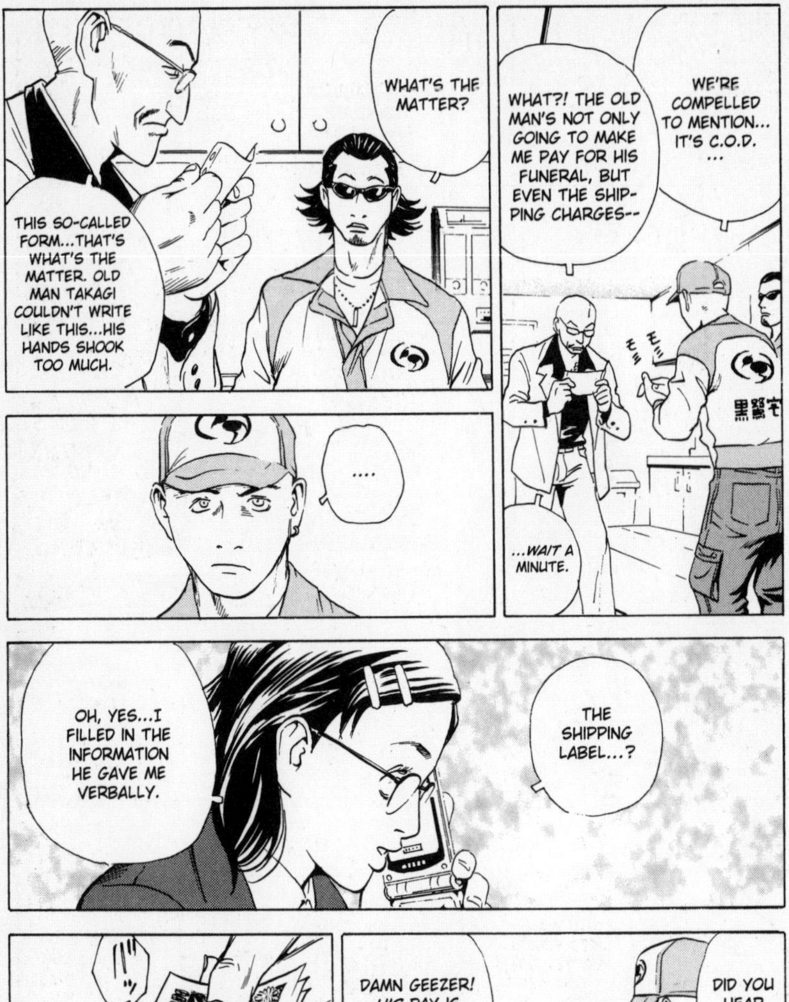
WE'RE COMPELLED TO MENTION... IT'S C.O.D. ...
WHAT?! THE OLD MAN'S NOT ONLY GOING TO MAKE ME PAY FOR HIS FUNERAL, BUT EVEN THE SHIP-PING CHARGES--
...*WAIT* A MINUTE.
WHAT'S THE MATTER?
THIS SO-CALLED FORM...THAT'S WHAT'S THE MATTER. OLD MAN TAKAGI COULDN'T WRITE LIKE THIS...HIS HANDS SHOOK TOO MUCH.
....
THE SHIPPING LABEL...?
OH, YES...I FILLED IN THE INFORMATION HE GAVE ME VERBALLY.
DID YOU HEAR THAT?
DAMN GEEZER! *HIS* DAY IS DONE, BUT HE'S STILL GOT TO RUIN *MINE!*
HERE. AND YOU BETTER NOT JUST POCKET THIS!

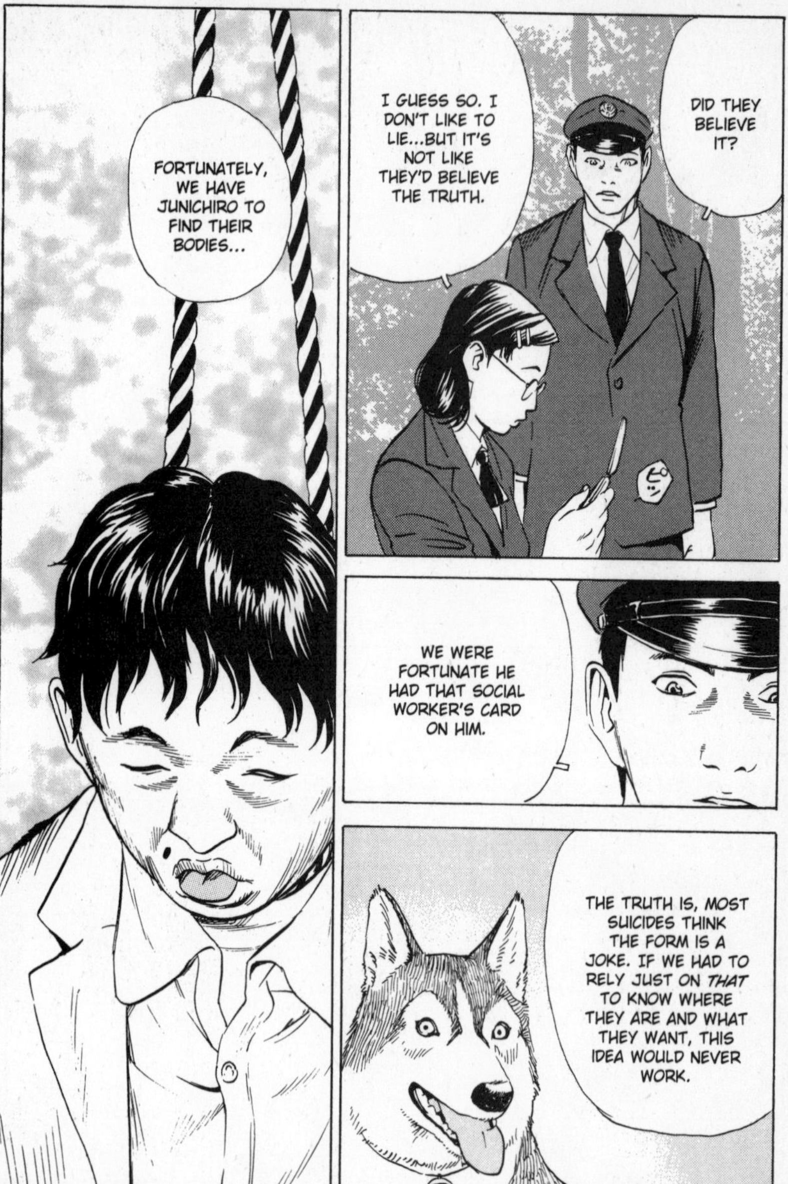
DID THEY BELIEVE IT?
I GUESS SO. I DON'T LIKE TO LIE...BUT IT'S NOT LIKE THEY'D BELIEVE THE TRUTH.
WE WERE FORTUNATE HE HAD THAT SOCIAL WORKER'S CARD ON HIM.
THE TRUTH IS, MOST SUICIDES THINK THE FORM IS A JOKE. IF WE HAD TO RELY JUST ON *THAT* TO KNOW WHERE THEY ARE AND WHAT THEY WANT, THIS IDEA WOULD NEVER WORK.
FORTUNATELY, WE HAVE JUNICHIRO TO FIND THEIR BODIES...

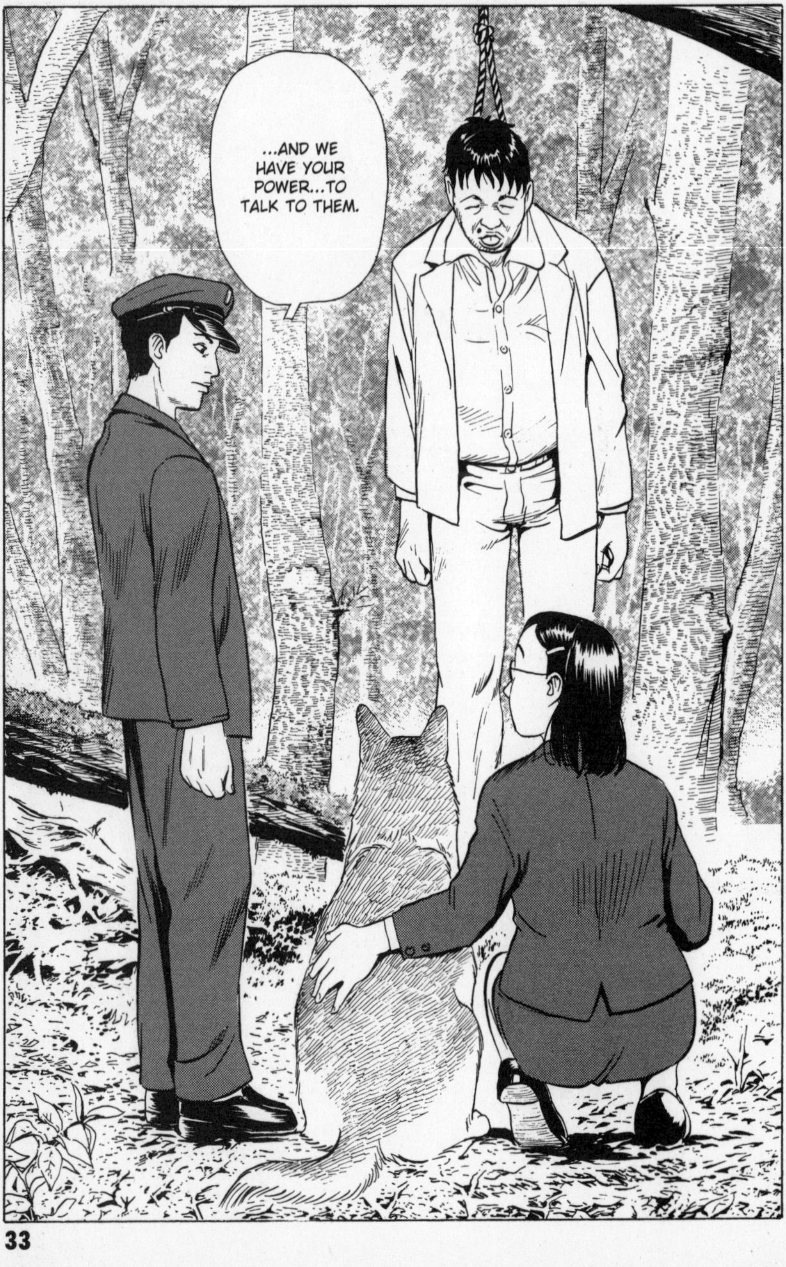
...AND WE HAVE YOUR POWER...TO TALK TO THEM.

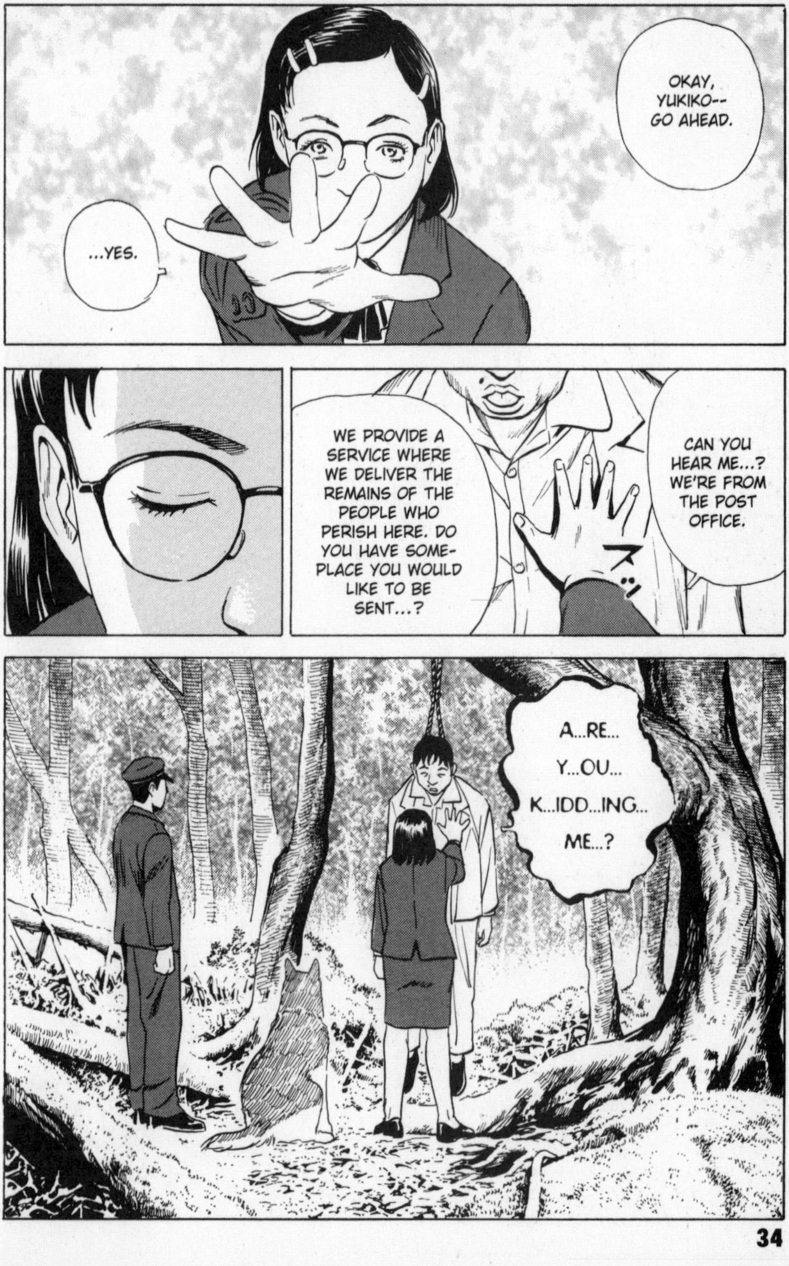
OKAY, YUKIKO-- GO AHEAD.
...YES.
CAN YOU HEAR ME...? WE'RE FROM THE POST OFFICE.
WE PROVIDE A SERVICE WHERE WE DELIVER THE REMAINS OF THE PEOPLE WHO PERISH HERE. DO YOU HAVE SOME-PLACE YOU WOULD LIKE TO BE SENT...?
スッ
A...RE... Y...OU... K...IDD...ING... ME...?

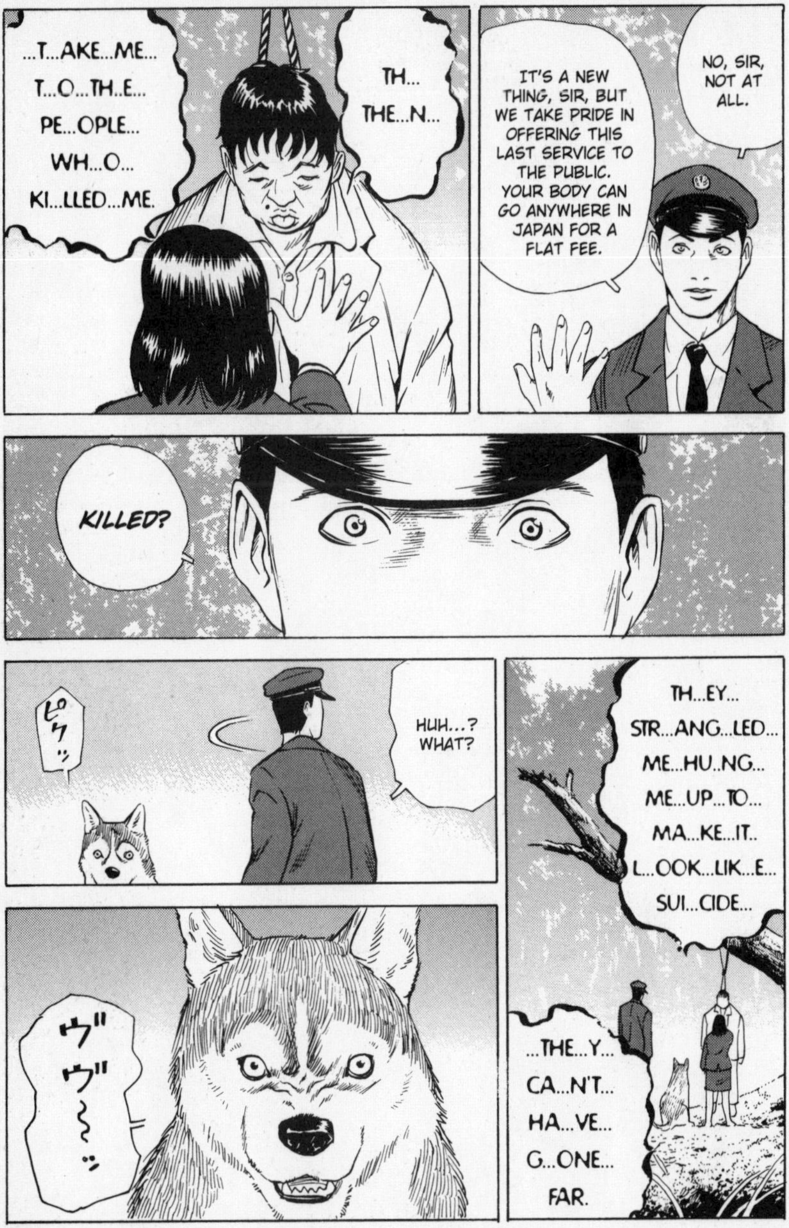
NO, SIR, NOT AT ALL.
IT'S A NEW THING, SIR, BUT WE TAKE PRIDE IN OFFERING THIS LAST SERVICE TO THE PUBLIC. YOUR BODY CAN GO ANYWHERE IN JAPAN FOR A FLAT FEE.
TH... THE...N...
...T...AKE...ME... T...O...TH..E... PE...OPLE... WH...O... KI...LLED...ME.
KILLED?
TH...EY... STR...ANG...LED... ME...HU..NG... ME...UP...TO... MA...KE...IT.. L...OOK...LIK...E... SUI...CIDE...
...THE...Y... CA...N'T... HA...VE... G...ONE... FAR.
HUH...? WHAT?
ピクッ
ヴヴ〜ッ

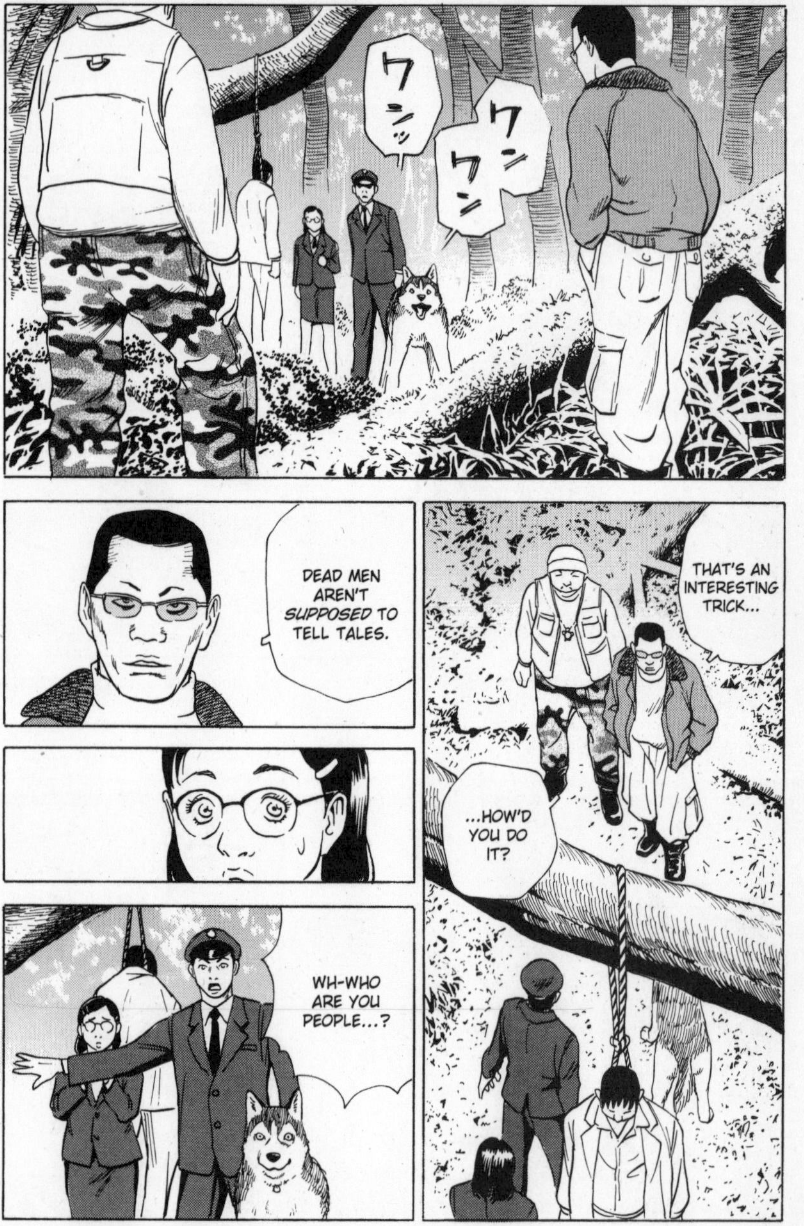
ワンワン
ワンッ
THAT'S AN INTERESTING TRICK...
...HOW'D YOU DO IT?
DEAD MEN AREN'T *SUPPOSED* TO TELL TALES.
WH-WHO ARE YOU PEOPLE...?

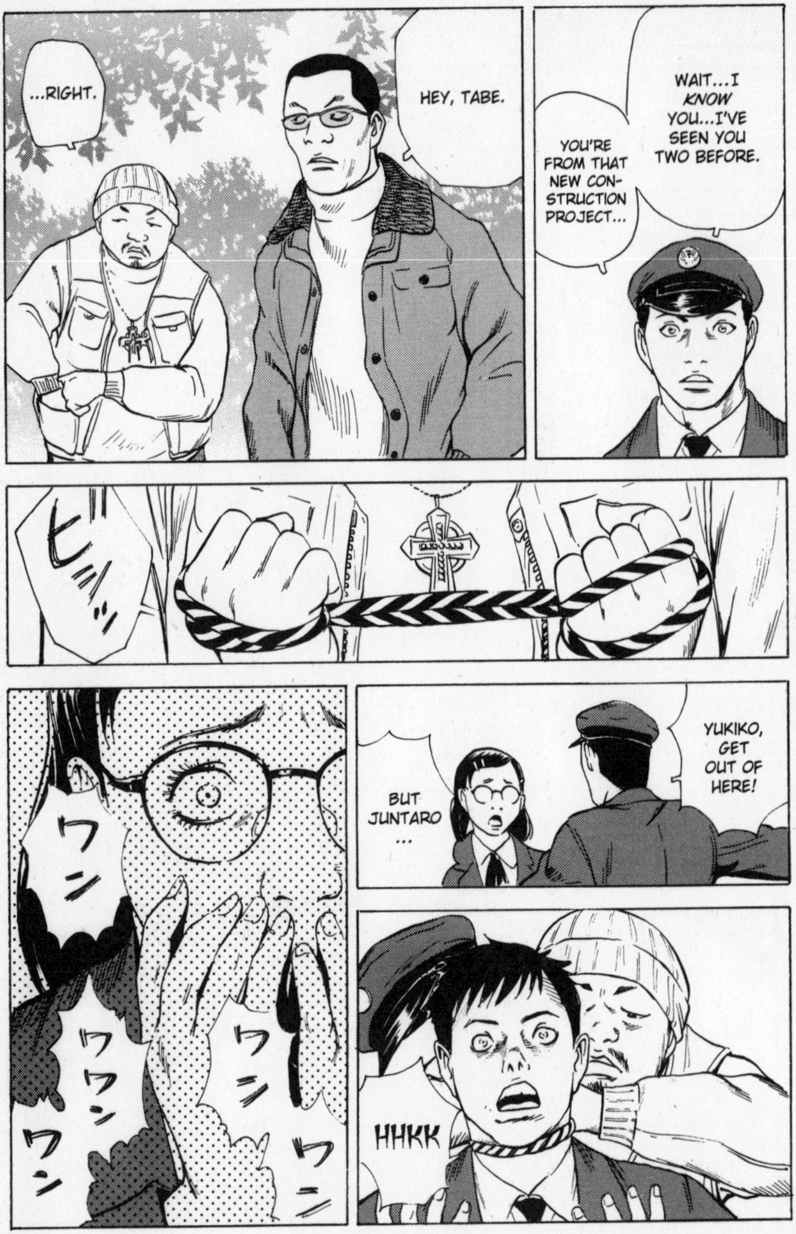
WAIT...I *KNOW* YOU...I'VE SEEN YOU TWO BEFORE.
YOU'RE FROM THAT NEW CON-STRUCTION PROJECT...
HEY, TABE.
...RIGHT.
ビシッ
YUKIKO, GET OUT OF HERE!
BUT JUNTARO ...
HHKK
ワン
ワンワン
ワン
ワン
ワン

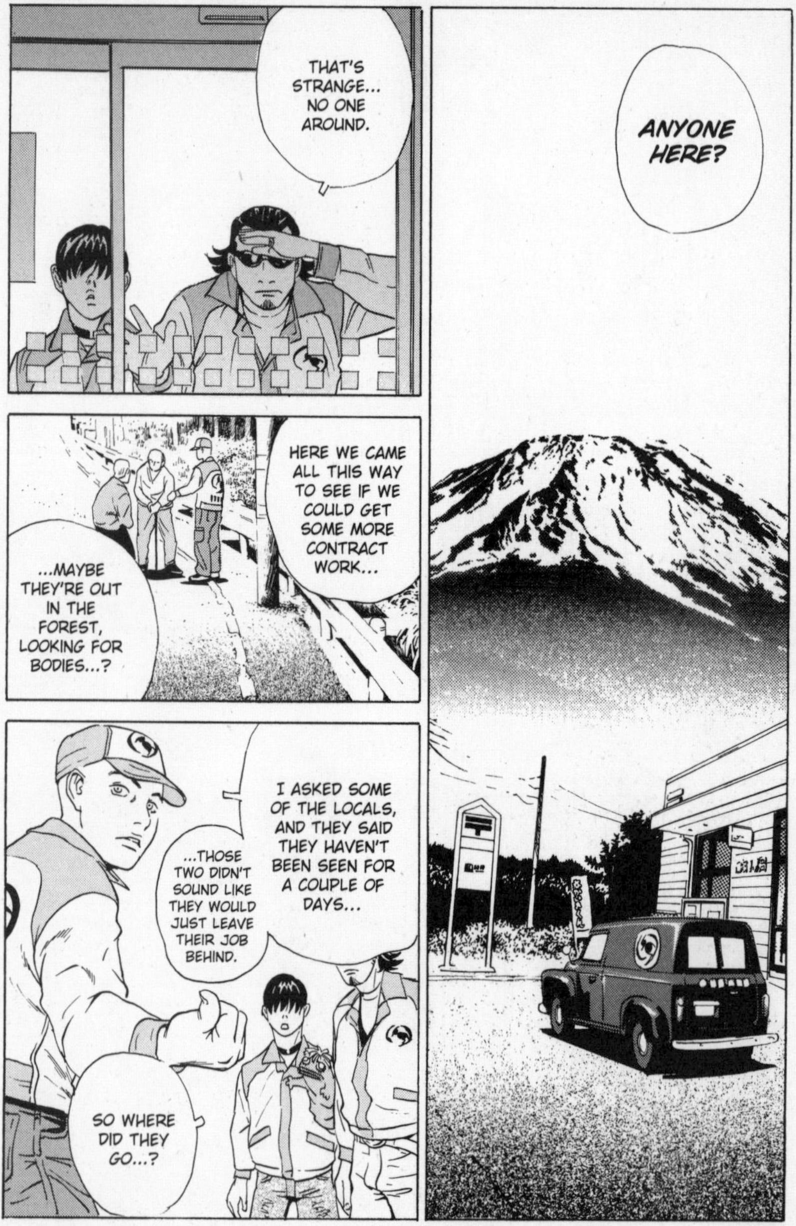
ANYONE HERE?
THAT'S STRANGE... NO ONE AROUND.
HERE WE CAME ALL THIS WAY TO SEE IF WE COULD GET SOME MORE CONTRACT WORK...
...MAYBE THEY'RE OUT IN THE FOREST, LOOKING FOR BODIES...?
I ASKED SOME OF THE LOCALS, AND THEY SAID THEY HAVEN'T BEEN SEEN FOR A COUPLE OF DAYS...
...THOSE TWO DIDN'T SOUND LIKE THEY WOULD JUST LEAVE THEIR JOB BEHIND.
SO WHERE DID THEY GO...?

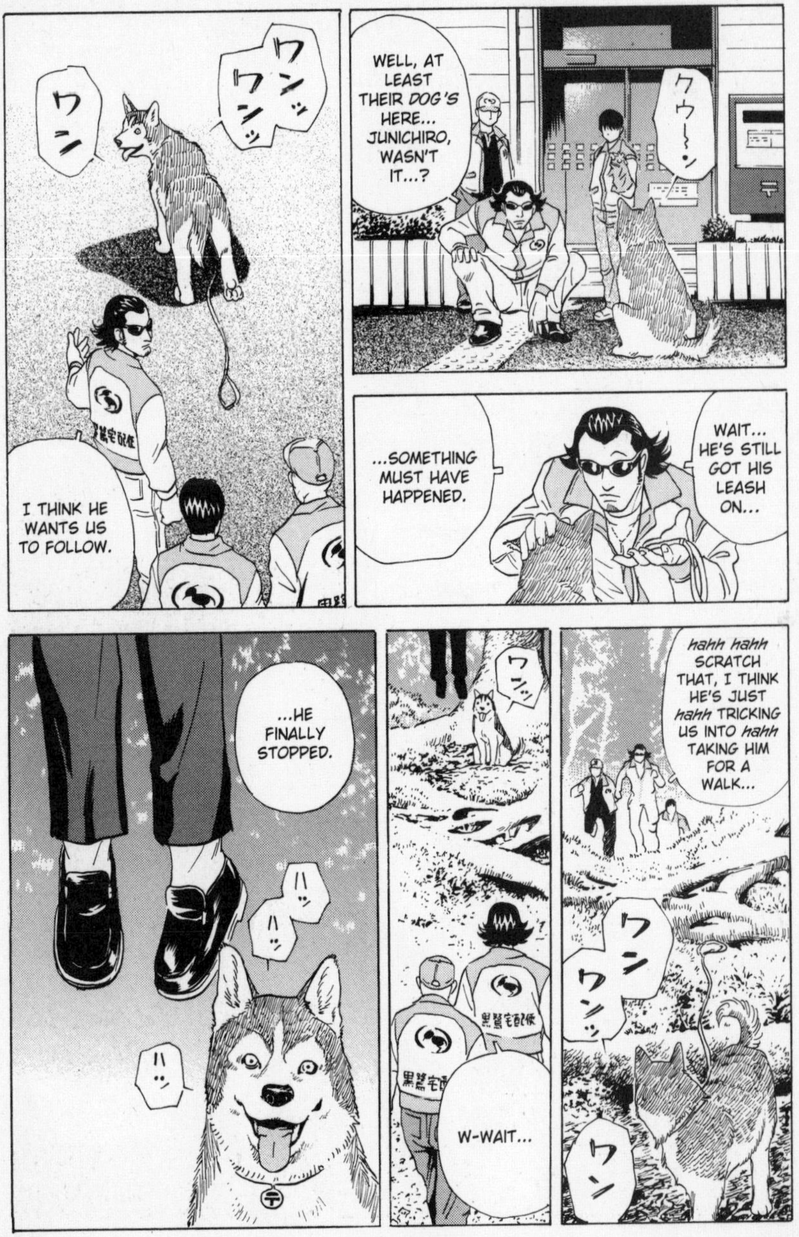
クゥ～ン
WELL, AT LEAST THEIR *DOG'S* HERE... JUNICHIRO, WASN'T IT...?
WAIT... HE'S STILL GOT HIS LEASH ON...
...SOMETHING MUST HAVE HAPPENED.
ワンッ ワンッ
ワン
I THINK HE WANTS US TO FOLLOW.
hahh hahh SCRATCH THAT, I THINK HE'S JUST *hahh* TRICKING US INTO *hahh* TAKING HIM FOR A WALK...
ワン ワンッ
ワン
ワンッ
黒鷺宅配便
W-WAIT...
...HE FINALLY STOPPED.
ハッ
ハッ
ハッ

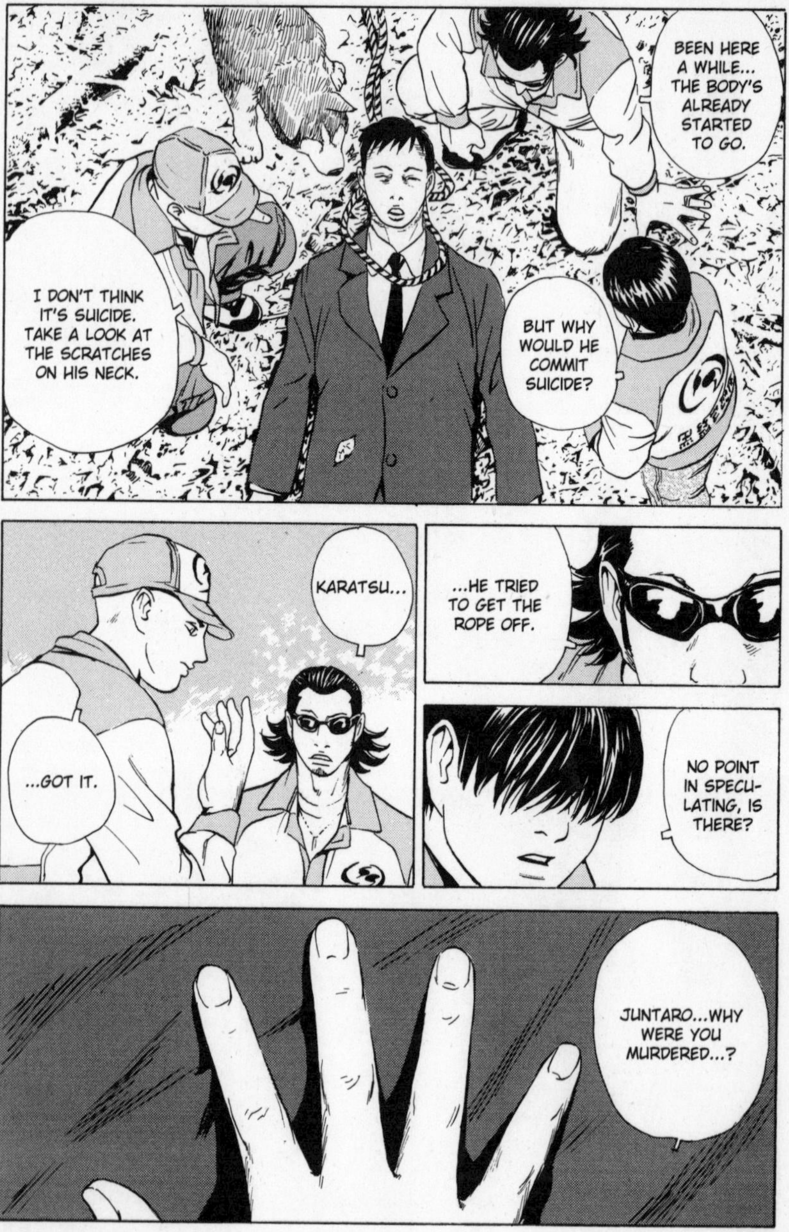
BEEN HERE A WHILE... THE BODY'S ALREADY STARTED TO GO.
BUT WHY WOULD HE COMMIT SUICIDE?
I DON'T THINK IT'S SUICIDE. TAKE A LOOK AT THE SCRATCHES ON HIS NECK.
...HE TRIED TO GET THE ROPE OFF.
NO POINT IN SPECU-LATING, IS THERE?
KARATSU...
...GOT IT.
JUNTARO...WHY WERE YOU MURDERED...?

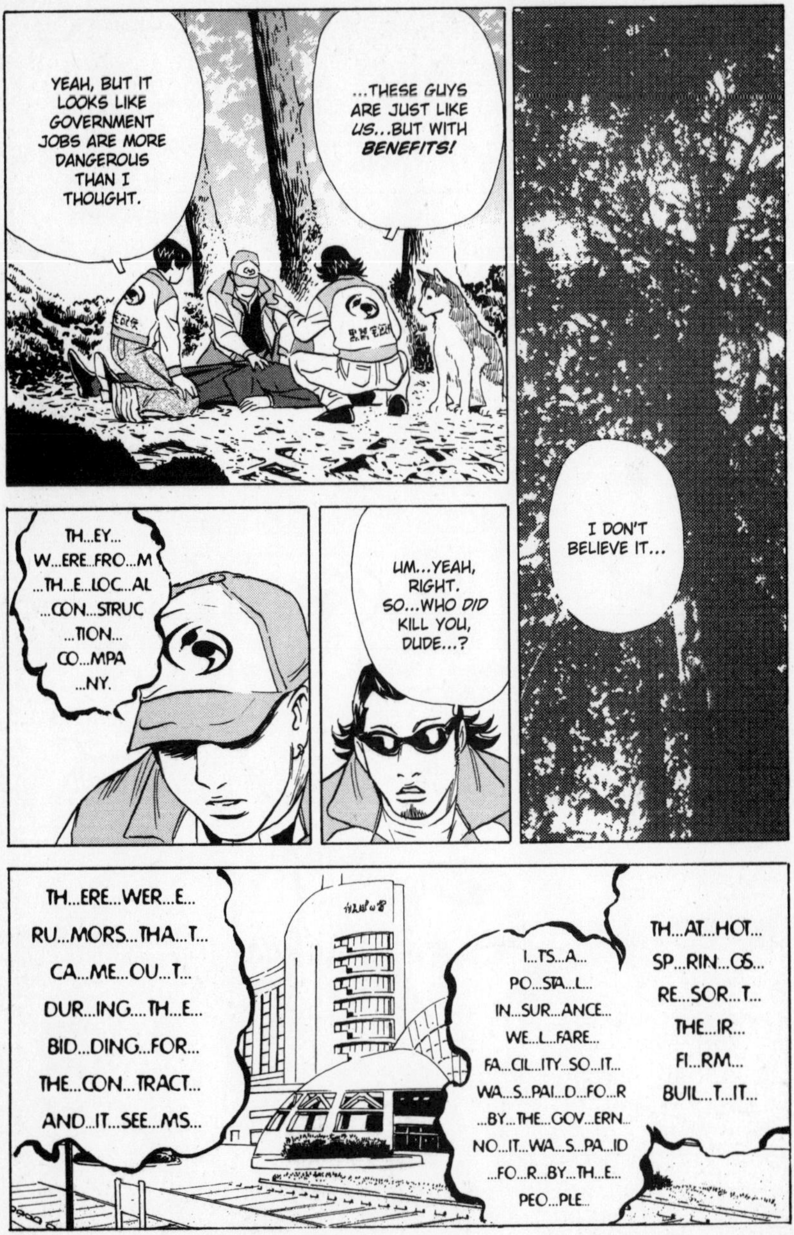
I DON'T BELIEVE IT...
...THESE GUYS ARE JUST LIKE *US*...BUT WITH ***BENEFITS!***
YEAH, BUT IT LOOKS LIKE GOVERNMENT JOBS ARE MORE DANGEROUS THAN I THOUGHT.
UM...YEAH, RIGHT. SO...WHO *DID* KILL YOU, DUDE...?
TH...EY... W...ERE...FRO...M ...TH...E...LOC...AL ...CON...STRUC ...TION... CO...MPA ...NY.
TH...AT...HOT... SP...RIN...GS... RE...SOR...T... THE...IR... FI...RM... BUIL...T...IT...
I...TS...A... PO...STA...L... IN...SUR...ANCE... WE...L...FARE... FA...CIL...ITY...SO...IT... WA...S...PAI...D...FO...R ...BY...THE...GOV...ERN... NO...IT...WA...S...PA...ID ...FO...R...BY...TH...E... PEO...PLE...
TH...ERE...WER...E... RU...MORS...THA...T... CA...ME...OU...T... DUR...ING...TH...E... BID...DING...FOR... THE...CON...TRACT... AND...IT...SEE...MS...

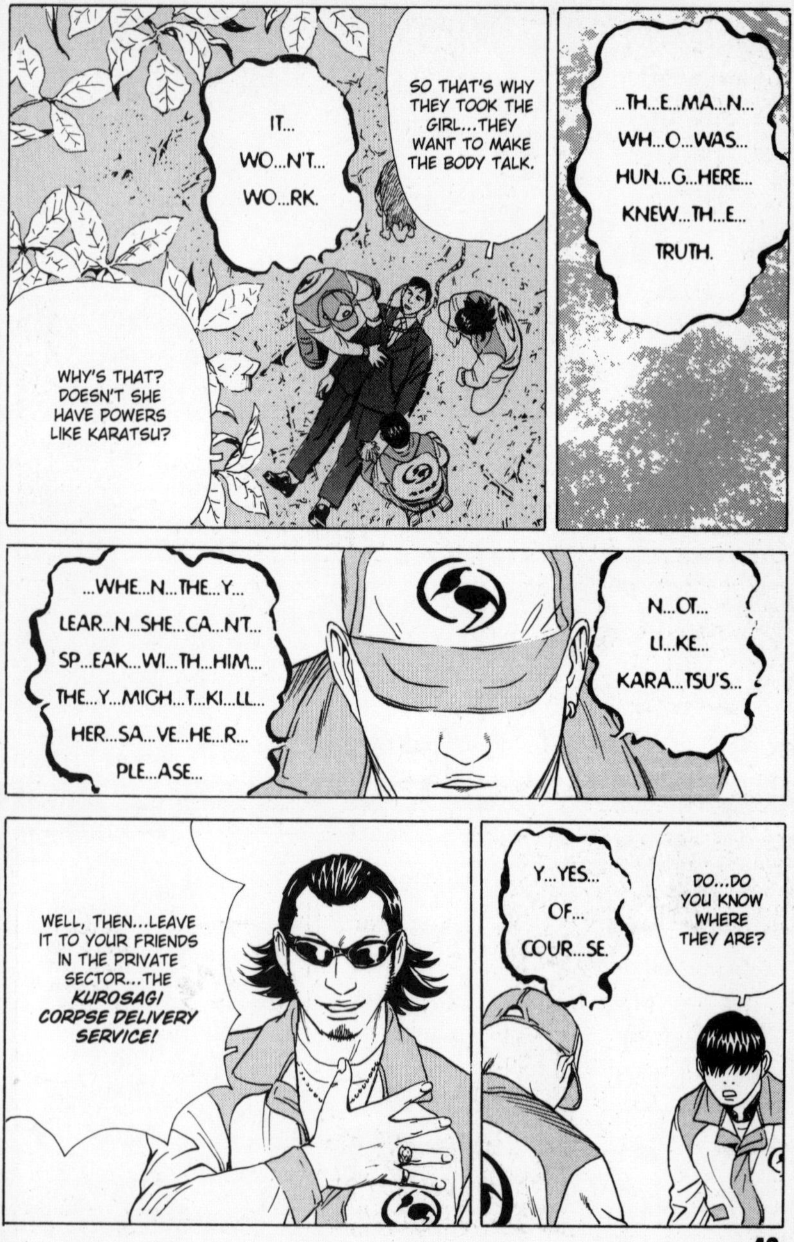
...TH...E...MA...N... WH...O...WAS... HUN...G...HERE... KNEW...TH...E... TRUTH.
SO THAT'S WHY THEY TOOK THE GIRL...THEY WANT TO MAKE THE BODY TALK.
IT... WO...N'T... WO...RK.
WHY'S THAT? DOESN'T SHE HAVE POWERS LIKE KARATSU?
N...OT... LI...KE... KARA...TSU'S...
...WHE...N...THE...Y... LEAR...N...SHE...CA...N'T... SP...EAK...WI...TH...HIM... THE...Y...MIGH...T...KI...LL... HER...SA...VE...HE...R... PLE...ASE...
DO...DO YOU KNOW WHERE THEY ARE?
Y...YES... OF... COUR...SE.
WELL, THEN...LEAVE IT TO YOUR FRIENDS IN THE PRIVATE SECTOR...THE ***KUROSAGI CORPSE DELIVERY SERVICE!***

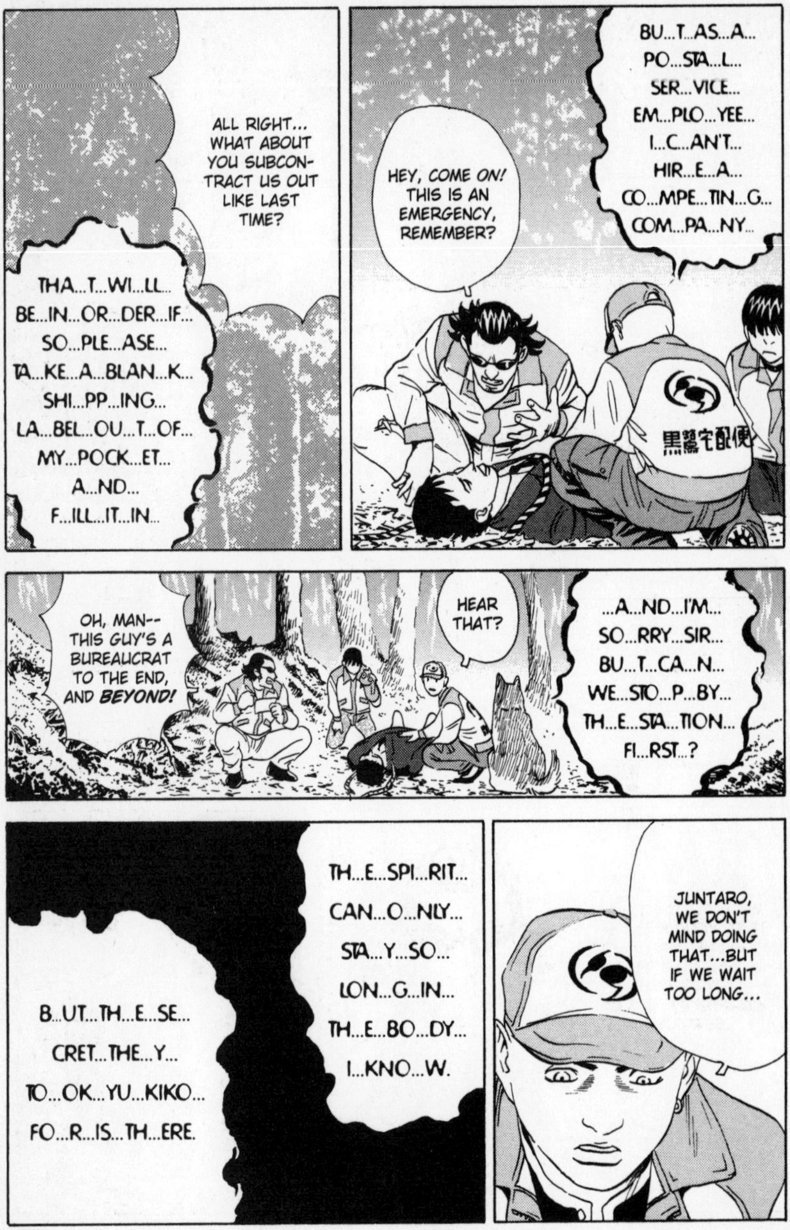
BU...T...AS...A... PO...STA...L... SER...VICE... EM...PLO...YEE... I...C...AN'T... HIR...E...A... CO...MPE...TIN...G... COM...PA...NY...
HEY, COME ON! THIS IS AN EMERGENCY, REMEMBER?
黒鷺宅配便
ALL RIGHT... WHAT ABOUT YOU SUBCON-TRACT US OUT LIKE LAST TIME?
THA...T...WI...LL... BE...IN...OR...DER...IF... SO...PLE...ASE... TA...KE...A...BLAN...K... SHI...PP...ING... LA...BEL...OU...T...OF... MY...POCK...ET... A...ND... F...ILL...IT...IN...
...A...ND...I'M... SO...RRY...SIR... BU...T...CA...N... WE...STO...P...BY... TH...E...STA...TION... FI...RST...?
HEAR THAT?
OH, MAN-- THIS GUY'S A BUREAUCRAT TO THE END, AND ***BEYOND!***
JUNTARO, WE DON'T MIND DOING THAT...BUT IF WE WAIT TOO LONG...
TH...E...SPI...RIT... CAN...O...NLY... STA...Y...SO... LON...G...IN... TH...E...BO...DY... I...KNO...W.
B...UT...TH...E...SE... CRET...THE...Y... TO...OK...YU...KIKO... FO...R...IS...TH...ERE.

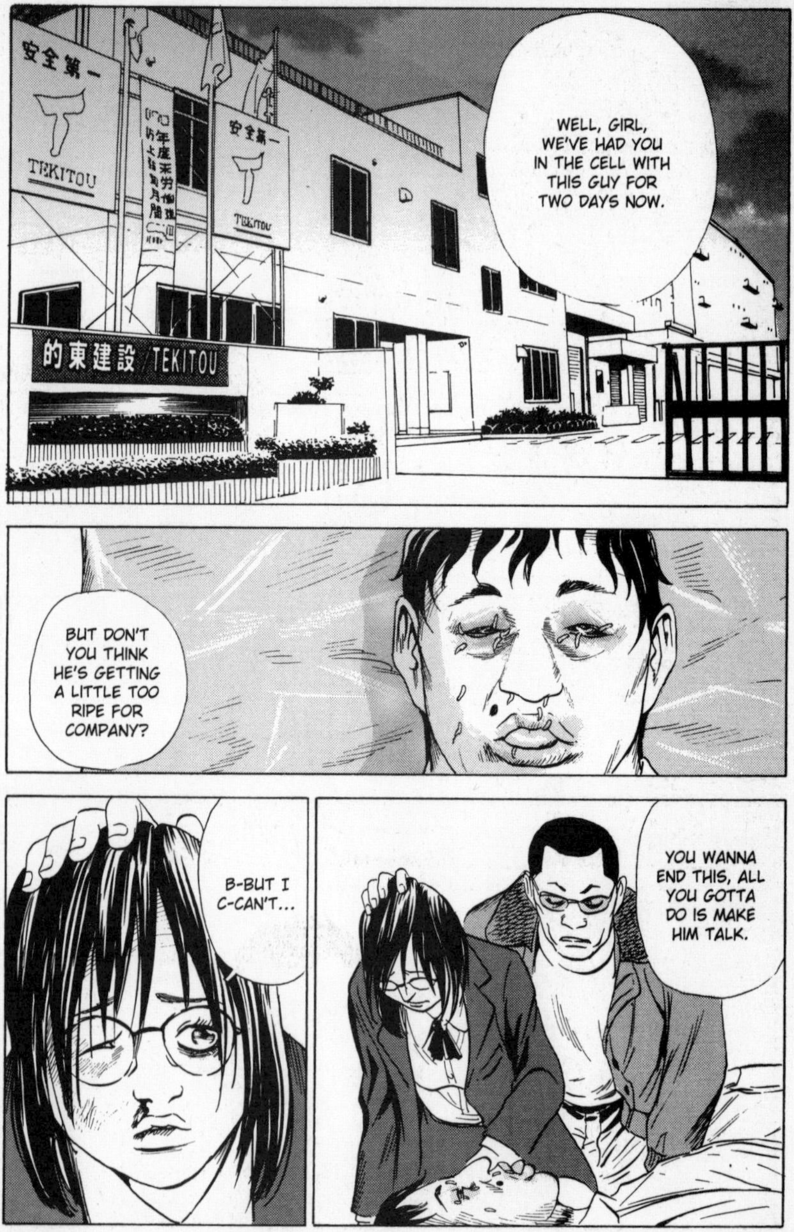
安全第一
TEKITOU
的東建設/TEKITOU
WELL, GIRL, WE'VE HAD YOU IN THE CELL WITH THIS GUY FOR TWO DAYS NOW.
BUT DON'T YOU THINK HE'S GETTING A LITTLE TOO RIPE FOR COMPANY?
YOU WANNA END THIS, ALL YOU GOTTA DO IS MAKE HIM TALK.
B-BUT I C-CAN'T...

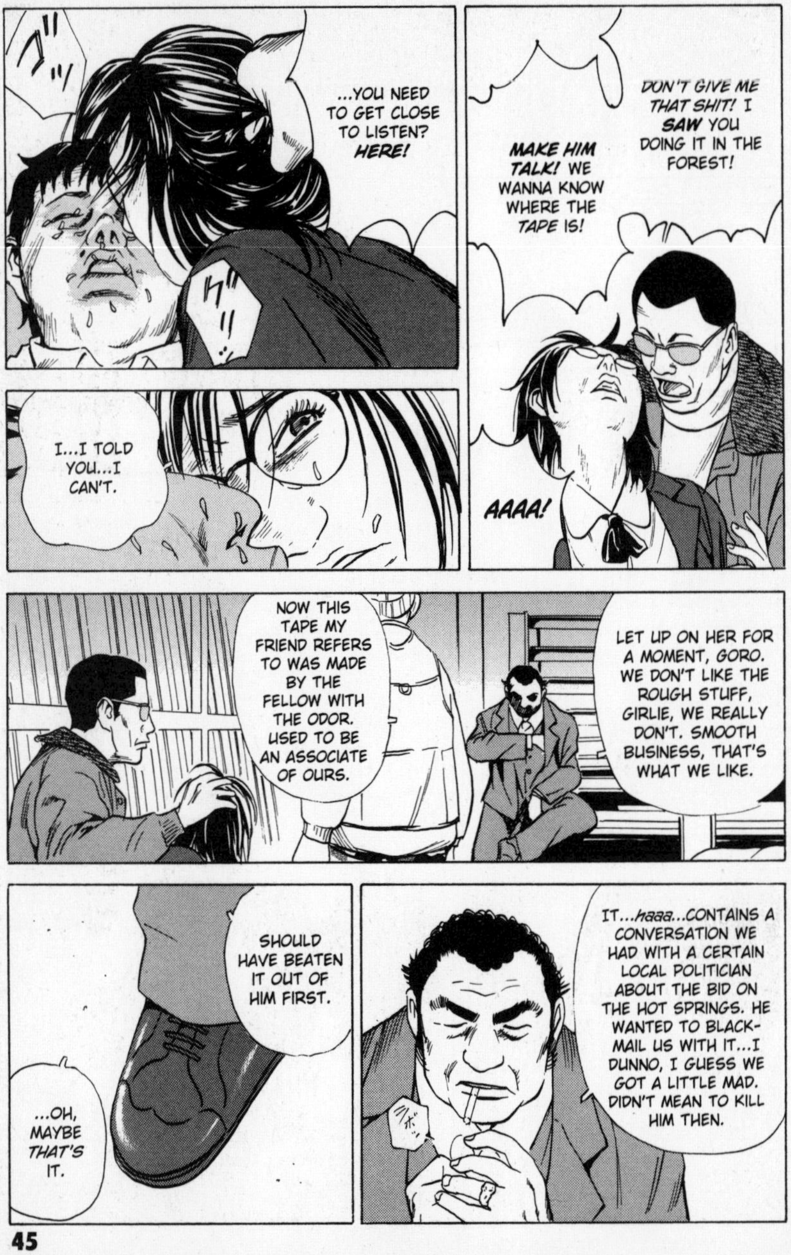
DON'T GIVE ME THAT SHIT! I SAW YOU DOING IT IN THE FOREST!
MAKE HIM TALK! WE WANNA KNOW WHERE THE TAPE IS!
AAAA!
...YOU NEED TO GET CLOSE TO LISTEN? HERE!
I...I TOLD YOU...I CAN'T.
LET UP ON HER FOR A MOMENT, GORO. WE DON'T LIKE THE ROUGH STUFF, GIRLIE, WE REALLY DON'T. SMOOTH BUSINESS, THAT'S WHAT WE LIKE.
NOW THIS TAPE MY FRIEND REFERS TO WAS MADE BY THE FELLOW WITH THE ODOR. USED TO BE AN ASSOCIATE OF OURS.
IT...haaa...CONTAINS A CONVERSATION WE HAD WITH A CERTAIN LOCAL POLITICIAN ABOUT THE BID ON THE HOT SPRINGS. HE WANTED TO BLACK-MAIL US WITH IT...I DUNNO, I GUESS WE GOT A LITTLE MAD. DIDN'T MEAN TO KILL HIM THEN.
SHOULD HAVE BEATEN IT OUT OF HIM FIRST.
...OH, MAYBE THAT'S IT.

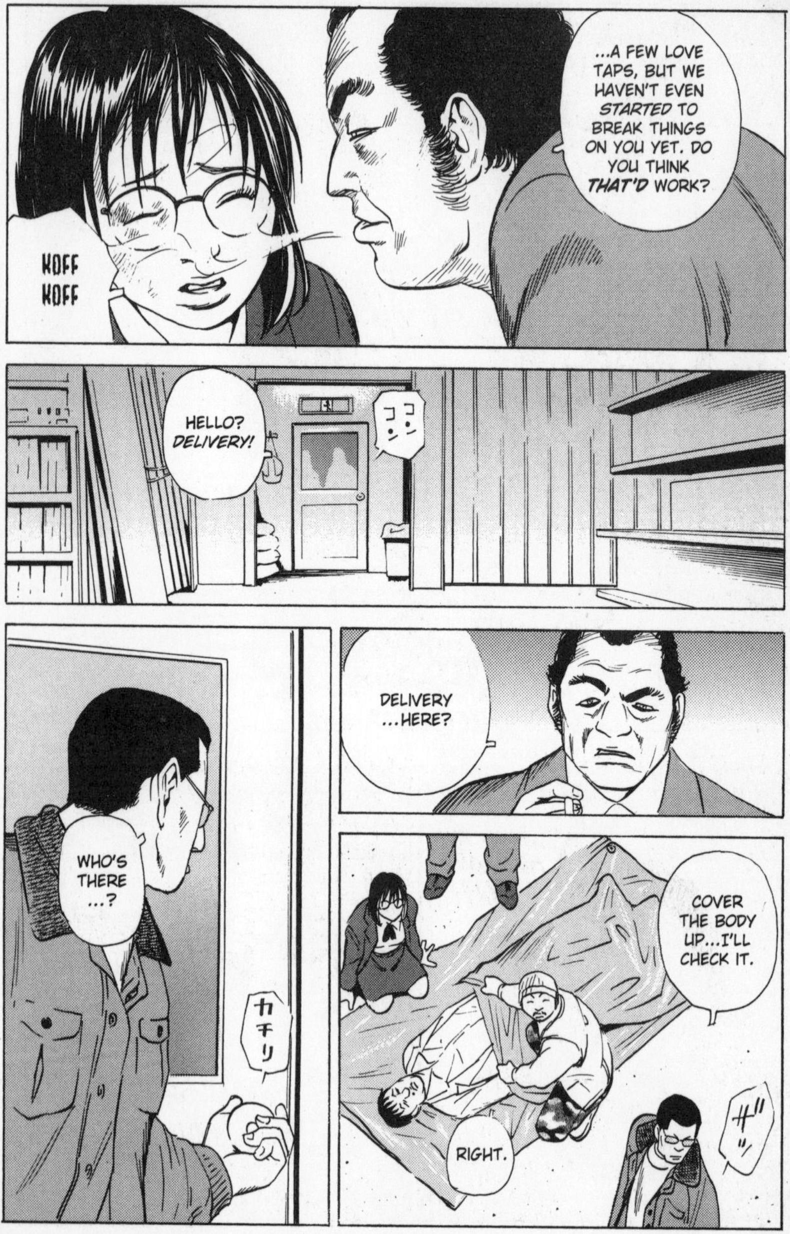
...A FEW LOVE TAPS, BUT WE HAVEN'T EVEN *STARTED* TO BREAK THINGS ON YOU YET. DO YOU THINK ***THAT'D*** WORK?
KOFF KOFF
コンコン
HELLO? *DELIVERY!*
DELIVERY ...HERE?
COVER THE BODY UP...I'LL CHECK IT.
ザッ
RIGHT.
WHO'S THERE ...?
カチリ

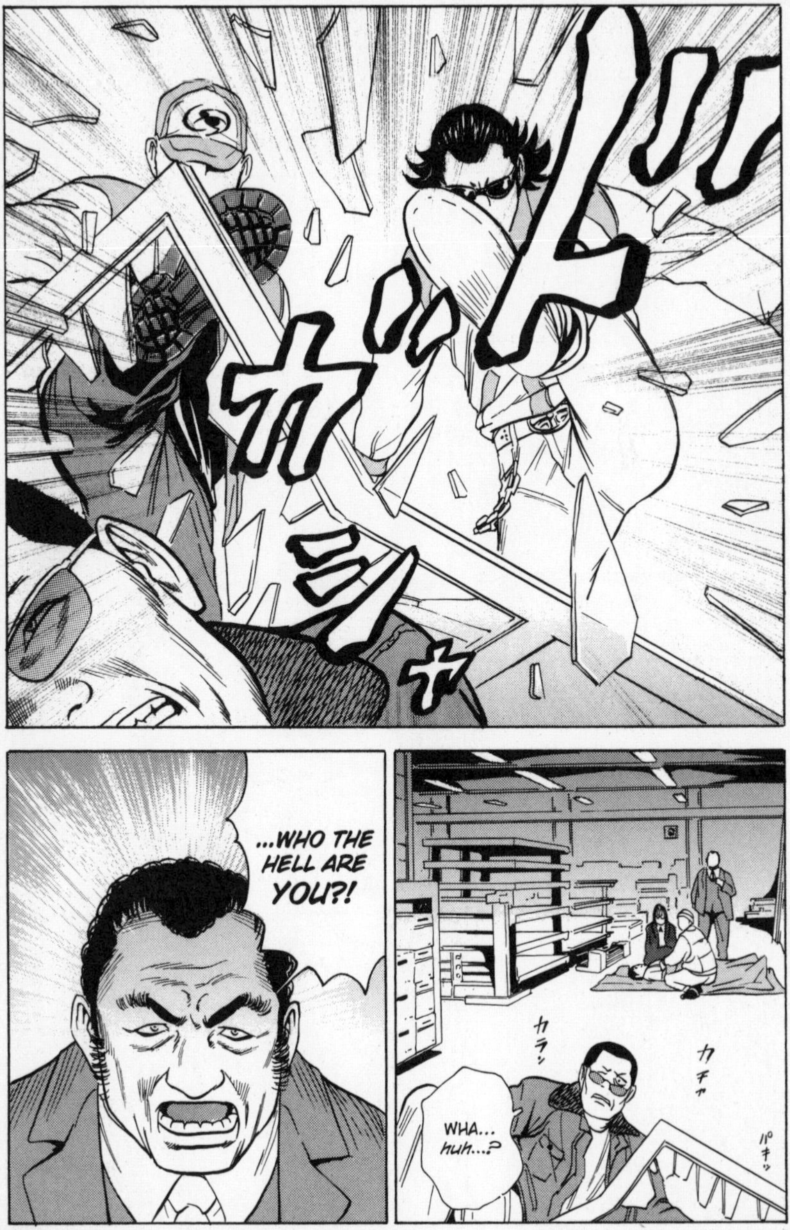
WHA... huh...?
カラン
カチャ
パキッ
...WHO THE HELL ARE YOU?!

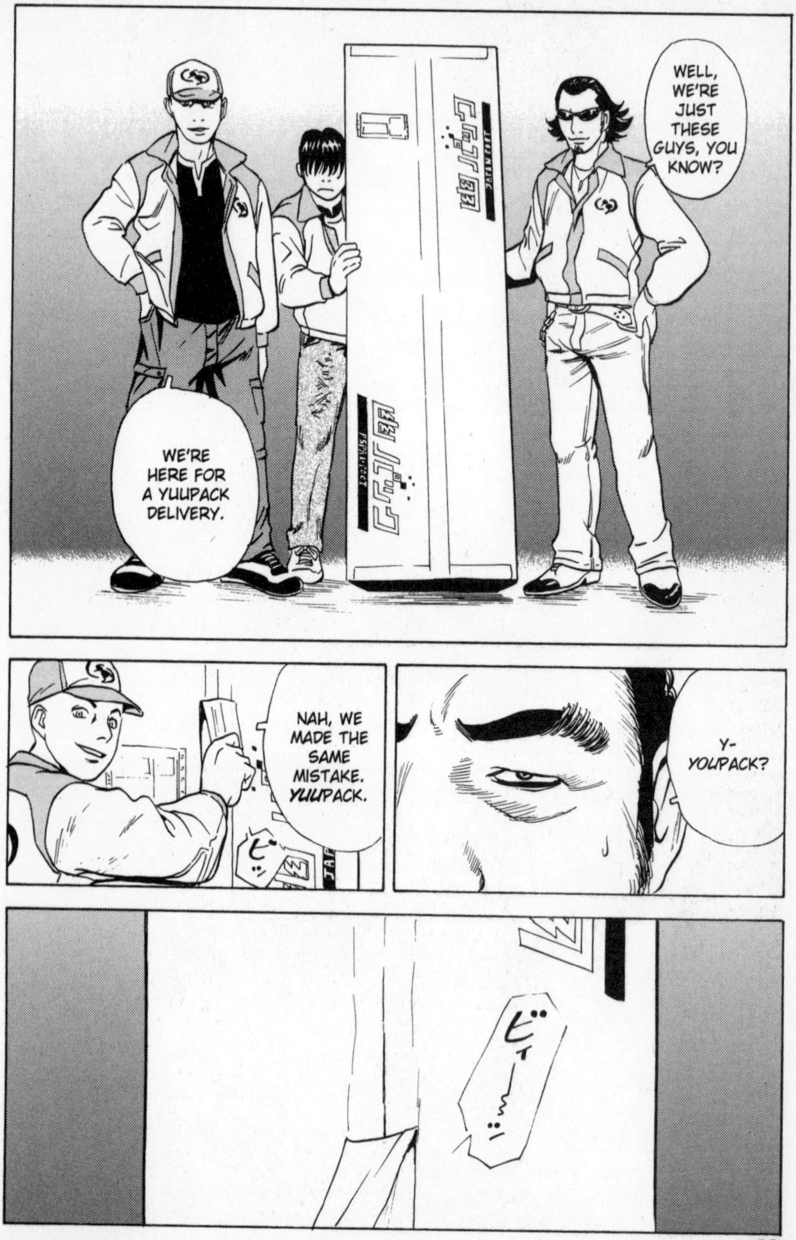
WELL, WE'RE JUST THESE GUYS, YOU KNOW?
WE'RE HERE FOR A YUUPACK DELIVERY.
Y- YOUPACK?
NAH, WE MADE THE SAME MISTAKE. YUUPACK.

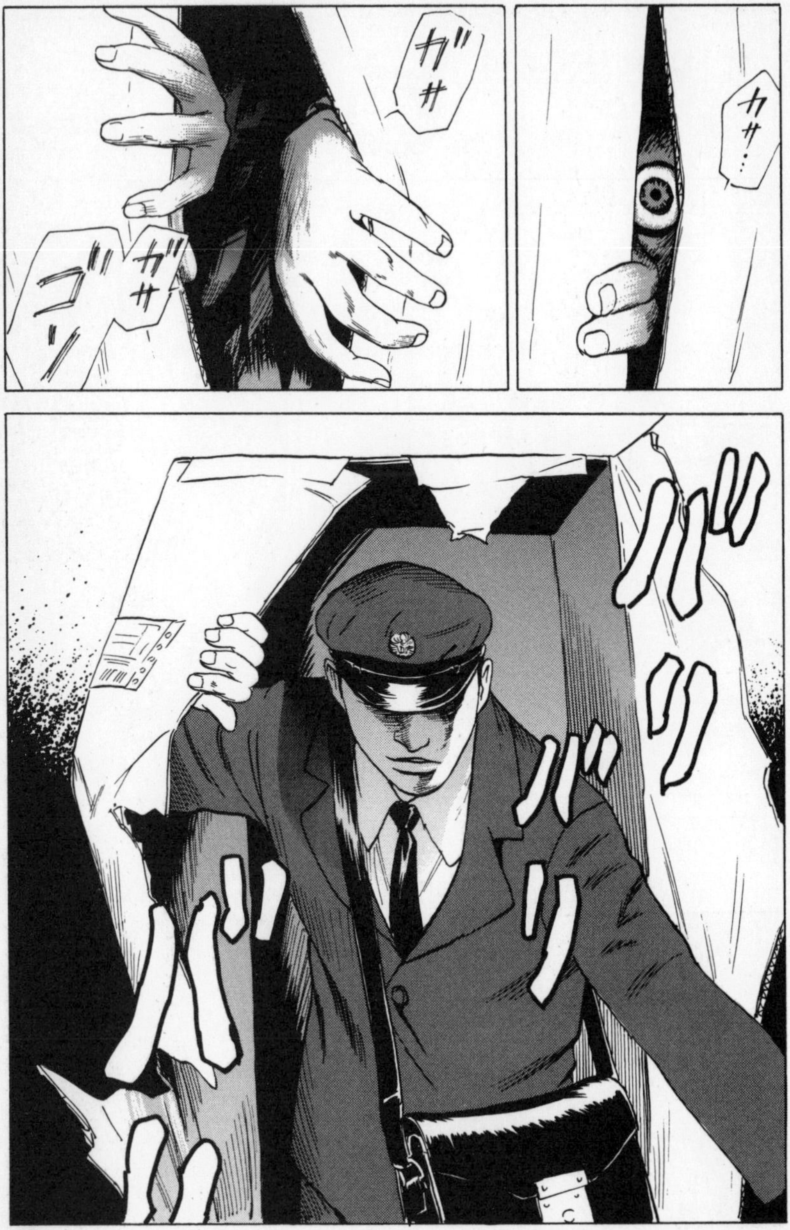
カサ…
ガサ
ガサ
ゴン
バリ
バリ

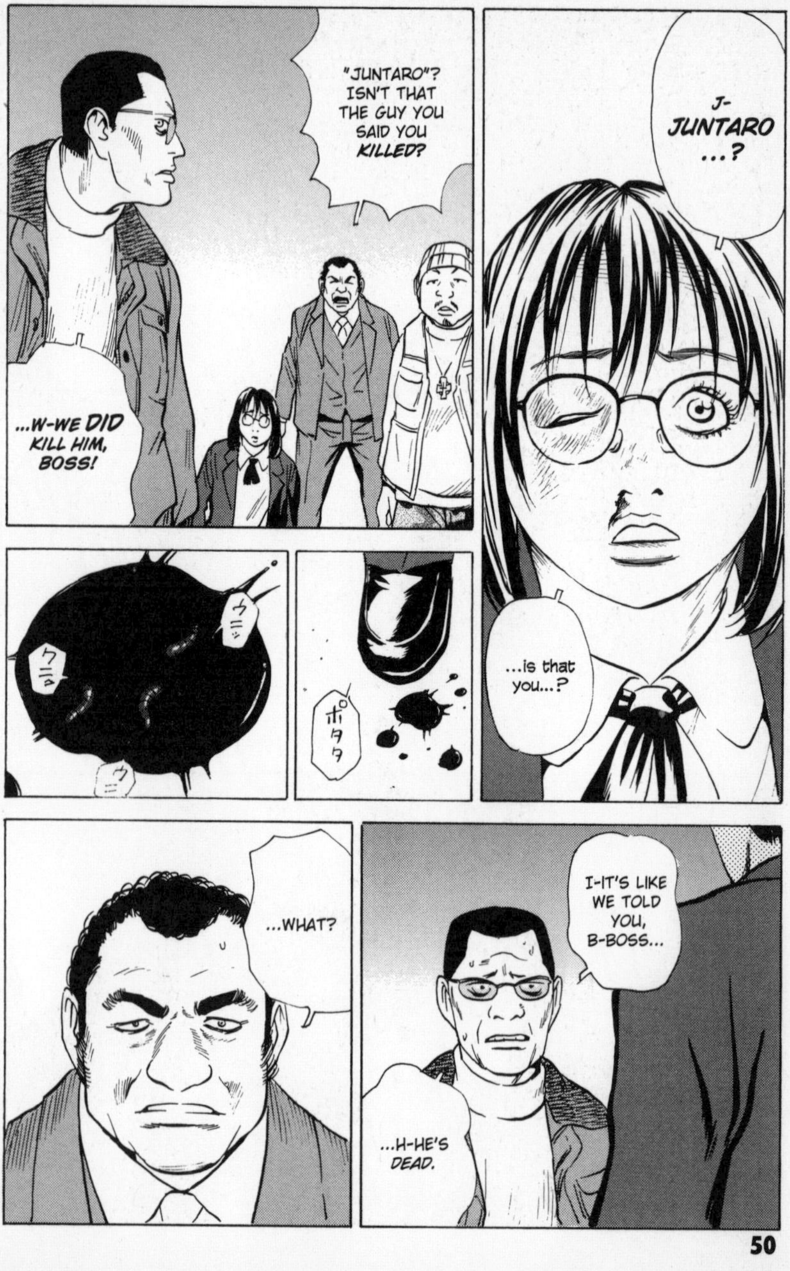
J-JUNTARO ...?
...is that you...?
"JUNTARO"? ISN'T THAT THE GUY YOU SAID YOU KILLED?
...W-WE DID KILL HIM, BOSS!
ポタタ
ウニッ
クニュ
ウニ
I-IT'S LIKE WE TOLD YOU, B-BOSS...
...H-HE'S DEAD.
...WHAT?

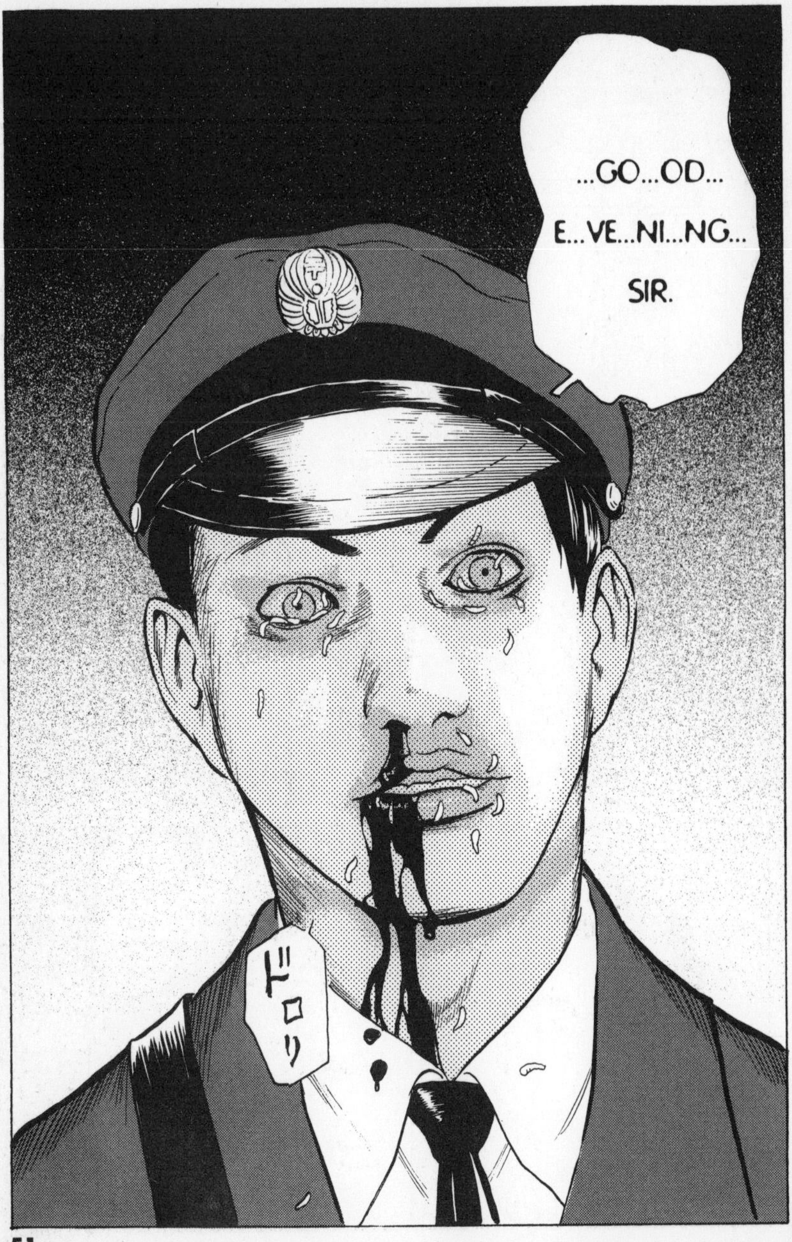
...GO...OD... E...VE...NI...NG... SIR.
ドロリ

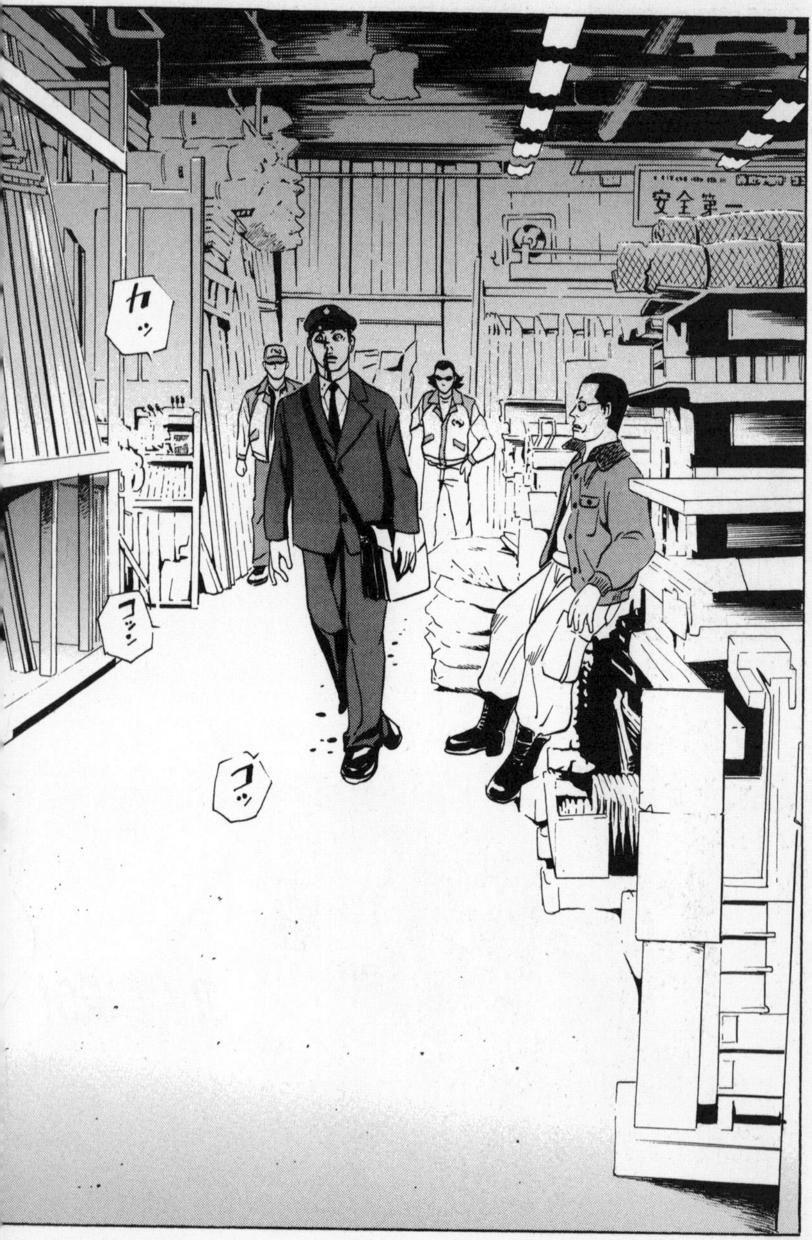
安全第一
カッ
コッン
コッ

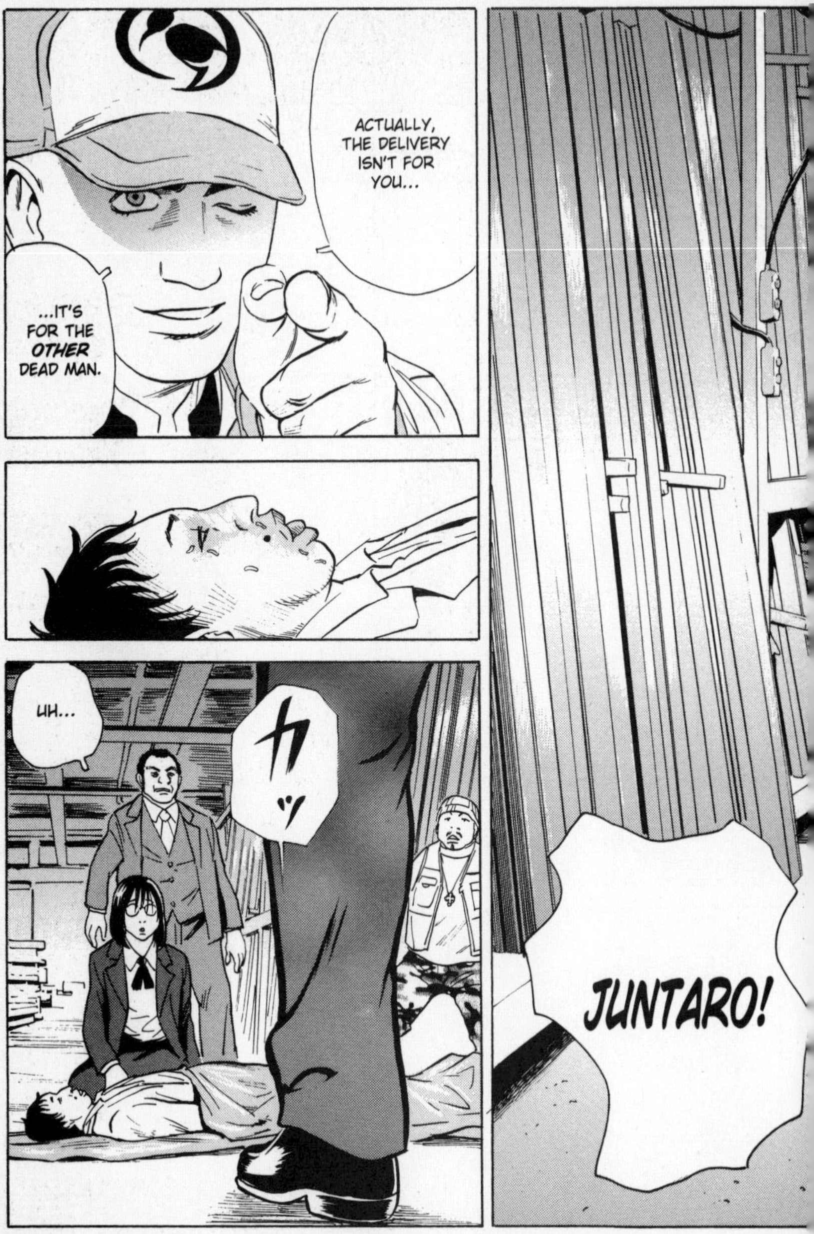
JUNTARO!
ACTUALLY, THE DELIVERY ISN'T FOR YOU...
...IT'S FOR THE *OTHER* DEAD MAN.
UH...
カッ

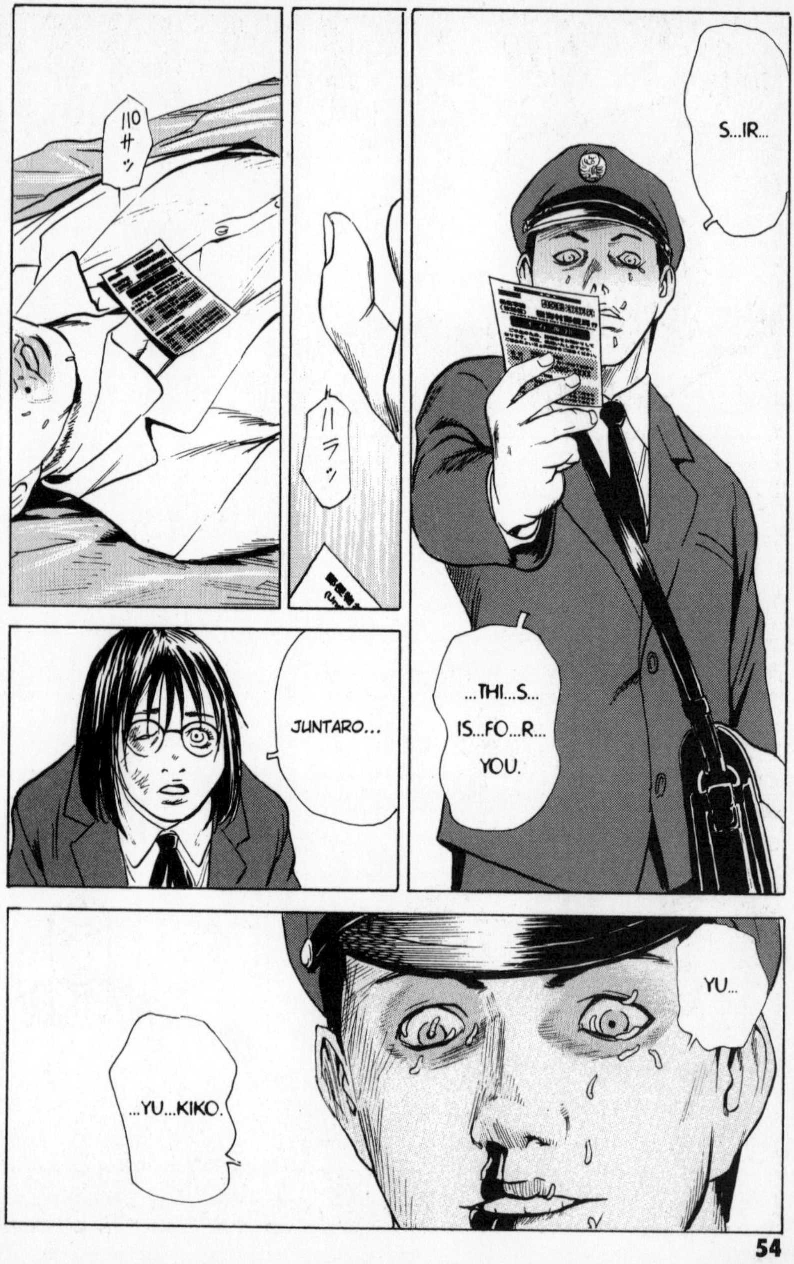
S...IR...
...THI...S...
IS...FO...R...
YOU.
ハラッ
バサッ
JUNTARO...
YU...
...YU...KIKO.

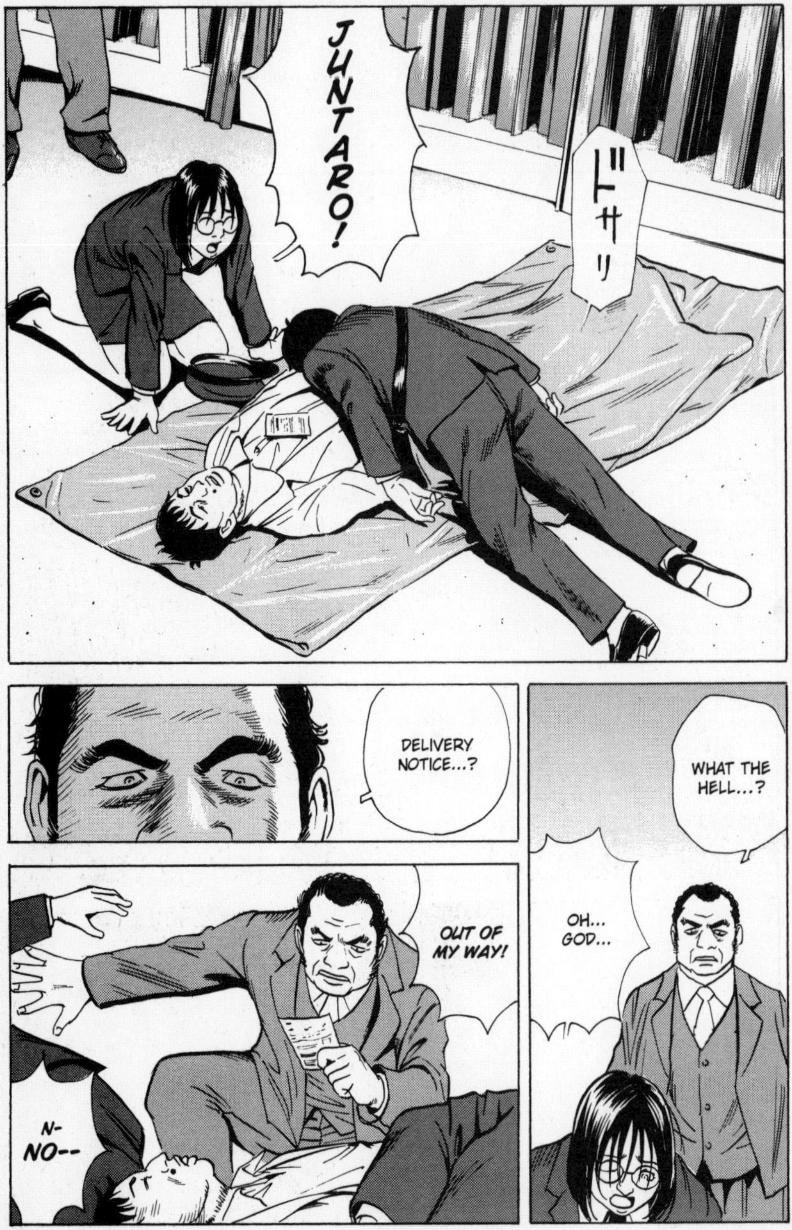
JUNTARO!
ドサリ
WHAT THE HELL...?
OH... GOD...
DELIVERY NOTICE...?
OUT OF MY WAY!
N- NO--

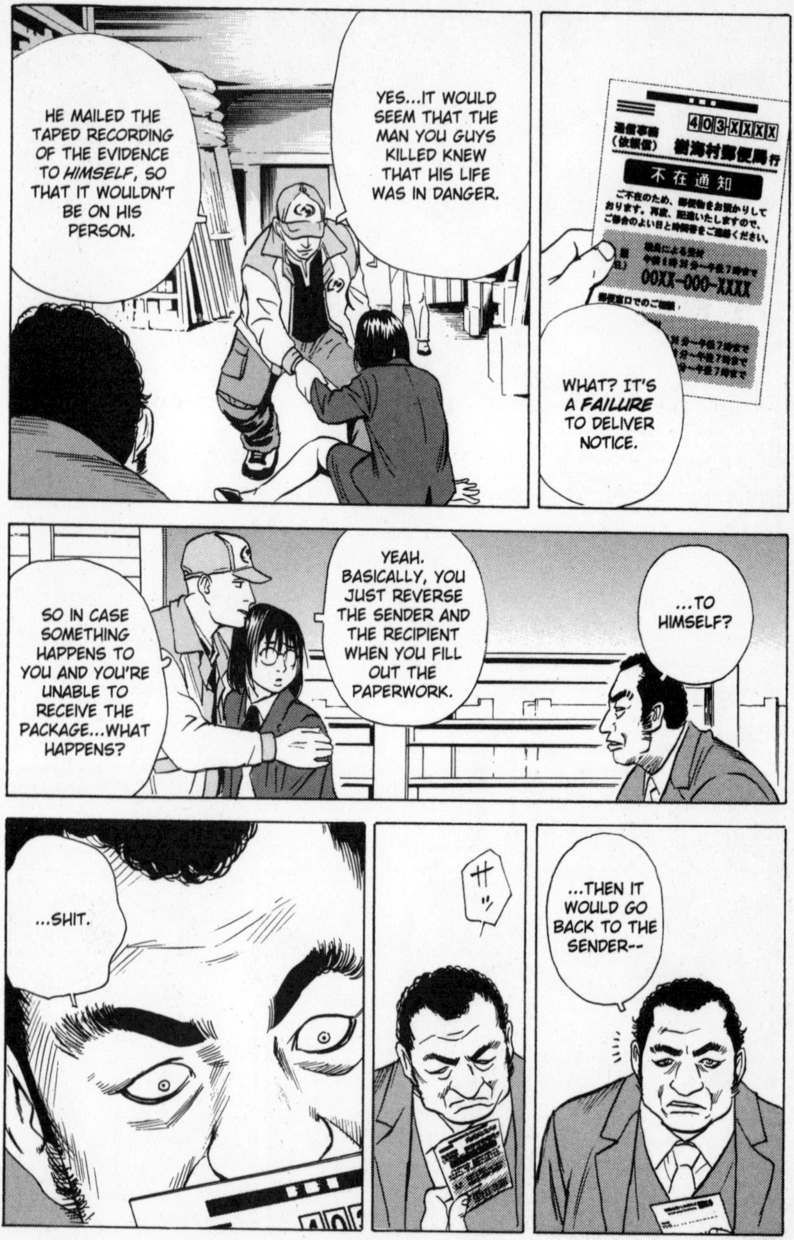
不在通知
WHAT? IT'S A *FAILURE* TO DELIVER NOTICE.
YES...IT WOULD SEEM THAT THE MAN YOU GUYS KILLED KNEW THAT HIS LIFE WAS IN DANGER.
HE MAILED THE TAPED RECORDING OF THE EVIDENCE TO *HIMSELF*, SO THAT IT WOULDN'T BE ON HIS PERSON.
...TO HIMSELF?
YEAH. BASICALLY, YOU JUST REVERSE THE SENDER AND THE RECIPIENT WHEN YOU FILL OUT THE PAPERWORK.
SO IN CASE SOMETHING HAPPENS TO YOU AND YOU'RE UNABLE TO RECEIVE THE PACKAGE...WHAT HAPPENS?
...THEN IT WOULD GO BACK TO THE SENDER--
ザッ
...SHIT.

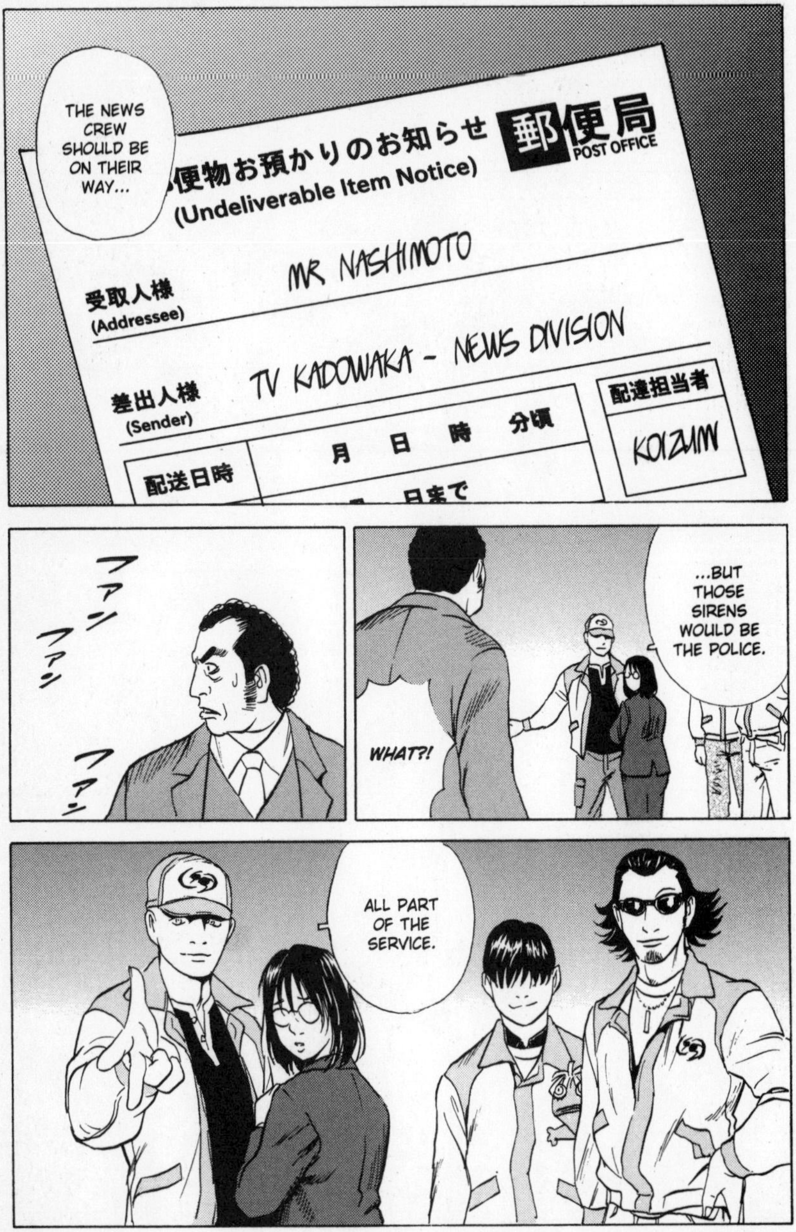
郵便局
POST OFFICE
便物お預かりのお知らせ
(Undeliverable Item Notice)
受取人様
(Addressee)
MR NASHIMOTO
差出人様
(Sender)
TV KADOWAKA - NEWS DIVISION
配達担当者
KOIZUMI
月 日 時 分頃
配送日時
THE NEWS CREW SHOULD BE ON THEIR WAY...
...BUT THOSE SIRENS WOULD BE THE POLICE.
WHAT?!
ファン
ファン
ファン
ALL PART OF THE SERVICE.

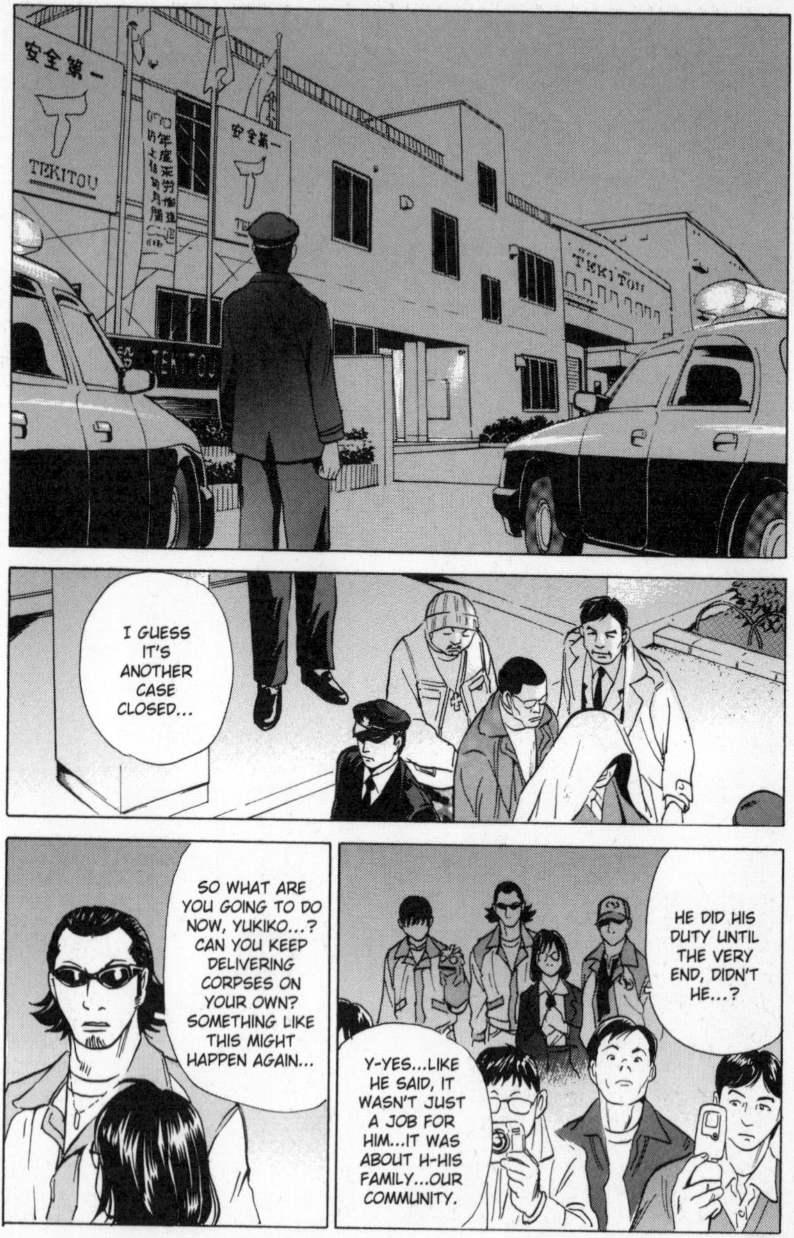
安全第一
TEKITOU
TEKITOU
I GUESS IT'S ANOTHER CASE CLOSED...
HE DID HIS DUTY UNTIL THE VERY END, DIDN'T HE...?
Y-YES...LIKE HE SAID, IT WASN'T JUST A JOB FOR HIM...IT WAS ABOUT H-HIS FAMILY...OUR COMMUNITY.
SO WHAT ARE YOU GOING TO DO NOW, YUKIKO...? CAN YOU KEEP DELIVERING CORPSES ON YOUR OWN? SOMETHING LIKE THIS MIGHT HAPPEN AGAIN...

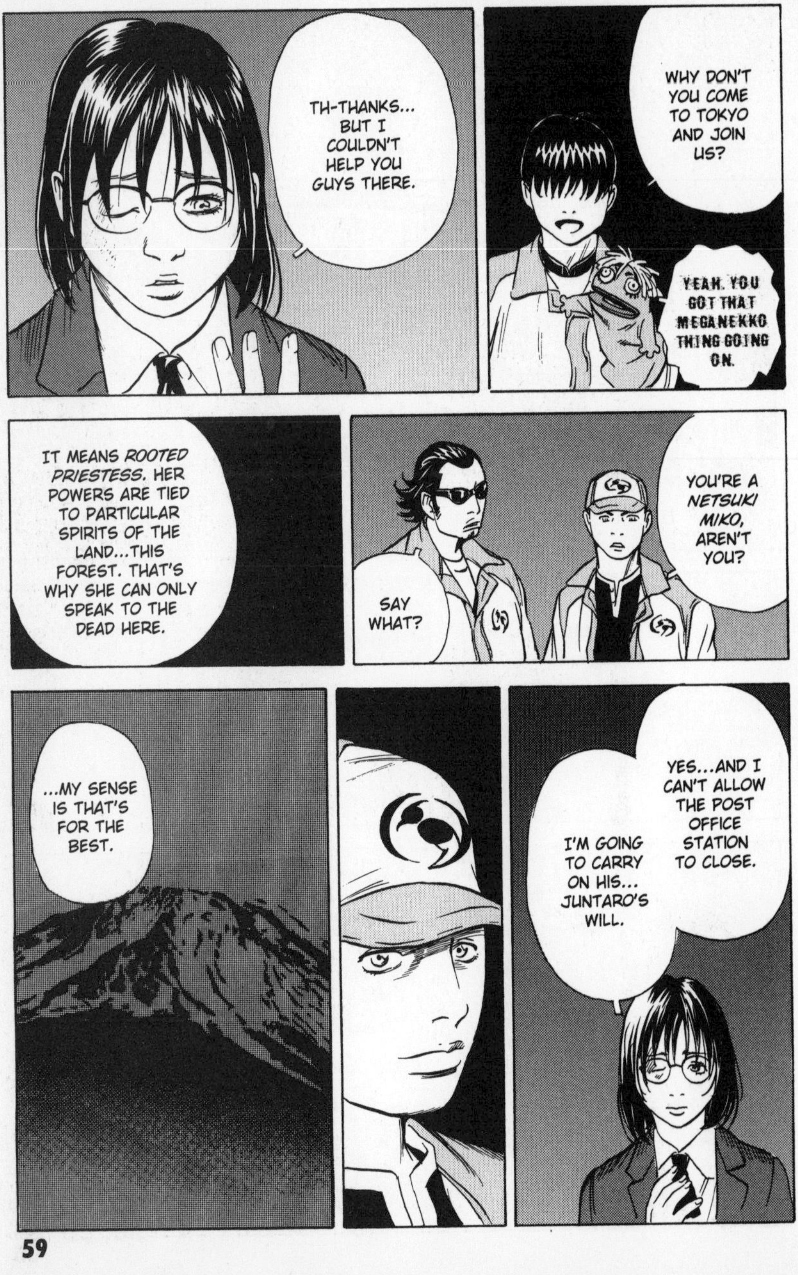
WHY DON'T YOU COME TO TOKYO AND JOIN US?
YEAH. YOU GOT THAT MEGANEKKO THING GOING ON.
TH-THANKS... BUT I COULDN'T HELP YOU GUYS THERE.
YOU'RE A *NETSUKI MIKO*, AREN'T YOU?
SAY WHAT?
IT MEANS *ROOTED PRIESTESS*. HER POWERS ARE TIED TO PARTICULAR SPIRITS OF THE LAND...THIS FOREST. THAT'S WHY SHE CAN ONLY SPEAK TO THE DEAD HERE.
YES...AND I CAN'T ALLOW THE POST OFFICE STATION TO CLOSE.
I'M GOING TO CARRY ON HIS... JUNTARO'S WILL.
...MY SENSE IS THAT'S FOR THE BEST.

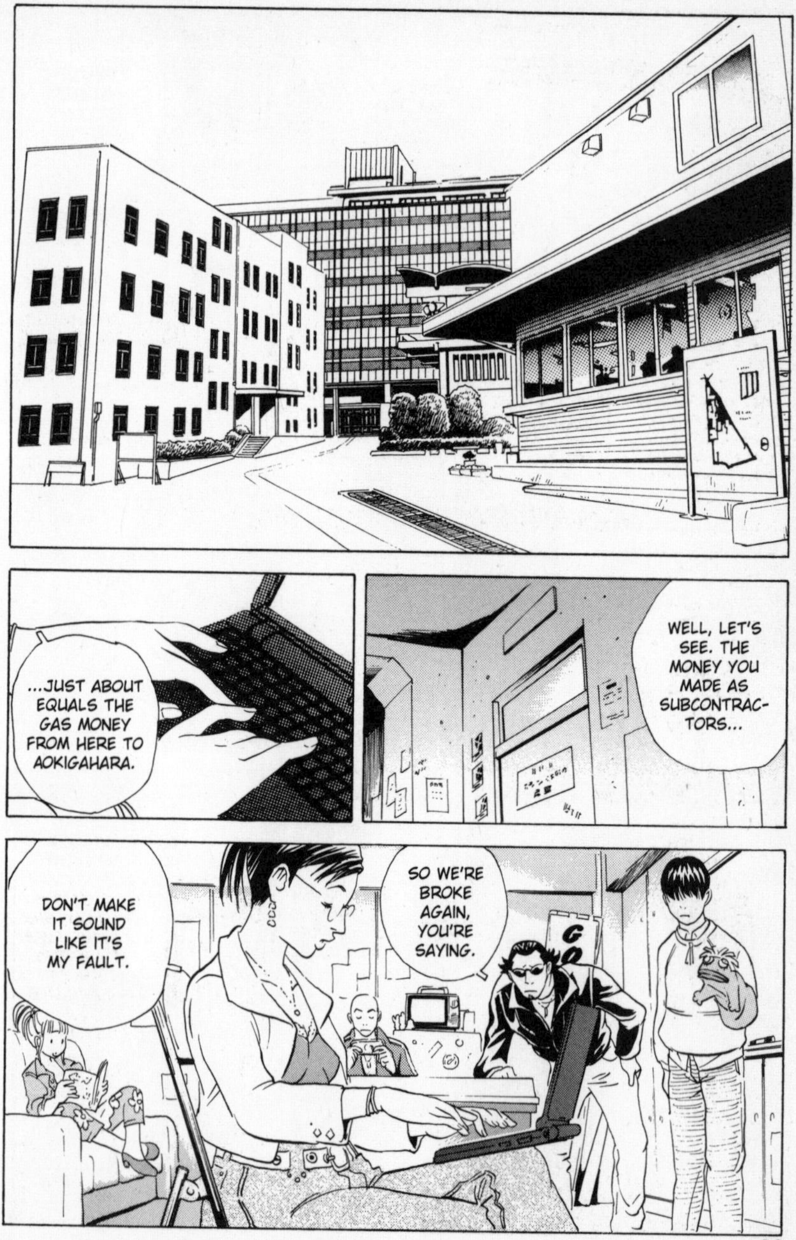
WELL, LET'S SEE. THE MONEY YOU MADE AS SUBCONTRAC-TORS...
...JUST ABOUT EQUALS THE GAS MONEY FROM HERE TO AOKIGAHARA.
SO WE'RE BROKE AGAIN, YOU'RE SAYING.
DON'T MAKE IT SOUND LIKE IT'S MY FAULT.

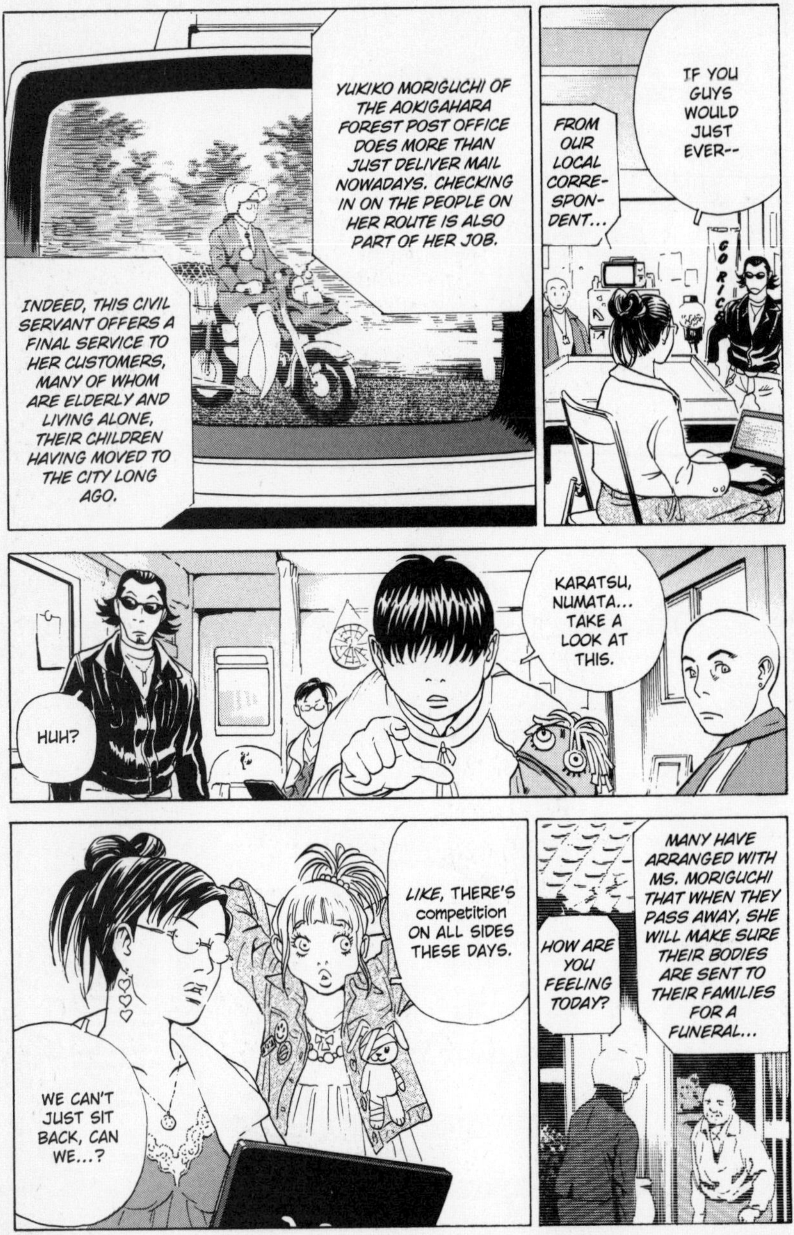
IF YOU GUYS WOULD JUST EVER--
FROM OUR LOCAL CORRESPONDENT...
YUKIKO MORIGUCHI OF THE AOKIGAHARA FOREST POST OFFICE DOES MORE THAN JUST DELIVER MAIL NOWADAYS. CHECKING IN ON THE PEOPLE ON HER ROUTE IS ALSO PART OF HER JOB.
INDEED, THIS CIVIL SERVANT OFFERS A FINAL SERVICE TO HER CUSTOMERS, MANY OF WHOM ARE ELDERLY AND LIVING ALONE, THEIR CHILDREN HAVING MOVED TO THE CITY LONG AGO.
KARATSU, NUMATA... TAKE A LOOK AT THIS.
HUH?
MANY HAVE ARRANGED WITH MS. MORIGUCHI THAT WHEN THEY PASS AWAY, SHE WILL MAKE SURE THEIR BODIES ARE SENT TO THEIR FAMILIES FOR A FUNERAL...
HOW ARE YOU FEELING TODAY?
LIKE, THERE'S competition ON ALL SIDES THESE DAYS.
WE CAN'T JUST SIT BACK, CAN WE...?

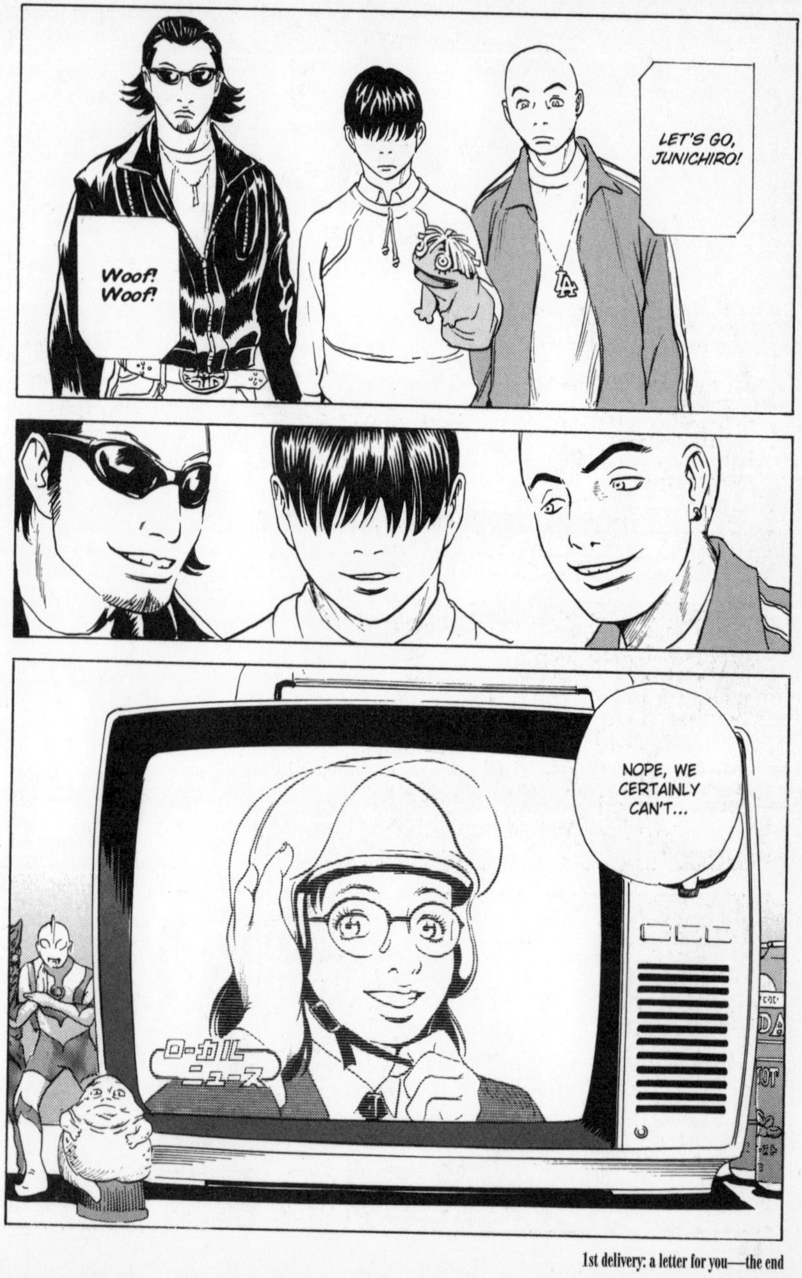
LET'S GO, JUNICHIRO!
Woof! Woof!
NOPE, WE CERTAINLY CAN'T...
ローカル ニュース

1st delivery: a letter for you—the end

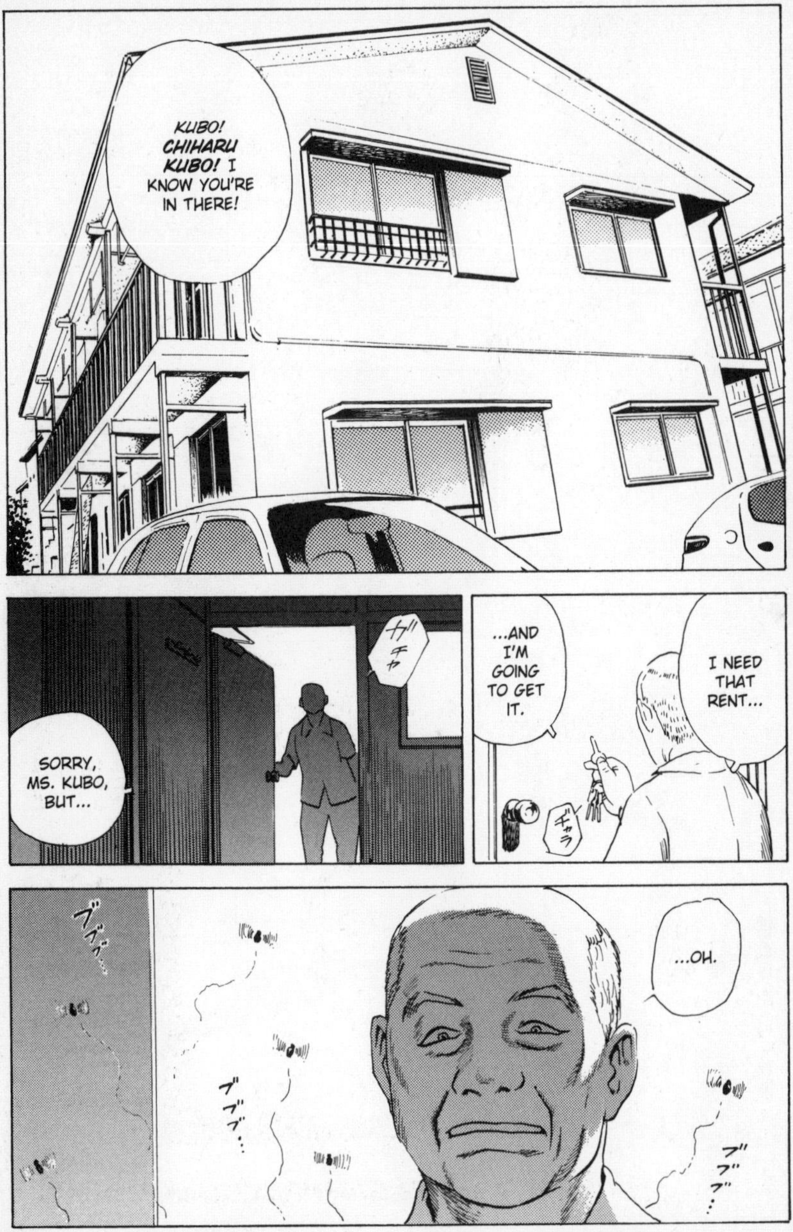
KUBO! CHIHARU KUBO! I KNOW YOU'RE IN THERE!
I NEED THAT RENT...
...AND I'M GOING TO GET IT.
ヂャラ
ガチャ
SORRY, MS. KUBO, BUT...
...OH.
ブブブ...
ブブブ...
ブブブ...

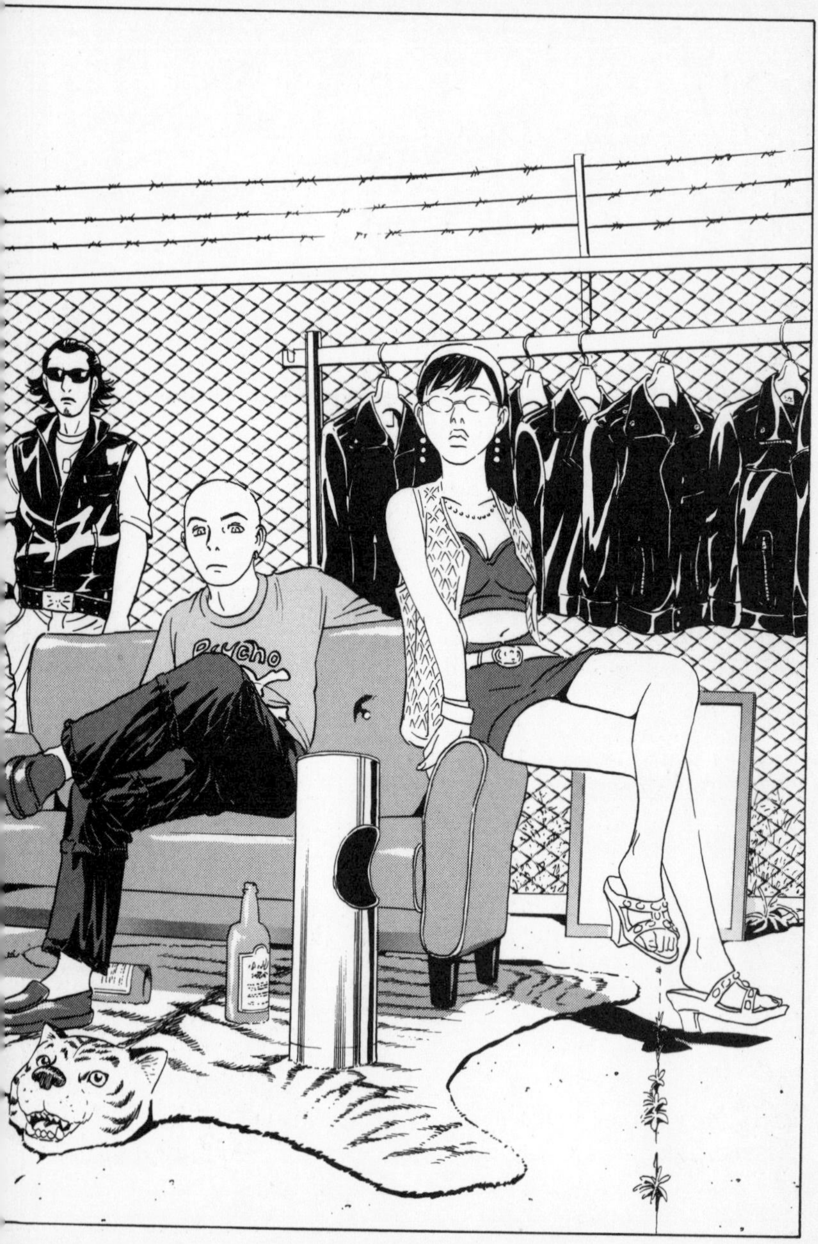
Psycho

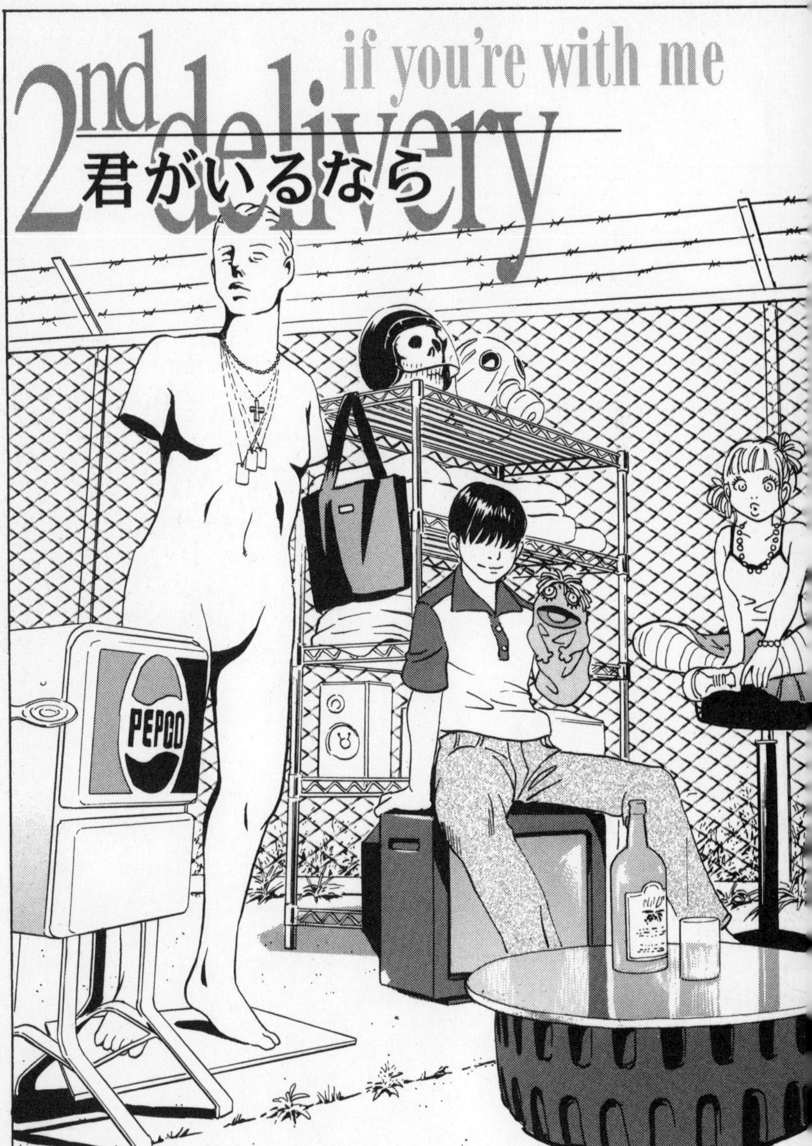
2nd delivery
if you're with me
君がいるなら
PEPOO

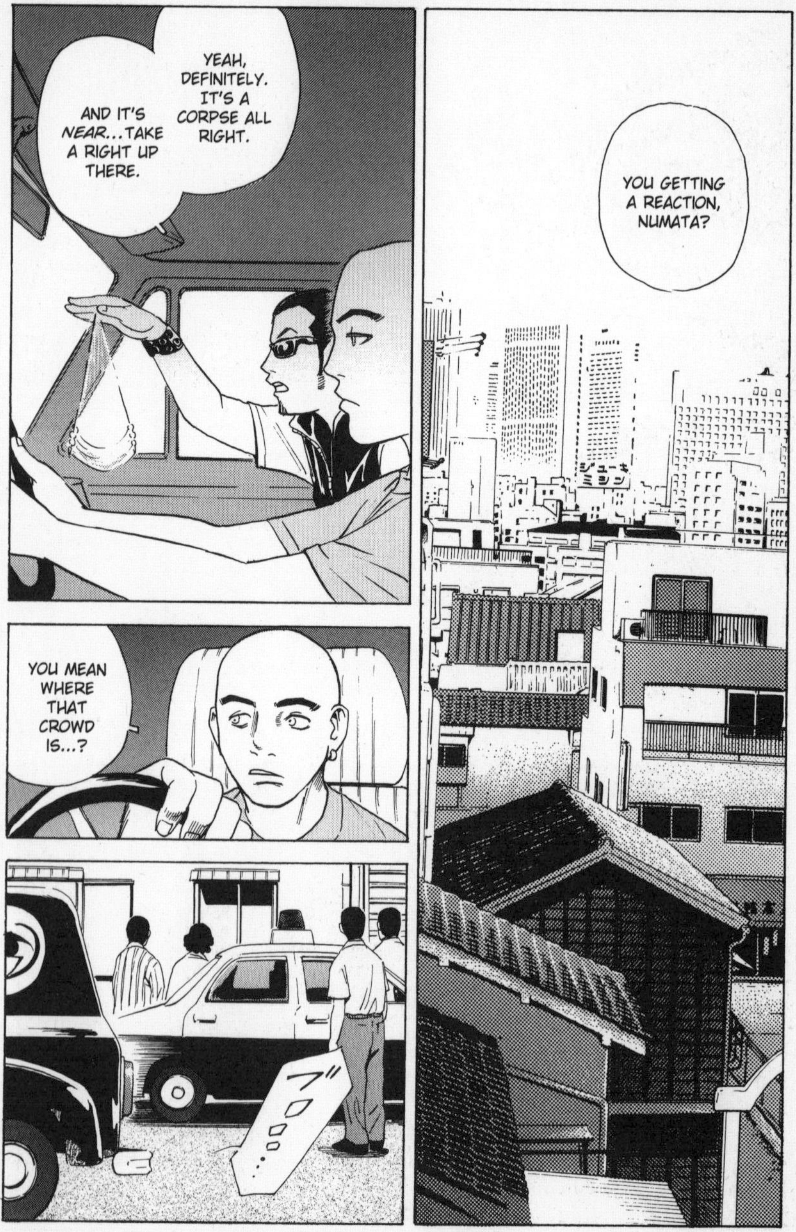
YOU GETTING A REACTION, NUMATA?
ジューキ ミシン
YEAH, DEFINITELY. IT'S A CORPSE ALL RIGHT.
AND IT'S *NEAR*...TAKE A RIGHT UP THERE.
YOU MEAN WHERE THAT CROWD IS...?
ブロロロ...

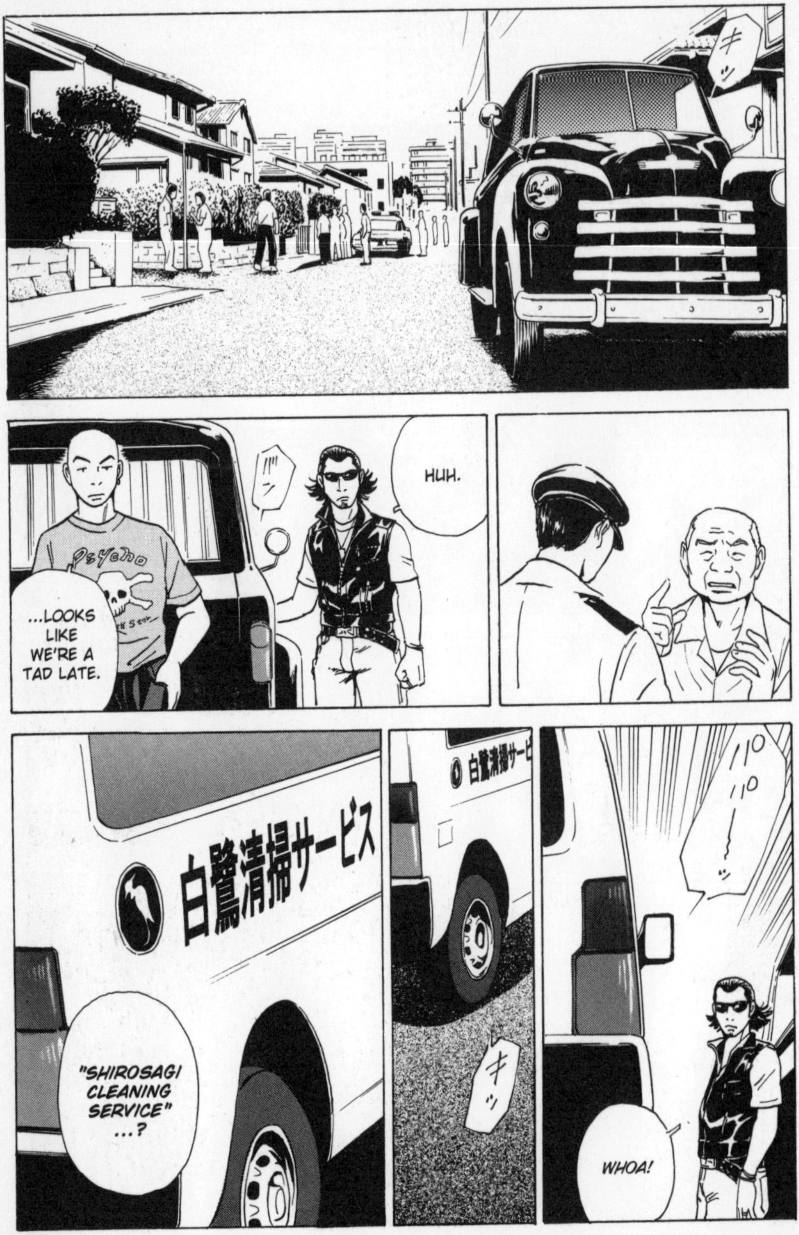
キッ
HUH.
バン
...LOOKS LIKE WE'RE A TAD LATE.
WHOA!
白鷺清掃サービ
キッ
白鷺清掃サービス
"SHIROSAGI CLEANING SERVICE" ...?

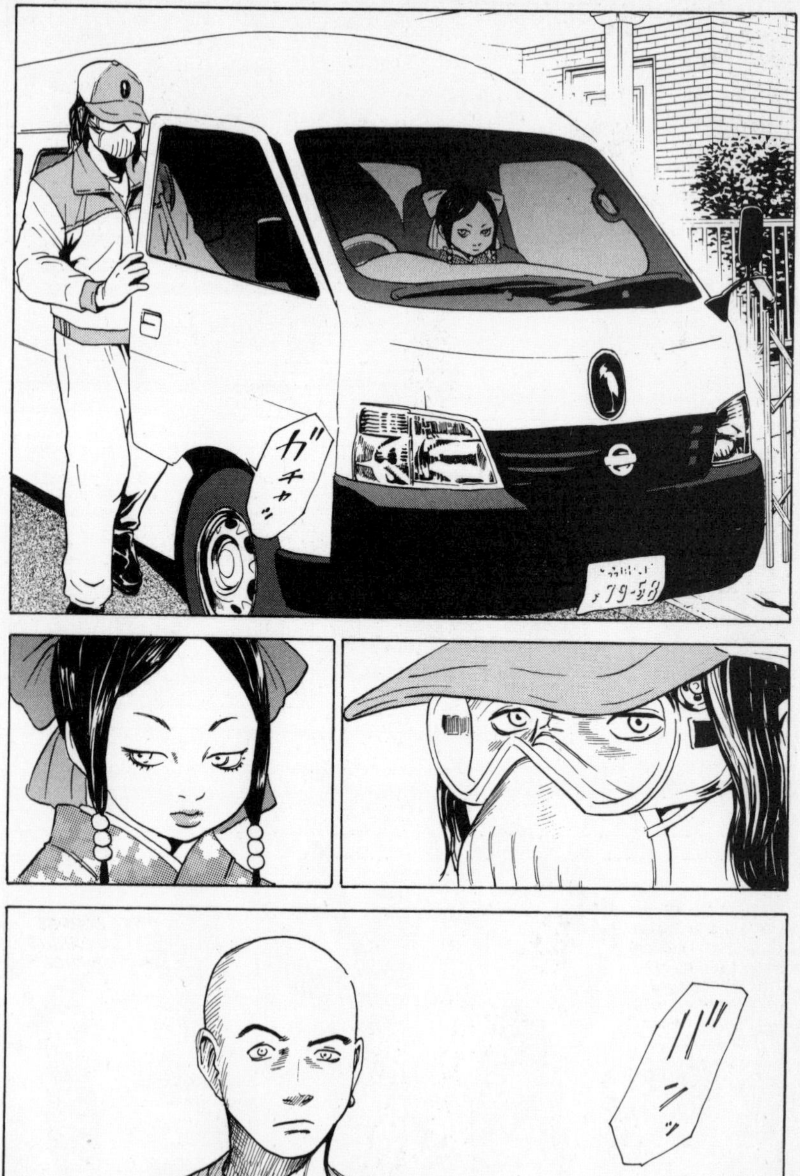
ガチャッ
バンッ

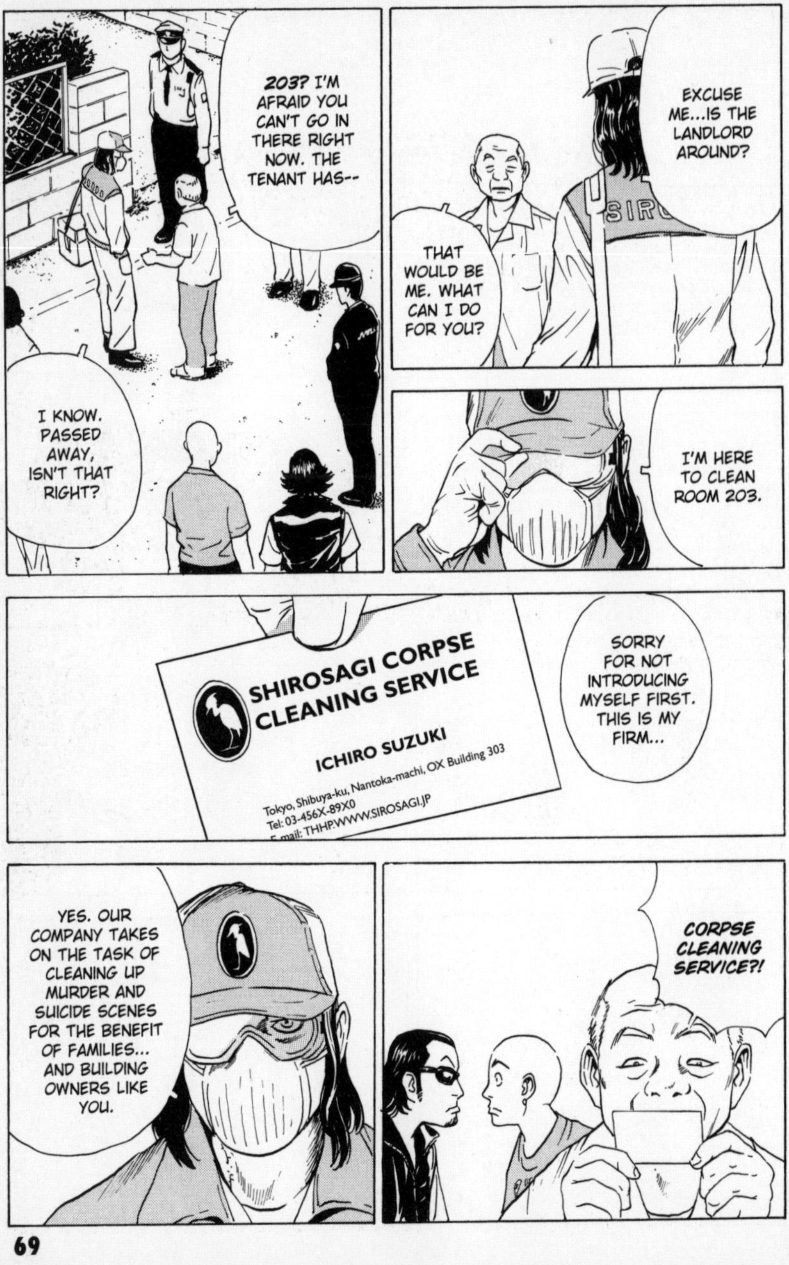
EXCUSE ME...IS THE LANDLORD AROUND?
THAT WOULD BE ME. WHAT CAN I DO FOR YOU?
I'M HERE TO CLEAN ROOM 203.
203? I'M AFRAID YOU CAN'T GO IN THERE RIGHT NOW. THE TENANT HAS--
I KNOW. PASSED AWAY, ISN'T THAT RIGHT?
SORRY FOR NOT INTRODUCING MYSELF FIRST. THIS IS MY FIRM...
SHIROSAGI CORPSE CLEANING SERVICE
ICHIRO SUZUKI
Tokyo, Shibuya-ku, Nantoka-machi, OX Building 303
Tel: 03-456X-89X0
CORPSE CLEANING SERVICE?!
YES. OUR COMPANY TAKES ON THE TASK OF CLEANING UP MURDER AND SUICIDE SCENES FOR THE BENEFIT OF FAMILIES... AND BUILDING OWNERS LIKE YOU.

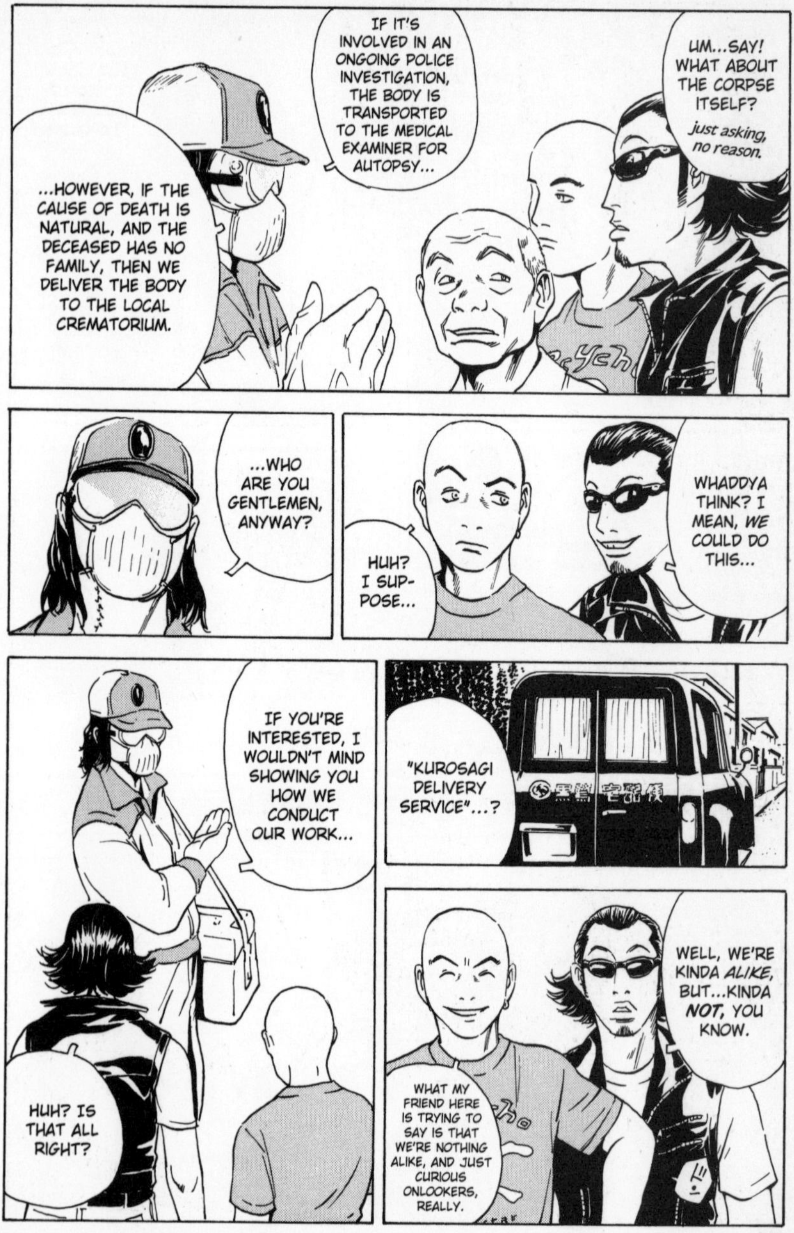
UM...SAY! WHAT ABOUT THE CORPSE ITSELF?
just asking, no reason.
IF IT'S INVOLVED IN AN ONGOING POLICE INVESTIGATION, THE BODY IS TRANSPORTED TO THE MEDICAL EXAMINER FOR AUTOPSY...
...HOWEVER, IF THE CAUSE OF DEATH IS NATURAL, AND THE DECEASED HAS NO FAMILY, THEN WE DELIVER THE BODY TO THE LOCAL CREMATORIUM.
WHADDYA THINK? I MEAN, *WE* COULD DO THIS...
HUH? I SUP-POSE...
...WHO ARE YOU GENTLEMEN, ANYWAY?
"KUROSAGI DELIVERY SERVICE"...?
黒鷺 宅配便
WELL, WE'RE KINDA *ALIKE*, BUT...KINDA ***NOT***, YOU KNOW.
WHAT MY FRIEND HERE IS TRYING TO SAY IS THAT WE'RE NOTHING ALIKE, AND JUST CURIOUS ONLOOKERS, REALLY.
IF YOU'RE INTERESTED, I WOULDN'T MIND SHOWING YOU HOW WE CONDUCT OUR WORK...
HUH? IS THAT ALL RIGHT?

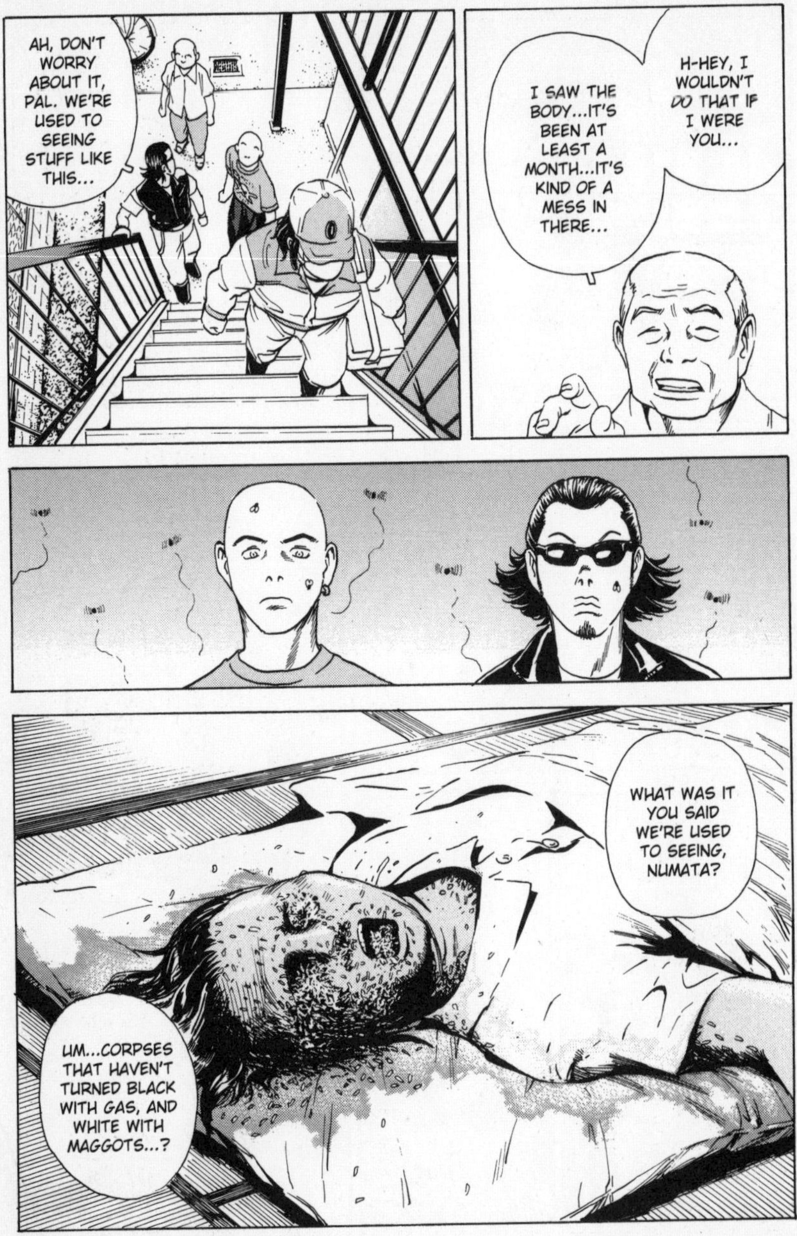
H-HEY, I WOULDN'T DO THAT IF I WERE YOU...
I SAW THE BODY...IT'S BEEN AT LEAST A MONTH...IT'S KIND OF A MESS IN THERE...
AH, DON'T WORRY ABOUT IT, PAL. WE'RE USED TO SEEING STUFF LIKE THIS...
WHAT WAS IT YOU SAID WE'RE USED TO SEEING, NUMATA?
UM...CORPSES THAT HAVEN'T TURNED BLACK WITH GAS, AND WHITE WITH MAGGOTS...?

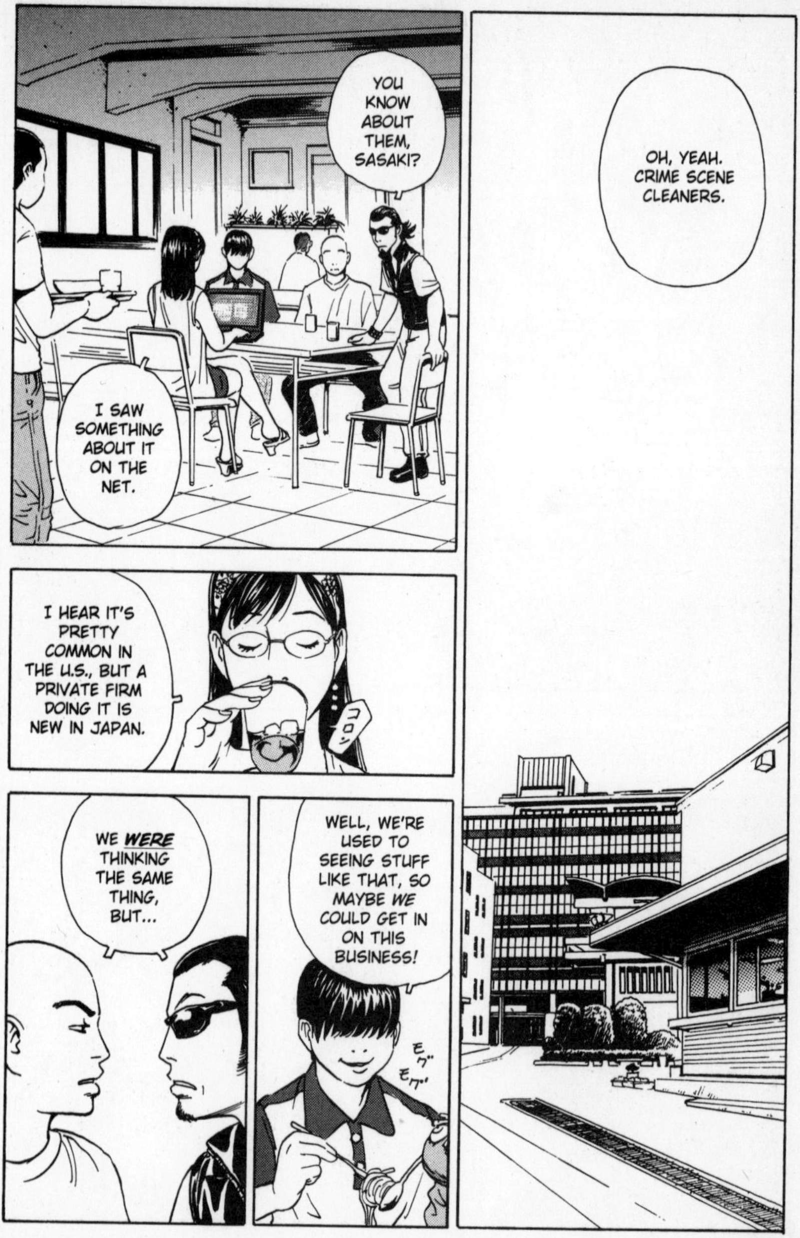
OH, YEAH. CRIME SCENE CLEANERS.
YOU KNOW ABOUT THEM, SASAKI?
I SAW SOMETHING ABOUT IT ON THE NET.
I HEAR IT'S PRETTY COMMON IN THE U.S., BUT A PRIVATE FIRM DOING IT IS NEW IN JAPAN.
コロン
WELL, WE'RE USED TO SEEING STUFF LIKE THAT, SO MAYBE *WE* COULD GET IN ON THIS BUSINESS!
モグ モグ
WE ***WERE*** THINKING THE SAME THING, BUT...

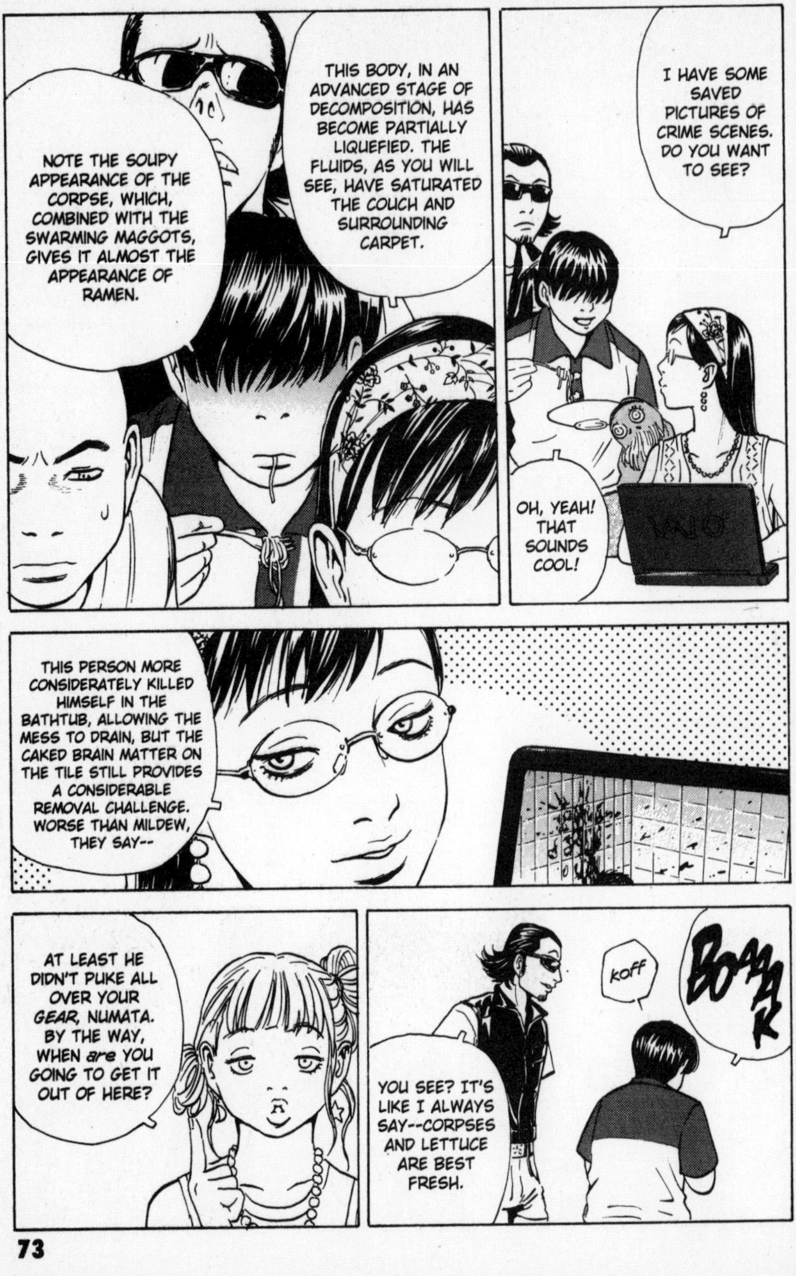
I HAVE SOME SAVED PICTURES OF CRIME SCENES. DO YOU WANT TO SEE?
OH, YEAH! THAT SOUNDS COOL!
THIS BODY, IN AN ADVANCED STAGE OF DECOMPOSITION, HAS BECOME PARTIALLY LIQUEFIED. THE FLUIDS, AS YOU WILL SEE, HAVE SATURATED THE COUCH AND SURROUNDING CARPET.
NOTE THE SOUPY APPEARANCE OF THE CORPSE, WHICH, COMBINED WITH THE SWARMING MAGGOTS, GIVES IT ALMOST THE APPEARANCE OF RAMEN.
THIS PERSON MORE CONSIDERATELY KILLED HIMSELF IN THE BATHTUB, ALLOWING THE MESS TO DRAIN, BUT THE CAKED BRAIN MATTER ON THE TILE STILL PROVIDES A CONSIDERABLE REMOVAL CHALLENGE. WORSE THAN MILDEW, THEY SAY--
BOAAAK
koff
YOU SEE? IT'S LIKE I ALWAYS SAY--CORPSES AND LETTUCE ARE BEST FRESH.
AT LEAST HE DIDN'T PUKE ALL OVER YOUR *GEAR*, NUMATA. BY THE WAY, WHEN *are* YOU GOING TO GET IT OUT OF HERE?

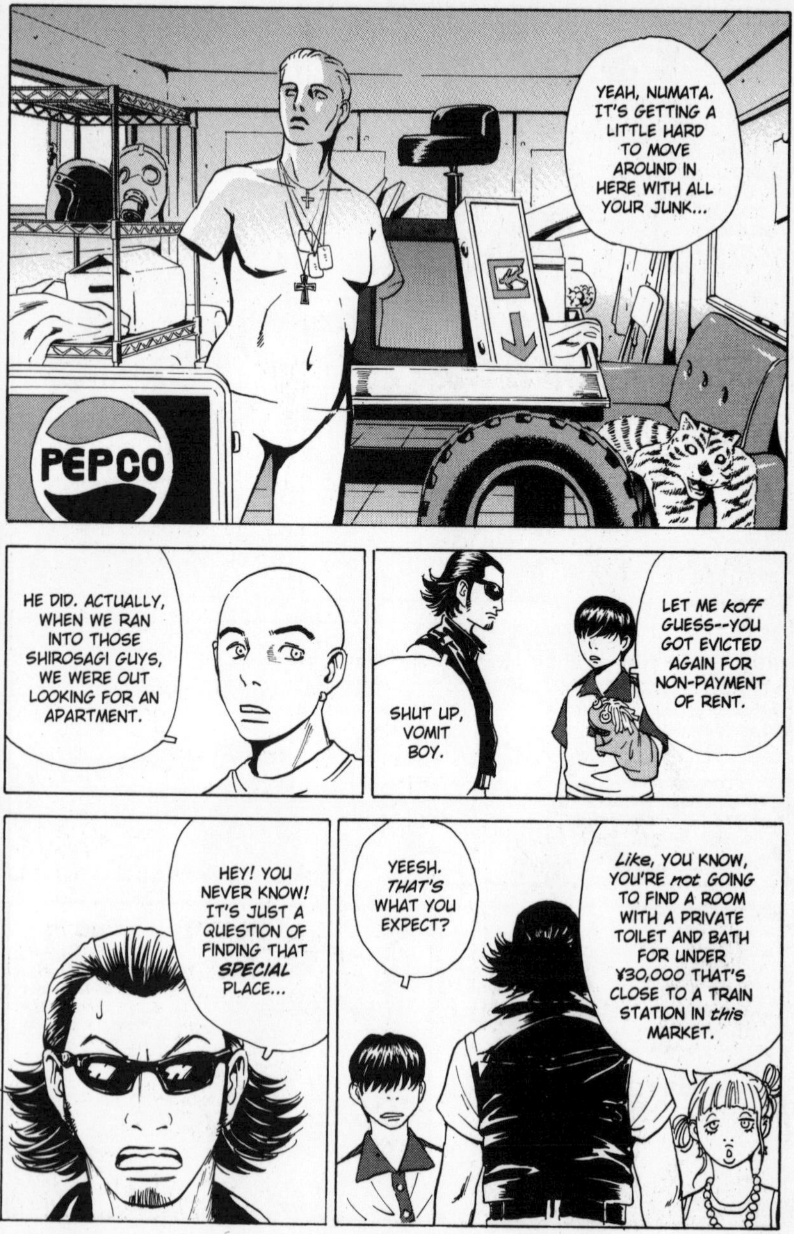
YEAH, NUMATA. IT'S GETTING A LITTLE HARD TO MOVE AROUND IN HERE WITH ALL YOUR JUNK...
PEPCO
LET ME *koff* GUESS--YOU GOT EVICTED AGAIN FOR NON-PAYMENT OF RENT.
SHUT UP, VOMIT BOY.
HE DID. ACTUALLY, WHEN WE RAN INTO THOSE SHIROSAGI GUYS, WE WERE OUT LOOKING FOR AN APARTMENT.
Like, YOU KNOW, YOU'RE *not* GOING TO FIND A ROOM WITH A PRIVATE TOILET AND BATH FOR UNDER ¥30,000 THAT'S CLOSE TO A TRAIN STATION IN *this* MARKET.
YEESH. *THAT'S* WHAT YOU EXPECT?
HEY! YOU NEVER KNOW! IT'S JUST A QUESTION OF FINDING THAT *SPECIAL* PLACE...

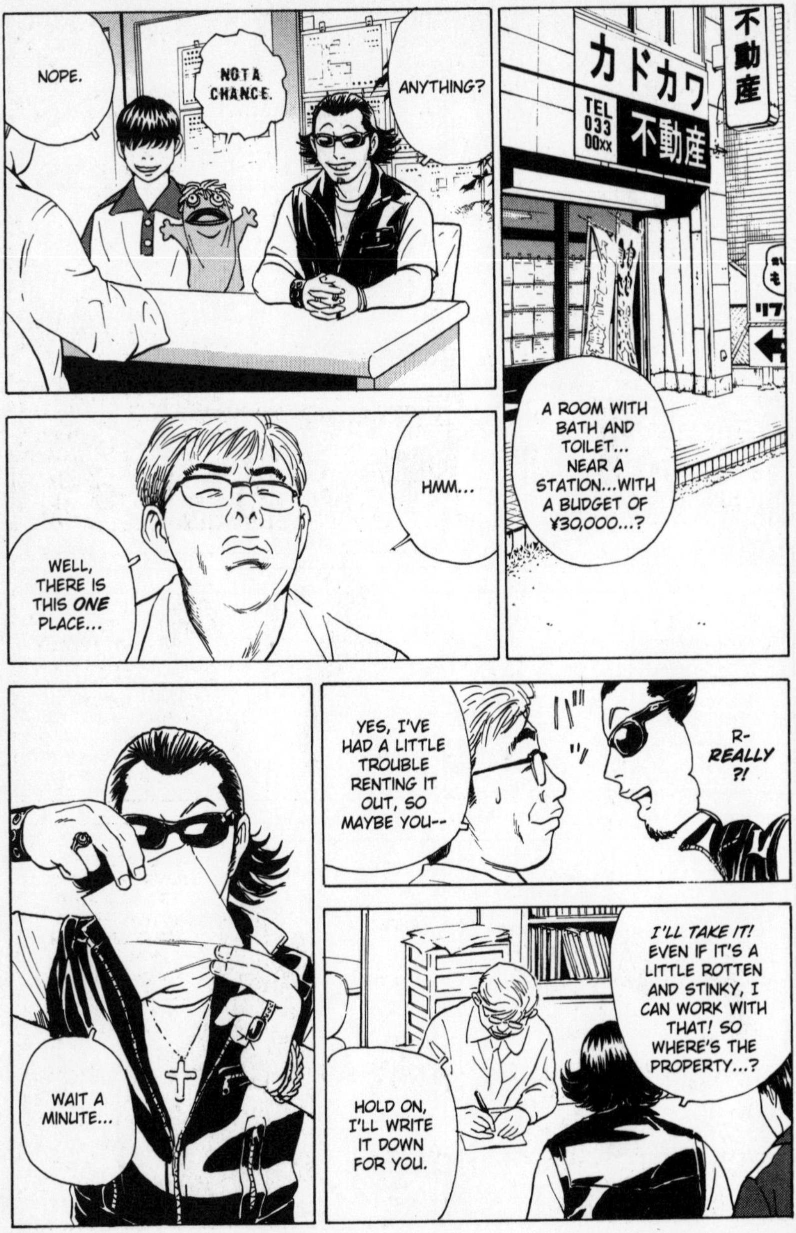
不動産
カドカワ
TEL 033 00XX
不動産
A ROOM WITH BATH AND TOILET... NEAR A STATION...WITH A BUDGET OF ¥30,000...?
ANYTHING?
NOT A CHANCE.
NOPE.
HMM...
WELL, THERE IS THIS *ONE* PLACE...
YES, I'VE HAD A LITTLE TROUBLE RENTING IT OUT, SO MAYBE YOU--
R- *REALLY ?!*
I'LL TAKE IT! EVEN IF IT'S A LITTLE ROTTEN AND STINKY, I CAN WORK WITH THAT! SO WHERE'S THE PROPERTY...?
HOLD ON, I'LL WRITE IT DOWN FOR YOU.
WAIT A MINUTE...

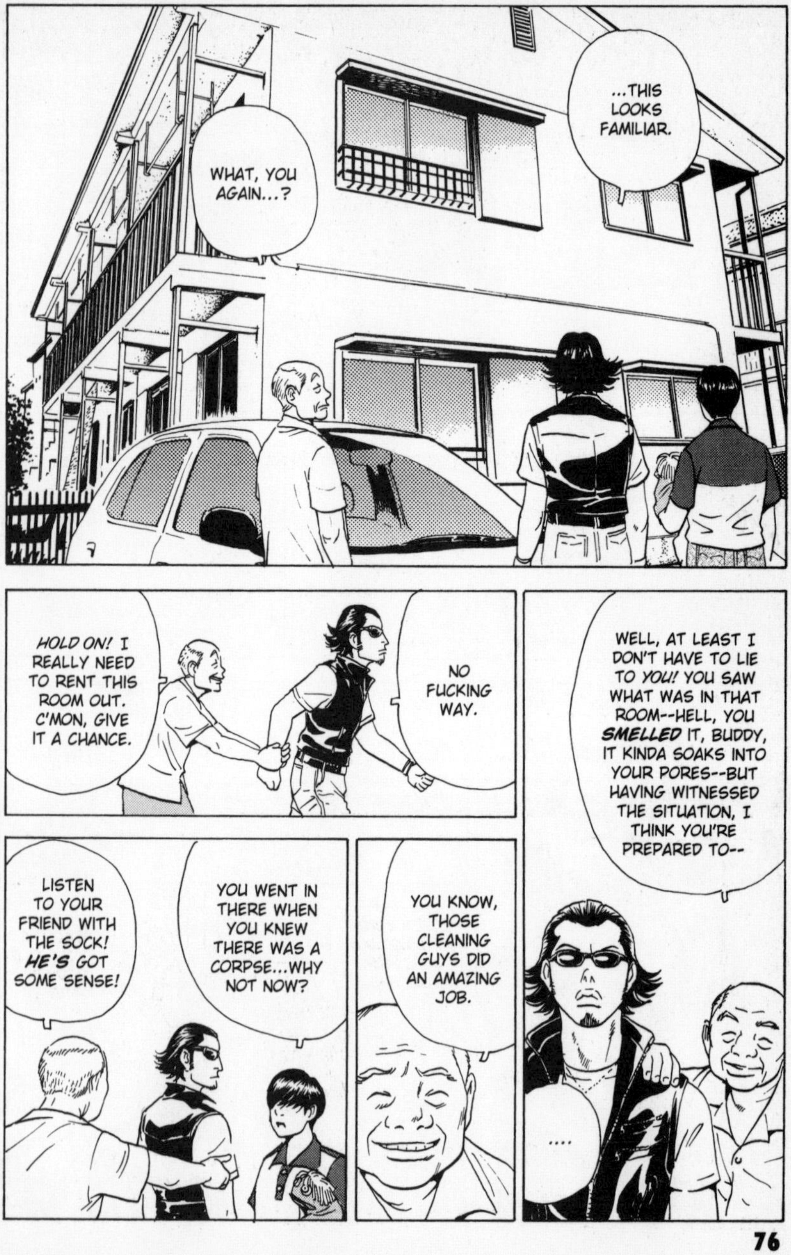

...THIS LOOKS FAMILIAR.
WHAT, YOU AGAIN...?
WELL, AT LEAST I DON'T HAVE TO LIE TO *YOU!* YOU SAW WHAT WAS IN THAT ROOM--HELL, YOU **SMELLED** IT, BUDDY, IT KINDA SOAKS INTO YOUR PORES--BUT HAVING WITNESSED THE SITUATION, I THINK YOU'RE PREPARED TO--
....
NO FUCKING WAY.
HOLD ON! I REALLY NEED TO RENT THIS ROOM OUT. C'MON, GIVE IT A CHANCE.
YOU KNOW, THOSE CLEANING GUYS DID AN AMAZING JOB.
YOU WENT IN THERE WHEN YOU KNEW THERE WAS A CORPSE...WHY NOT NOW?
LISTEN TO YOUR FRIEND WITH THE SOCK! ***HE'S*** GOT SOME SENSE!

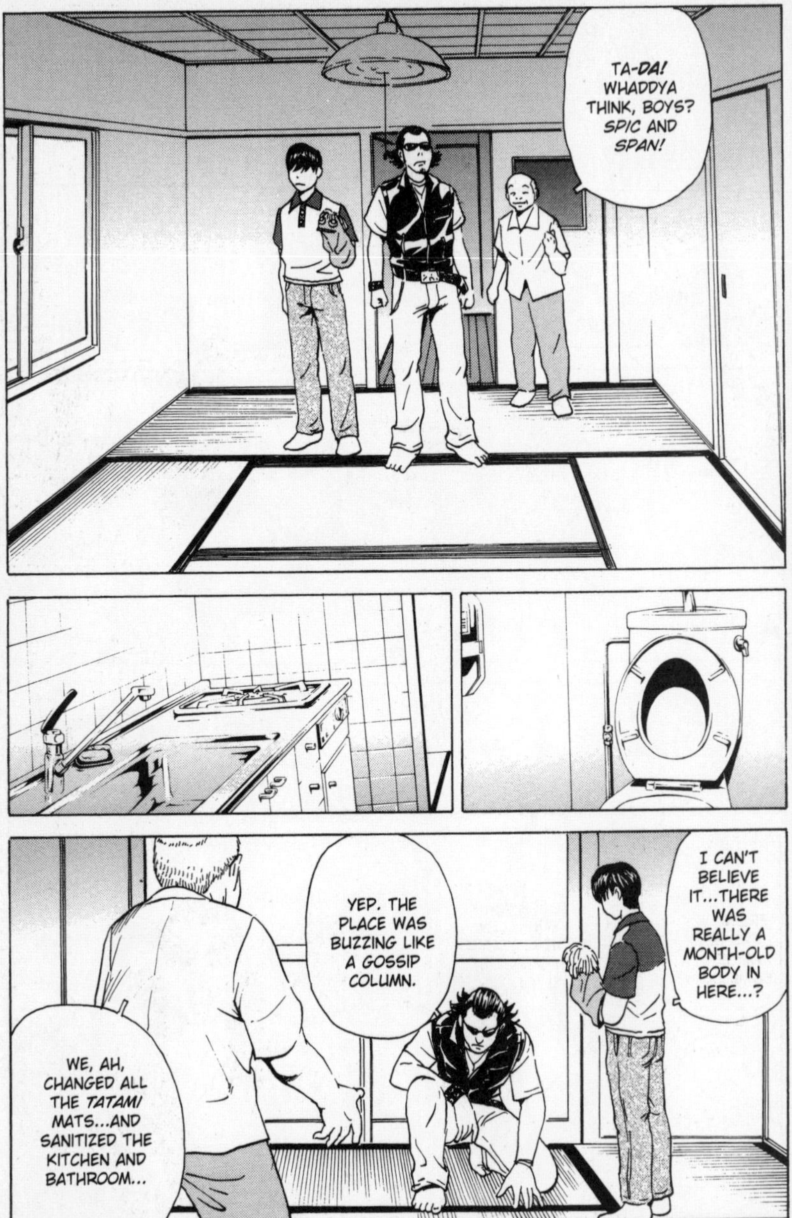
TA-DA! WHADDYA THINK, BOYS? *SPIC AND SPAN!*
I CAN'T BELIEVE IT...THERE WAS REALLY A MONTH-OLD BODY IN HERE...?
YEP. THE PLACE WAS BUZZING LIKE A GOSSIP COLUMN.
WE, AH, CHANGED ALL THE *TATAMI* MATS...AND SANITIZED THE KITCHEN AND BATHROOM...

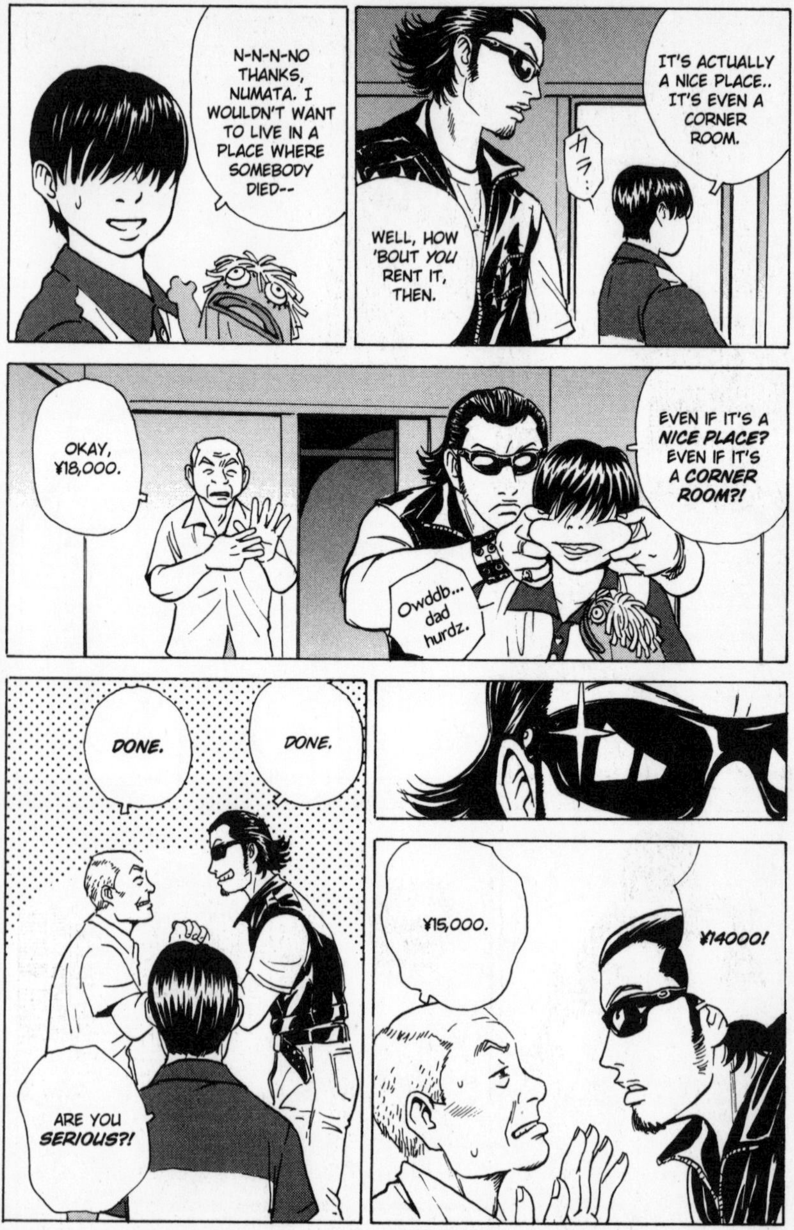
IT'S ACTUALLY A NICE PLACE.. IT'S EVEN A CORNER ROOM.
カラ…
WELL, HOW 'BOUT YOU RENT IT, THEN.
N-N-N-NO THANKS, NUMATA. I WOULDN'T WANT TO LIVE IN A PLACE WHERE SOMEBODY DIED--
EVEN IF IT'S A NICE PLACE? EVEN IF IT'S A CORNER ROOM?!
Owddb... dad hurdz.
OKAY, ¥18,000.
¥14000!
¥15,000.
DONE.
DONE.
ARE YOU SERIOUS?!

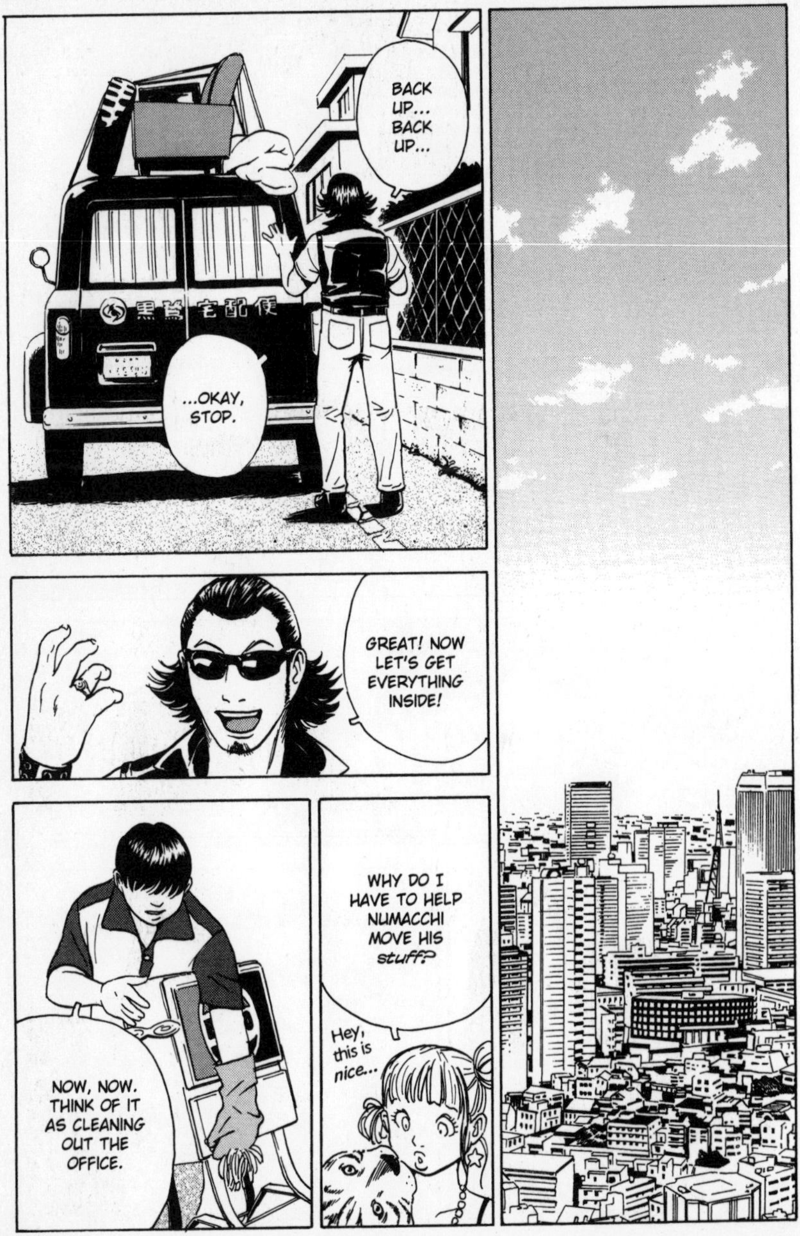
BACK UP... BACK UP...
黒鷺宅配便
...OKAY, STOP.
GREAT! NOW LET'S GET EVERYTHING INSIDE!
WHY DO I HAVE TO HELP NUMACCHI MOVE HIS *stuff?*
Hey, this is *nice...*
NOW, NOW. THINK OF IT AS CLEANING OUT THE OFFICE.

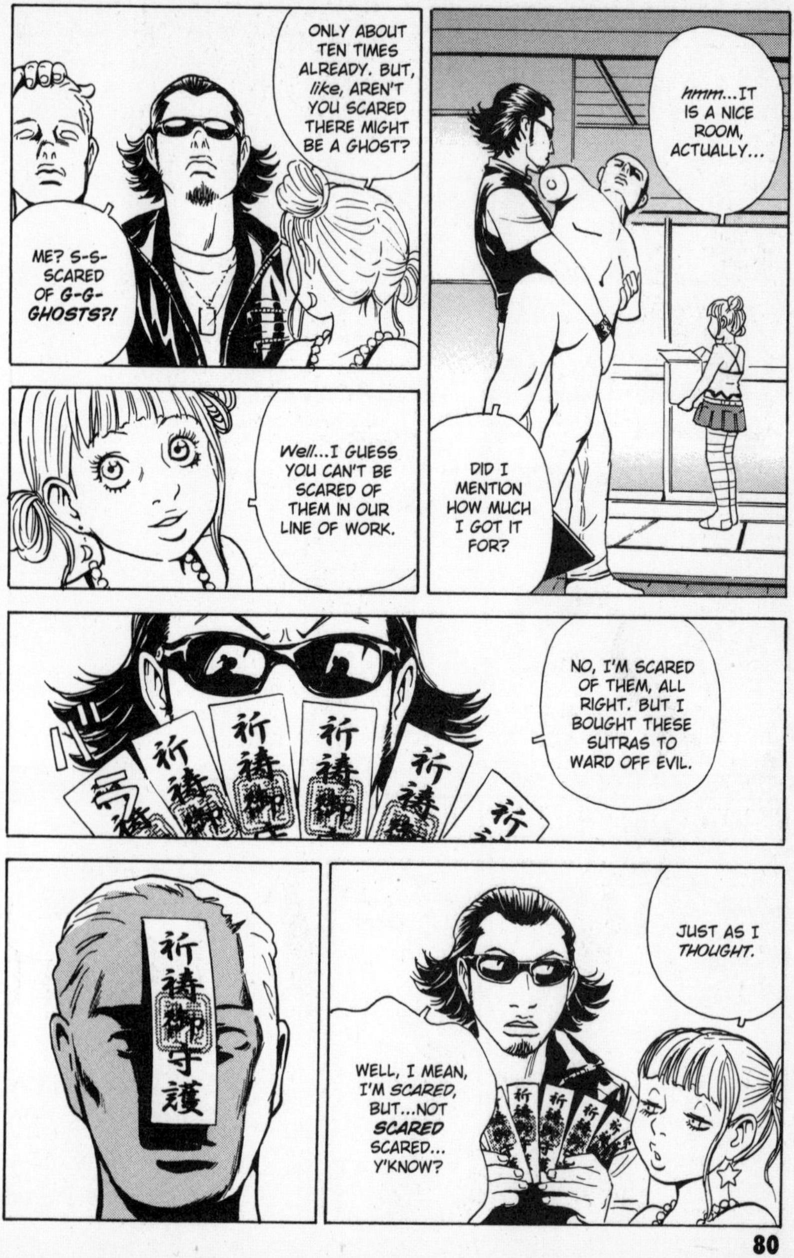
hmmm...IT IS A NICE ROOM, ACTUALLY...
DID I MENTION HOW MUCH I GOT IT FOR?
ONLY ABOUT TEN TIMES ALREADY. BUT, *like*, AREN'T YOU SCARED THERE MIGHT BE A GHOST?
ME? S-S-SCARED OF *G-G-GHOSTS?!*
Well...I GUESS YOU CAN'T BE SCARED OF THEM IN OUR LINE OF WORK.
NO, I'M SCARED OF THEM, ALL RIGHT. BUT I BOUGHT THESE SUTRAS TO WARD OFF EVIL.
JUST AS I *THOUGHT.*
WELL, I MEAN, I'M *SCARED,* BUT...NOT ***SCARED*** SCARED... Y'KNOW?
祈祷御守護

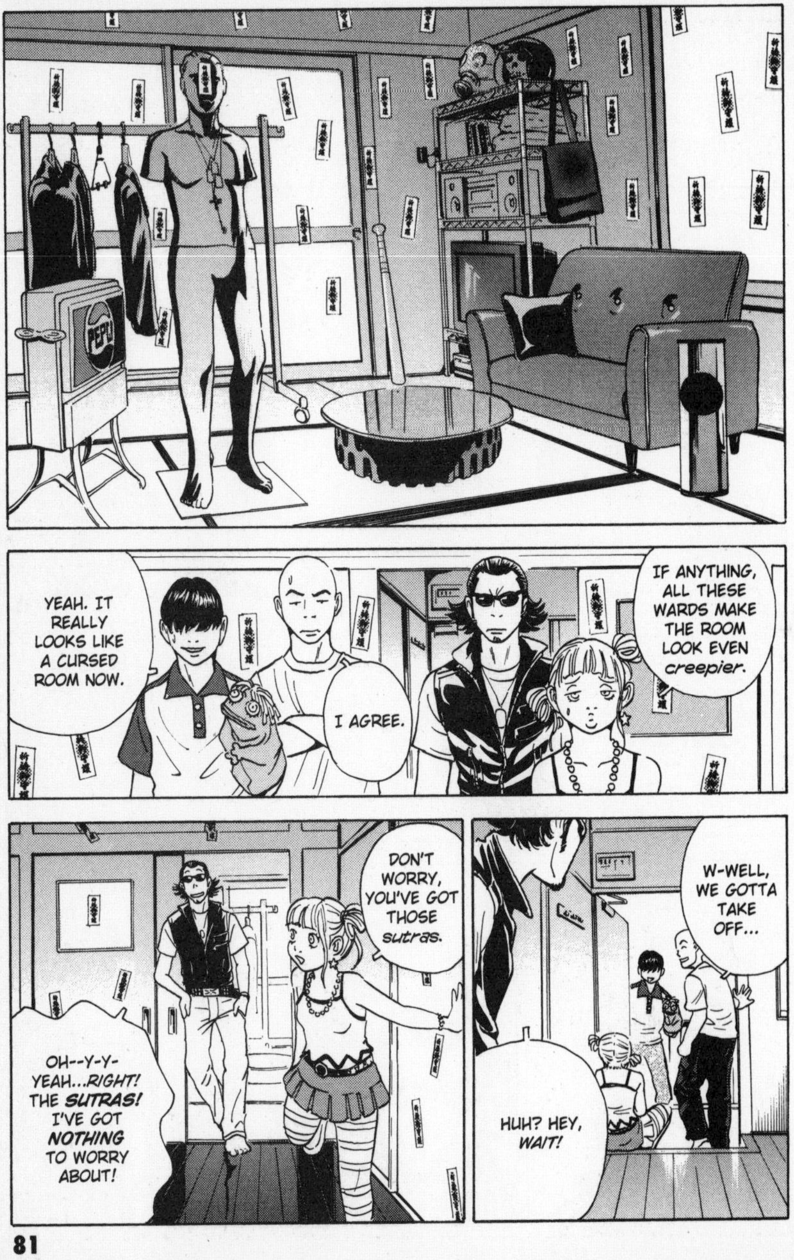
IF ANYTHING, ALL THESE WARDS MAKE THE ROOM LOOK EVEN *creepier*.
I AGREE.
YEAH. IT REALLY LOOKS LIKE A CURSED ROOM NOW.
W-WELL, WE GOTTA TAKE OFF...
HUH? HEY, *WAIT!*
DON'T WORRY, YOU'VE GOT THOSE *sutras*.
OH--Y-Y-YEAH...*RIGHT!* THE ***SUTRAS!*** I'VE GOT ***NOTHING*** TO WORRY ABOUT!

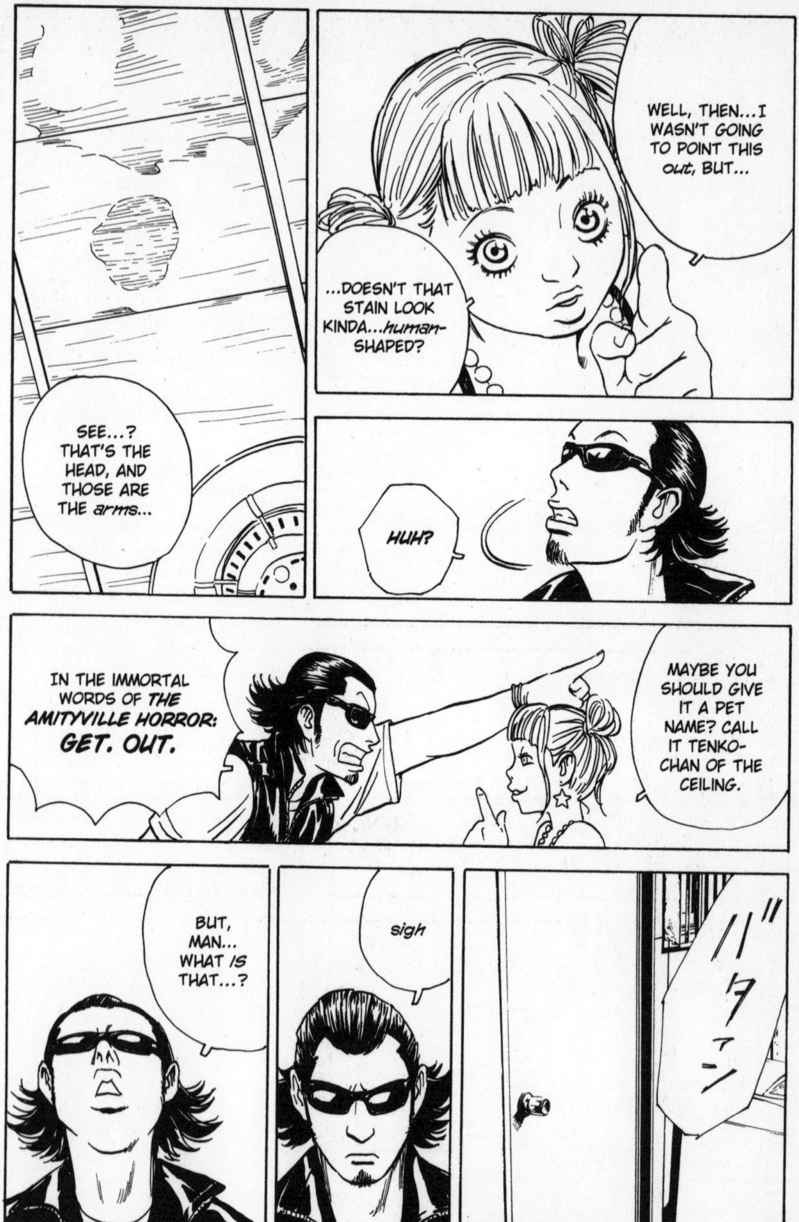
WELL, THEN...I WASN'T GOING TO POINT THIS *out*, BUT...
...DOESN'T THAT STAIN LOOK KINDA...*human*-SHAPED?
HUH?
SEE...? THAT'S THE HEAD, AND THOSE ARE THE *arms*...
MAYBE YOU SHOULD GIVE IT A PET NAME? CALL IT TENKO-CHAN OF THE CEILING.
IN THE IMMORTAL WORDS OF *THE AMITYVILLE HORROR*: **GET. OUT.**
sigh
BUT, MAN... WHAT *IS* THAT...?

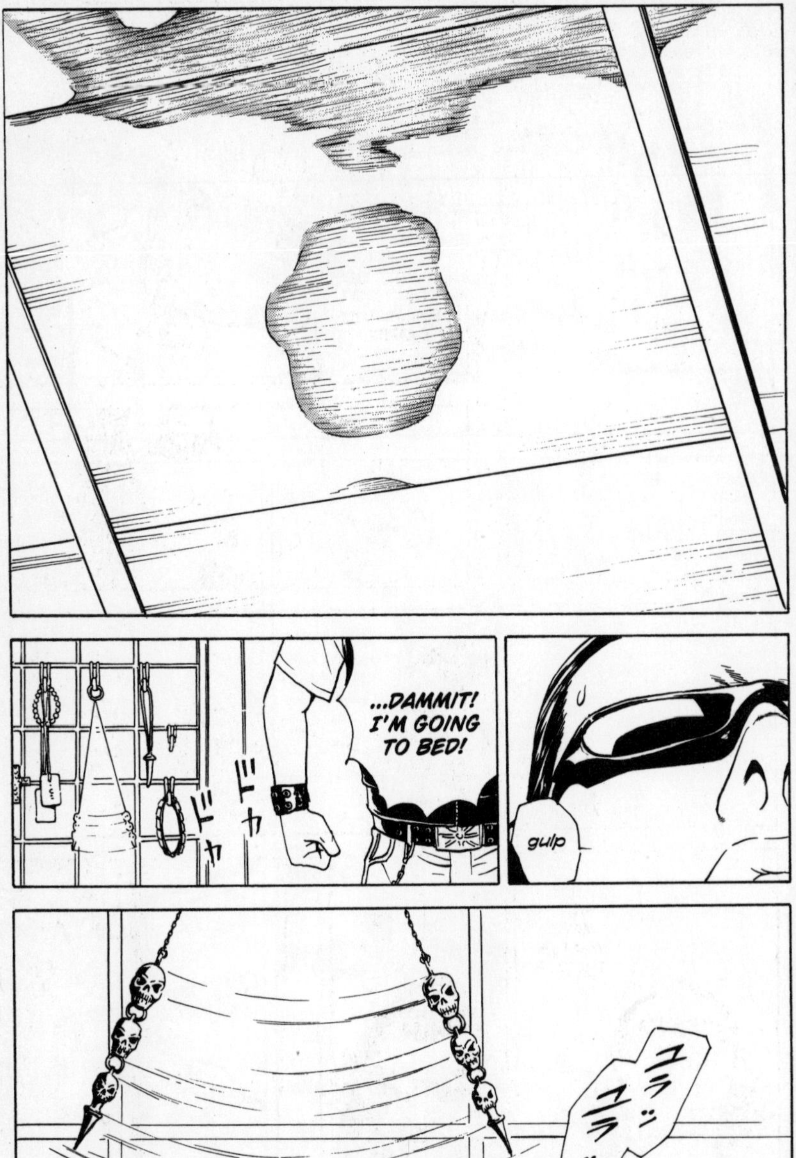
gulp
...DAMMIT! I'M GOING TO BED!
ドカ
ドカ
ユラッ
ユラッ

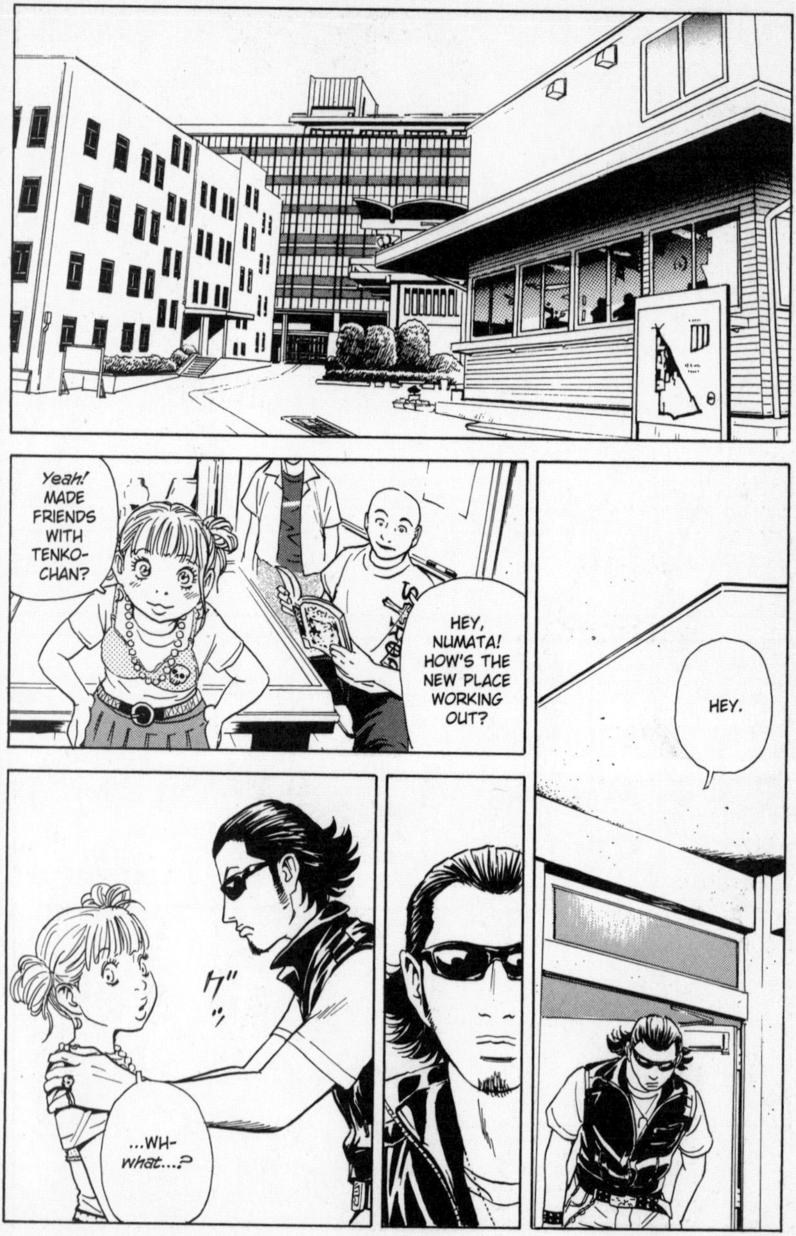
HEY.
HEY, NUMATA! HOW'S THE NEW PLACE WORKING OUT?
Yeah! MADE FRIENDS WITH TENKO-CHAN?
グッ
...WH- what...?

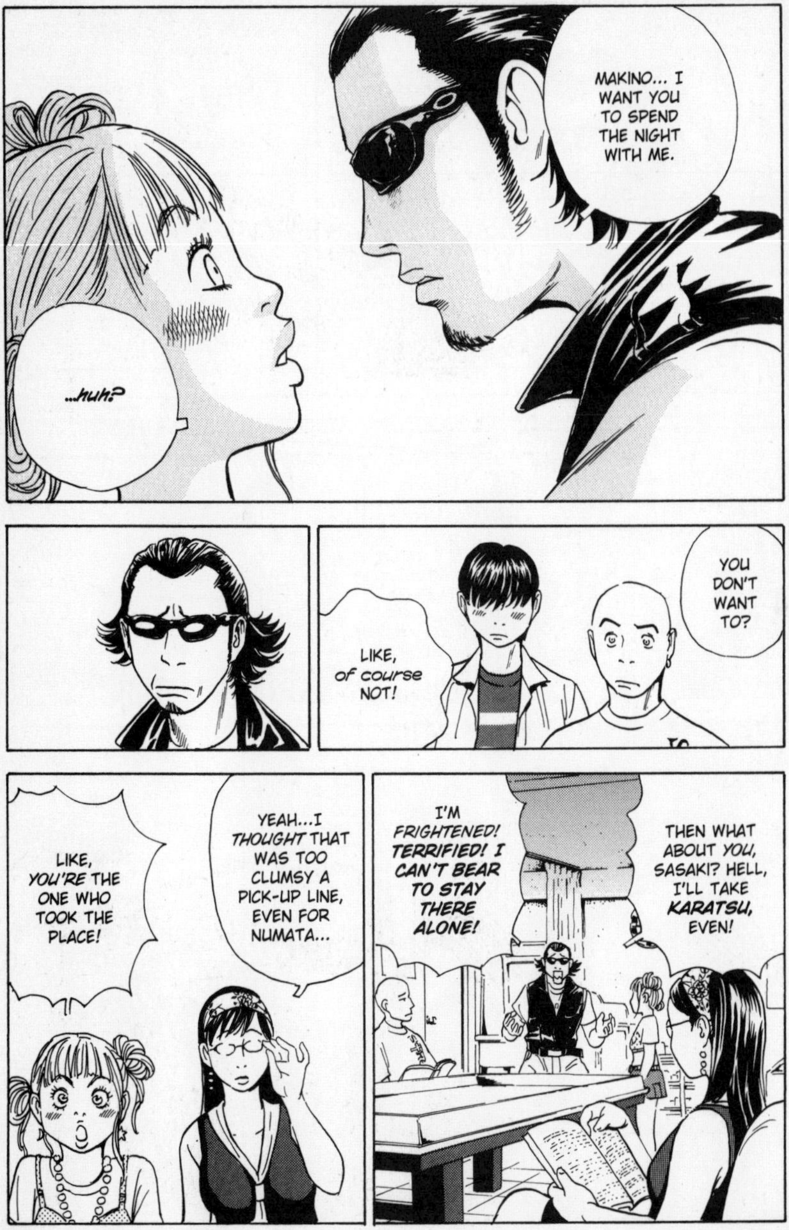
MAKINO... I WANT YOU TO SPEND THE NIGHT WITH ME.
...huh?
YOU DON'T WANT TO?
LIKE, of course NOT!
THEN WHAT ABOUT *YOU*, SASAKI? HELL, I'LL TAKE ***KARATSU***, EVEN!
I'M *FRIGHTENED!* ***TERRIFIED! I CAN'T BEAR TO STAY THERE ALONE!***
YEAH...I *THOUGHT* THAT WAS TOO CLUMSY A PICK-UP LINE, EVEN FOR NUMATA...
LIKE, *YOU'RE* THE ONE WHO TOOK THE PLACE!

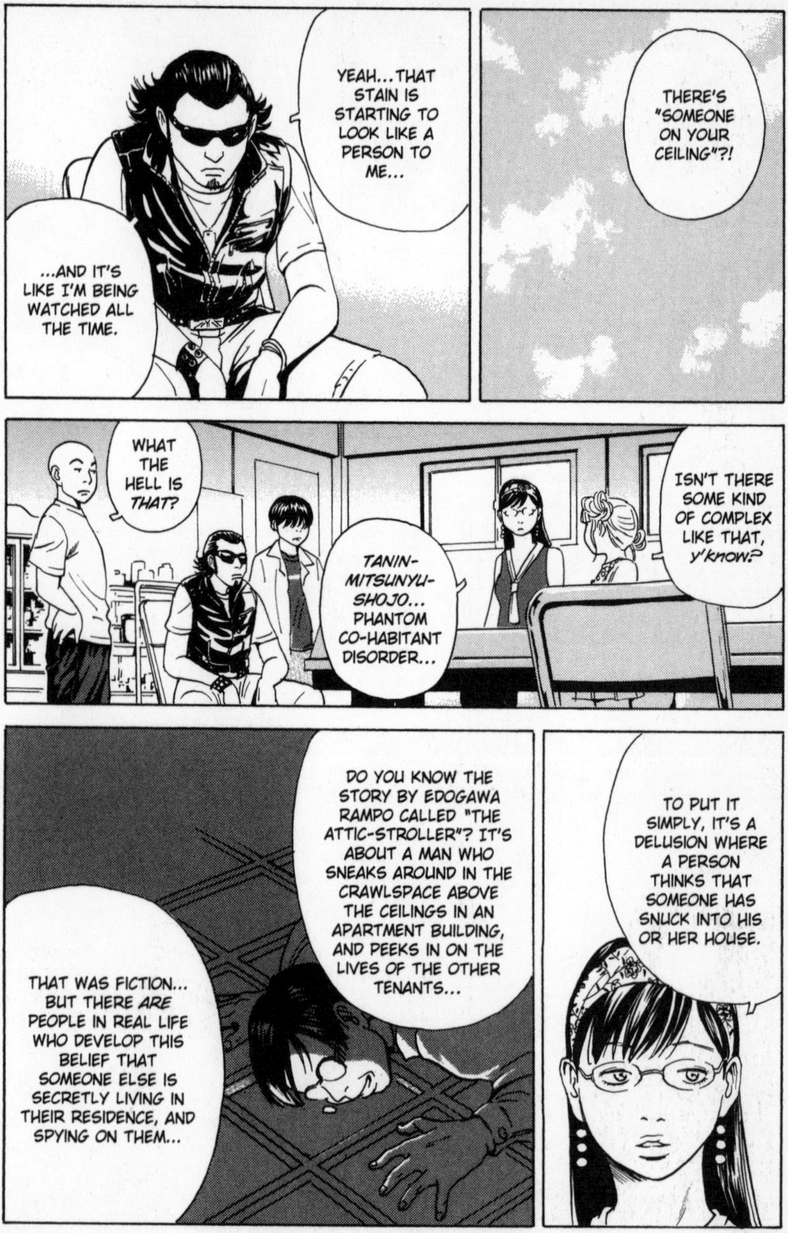
THERE'S "SOMEONE ON YOUR CEILING"?!
YEAH...THAT STAIN IS STARTING TO LOOK LIKE A PERSON TO ME...
...AND IT'S LIKE I'M BEING WATCHED ALL THE TIME.
ISN'T THERE SOME KIND OF COMPLEX LIKE THAT, *y'know?*
TANIN-MITSUNYU-SHOJO... PHANTOM CO-HABITANT DISORDER...
WHAT THE HELL IS *THAT?*
TO PUT IT SIMPLY, IT'S A DELUSION WHERE A PERSON THINKS THAT SOMEONE HAS SNUCK INTO HIS OR HER HOUSE.
DO YOU KNOW THE STORY BY EDOGAWA RAMPO CALLED "THE ATTIC-STROLLER"? IT'S ABOUT A MAN WHO SNEAKS AROUND IN THE CRAWLSPACE ABOVE THE CEILINGS IN AN APARTMENT BUILDING, AND PEEKS IN ON THE LIVES OF THE OTHER TENANTS...
THAT WAS FICTION... BUT THERE *ARE* PEOPLE IN REAL LIFE WHO DEVELOP THIS BELIEF THAT SOMEONE ELSE IS SECRETLY LIVING IN THEIR RESIDENCE, AND SPYING ON THEM...

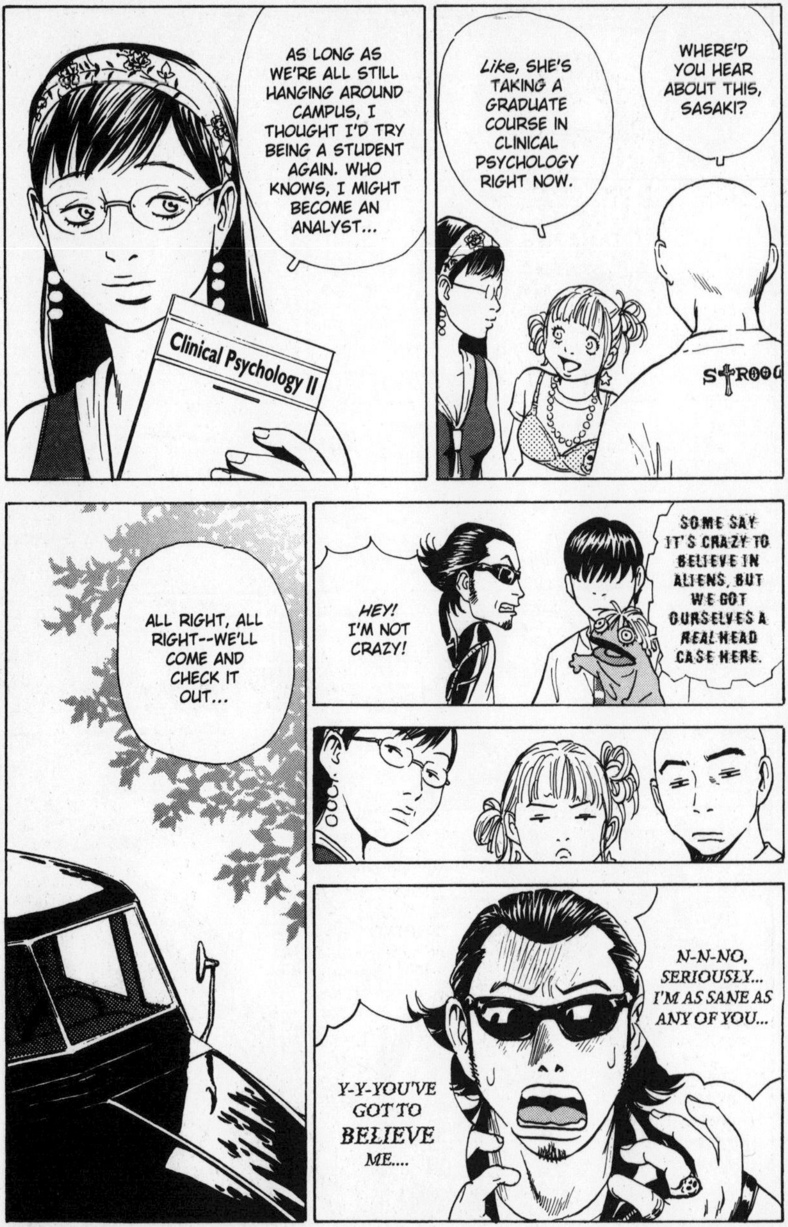
WHERE'D YOU HEAR ABOUT THIS, SASAKI?
Like, SHE'S TAKING A GRADUATE COURSE IN CLINICAL PSYCHOLOGY RIGHT NOW.
AS LONG AS WE'RE ALL STILL HANGING AROUND CAMPUS, I THOUGHT I'D TRY BEING A STUDENT AGAIN. WHO KNOWS, I MIGHT BECOME AN ANALYST...
Clinical Psychology II
SOME SAY IT'S CRAZY TO BELIEVE IN ALIENS, BUT WE GOT OURSELVES A REAL HEAD CASE HERE.
HEY! I'M NOT CRAZY!
N-N-NO, SERIOUSLY... I'M AS SANE AS ANY OF YOU...
Y-Y-YOU'VE GOT TO BELIEVE ME....
ALL RIGHT, ALL RIGHT--WE'LL COME AND CHECK IT OUT...

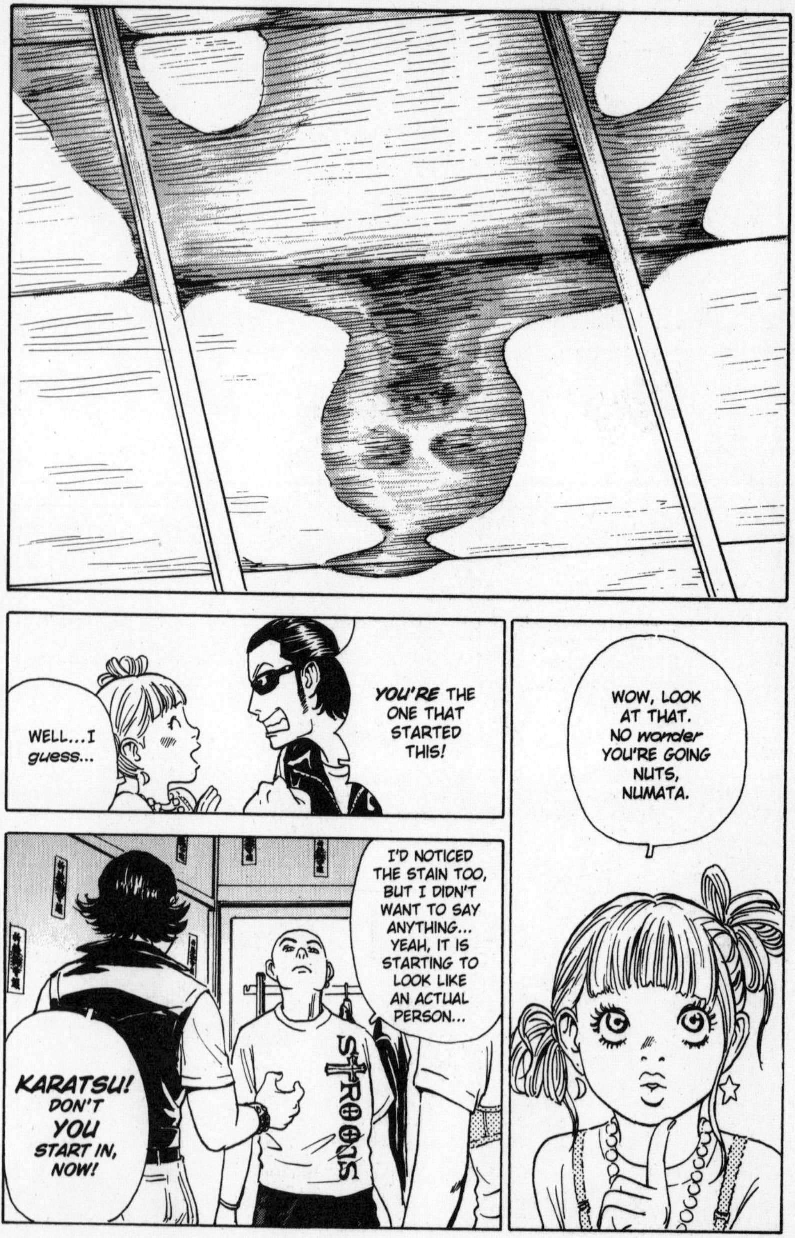
WOW, LOOK AT THAT. NO *wonder* YOU'RE GOING NUTS, NUMATA.
YOU'RE THE ONE THAT STARTED THIS!
WELL...I *guess*...
I'D NOTICED THE STAIN TOO, BUT I DIDN'T WANT TO SAY ANYTHING... YEAH, IT IS STARTING TO LOOK LIKE AN ACTUAL PERSON...
KARATSU! DON'T ***YOU*** START IN, NOW!

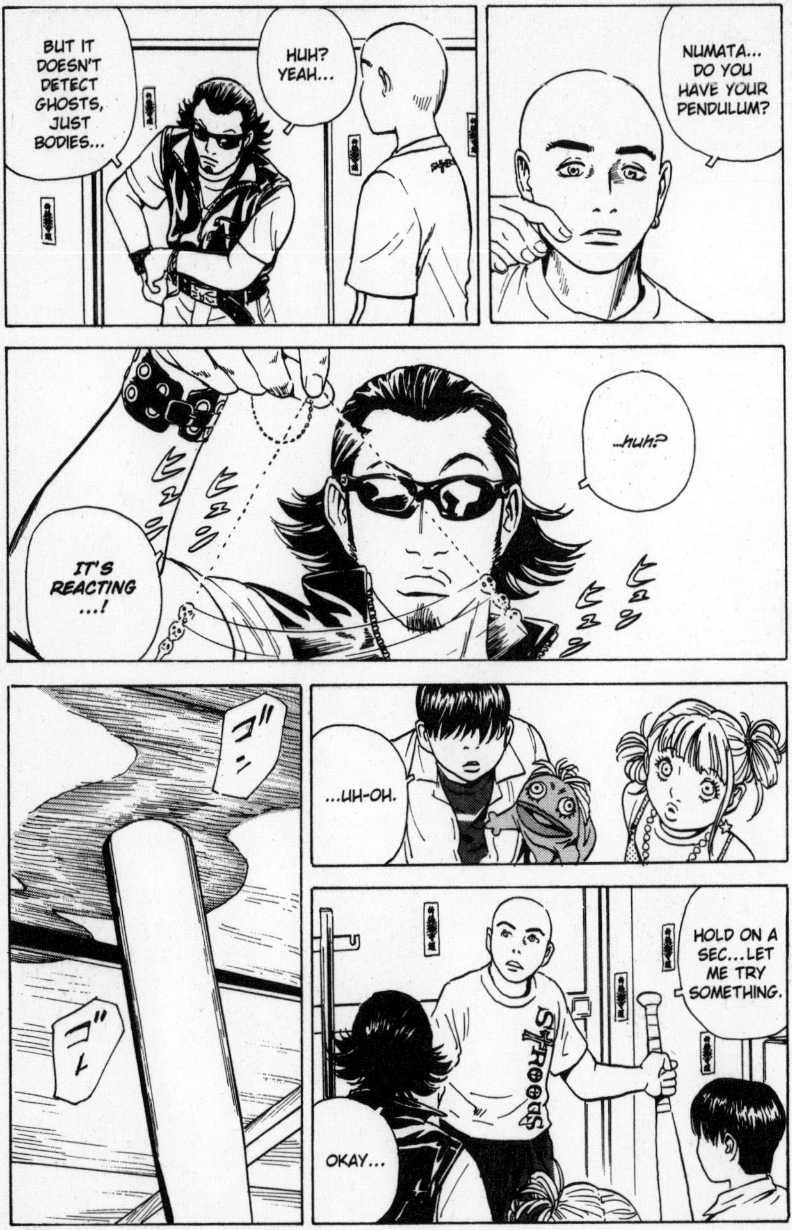
NUMATA... DO YOU HAVE YOUR PENDULUM?
HUH? YEAH...
BUT IT DOESN'T DETECT GHOSTS, JUST BODIES...
...huh?
IT'S REACTING ...!
...UH-OH.
HOLD ON A SEC...LET ME TRY SOMETHING.
OKAY...

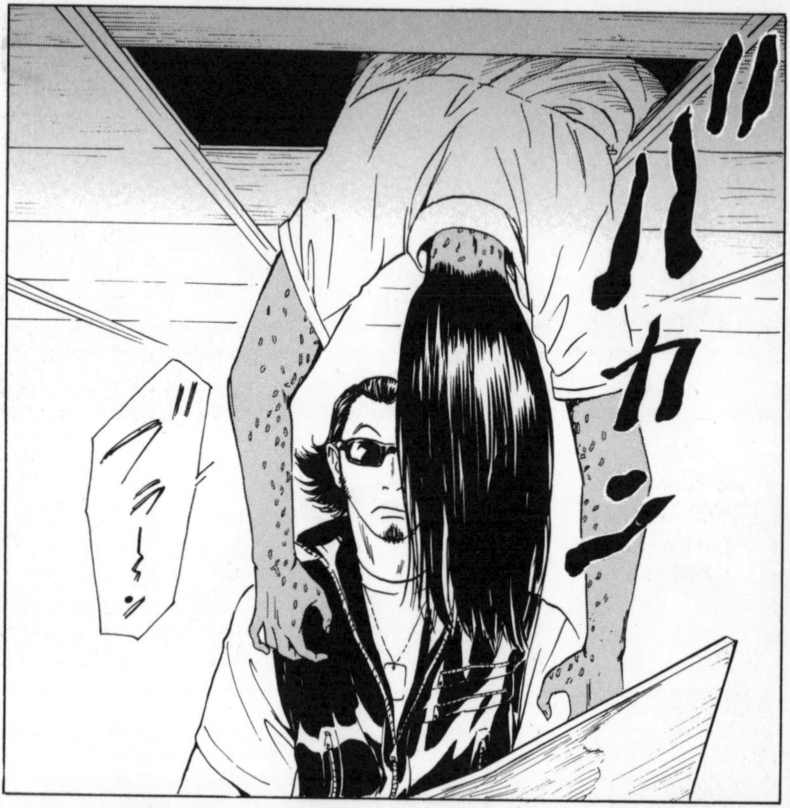
バカン
ブラ〜ン
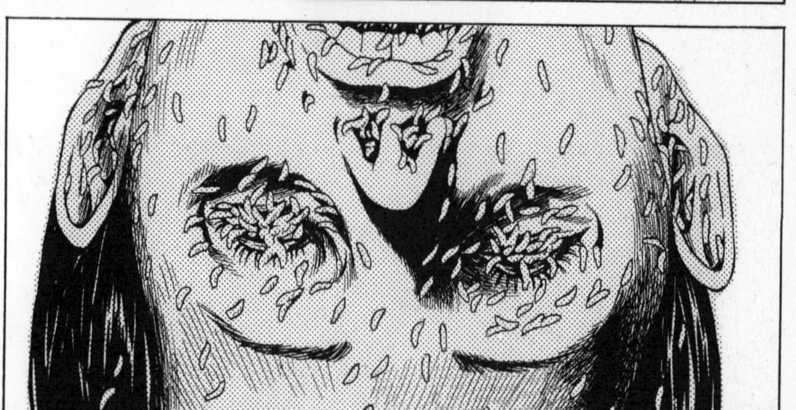

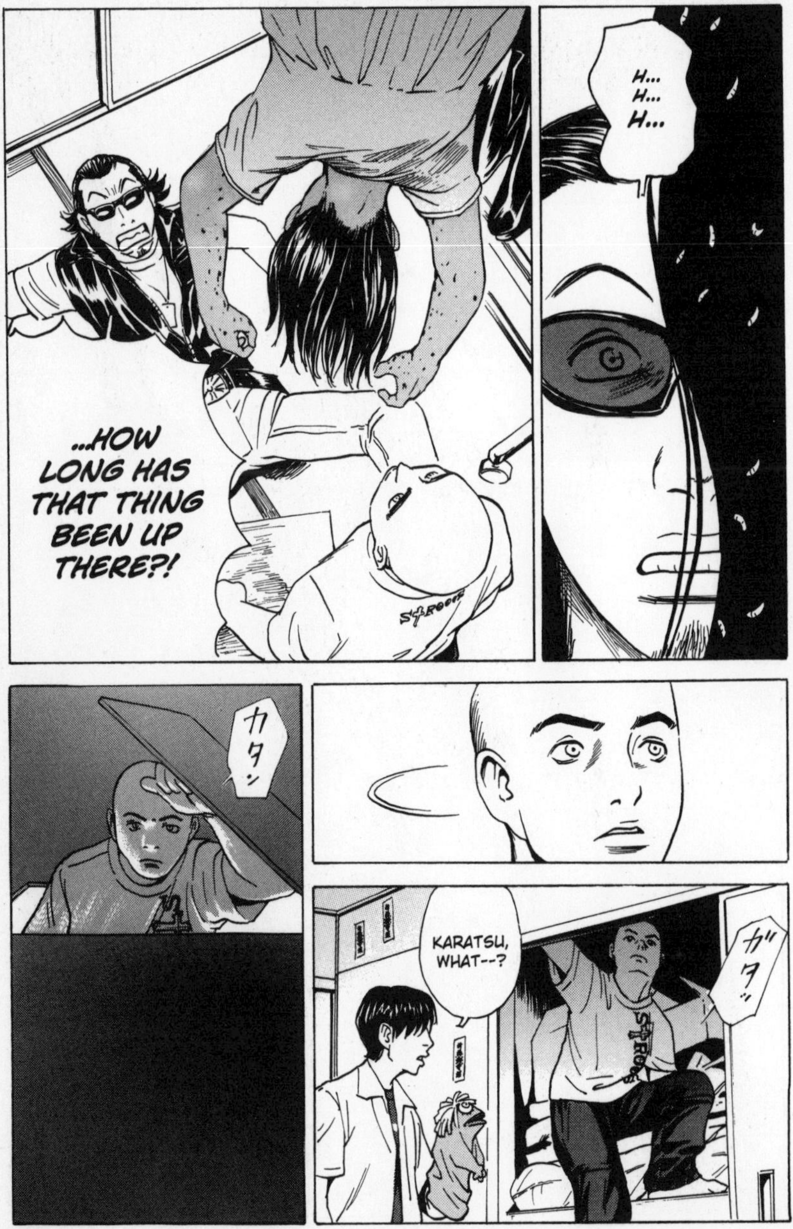
H...
H...
H...
...HOW LONG HAS THAT THING BEEN UP THERE?!
ガタッ
KARATSU, WHAT--?
カタン

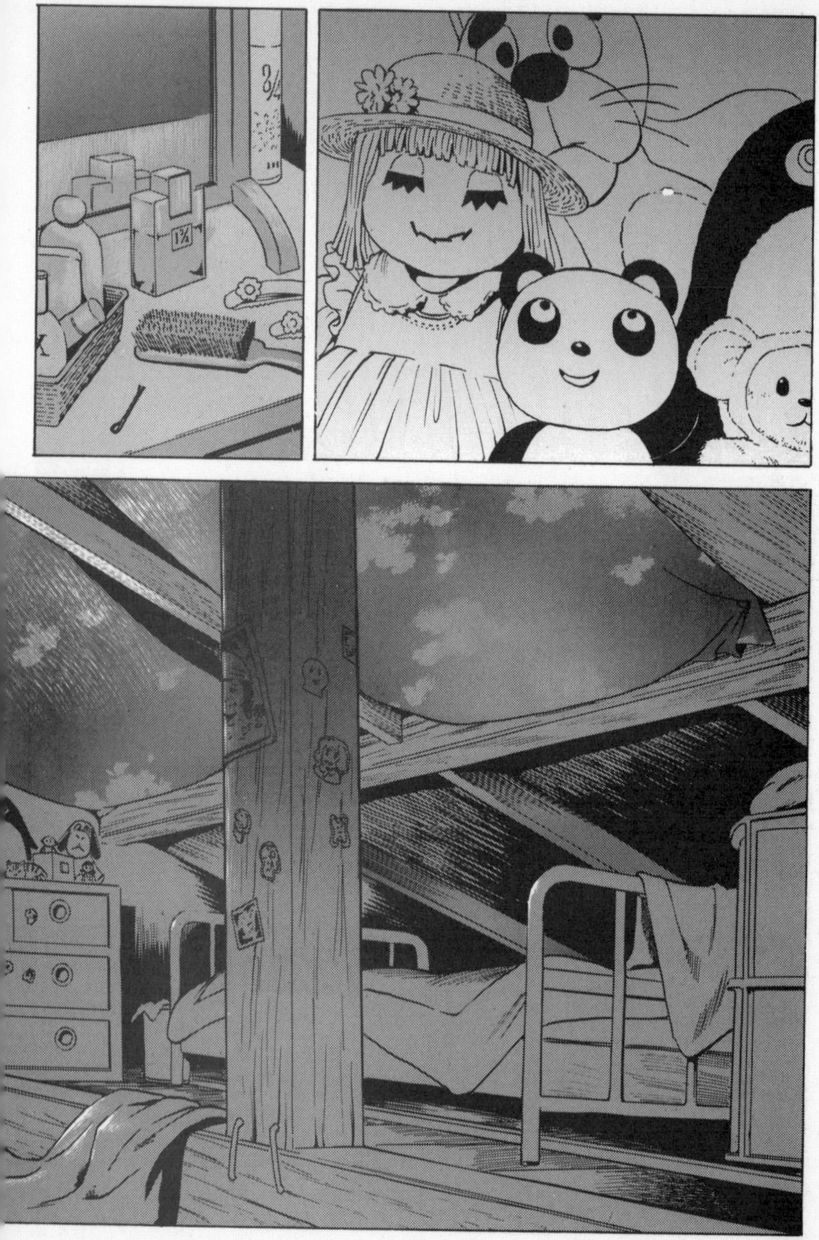
3/4
1¾

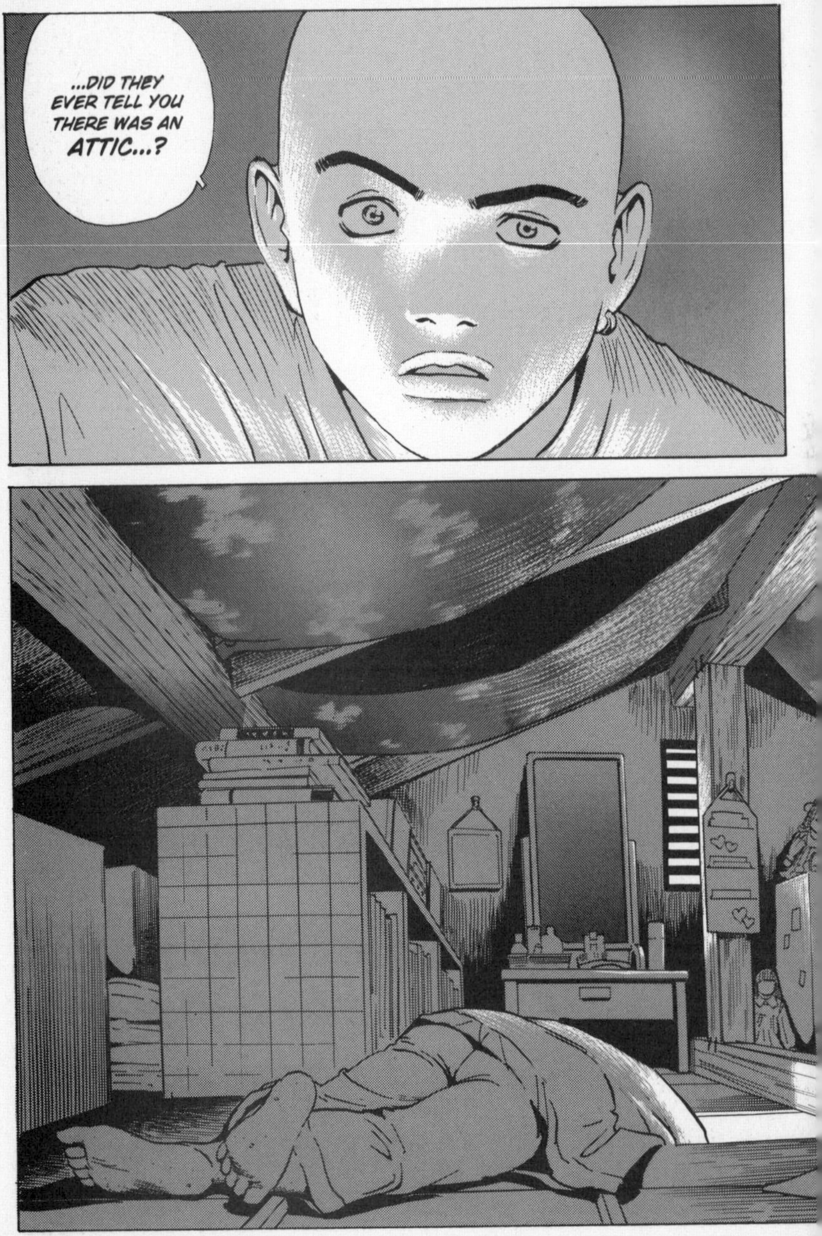
...DID THEY EVER TELL YOU THERE WAS AN ATTIC...?

2nd delivery: if you're with me—the end

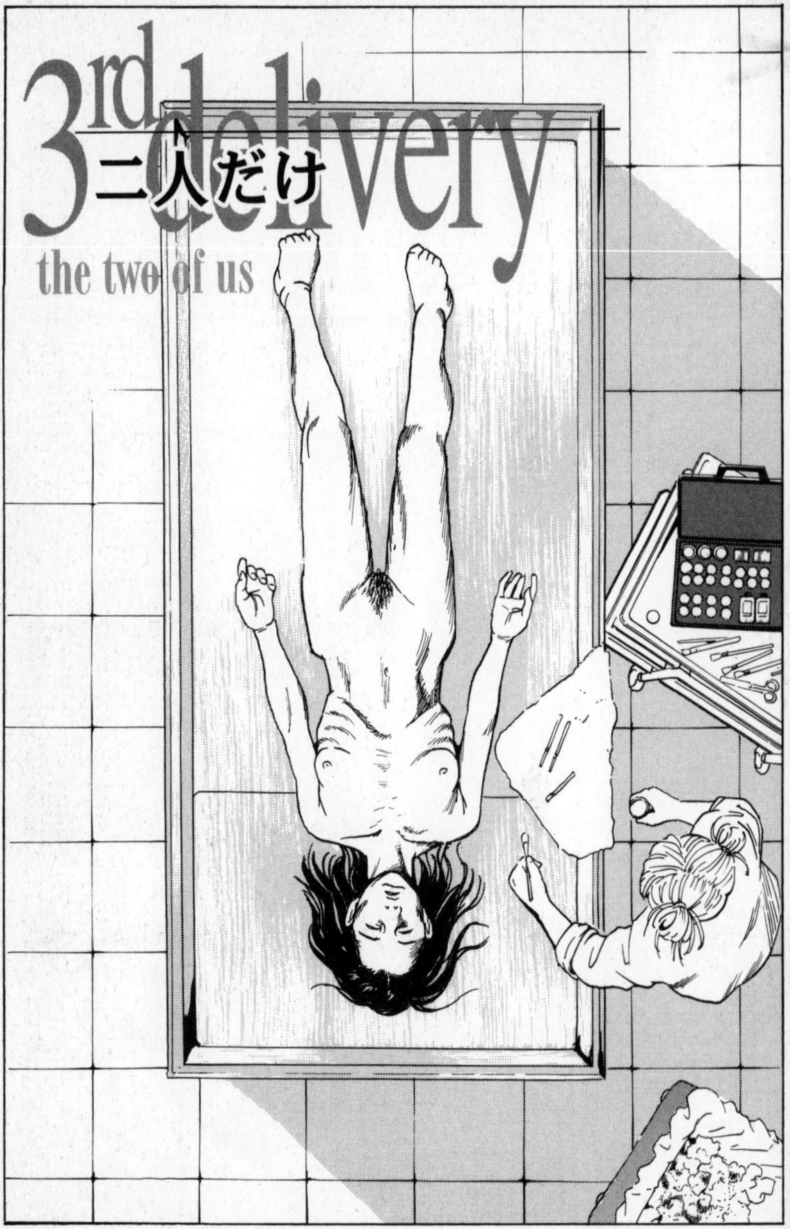
3rd delivery
二人だけ
the two of us

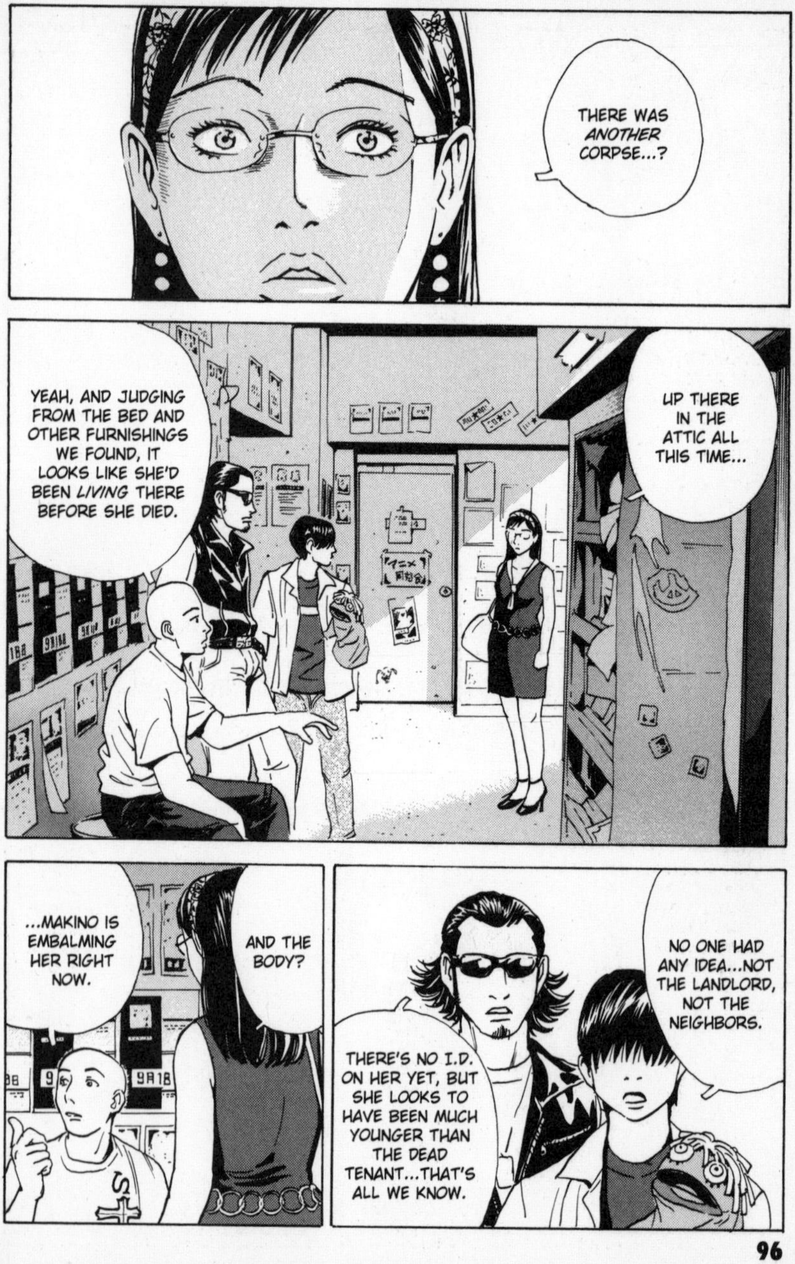
THERE WAS *ANOTHER* CORPSE...?
UP THERE IN THE ATTIC ALL THIS TIME...
YEAH, AND JUDGING FROM THE BED AND OTHER FURNISHINGS WE FOUND, IT LOOKS LIKE SHE'D BEEN *LIVING* THERE BEFORE SHE DIED.
NO ONE HAD ANY IDEA...NOT THE LANDLORD, NOT THE NEIGHBORS.
THERE'S NO I.D. ON HER YET, BUT SHE LOOKS TO HAVE BEEN MUCH YOUNGER THAN THE DEAD TENANT...THAT'S ALL WE KNOW.
AND THE BODY?
...MAKINO IS EMBALMING HER RIGHT NOW.

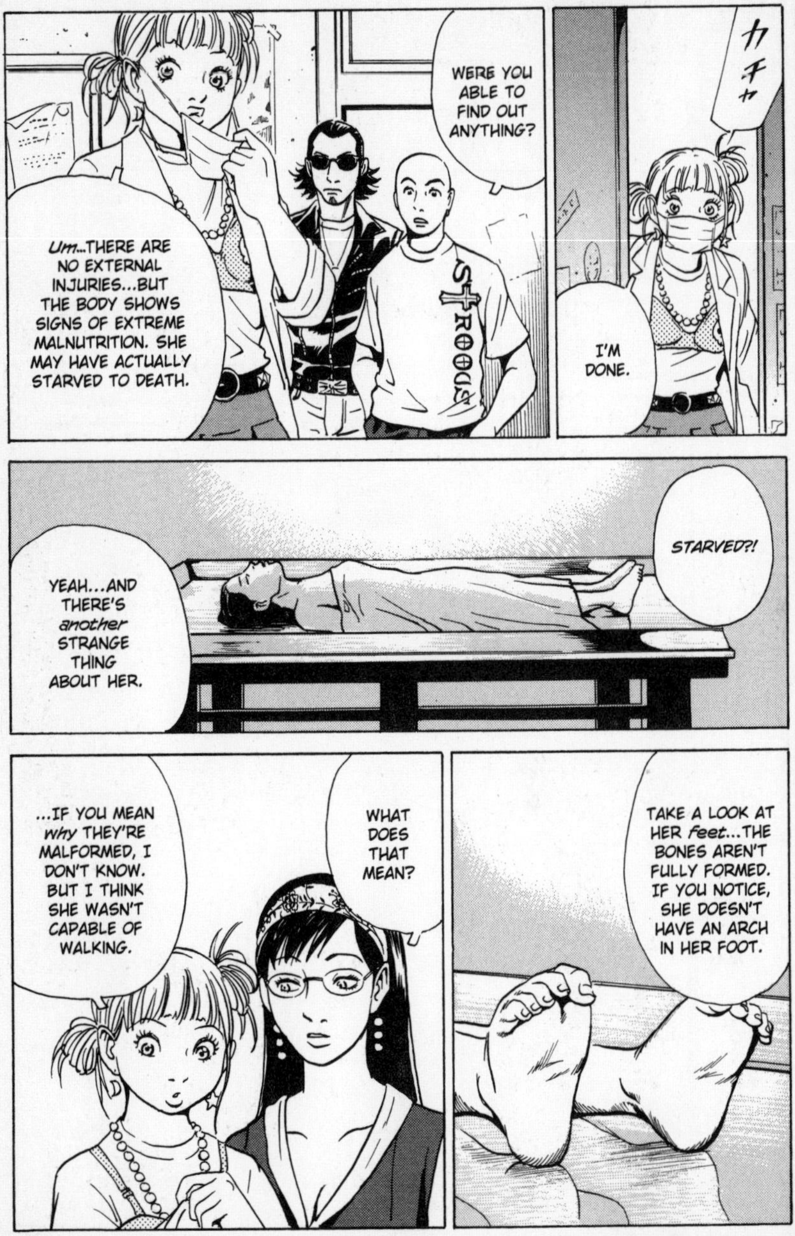

カチャ
I'M DONE.
WERE YOU ABLE TO FIND OUT ANYTHING?
Um...THERE ARE NO EXTERNAL INJURIES...BUT THE BODY SHOWS SIGNS OF EXTREME MALNUTRITION. SHE MAY HAVE ACTUALLY STARVED TO DEATH.
STARVED?!
YEAH...AND THERE'S *another* STRANGE THING ABOUT HER.
TAKE A LOOK AT HER *feet*...THE BONES AREN'T FULLY FORMED. IF YOU NOTICE, SHE DOESN'T HAVE AN ARCH IN HER FOOT.
WHAT DOES THAT MEAN?
...IF YOU MEAN *why* THEY'RE MALFORMED, I DON'T KNOW. BUT I THINK SHE WASN'T CAPABLE OF WALKING.

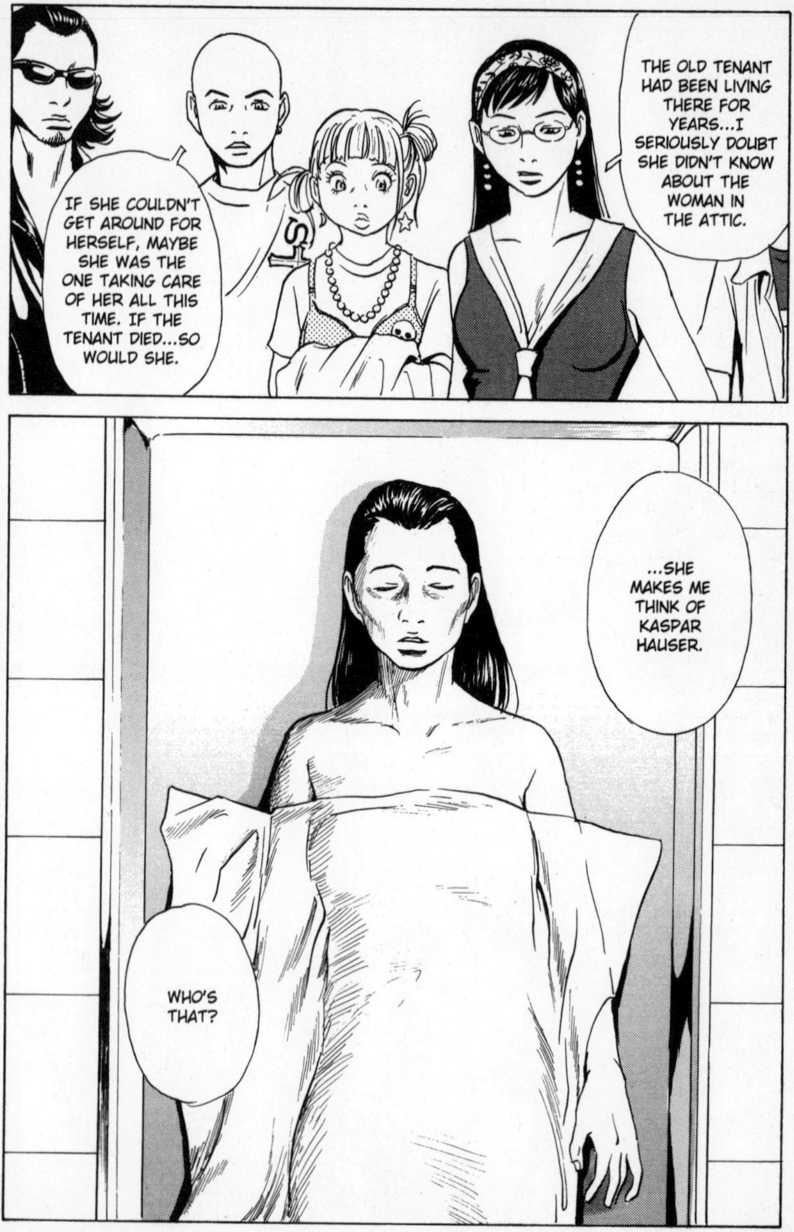
THE OLD TENANT HAD BEEN LIVING THERE FOR YEARS...I SERIOUSLY DOUBT SHE DIDN'T KNOW ABOUT THE WOMAN IN THE ATTIC.
IF SHE COULDN'T GET AROUND FOR HERSELF, MAYBE SHE WAS THE ONE TAKING CARE OF HER ALL THIS TIME. IF THE TENANT DIED...SO WOULD SHE.
...SHE MAKES ME THINK OF KASPAR HAUSER.
WHO'S THAT?

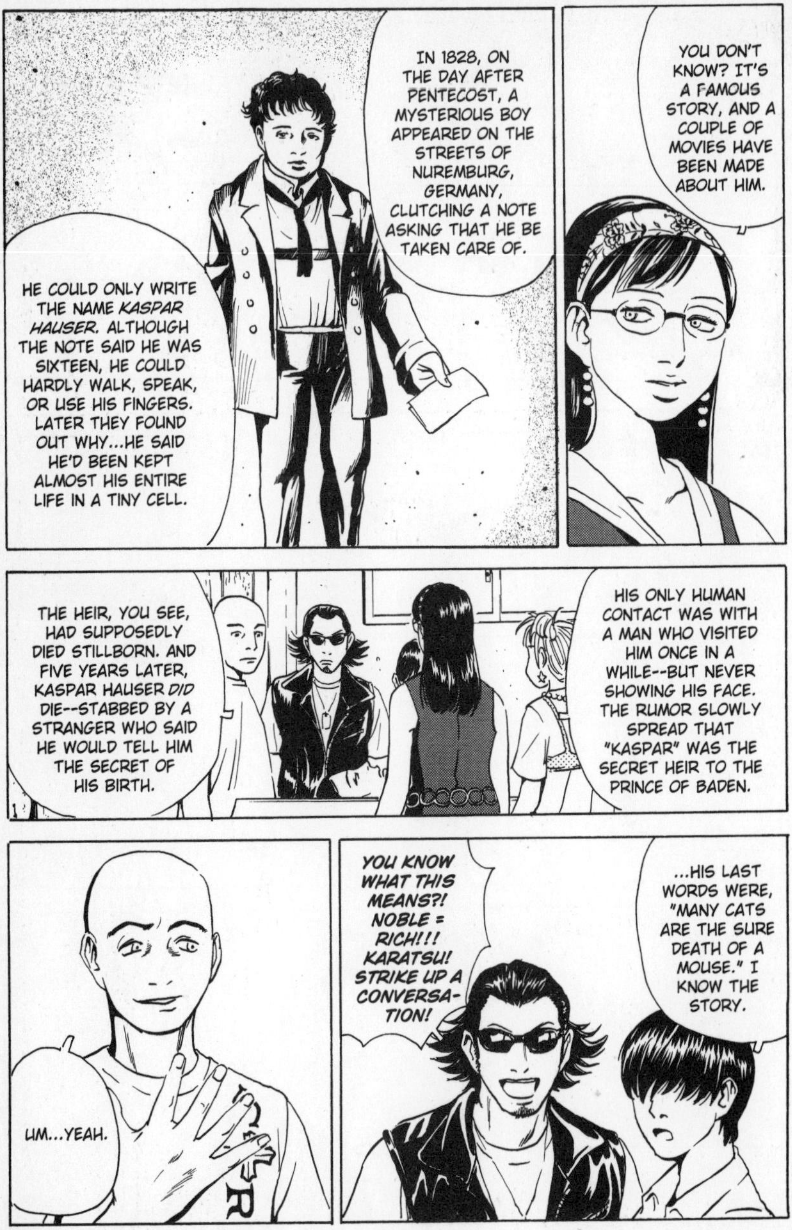
YOU DON'T KNOW? IT'S A FAMOUS STORY, AND A COUPLE OF MOVIES HAVE BEEN MADE ABOUT HIM.
IN 1828, ON THE DAY AFTER PENTECOST, A MYSTERIOUS BOY APPEARED ON THE STREETS OF NUREMBURG, GERMANY, CLUTCHING A NOTE ASKING THAT HE BE TAKEN CARE OF.
HE COULD ONLY WRITE THE NAME *KASPAR HAUSER*. ALTHOUGH THE NOTE SAID HE WAS SIXTEEN, HE COULD HARDLY WALK, SPEAK, OR USE HIS FINGERS. LATER THEY FOUND OUT WHY...HE SAID HE'D BEEN KEPT ALMOST HIS ENTIRE LIFE IN A TINY CELL.
HIS ONLY HUMAN CONTACT WAS WITH A MAN WHO VISITED HIM ONCE IN A WHILE--BUT NEVER SHOWING HIS FACE. THE RUMOR SLOWLY SPREAD THAT "KASPAR" WAS THE SECRET HEIR TO THE PRINCE OF BADEN.
THE HEIR, YOU SEE, HAD SUPPOSEDLY DIED STILLBORN. AND FIVE YEARS LATER, KASPAR HAUSER *DID* DIE--STABBED BY A STRANGER WHO SAID HE WOULD TELL HIM THE SECRET OF HIS BIRTH.
...HIS LAST WORDS WERE, "MANY CATS ARE THE SURE DEATH OF A MOUSE." I KNOW THE STORY.
YOU KNOW WHAT THIS MEANS?! NOBLE = RICH!!! KARATSU! STRIKE UP A CONVERSATION!
UM...YEAH.

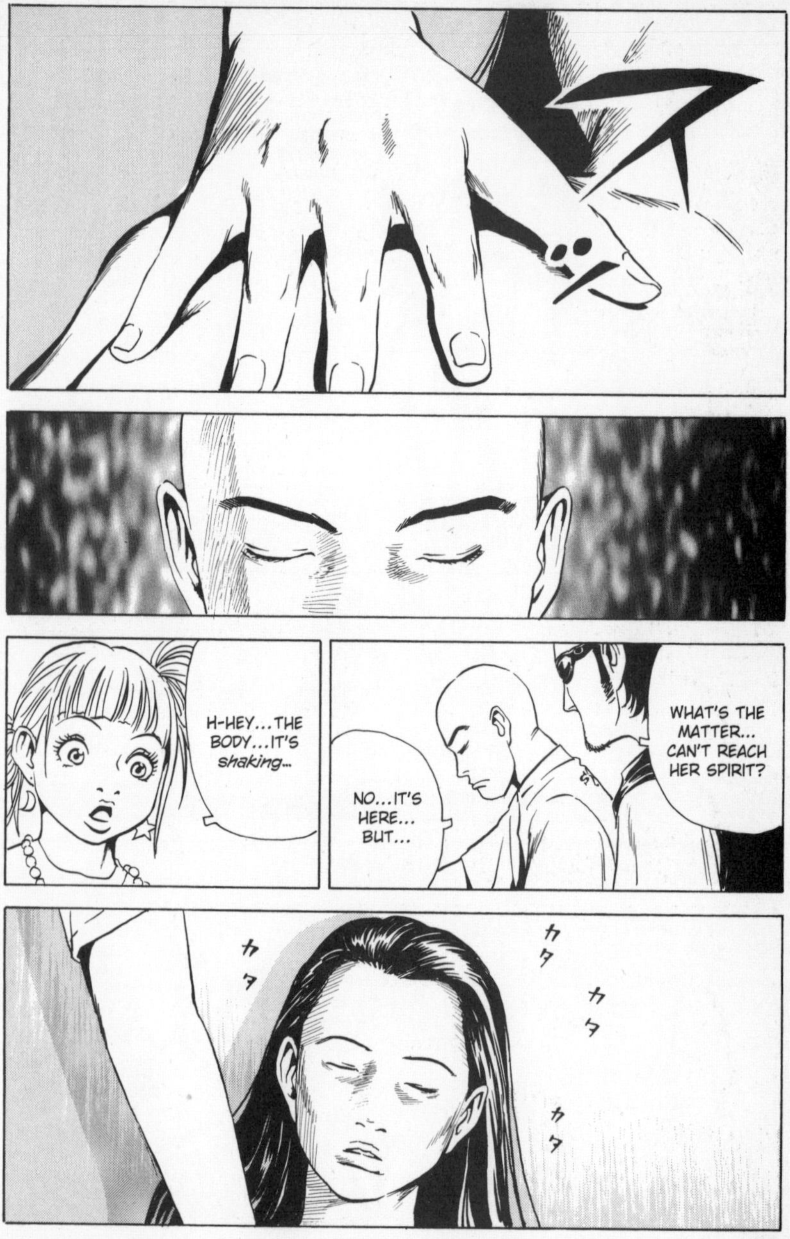
WHAT'S THE MATTER... CAN'T REACH HER SPIRIT?
NO...IT'S HERE... BUT...
H-HEY...THE BODY...IT'S *shaking*...
カタ
カタ
カタ
カタ

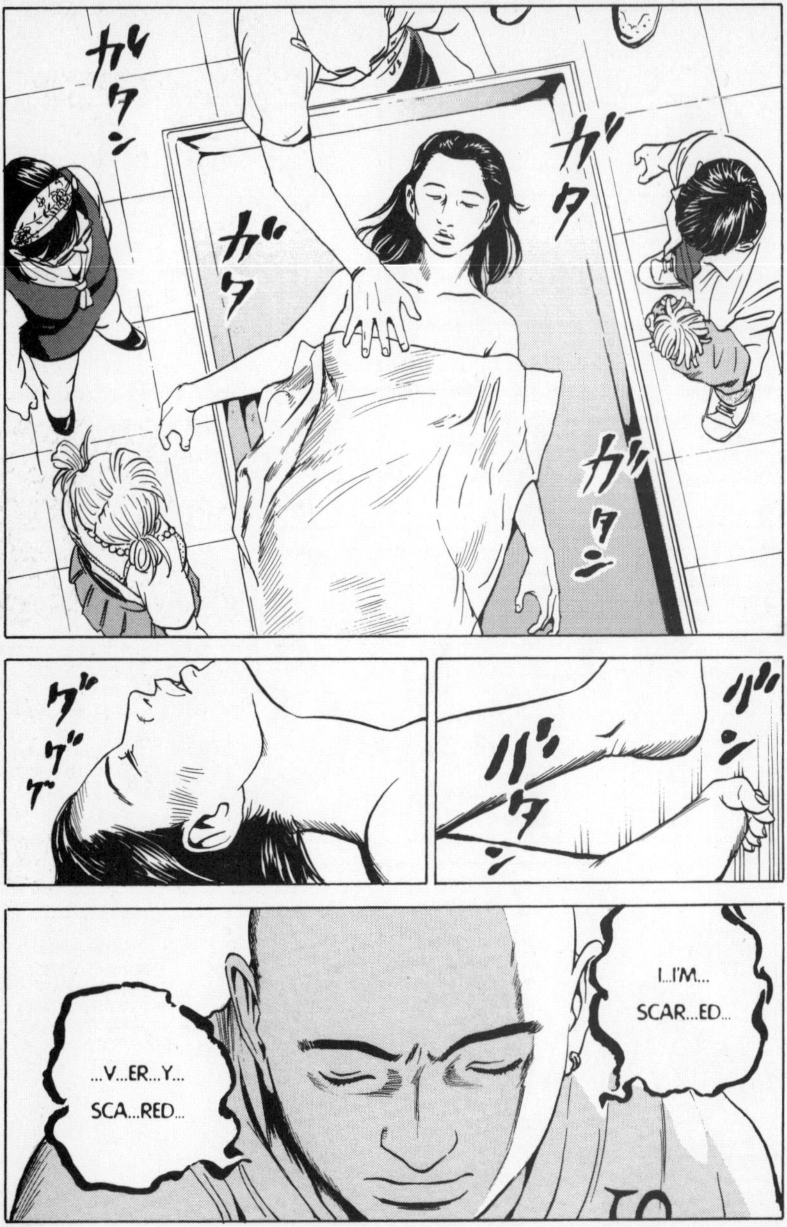
ガタ
ガタン
ガタン
ガタ
バン
バタン
グググ
I...I'M...
SCAR...ED...
...V...ER...Y...
SCA...RED...

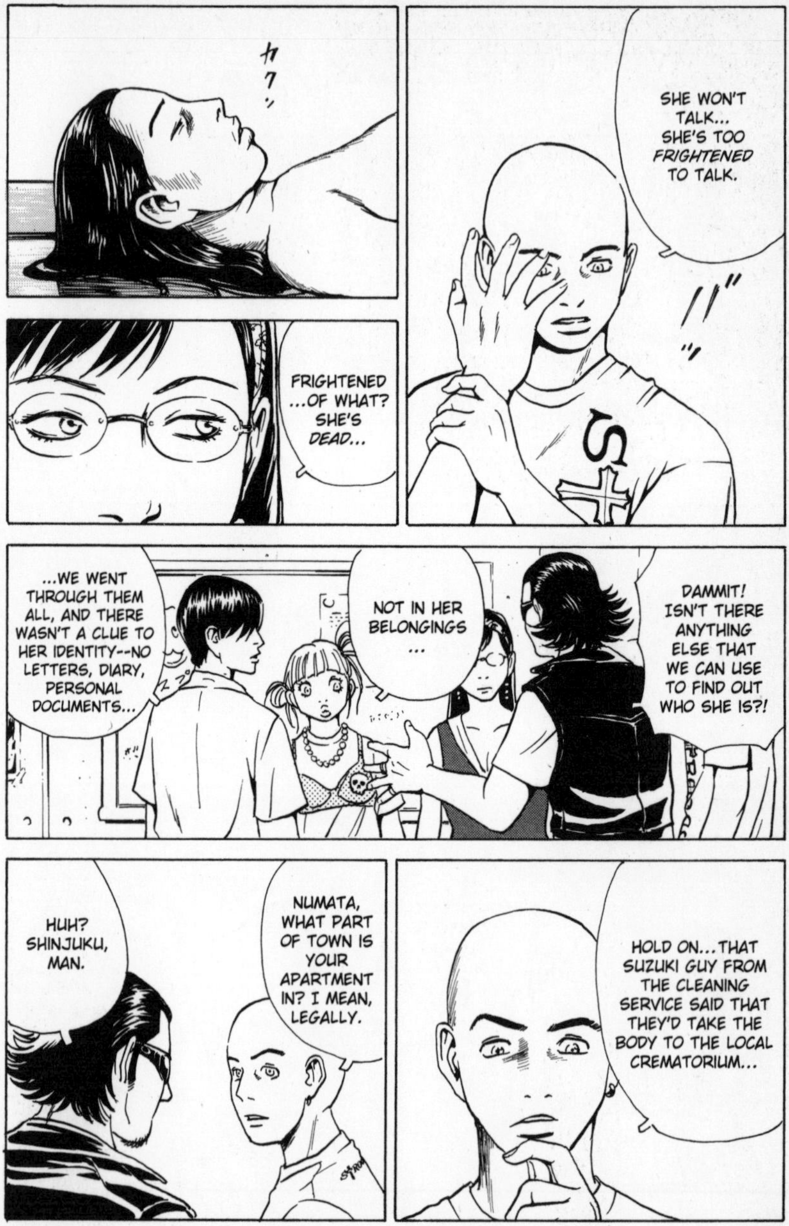
SHE WON'T TALK... SHE'S TOO *FRIGHTENED* TO TALK.
カクッ
FRIGHTENED ...OF WHAT? SHE'S *DEAD*...
DAMMIT! ISN'T THERE ANYTHING ELSE THAT WE CAN USE TO FIND OUT WHO SHE IS?!
NOT IN HER BELONGINGS ...
...WE WENT THROUGH THEM ALL, AND THERE WASN'T A CLUE TO HER IDENTITY--NO LETTERS, DIARY, PERSONAL DOCUMENTS...
HOLD ON...THAT SUZUKI GUY FROM THE CLEANING SERVICE SAID THAT THEY'D TAKE THE BODY TO THE LOCAL CREMATORIUM...
NUMATA, WHAT PART OF TOWN IS YOUR APARTMENT IN? I MEAN, LEGALLY.
HUH? SHINJUKU, MAN.

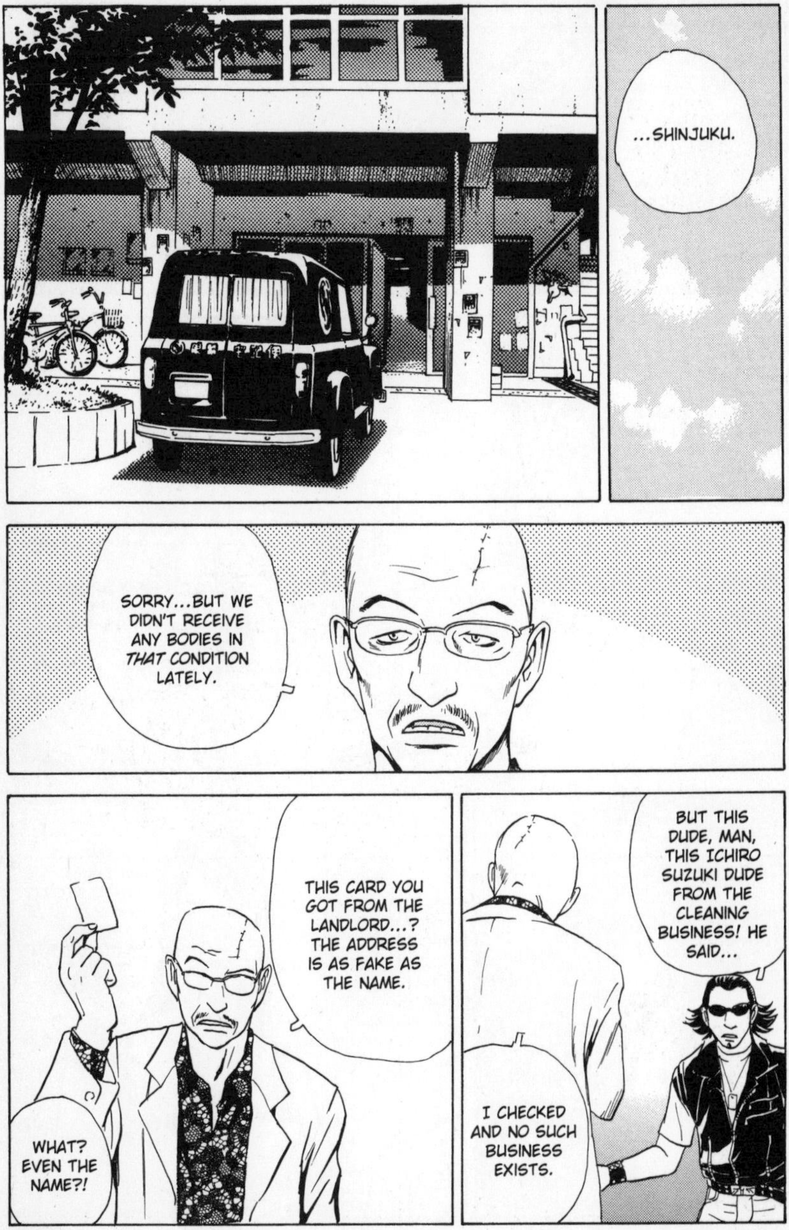
...SHINJUKU.
SORRY...BUT WE DIDN'T RECEIVE ANY BODIES IN *THAT* CONDITION LATELY.
BUT THIS DUDE, MAN, THIS ICHIRO SUZUKI DUDE FROM THE CLEANING BUSINESS! HE SAID...
I CHECKED AND NO SUCH BUSINESS EXISTS.
THIS CARD YOU GOT FROM THE LANDLORD...? THE ADDRESS IS AS FAKE AS THE NAME.
WHAT? EVEN THE NAME?!

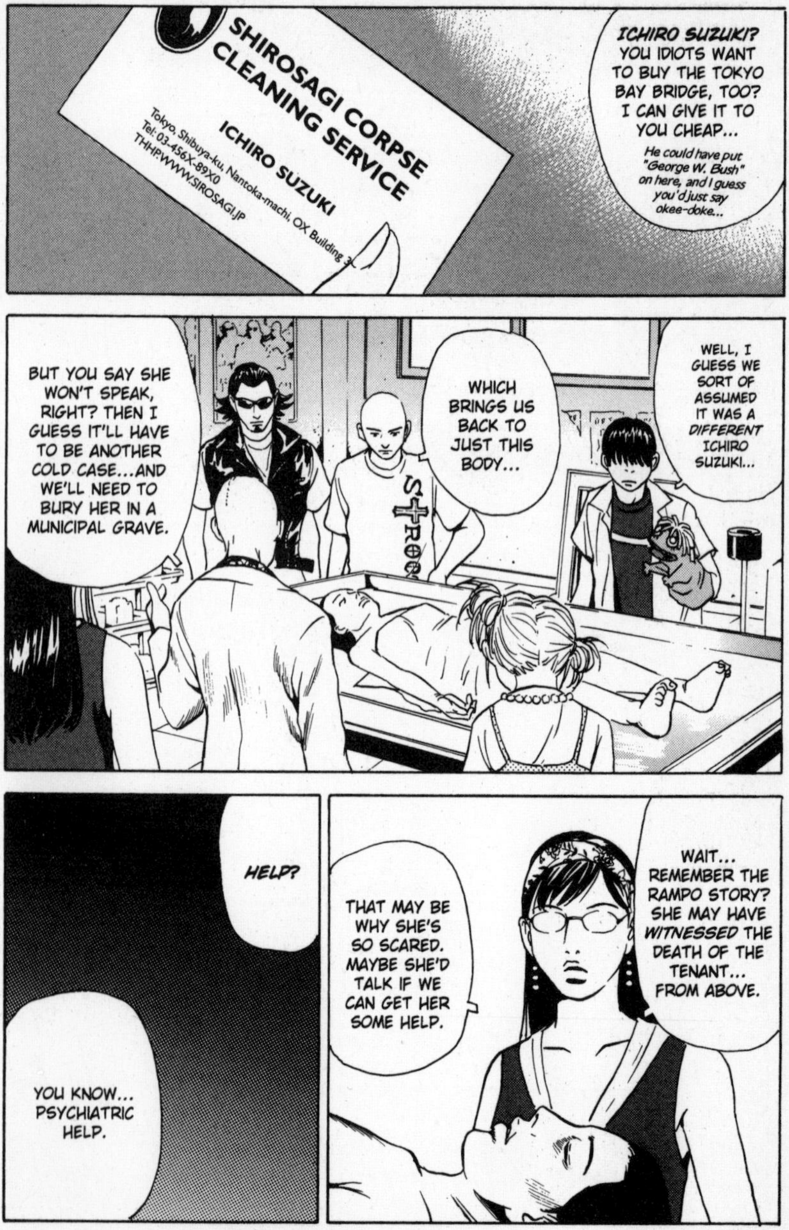
ICHIRO SUZUKI? YOU IDIOTS WANT TO BUY THE TOKYO BAY BRIDGE, TOO? I CAN GIVE IT TO YOU CHEAP...
He could have put "George W. Bush" on here, and I guess you'd just say okee-doke...
SHIROSAGI CORPSE CLEANING SERVICE
ICHIRO SUZUKI
Tokyo, Shibuya-ku, Nantoka-machi, OX Building 3
Tel: 03-456X-89X0
THHP:WWW.SIROSAGI.JP
WELL, I GUESS WE SORT OF ASSUMED IT WAS A DIFFERENT ICHIRO SUZUKI...
WHICH BRINGS US BACK TO JUST THIS BODY...
BUT YOU SAY SHE WON'T SPEAK, RIGHT? THEN I GUESS IT'LL HAVE TO BE ANOTHER COLD CASE...AND WE'LL NEED TO BURY HER IN A MUNICIPAL GRAVE.
WAIT... REMEMBER THE RAMPO STORY? SHE MAY HAVE WITNESSED THE DEATH OF THE TENANT... FROM ABOVE.
THAT MAY BE WHY SHE'S SO SCARED. MAYBE SHE'D TALK IF WE CAN GET HER SOME HELP.
HELP?
YOU KNOW... PSYCHIATRIC HELP.

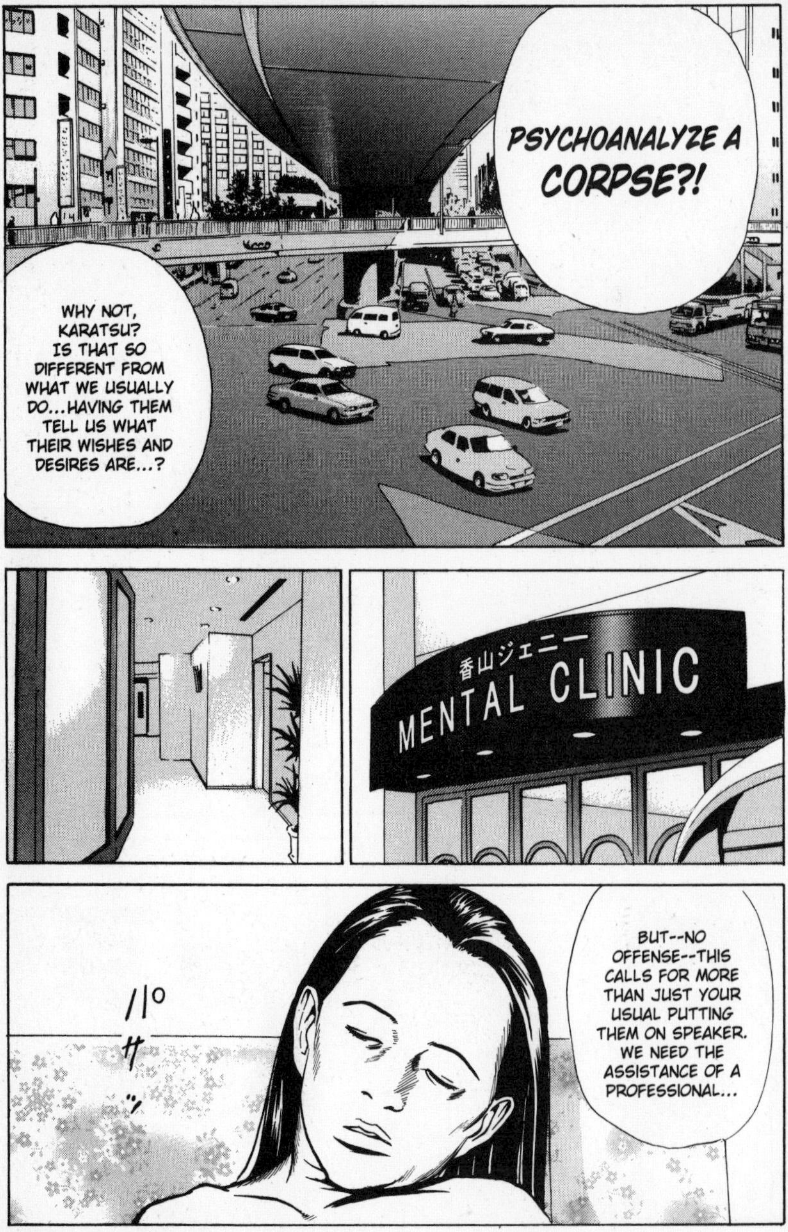
PSYCHOANALYZE A CORPSE?!
WHY NOT, KARATSU? IS THAT SO DIFFERENT FROM WHAT WE USUALLY DO...HAVING THEM TELL US WHAT THEIR WISHES AND DESIRES ARE...?
香山ジェニー
MENTAL CLINIC
BUT--NO OFFENSE--THIS CALLS FOR MORE THAN JUST YOUR USUAL PUTTING THEM ON SPEAKER. WE NEED THE ASSISTANCE OF A PROFESSIONAL...

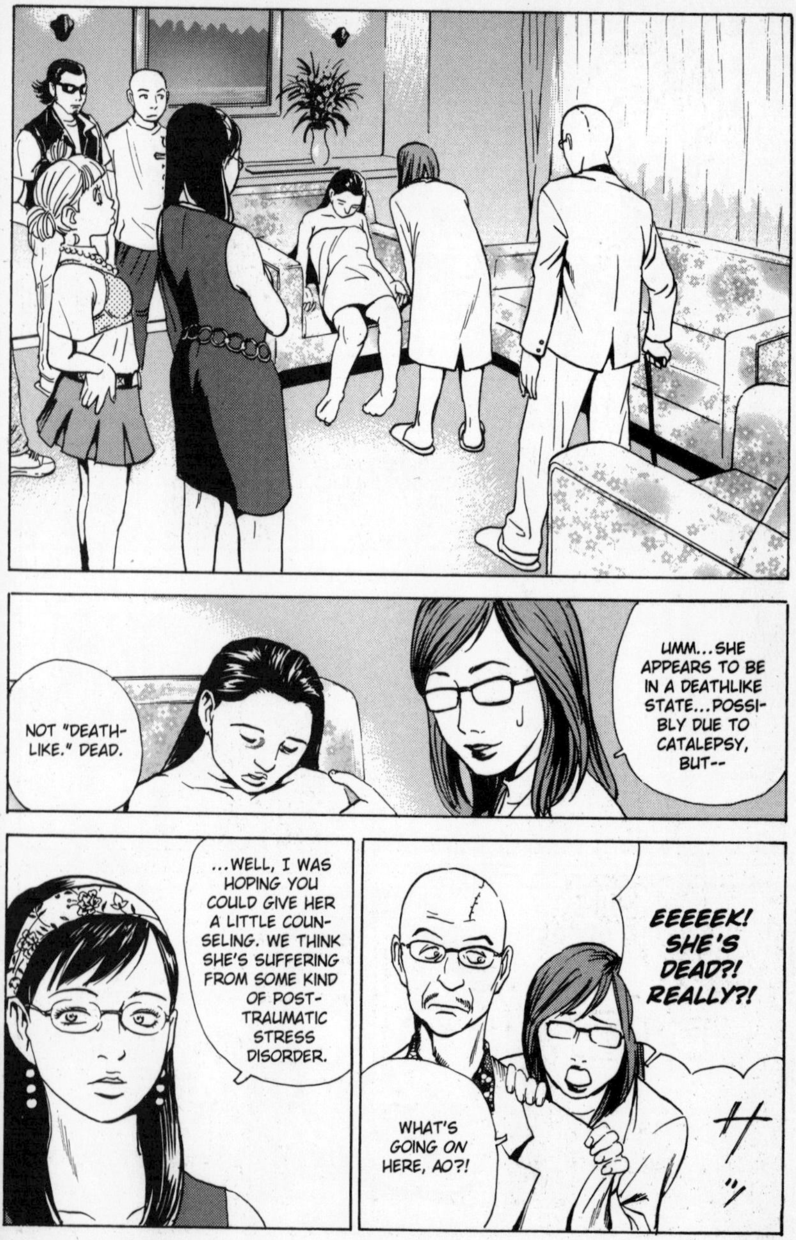
UMM...SHE APPEARS TO BE IN A DEATHLIKE STATE...POSSIBLY DUE TO CATALEPSY, BUT--
NOT "DEATH-LIKE." DEAD.
EEEEEK! SHE'S DEAD?! REALLY?!
WHAT'S GOING ON HERE, AO?!
...WELL, I WAS HOPING YOU COULD GIVE HER A LITTLE COUNSELING. WE THINK SHE'S SUFFERING FROM SOME KIND OF POST-TRAUMATIC STRESS DISORDER.

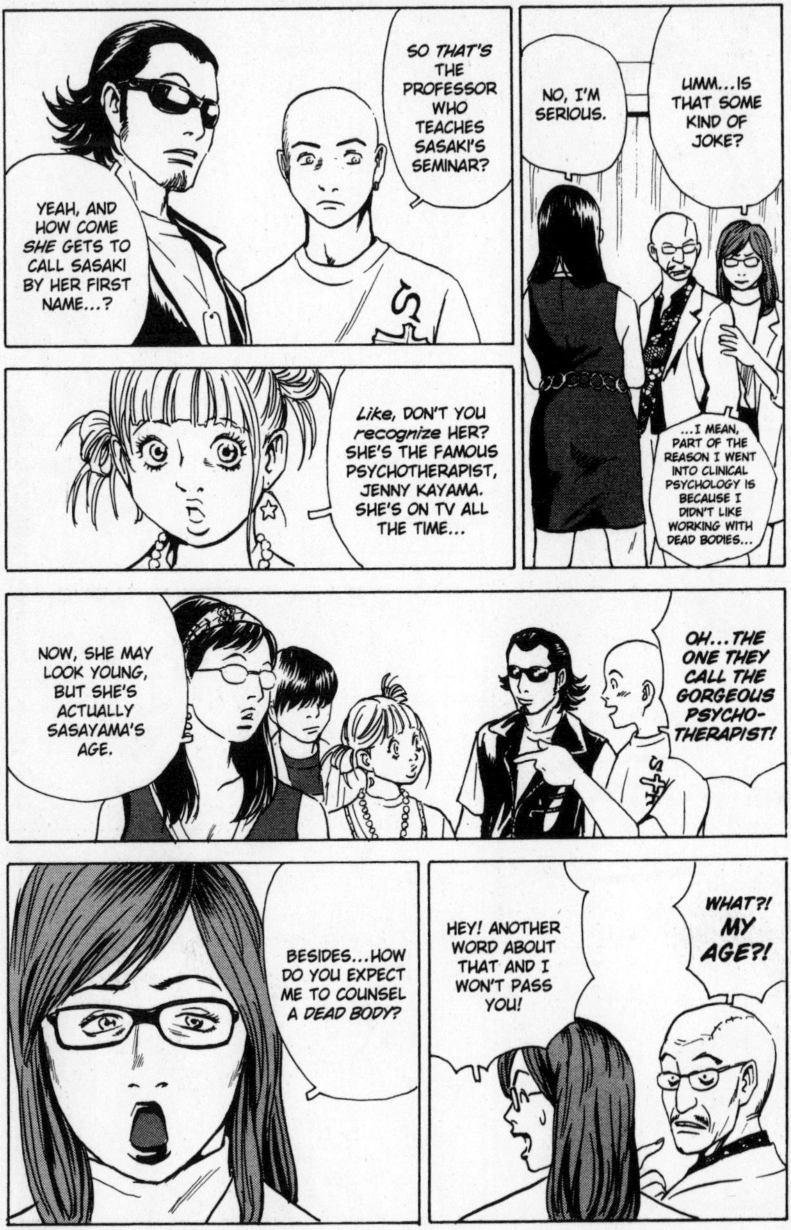
UMM...IS THAT SOME KIND OF JOKE?
NO, I'M SERIOUS.
...I MEAN, PART OF THE REASON I WENT INTO CLINICAL PSYCHOLOGY IS BECAUSE I DIDN'T LIKE WORKING WITH DEAD BODIES...
SO *THAT'S* THE PROFESSOR WHO TEACHES SASAKI'S SEMINAR?
YEAH, AND HOW COME *SHE* GETS TO CALL SASAKI BY HER FIRST NAME...?
Like, DON'T YOU *recognize* HER? SHE'S THE FAMOUS PSYCHOTHERAPIST, JENNY KAYAMA. SHE'S ON TV ALL THE TIME...
OH...THE ONE THEY CALL THE GORGEOUS PSYCHO-THERAPIST!
NOW, SHE MAY LOOK YOUNG, BUT SHE'S ACTUALLY SASAYAMA'S AGE.
WHAT?! MY AGE?!
HEY! ANOTHER WORD ABOUT THAT AND I WON'T PASS YOU!
BESIDES...HOW DO YOU EXPECT ME TO COUNSEL A *DEAD BODY?*

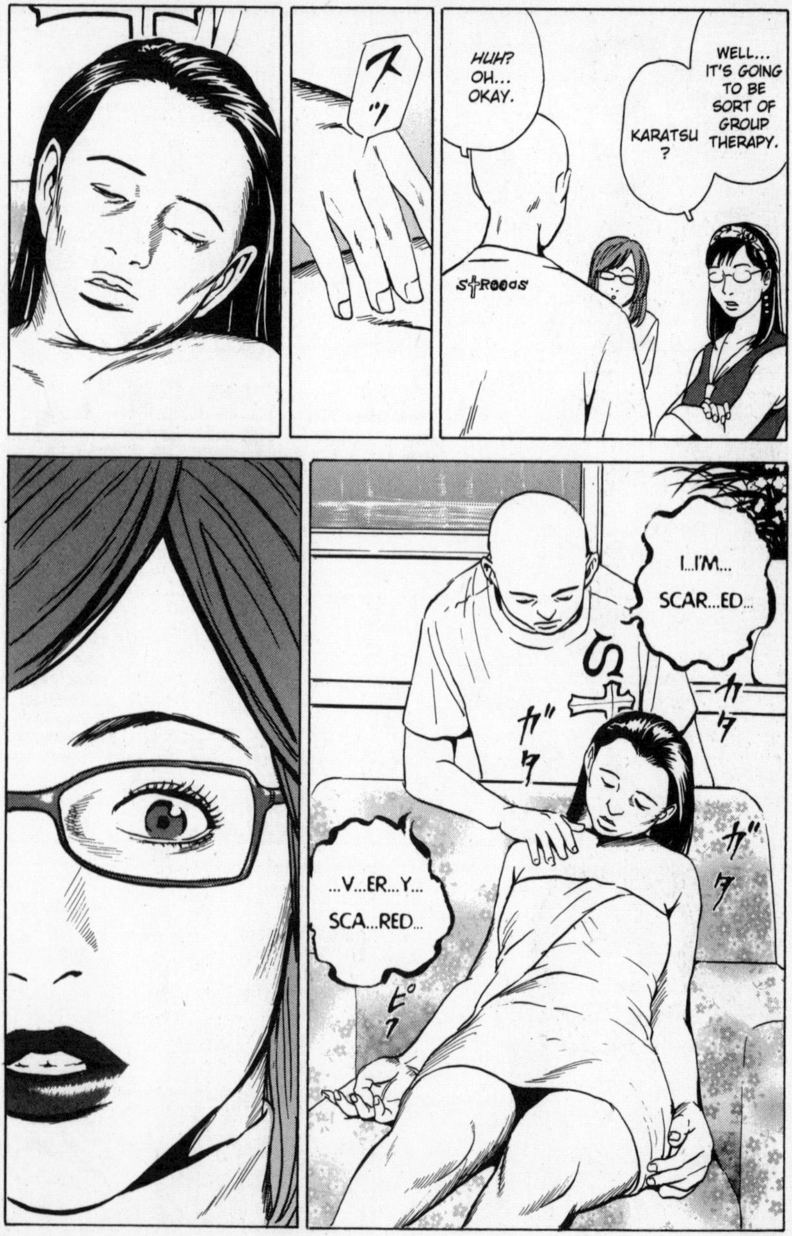
WELL... IT'S GOING TO BE SORT OF GROUP THERAPY.
KARATSU?
HUH? OH... OKAY.
スッ
I...I'M... SCAR...ED...
カタ
ガタ
ガタ
...V...ER...Y... SCA...RED...
ピク

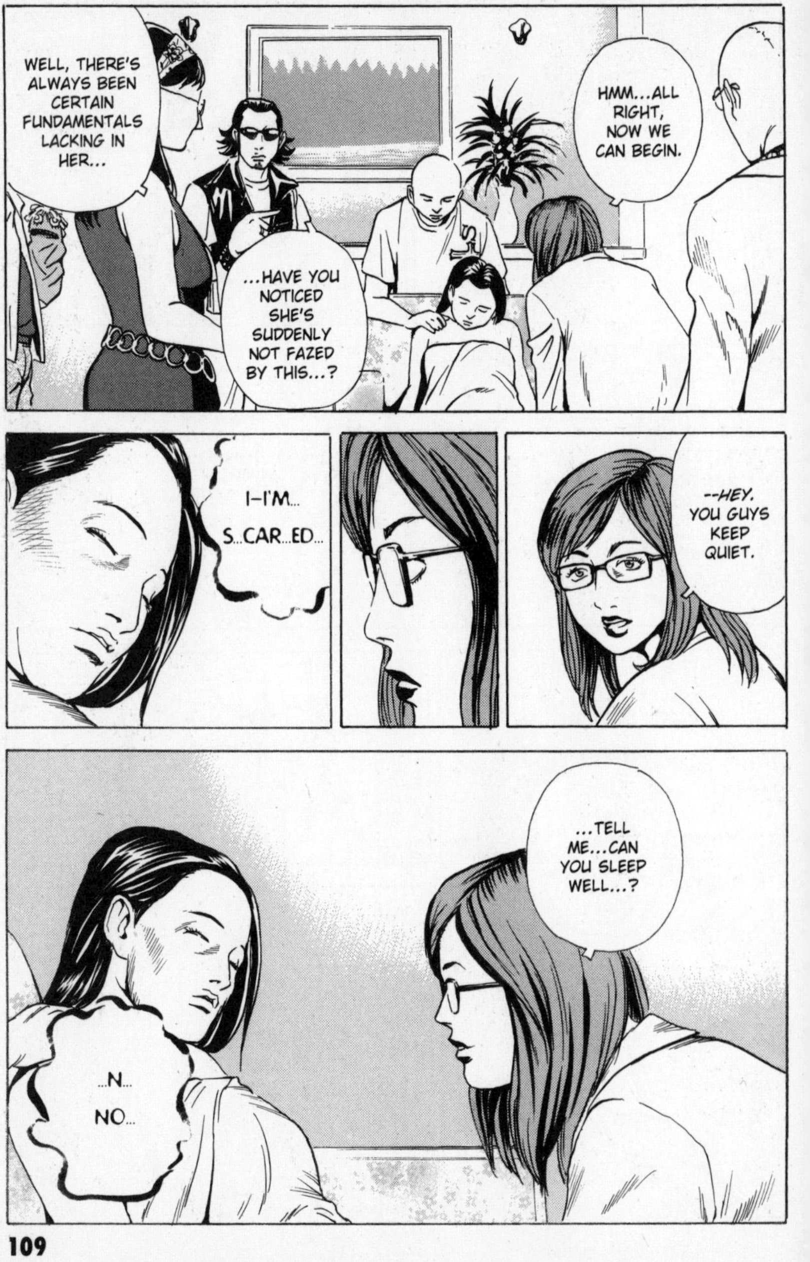
HMM...ALL RIGHT, NOW WE CAN BEGIN.
WELL, THERE'S ALWAYS BEEN CERTAIN FUNDAMENTALS LACKING IN HER...
...HAVE YOU NOTICED SHE'S SUDDENLY NOT FAZED BY THIS...?
--HEY. YOU GUYS KEEP QUIET.
I-I'M... S...CAR...ED...
...TELL ME...CAN YOU SLEEP WELL...?
...N... NO...

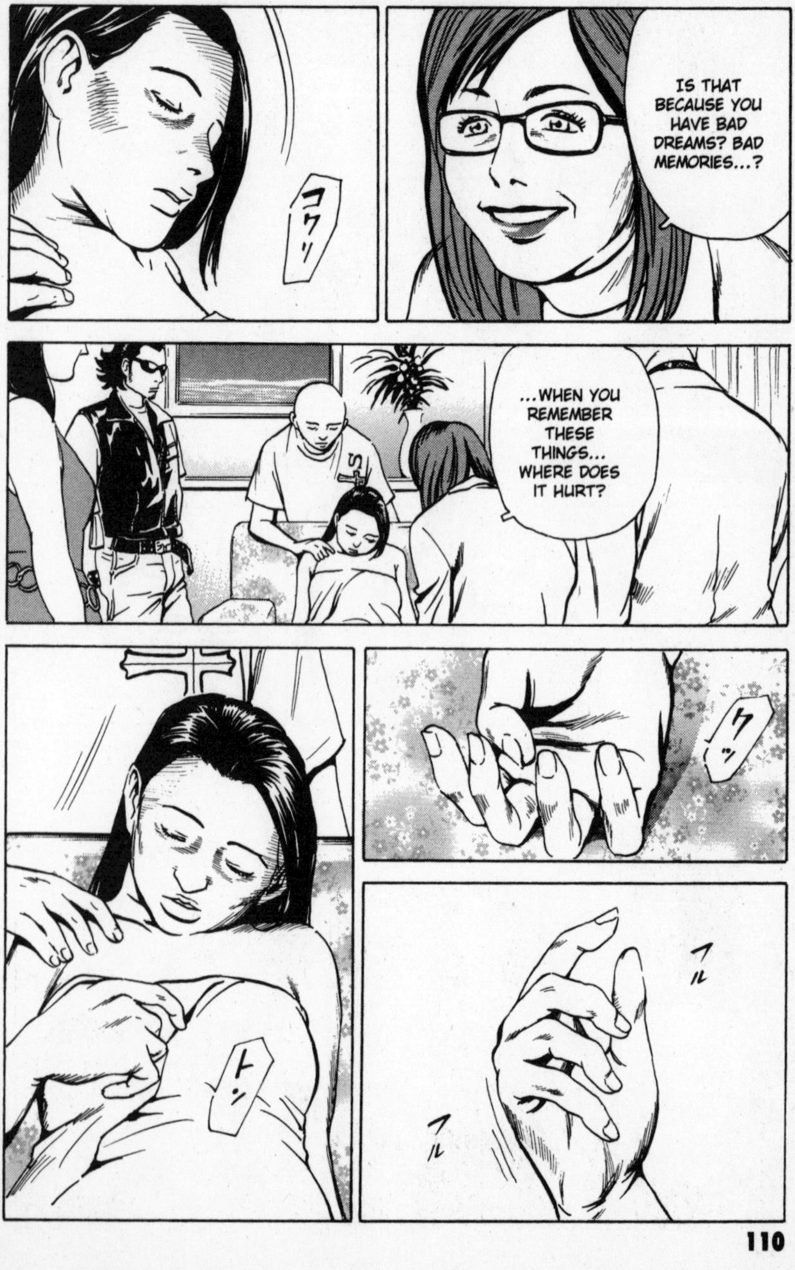
IS THAT BECAUSE YOU HAVE BAD DREAMS? BAD MEMORIES...?
コクッ
...WHEN YOU REMEMBER THESE THINGS... WHERE DOES IT HURT?
クッ
フル
フル
トン

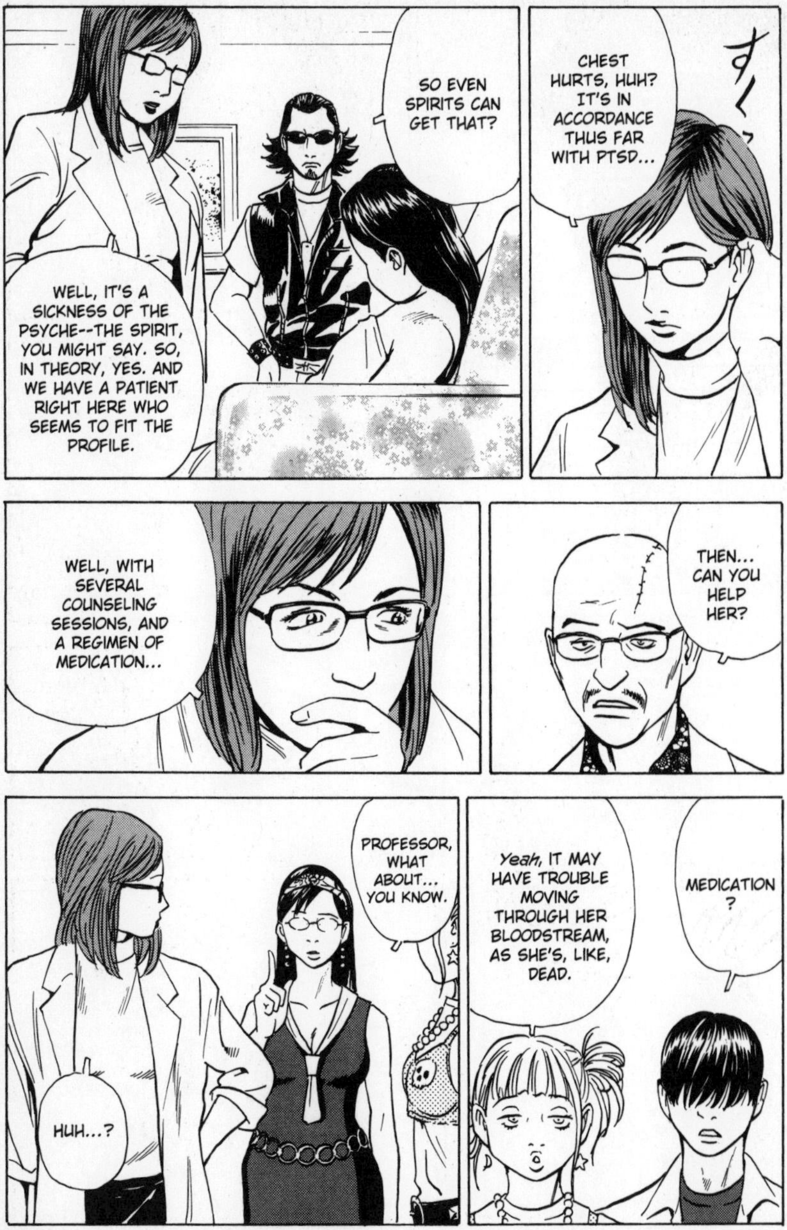
すく
CHEST HURTS, HUH? IT'S IN ACCORDANCE THUS FAR WITH PTSD...
SO EVEN SPIRITS CAN GET THAT?
WELL, IT'S A SICKNESS OF THE PSYCHE--THE SPIRIT, YOU MIGHT SAY. SO, IN THEORY, YES. AND WE HAVE A PATIENT RIGHT HERE WHO SEEMS TO FIT THE PROFILE.
THEN... CAN YOU HELP HER?
WELL, WITH SEVERAL COUNSELING SESSIONS, AND A REGIMEN OF MEDICATION...
MEDICATION ?
Yeah, IT MAY HAVE TROUBLE MOVING THROUGH HER BLOODSTREAM, AS SHE'S, LIKE, DEAD.
PROFESSOR, WHAT ABOUT... YOU KNOW.
HUH...?

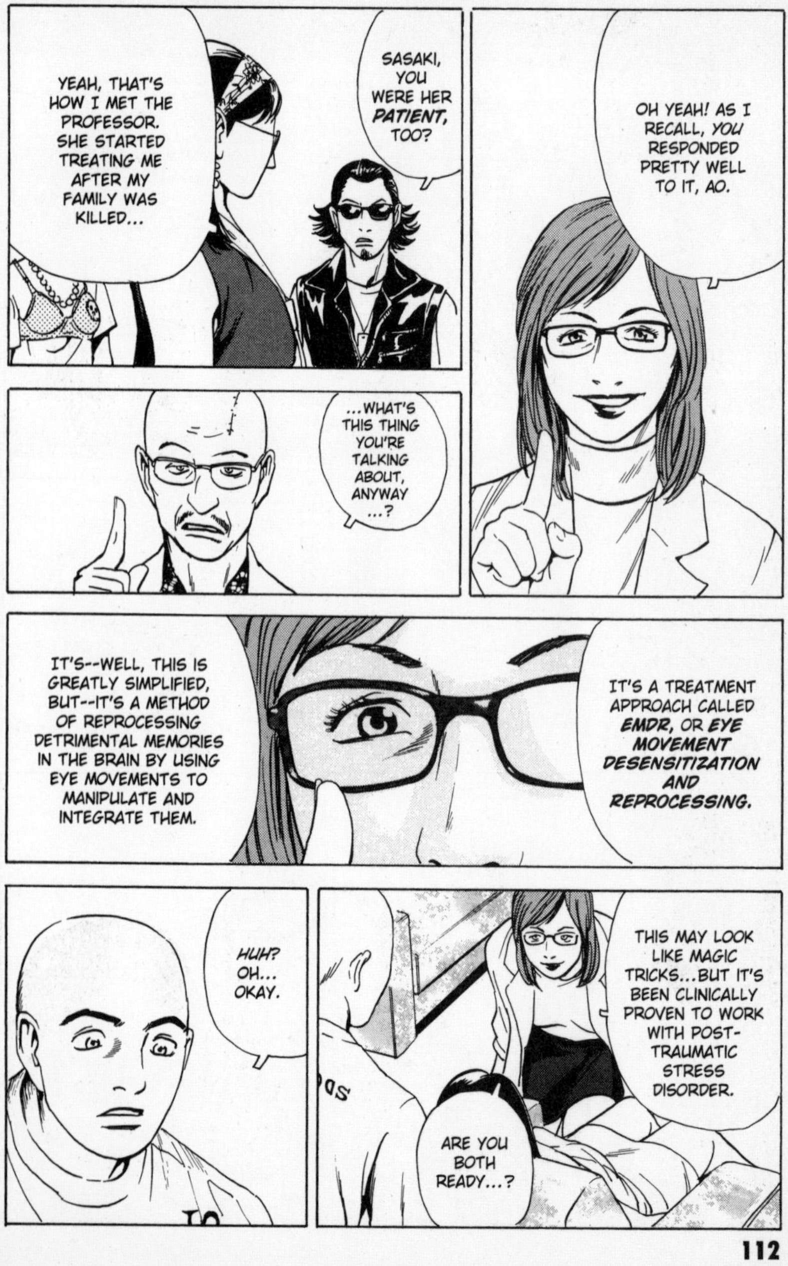
OH YEAH! AS I RECALL, YOU RESPONDED PRETTY WELL TO IT, AO.
SASAKI, YOU WERE HER PATIENT, TOO?
YEAH, THAT'S HOW I MET THE PROFESSOR. SHE STARTED TREATING ME AFTER MY FAMILY WAS KILLED...
...WHAT'S THIS THING YOU'RE TALKING ABOUT, ANYWAY ...?
IT'S A TREATMENT APPROACH CALLED EMDR, OR EYE MOVEMENT DESENSITIZATION AND REPROCESSING.
IT'S--WELL, THIS IS GREATLY SIMPLIFIED, BUT--IT'S A METHOD OF REPROCESSING DETRIMENTAL MEMORIES IN THE BRAIN BY USING EYE MOVEMENTS TO MANIPULATE AND INTEGRATE THEM.
THIS MAY LOOK LIKE MAGIC TRICKS...BUT IT'S BEEN CLINICALLY PROVEN TO WORK WITH POST-TRAUMATIC STRESS DISORDER.
ARE YOU BOTH READY...?
HUH? OH... OKAY.

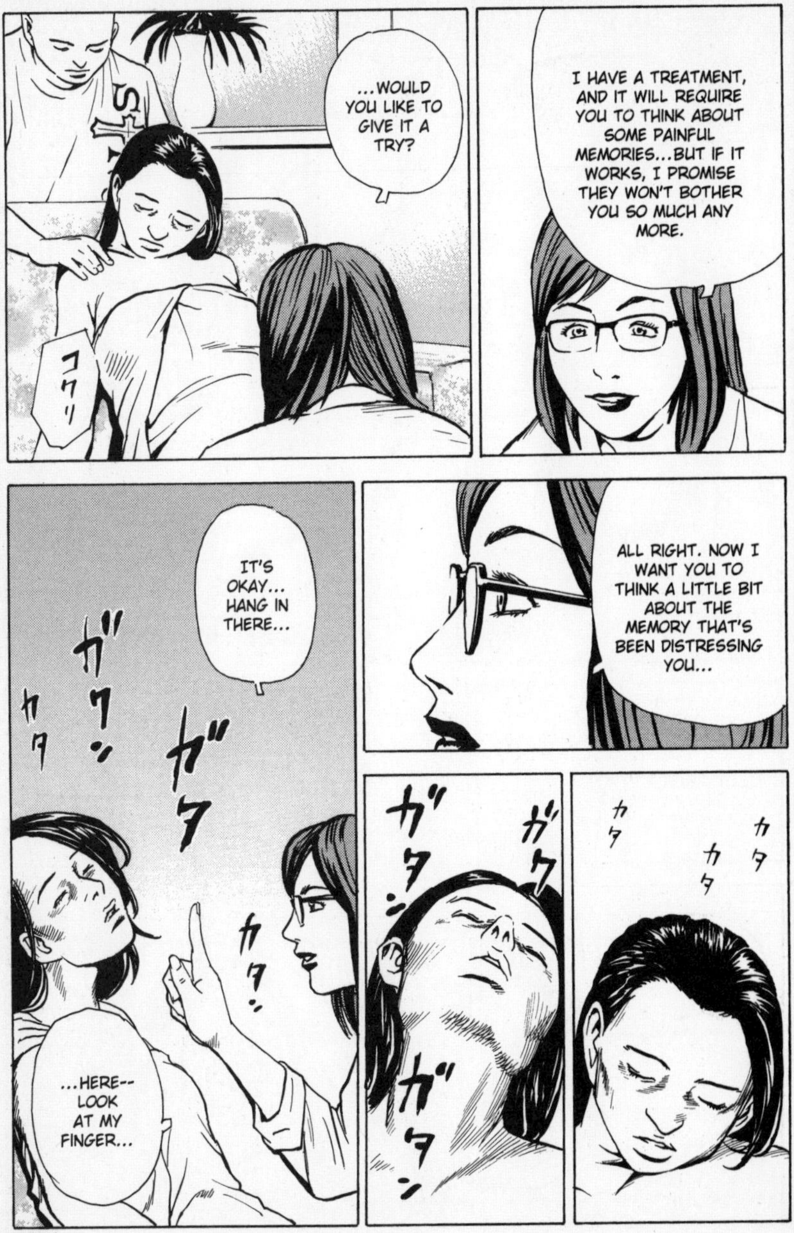
I HAVE A TREATMENT, AND IT WILL REQUIRE YOU TO THINK ABOUT SOME PAINFUL MEMORIES...BUT IF IT WORKS, I PROMISE THEY WON'T BOTHER YOU SO MUCH ANY MORE.
...WOULD YOU LIKE TO GIVE IT A TRY?
コクッ
ALL RIGHT. NOW I WANT YOU TO THINK A LITTLE BIT ABOUT THE MEMORY THAT'S BEEN DISTRESSING YOU...
カタ
カタ
カタ
ガクッ
ガタン
ガタン
IT'S OKAY... HANG IN THERE...
ガクッ
カタ
ガタ
カタ
...HERE-- LOOK AT MY FINGER...

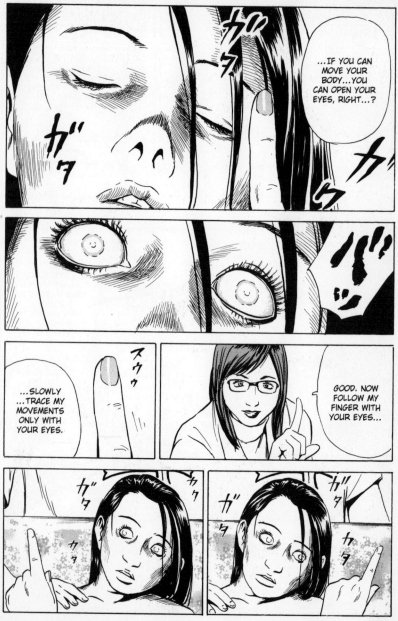

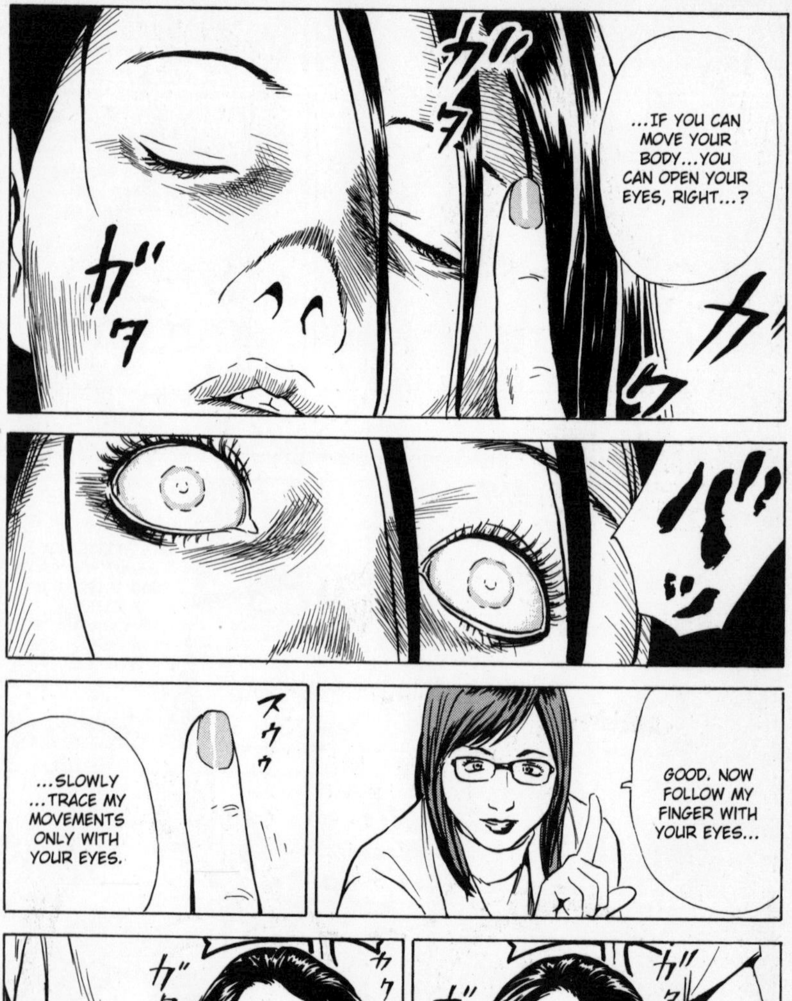
ガタ
...IF YOU CAN MOVE YOUR BODY...YOU CAN OPEN YOUR EYES, RIGHT...?
カク
ガタ
バッ
GOOD. NOW FOLLOW MY FINGER WITH YOUR EYES...
スウゥ
...SLOWLY ...TRACE MY MOVEMENTS ONLY WITH YOUR EYES.
ガタ
ガタ
カタ
カク
ガタ
カタ

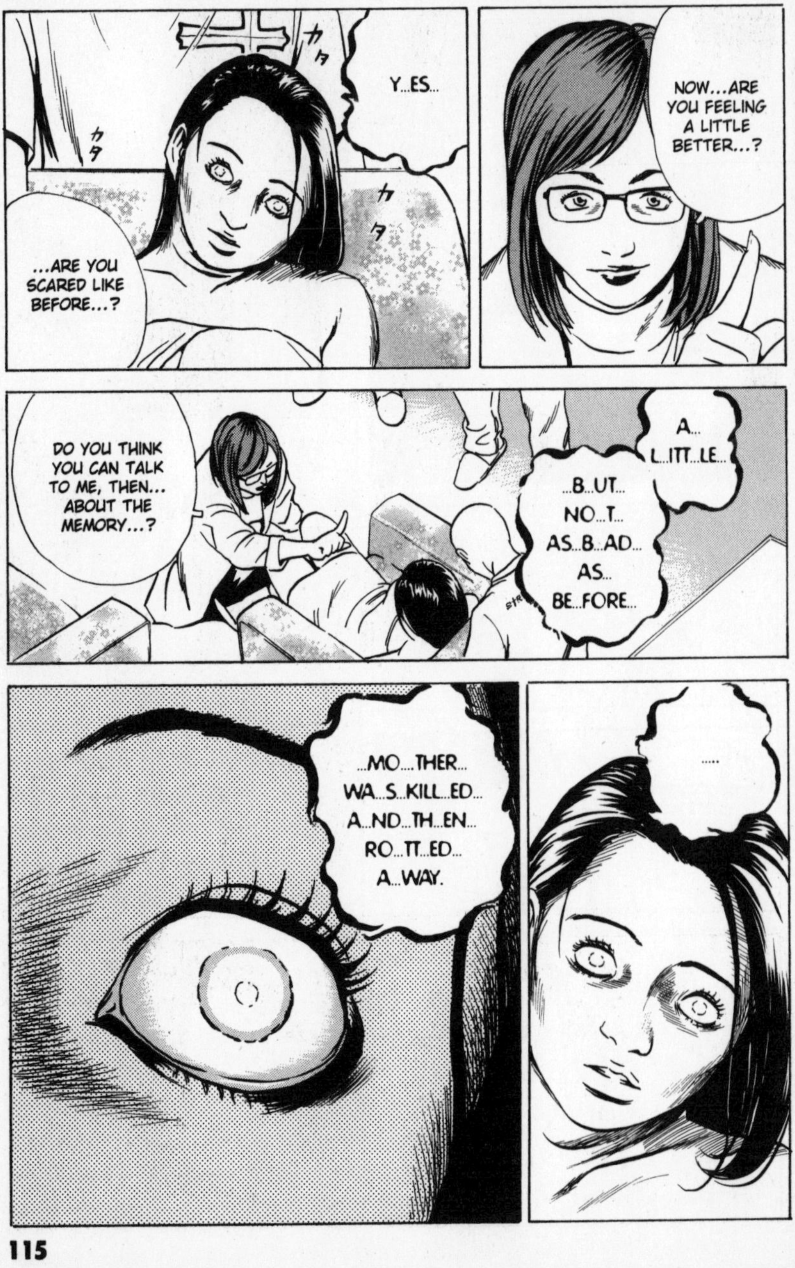
NOW...ARE YOU FEELING A LITTLE BETTER...?
Y...ES...
カタ
カタ
カタ
...ARE YOU SCARED LIKE BEFORE...?
A... L...ITT...LE...
...B...UT... NO...T... AS...B...AD... AS... BE...FORE...
DO YOU THINK YOU CAN TALK TO ME, THEN... ABOUT THE MEMORY...?
....
...MO....THER... WA...S...KILL...ED... A...ND...TH...EN... RO...TT...ED... A...WAY.

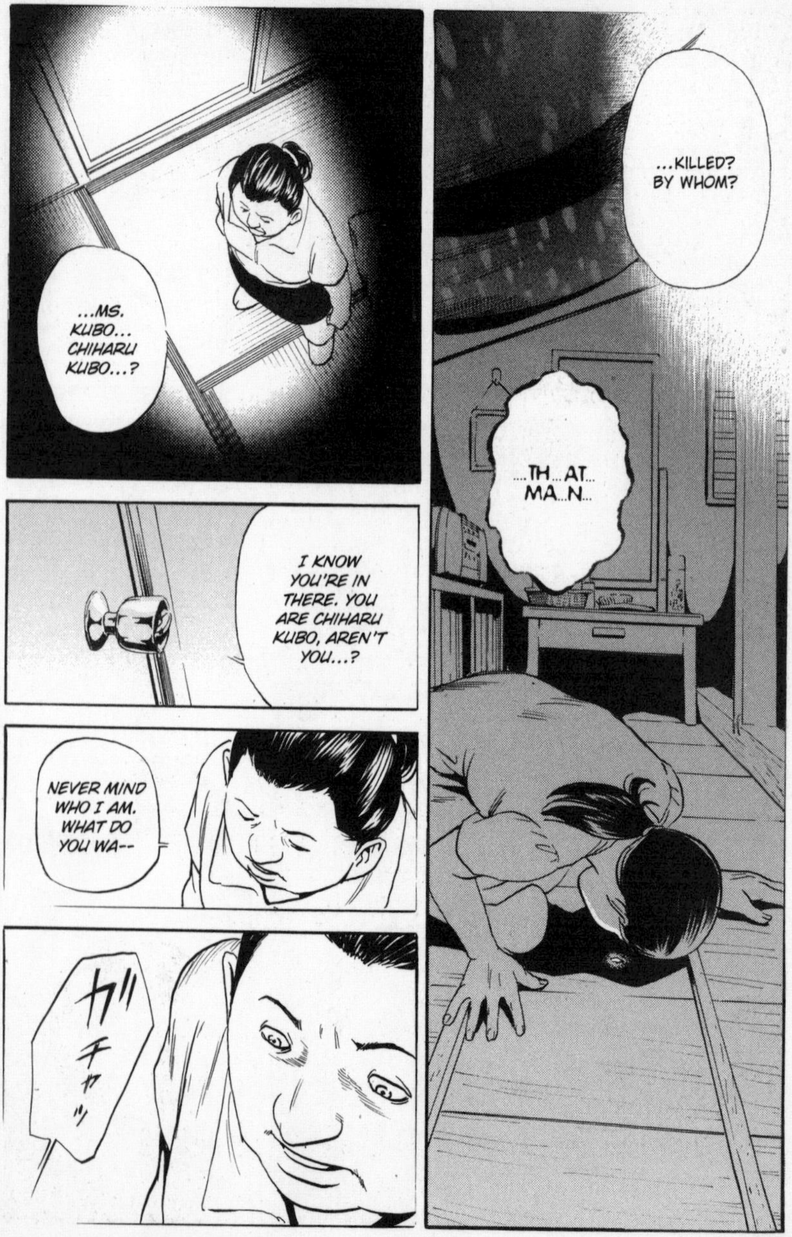
...KILLED? BY WHOM?
...TH...AT... MA...N...
...MS. KUBO... CHIHARU KUBO...?
I KNOW YOU'RE IN THERE. YOU ARE CHIHARU KUBO, AREN'T YOU...?
NEVER MIND WHO I AM. WHAT DO YOU WA--
ガチャッ

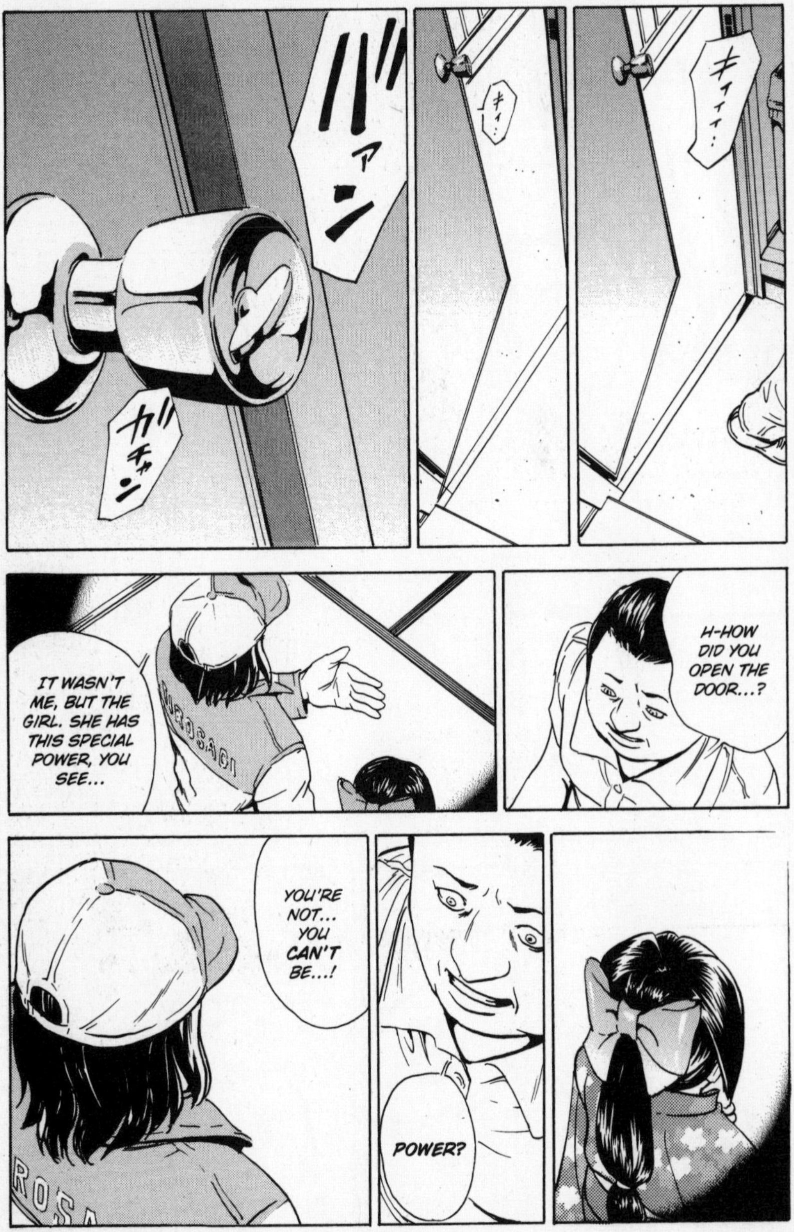
キィィィ…
キィ…
バァーン
ガチャン
H-HOW DID YOU OPEN THE DOOR...?
IT WASN'T ME, BUT THE GIRL. SHE HAS THIS SPECIAL POWER, YOU SEE...
YOU'RE NOT... YOU CAN'T BE...!
POWER?

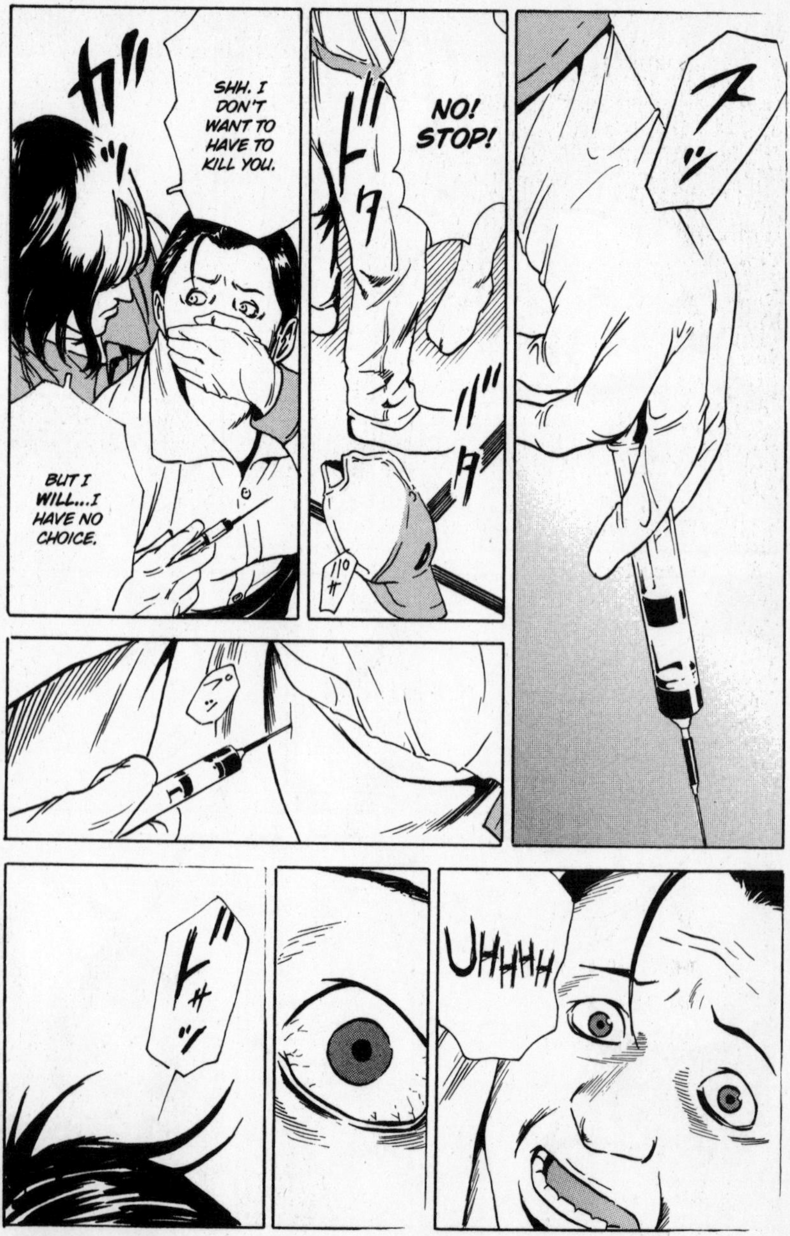
NO! STOP!
SHH. I DON'T WANT TO HAVE TO KILL YOU.
BUT I WILL...I HAVE NO CHOICE.
UHHHH

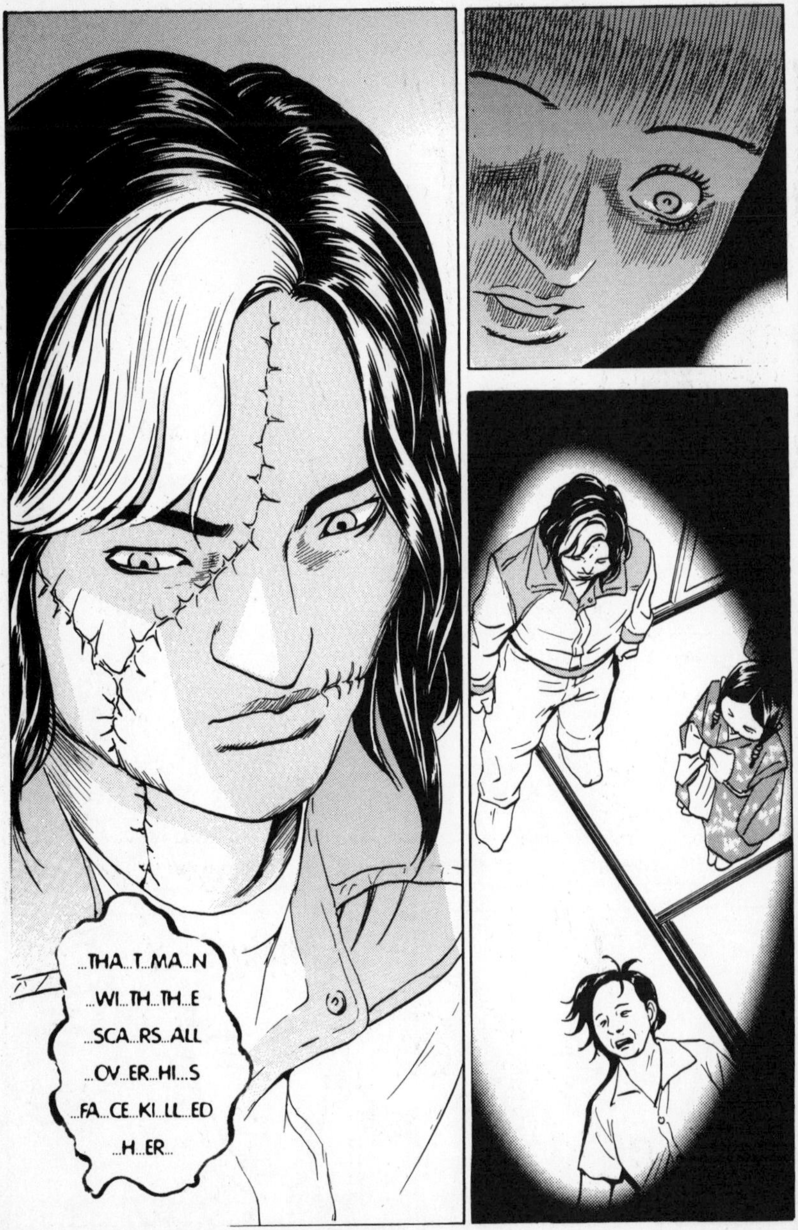
...THA...T...MA...N
...WI...TH...TH...E
...SCA...RS...ALL
...OV...ER...HI...S
...FA...CE...KI...LL...ED
...H...ER...

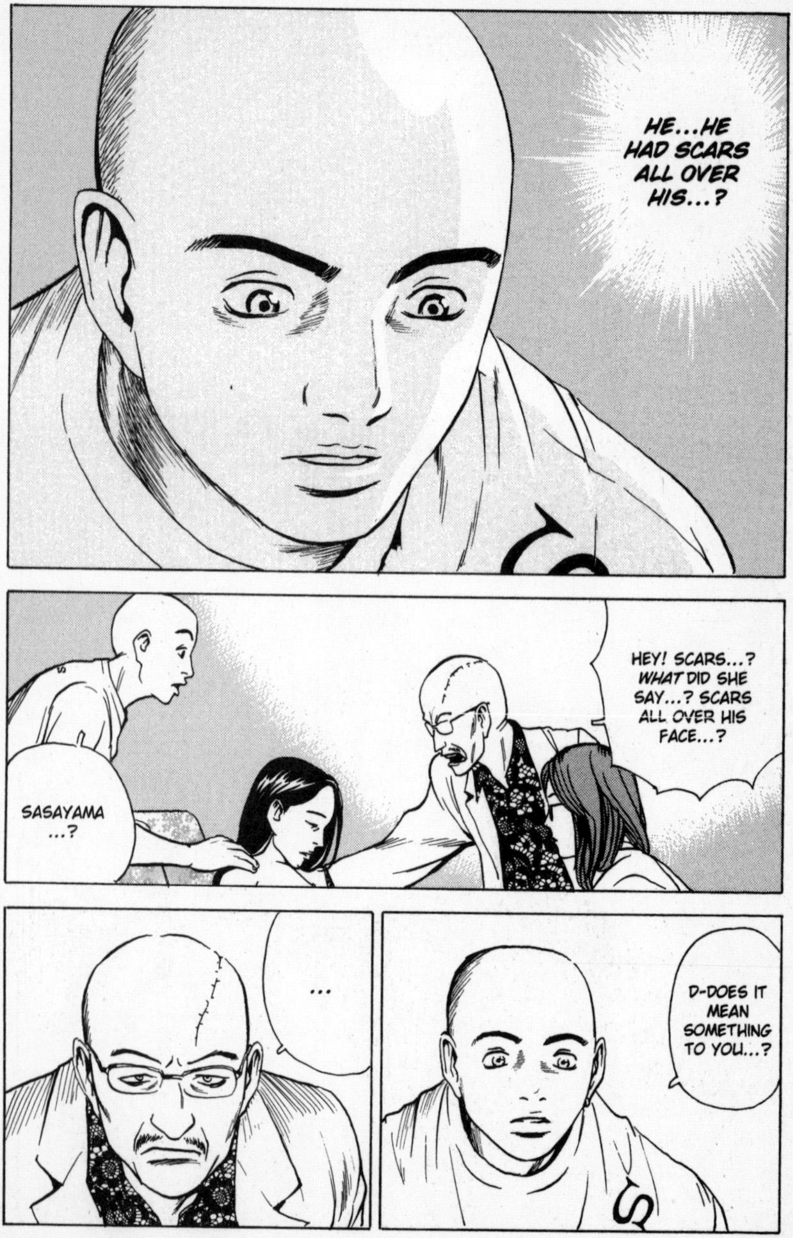
HE...HE HAD SCARS ALL OVER HIS...?
HEY! SCARS...? *WHAT* DID SHE SAY...? SCARS ALL OVER HIS FACE...?
SASAYAMA ...?
D-DOES IT MEAN SOMETHING TO YOU...?
...

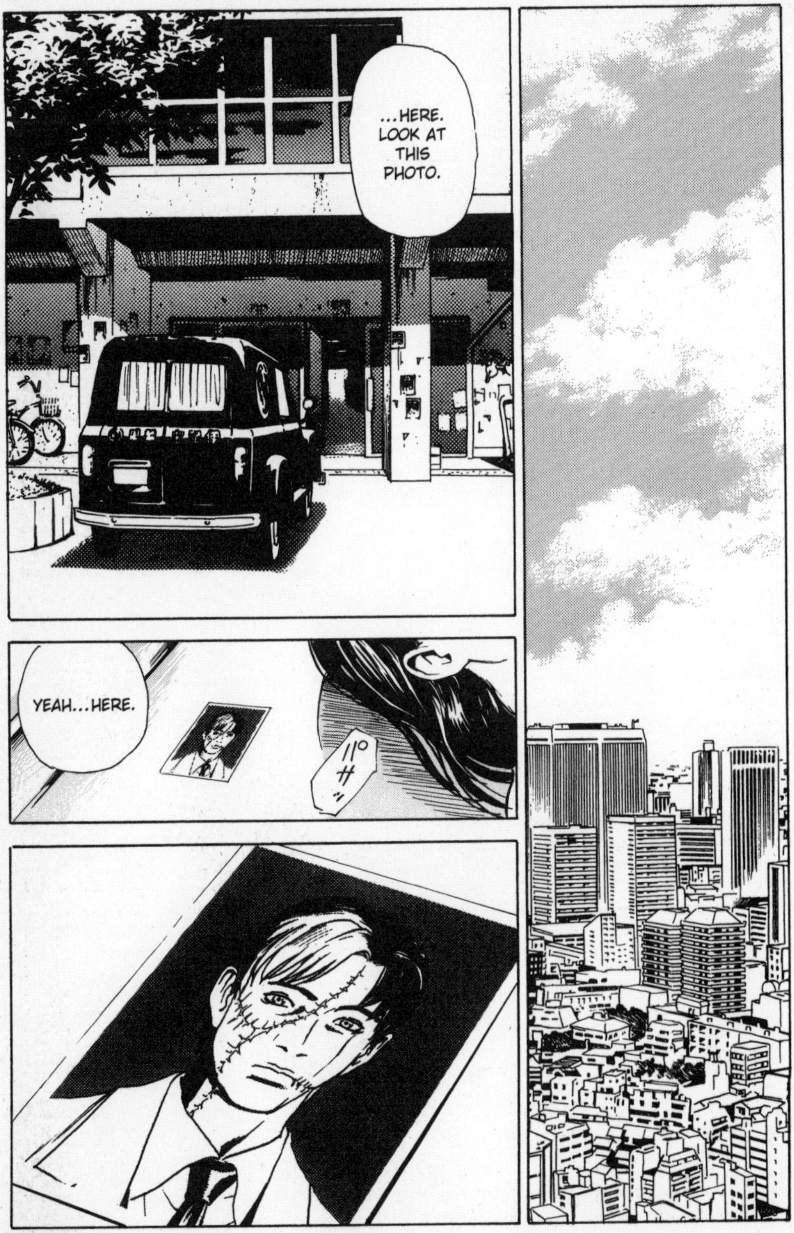
...HERE. LOOK AT THIS PHOTO.
YEAH...HERE.
パサッ

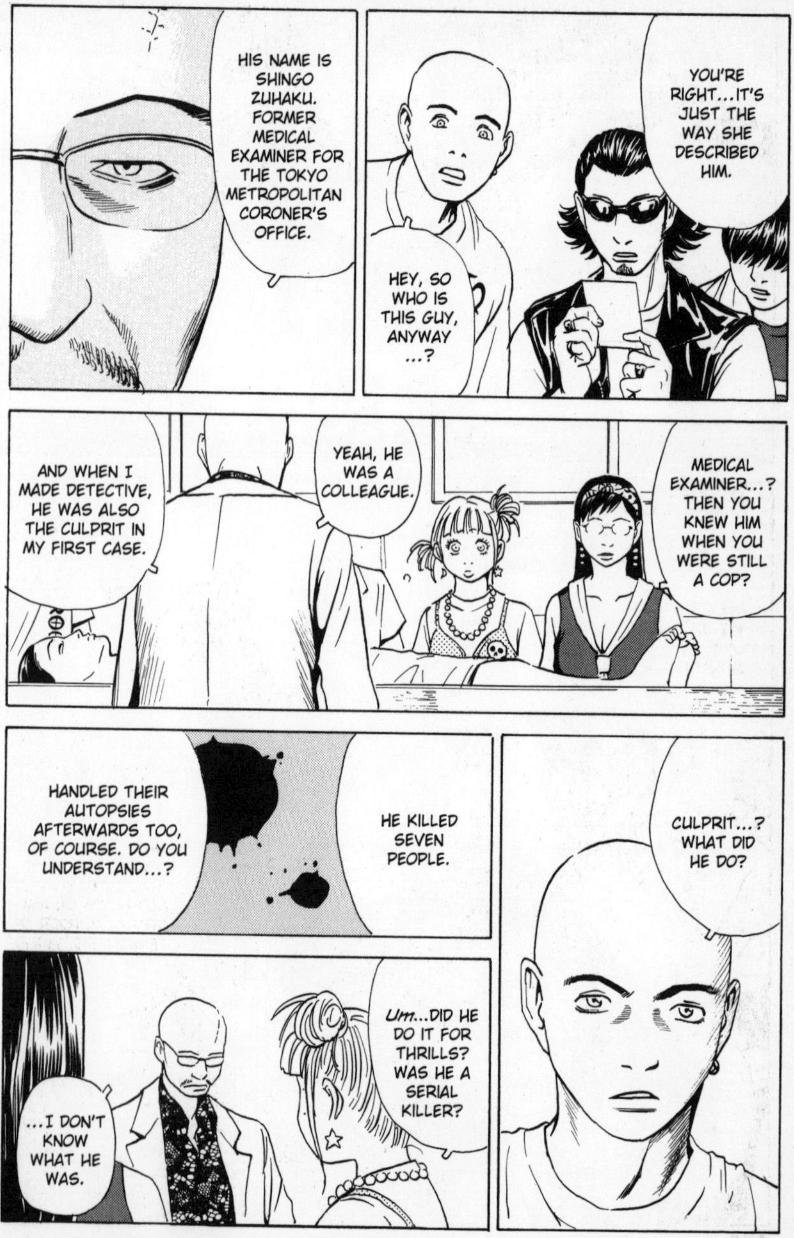
YOU'RE RIGHT...IT'S JUST THE WAY SHE DESCRIBED HIM.
HEY, SO WHO IS THIS GUY, ANYWAY ...?
HIS NAME IS SHINGO ZUHAKU. FORMER MEDICAL EXAMINER FOR THE TOKYO METROPOLITAN CORONER'S OFFICE.
MEDICAL EXAMINER...? THEN YOU KNEW HIM WHEN YOU WERE STILL A COP?
YEAH, HE WAS A COLLEAGUE.
AND WHEN I MADE DETECTIVE, HE WAS ALSO THE CULPRIT IN MY FIRST CASE.
CULPRIT...? WHAT DID HE DO?
HE KILLED SEVEN PEOPLE.
HANDLED THEIR AUTOPSIES AFTERWARDS TOO, OF COURSE. DO YOU UNDERSTAND...?
Um...DID HE DO IT FOR THRILLS? WAS HE A SERIAL KILLER?
...I DON'T KNOW WHAT HE WAS.

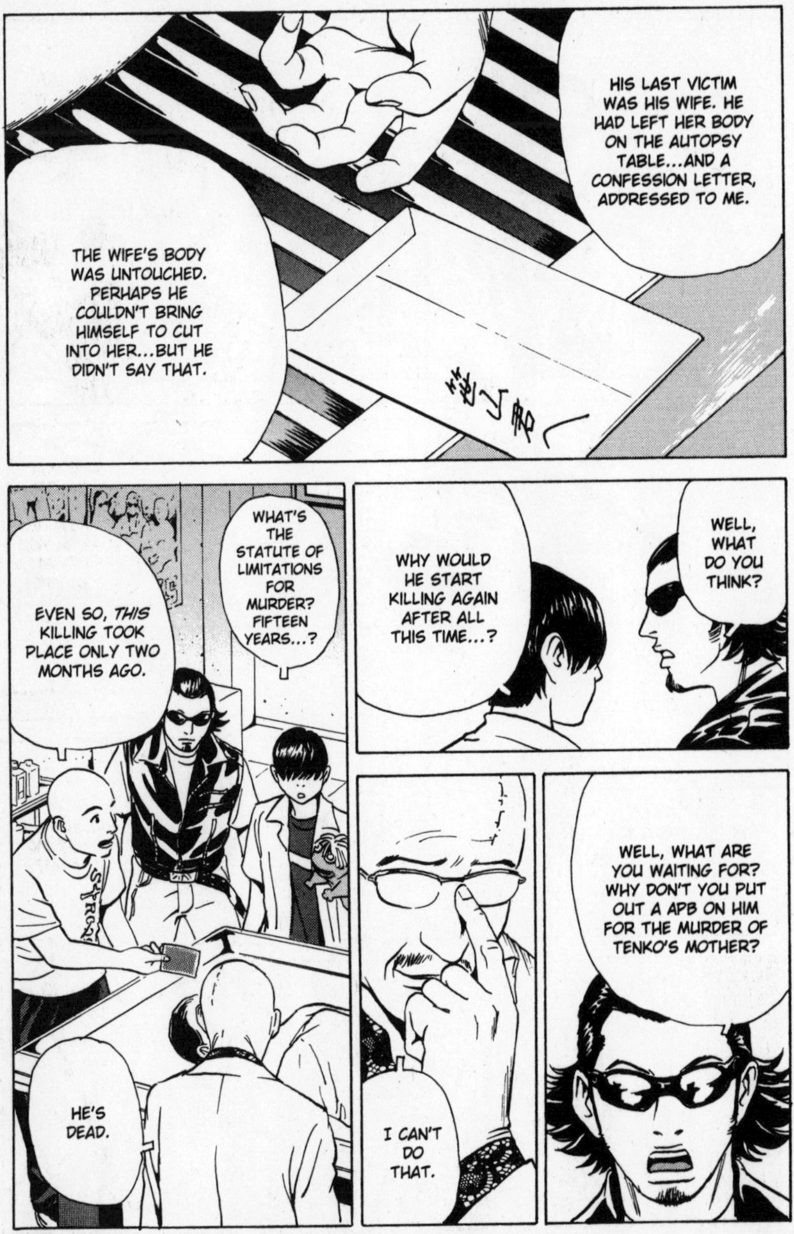
HIS LAST VICTIM WAS HIS WIFE. HE HAD LEFT HER BODY ON THE AUTOPSY TABLE...AND A CONFESSION LETTER, ADDRESSED TO ME.
THE WIFE'S BODY WAS UNTOUCHED. PERHAPS HE COULDN'T BRING HIMSELF TO CUT INTO HER...BUT HE DIDN'T SAY THAT.
WELL, WHAT DO YOU THINK?
WHY WOULD HE START KILLING AGAIN AFTER ALL THIS TIME...?
WELL, WHAT ARE YOU WAITING FOR? WHY DON'T YOU PUT OUT A APB ON HIM FOR THE MURDER OF TENKO'S MOTHER?
I CAN'T DO THAT.
WHAT'S THE STATUTE OF LIMITATIONS FOR MURDER? FIFTEEN YEARS...?
EVEN SO, *THIS* KILLING TOOK PLACE ONLY TWO MONTHS AGO.
HE'S DEAD.

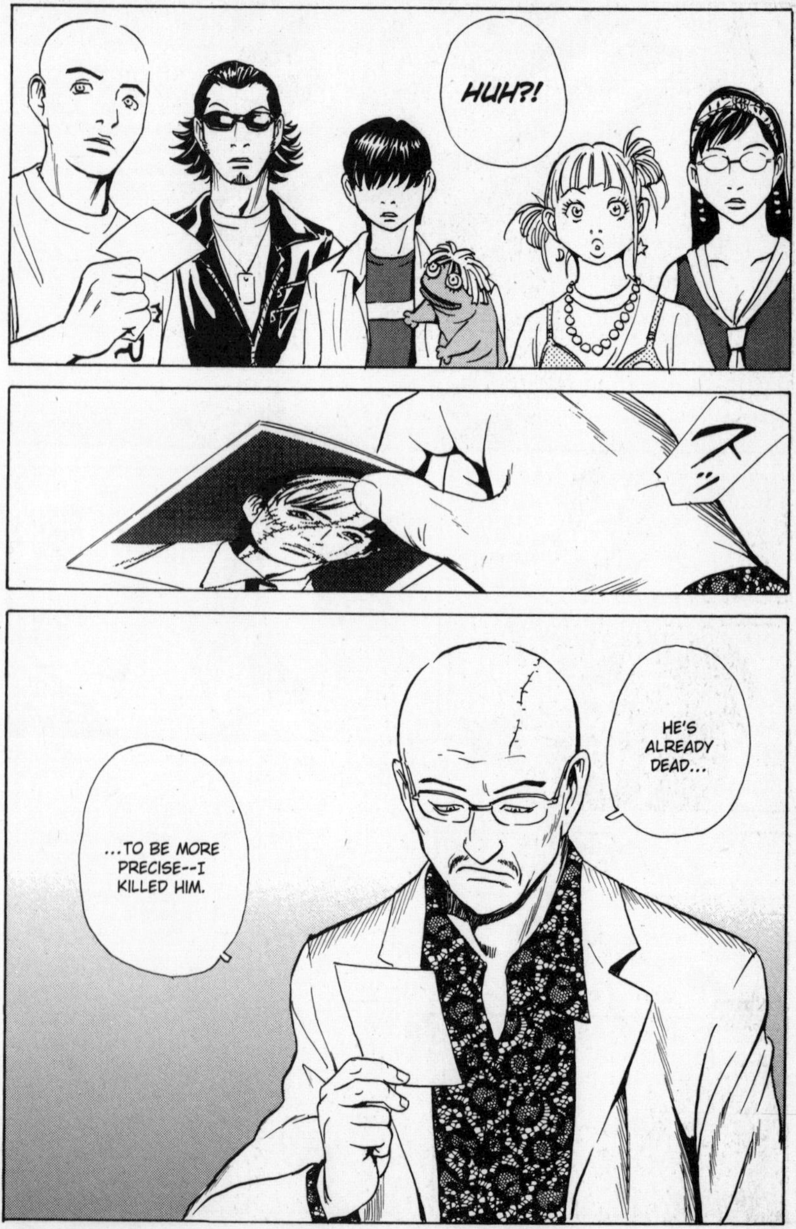
HUH?!
HE'S ALREADY DEAD...
...TO BE MORE PRECISE--I KILLED HIM.

3rd delivery: the two of us—the end

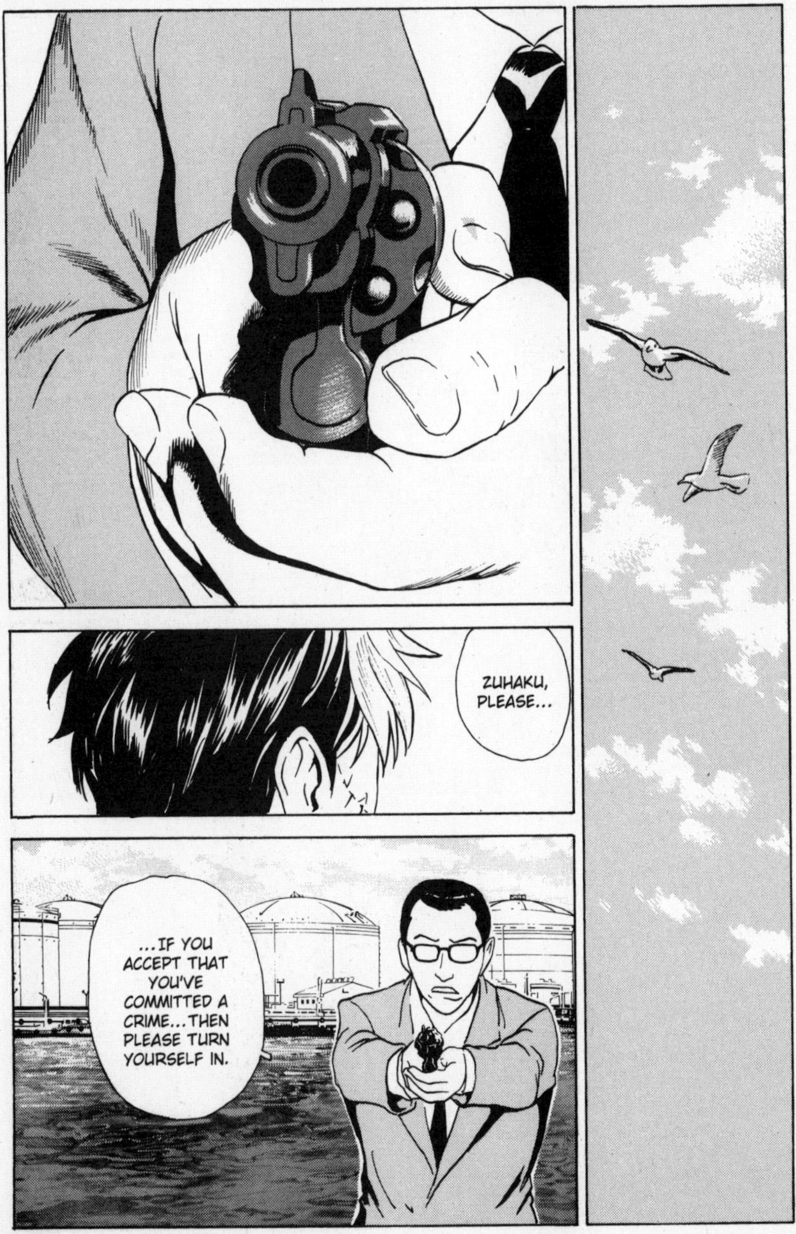
ZUHAKU, PLEASE...
...IF YOU ACCEPT THAT YOU'VE COMMITTED A CRIME...THEN PLEASE TURN YOURSELF IN.

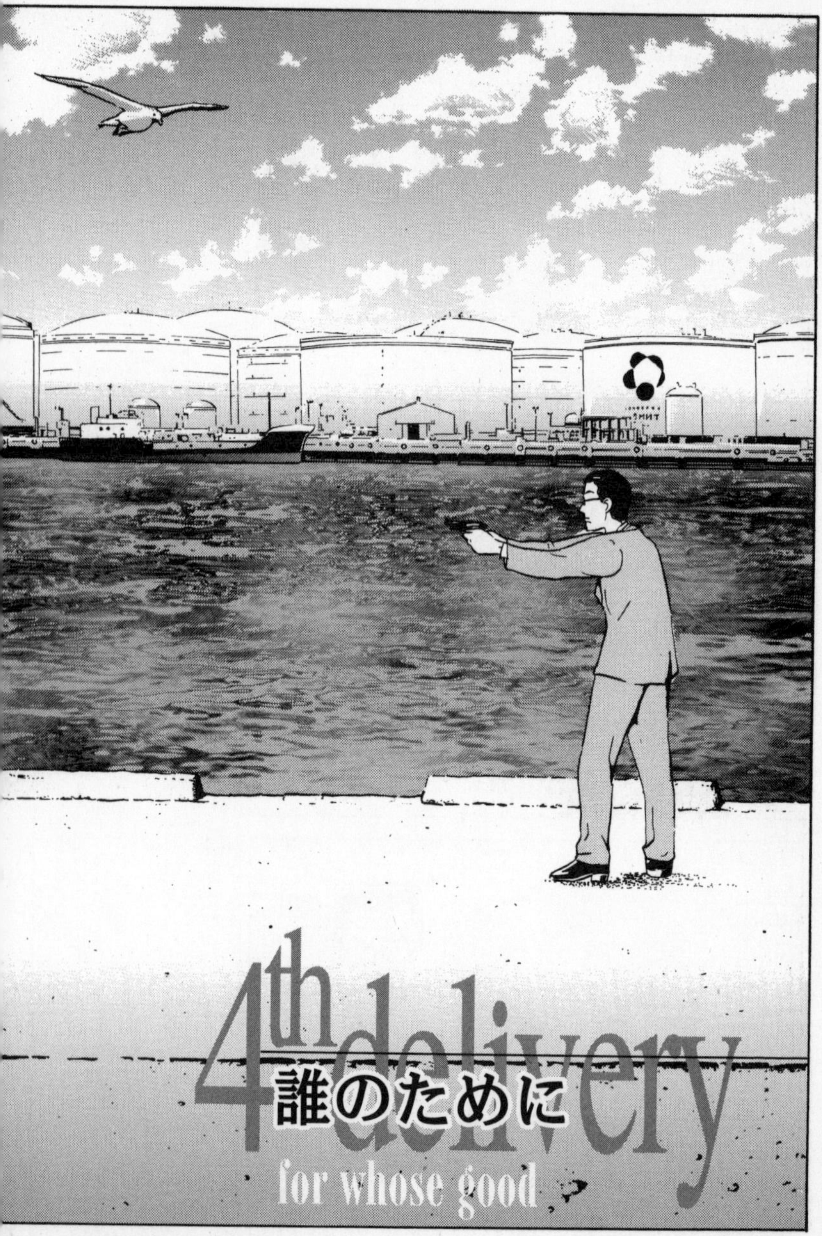
4th delivery
誰のために
for whose good

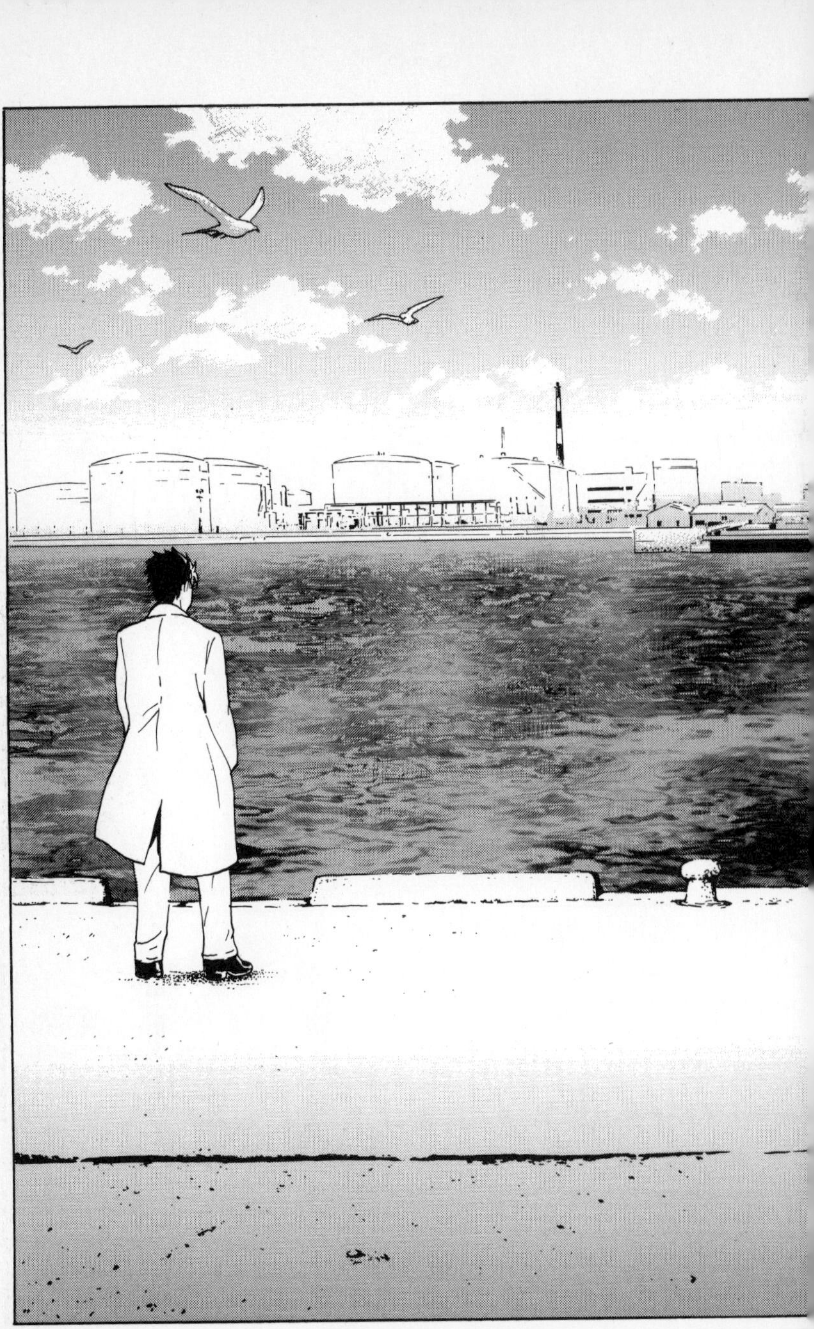

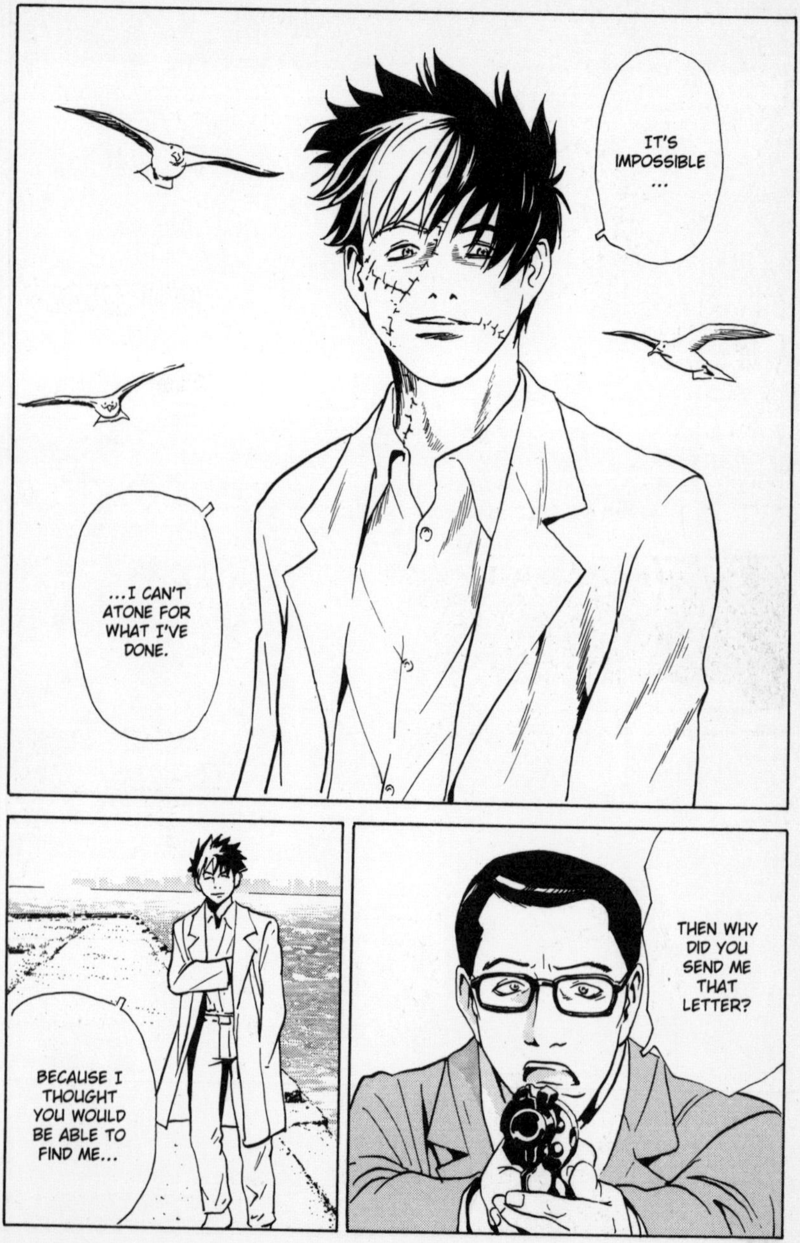
IT'S IMPOSSIBLE ...
...I CAN'T ATONE FOR WHAT I'VE DONE.
THEN WHY DID YOU SEND ME THAT LETTER?
BECAUSE I THOUGHT YOU WOULD BE ABLE TO FIND ME...

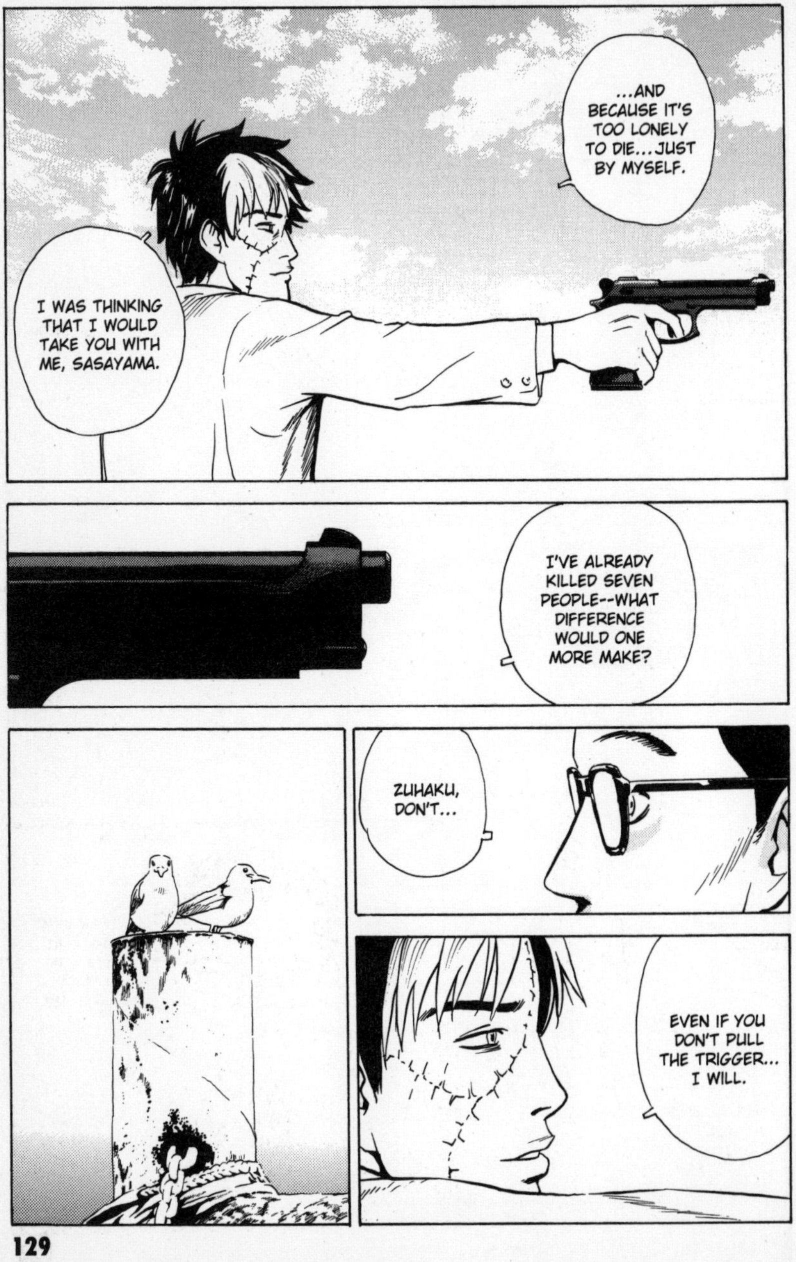
...AND BECAUSE IT'S TOO LONELY TO DIE... JUST BY MYSELF.
I WAS THINKING THAT I WOULD TAKE YOU WITH ME, SASAYAMA.
I'VE ALREADY KILLED SEVEN PEOPLE--WHAT DIFFERENCE WOULD ONE MORE MAKE?
ZUHAKU, DON'T...
EVEN IF YOU DON'T PULL THE TRIGGER... I WILL.

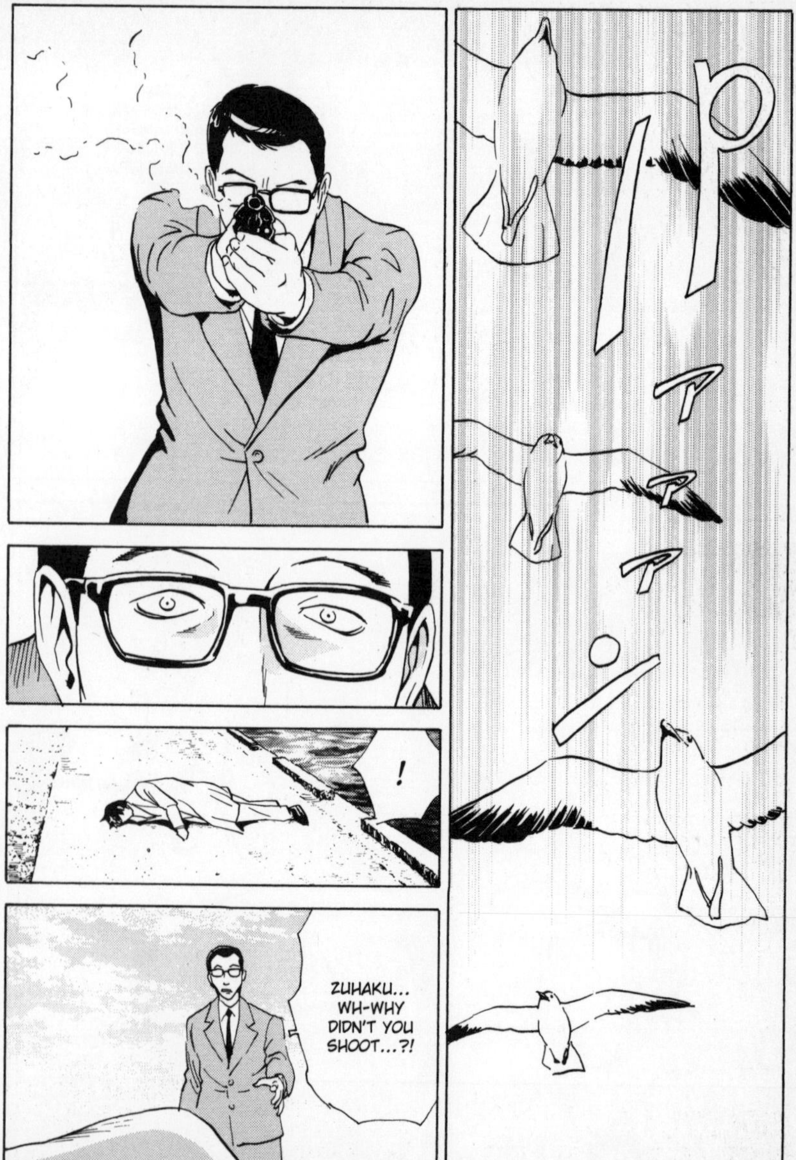
パァァァン
!
ZUHAKU... WH-WHY DIDN'T YOU SHOOT...?!

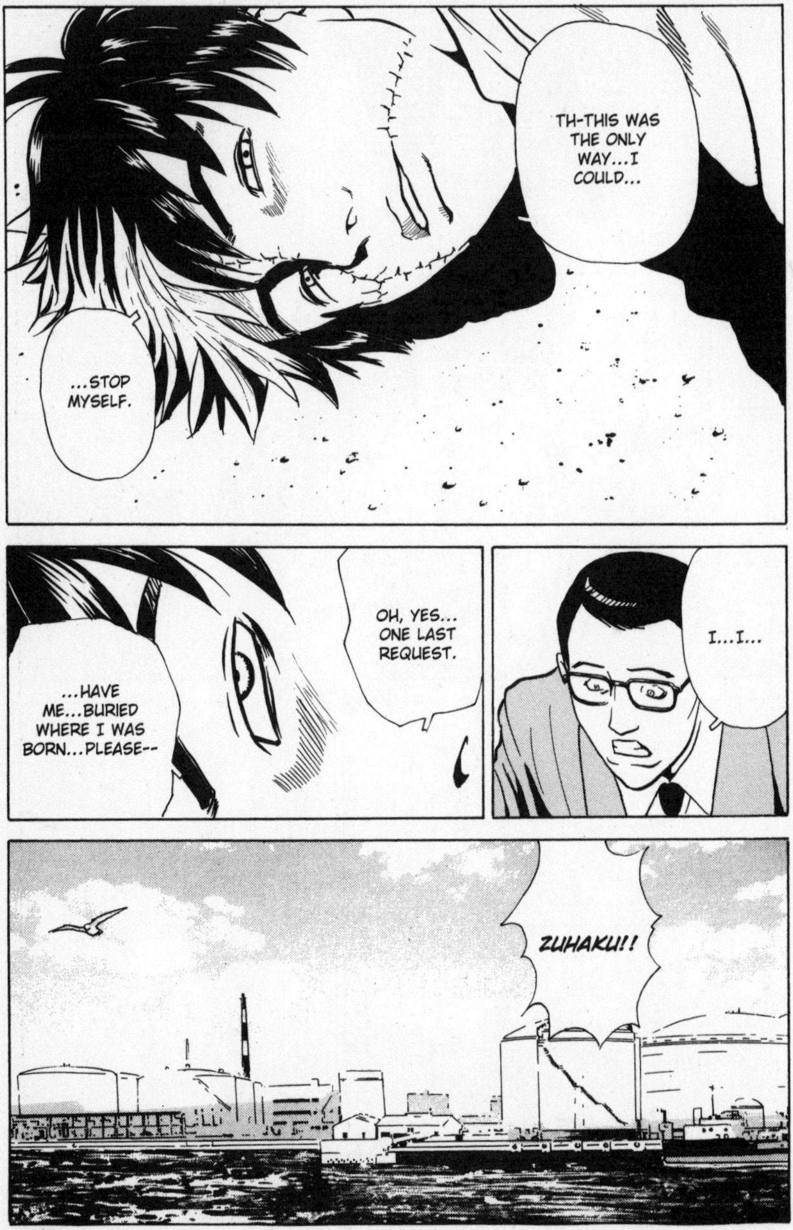
TH-THIS WAS THE ONLY WAY...I COULD...
...STOP MYSELF.
I...I...
OH, YES... ONE LAST REQUEST.
...HAVE ME...BURIED WHERE I WAS BORN...PLEASE--
ZUHAKU!!

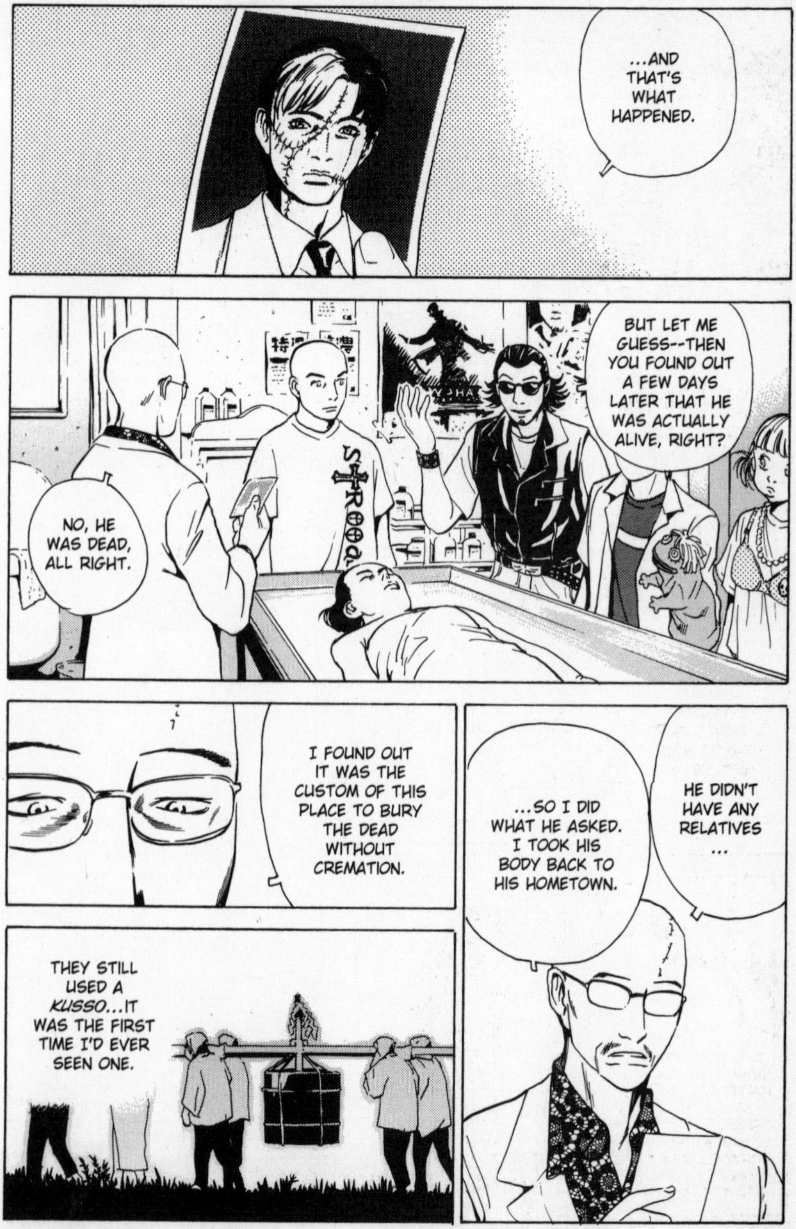
...AND THAT'S WHAT HAPPENED.
BUT LET ME GUESS--THEN YOU FOUND OUT A FEW DAYS LATER THAT HE WAS ACTUALLY ALIVE, RIGHT?
NO, HE WAS DEAD, ALL RIGHT.
HE DIDN'T HAVE ANY RELATIVES ...
...SO I DID WHAT HE ASKED. I TOOK HIS BODY BACK TO HIS HOMETOWN.
I FOUND OUT IT WAS THE CUSTOM OF THIS PLACE TO BURY THE DEAD WITHOUT CREMATION.
THEY STILL USED A *KUSSO*...IT WAS THE FIRST TIME I'D EVER SEEN ONE.

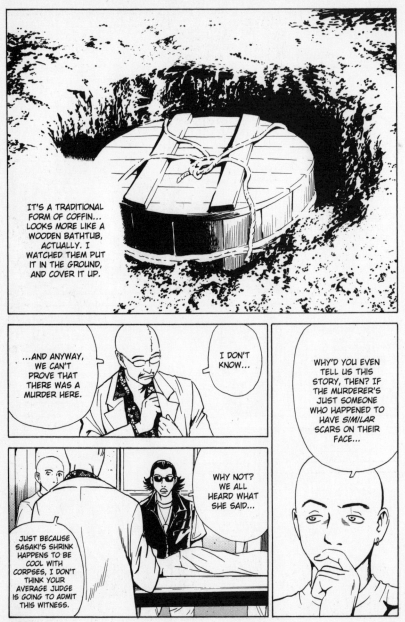

IT'S A TRADITIONAL FORM OF COFFIN... LOOKS MORE LIKE A WOODEN BATHTUB, ACTUALLY. I WATCHED THEM PUT IT IN THE GROUND, AND COVER IT UP.
WHY'D YOU EVEN TELL US THIS STORY, THEN? IF THE MURDERER'S JUST SOMEONE WHO HAPPENED TO HAVE *SIMILAR* SCARS ON THEIR FACE...
I DON'T KNOW...
...AND ANYWAY, WE CAN'T PROVE THAT THERE WAS A MURDER HERE.
WHY NOT? WE ALL HEARD WHAT SHE SAID...
JUST BECAUSE SASAKI'S SHRINK HAPPENS TO BE COOL WITH CORPSES, I DON'T THINK YOUR AVERAGE JUDGE IS GOING TO ADMIT THIS WITNESS.

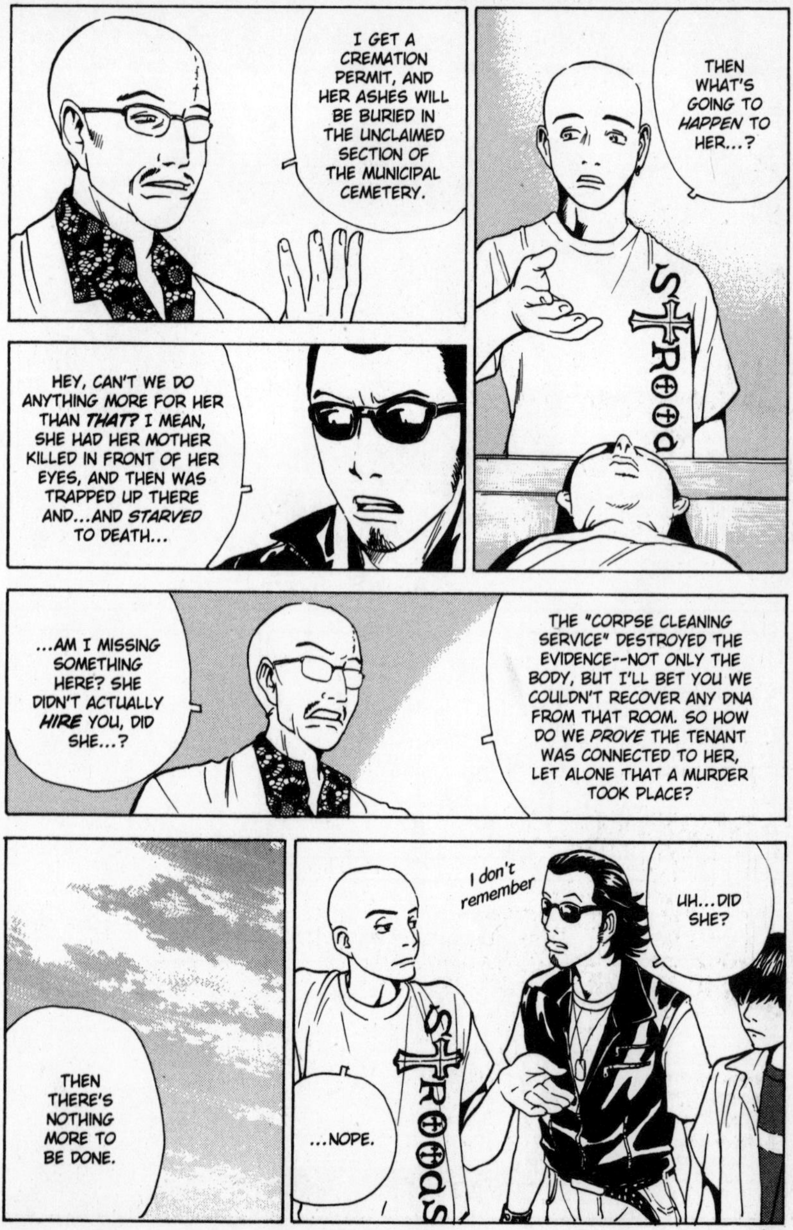
THEN WHAT'S GOING TO *HAPPEN* TO HER...?
I GET A CREMATION PERMIT, AND HER ASHES WILL BE BURIED IN THE UNCLAIMED SECTION OF THE MUNICIPAL CEMETERY.
HEY, CAN'T WE DO ANYTHING MORE FOR HER THAN ***THAT?*** I MEAN, SHE HAD HER MOTHER KILLED IN FRONT OF HER EYES, AND THEN WAS TRAPPED UP THERE AND...AND ***STARVED*** TO DEATH...
THE "CORPSE CLEANING SERVICE" DESTROYED THE EVIDENCE--NOT ONLY THE BODY, BUT I'LL BET YOU WE COULDN'T RECOVER ANY DNA FROM THAT ROOM. SO HOW DO WE *PROVE* THE TENANT WAS CONNECTED TO HER, LET ALONE THAT A MURDER TOOK PLACE?
...AM I MISSING SOMETHING HERE? SHE DIDN'T ACTUALLY ***HIRE*** YOU, DID SHE...?
UH...DID SHE?
I don't remember
...NOPE.
THEN THERE'S NOTHING MORE TO BE DONE.

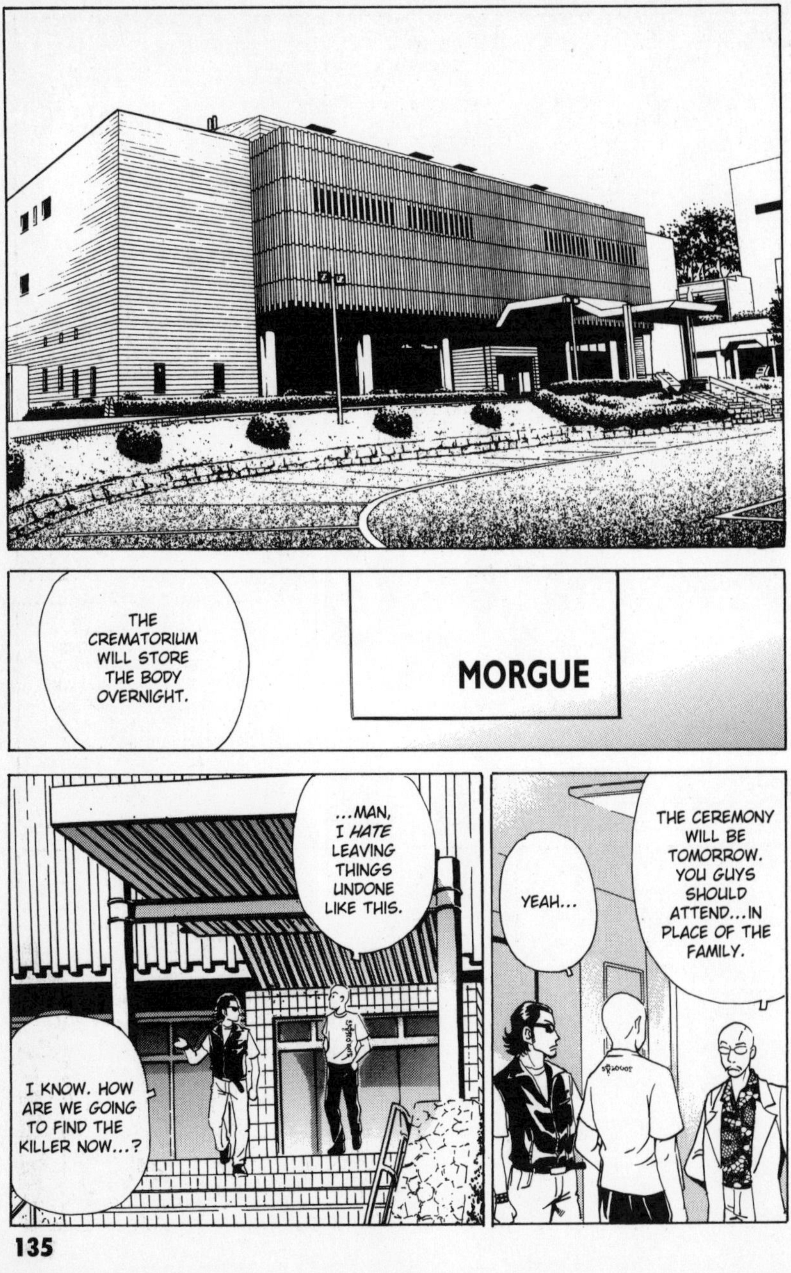
MORGUE
THE CREMATORIUM WILL STORE THE BODY OVERNIGHT.
THE CEREMONY WILL BE TOMORROW. YOU GUYS SHOULD ATTEND...IN PLACE OF THE FAMILY.
YEAH...
...MAN, I *HATE* LEAVING THINGS UNDONE LIKE THIS.
I KNOW. HOW ARE WE GOING TO FIND THE KILLER NOW...?

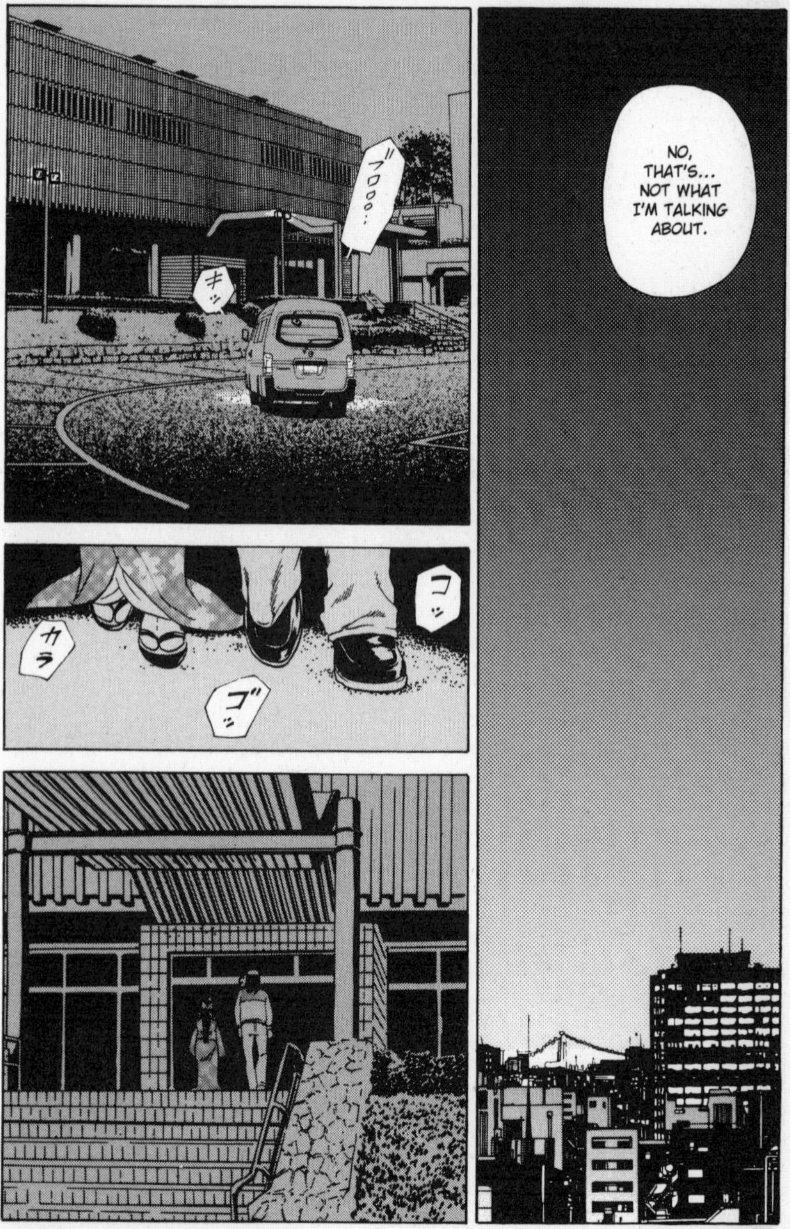
NO, THAT'S... NOT WHAT I'M TALKING ABOUT.
ブロoo..
キッ
コッ
カラ
ゴッ

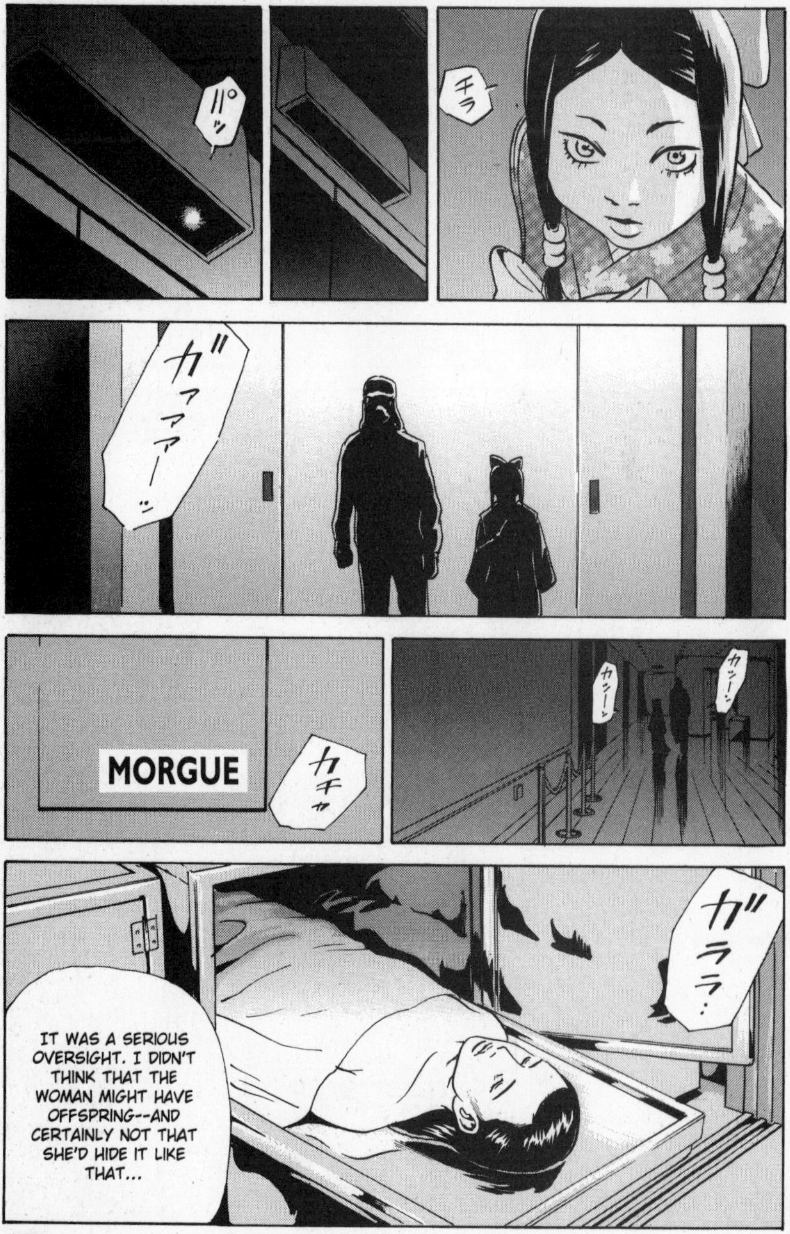
チラ
パッ
ガァァァー…ッ
カシーン
カシーン
MORGUE
カチャ
ガララ…
IT WAS A SERIOUS OVERSIGHT. I DIDN'T THINK THAT THE WOMAN MIGHT HAVE OFFSPRING--AND CERTAINLY NOT THAT SHE'D HIDE IT LIKE THAT...

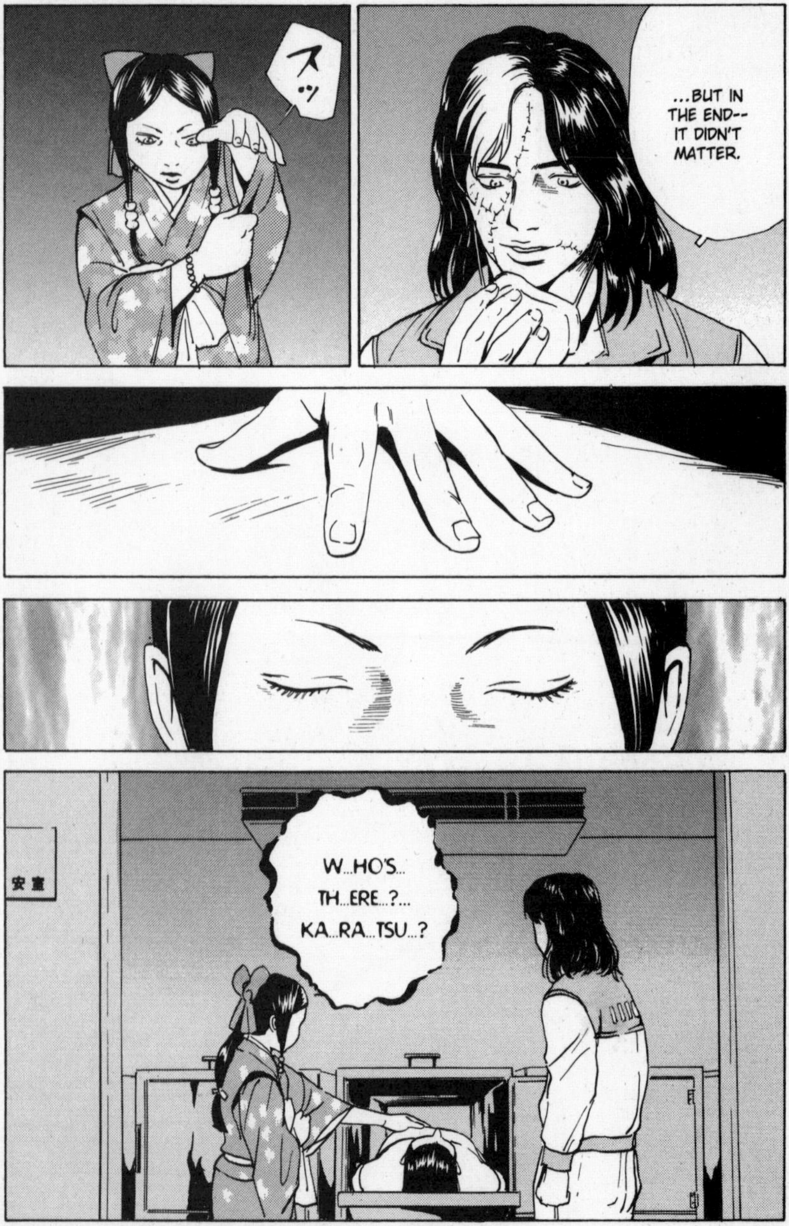
...BUT IN THE END-- IT DIDN'T MATTER.
スッ
W...HO'S... TH...ERE...?... KA...RA...TSU...?
安室

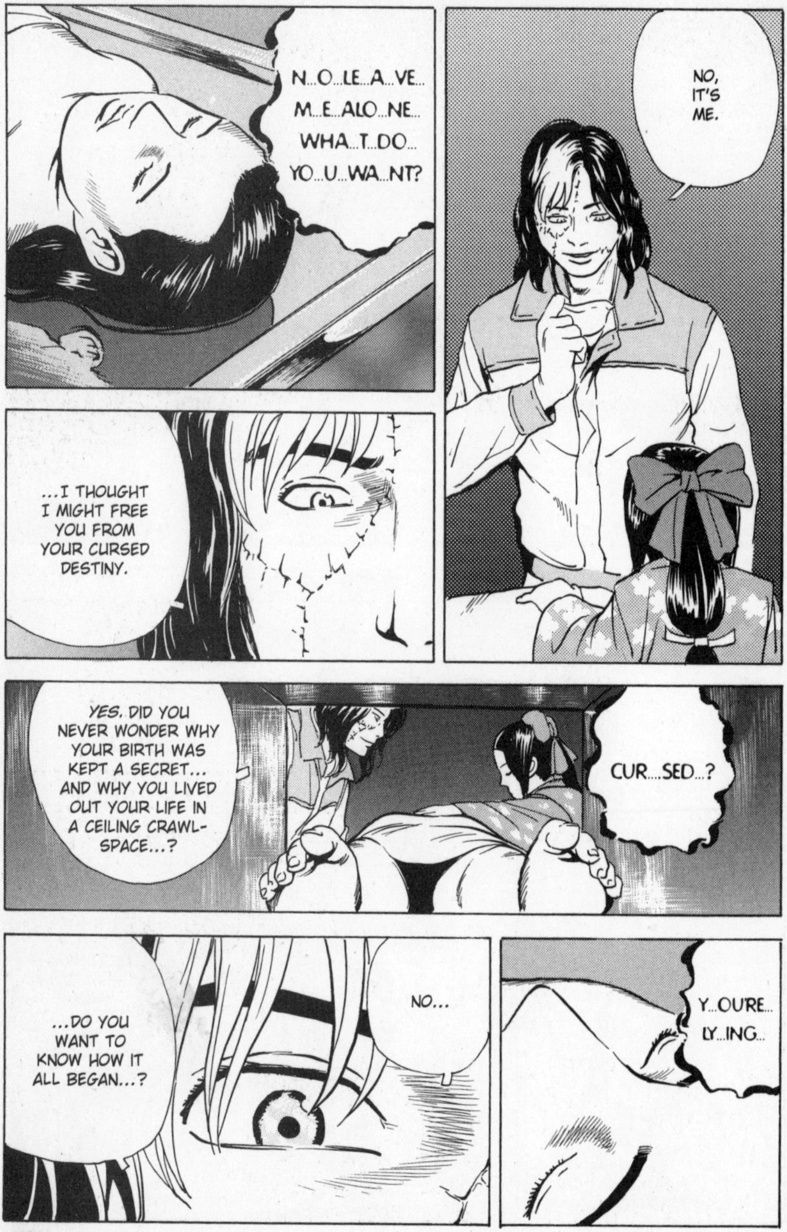
NO, IT'S ME.
N...O...LE...A...VE... M...E...ALO...NE... WHA...T...DO... YO...U...WA...NT?
...I THOUGHT I MIGHT FREE YOU FROM YOUR CURSED DESTINY.
CUR....SED...?
YES. DID YOU NEVER WONDER WHY YOUR BIRTH WAS KEPT A SECRET... AND WHY YOU LIVED OUT YOUR LIFE IN A CEILING CRAWL-SPACE...?
Y...OU'RE... LY...ING...
NO...
...DO YOU WANT TO KNOW HOW IT ALL BEGAN...?

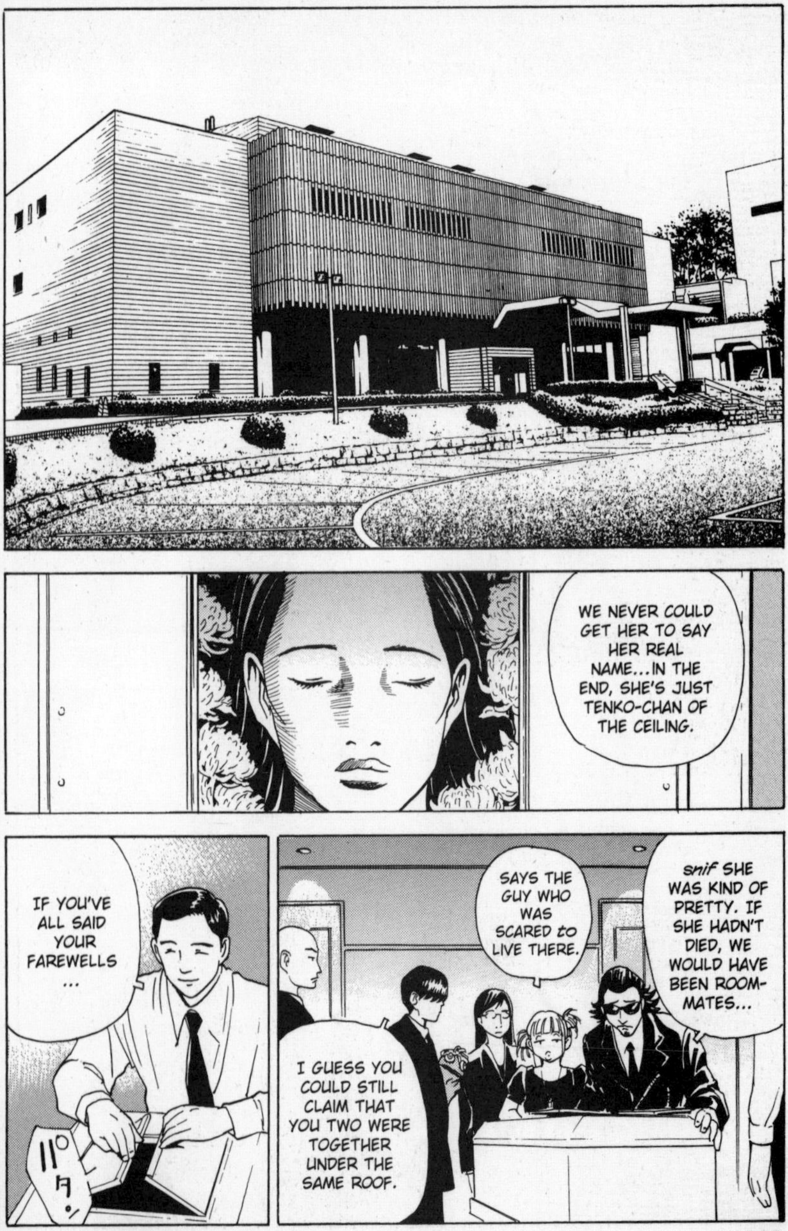
WE NEVER COULD GET HER TO SAY HER REAL NAME...IN THE END, SHE'S JUST TENKO-CHAN OF THE CEILING.
snif SHE WAS KIND OF PRETTY. IF SHE HADN'T DIED, WE WOULD HAVE BEEN ROOM-MATES...
SAYS THE GUY WHO WAS SCARED *to* LIVE THERE.
I GUESS YOU COULD STILL CLAIM THAT YOU TWO WERE TOGETHER UNDER THE SAME ROOF.
IF YOU'VE ALL SAID YOUR FAREWELLS ...
パタ。

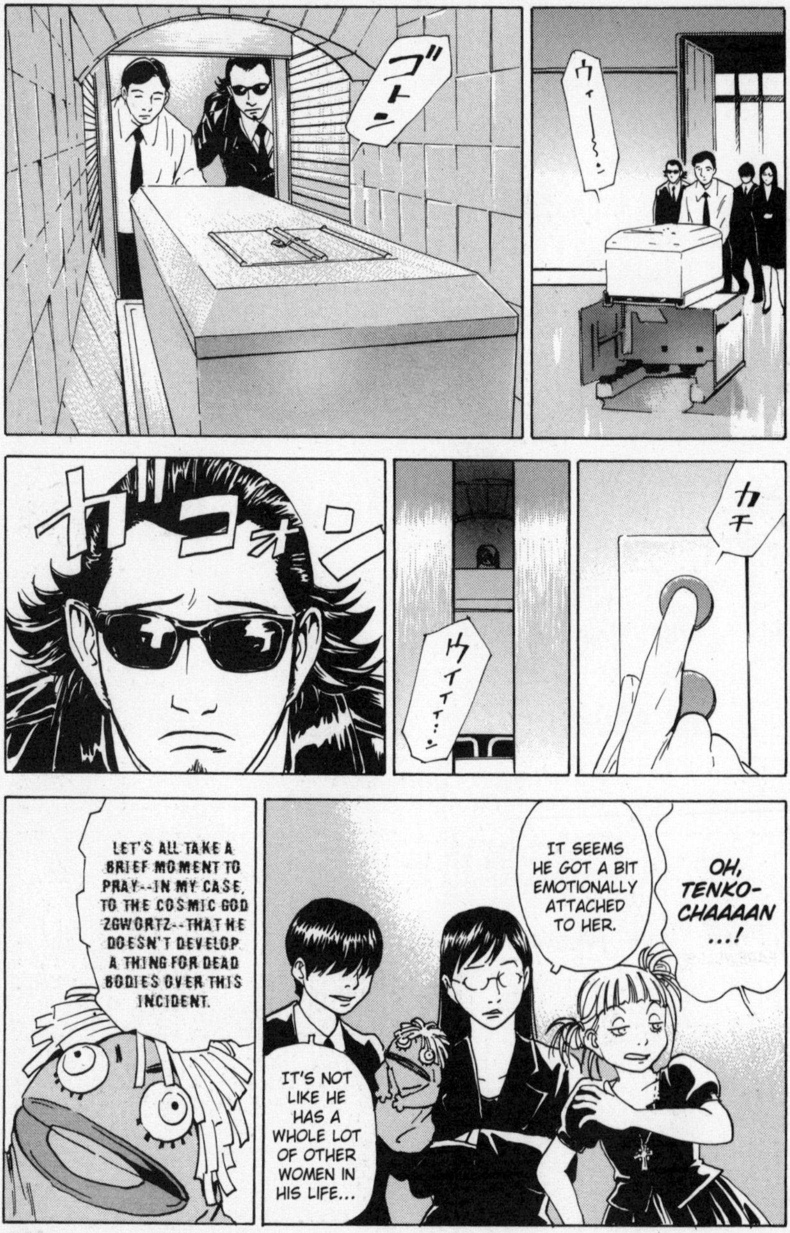
ウィー〜〜ン
ゴトン
カチ
ウイイイ…ン
ガコォン
OH, TENKO-CHAAAAN...!
IT SEEMS HE GOT A BIT EMOTIONALLY ATTACHED TO HER.
IT'S NOT LIKE HE HAS A WHOLE LOT OF OTHER WOMEN IN HIS LIFE...
LET'S ALL TAKE A BRIEF MOMENT TO PRAY--IN MY CASE, TO THE COSMIC GOD ZGWORTZ--THAT HE DOESN'T DEVELOP A THING FOR DEAD BODIES OVER THIS INCIDENT.

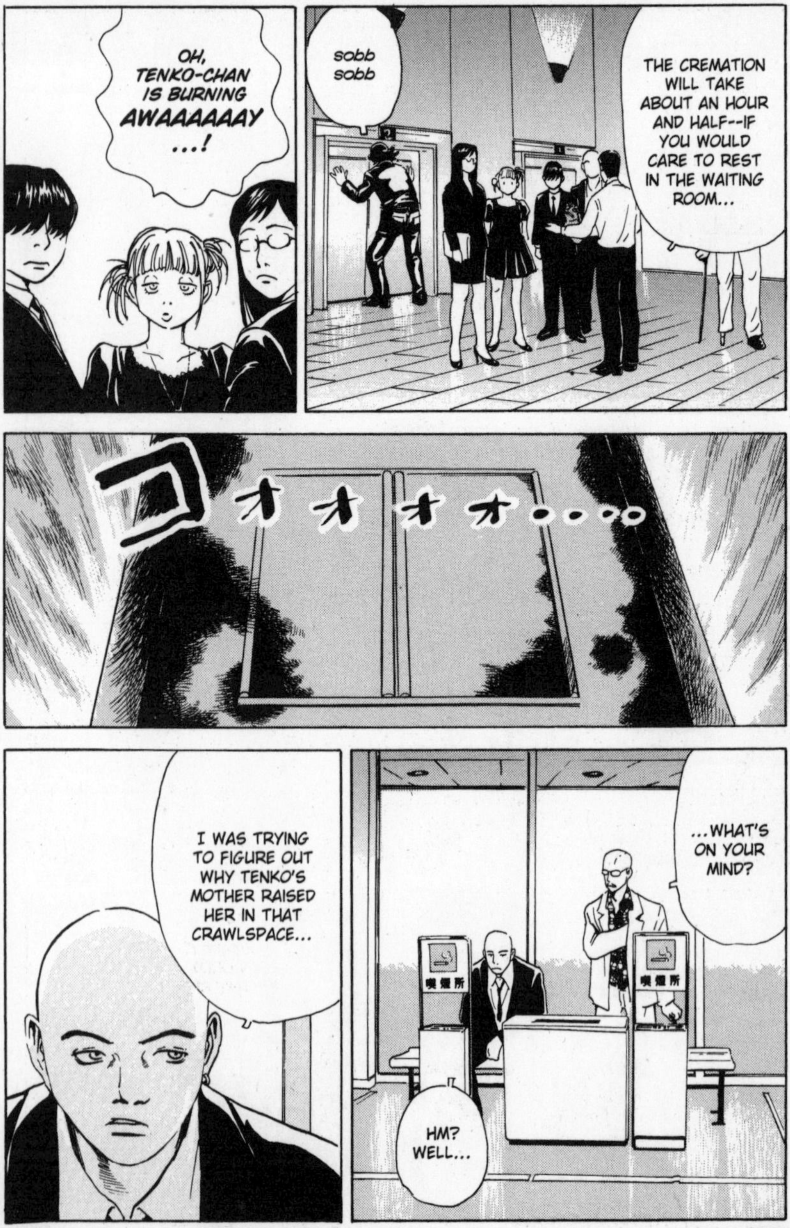
THE CREMATION WILL TAKE ABOUT AN HOUR AND HALF--IF YOU WOULD CARE TO REST IN THE WAITING ROOM...
sobb sobb
OH, TENKO-CHAN IS BURNING AWAAAAAAY ...!
コオオオオ....
...WHAT'S ON YOUR MIND?
喫煙所
喫煙所
HM? WELL...
I WAS TRYING TO FIGURE OUT WHY TENKO'S MOTHER RAISED HER IN THAT CRAWLSPACE...

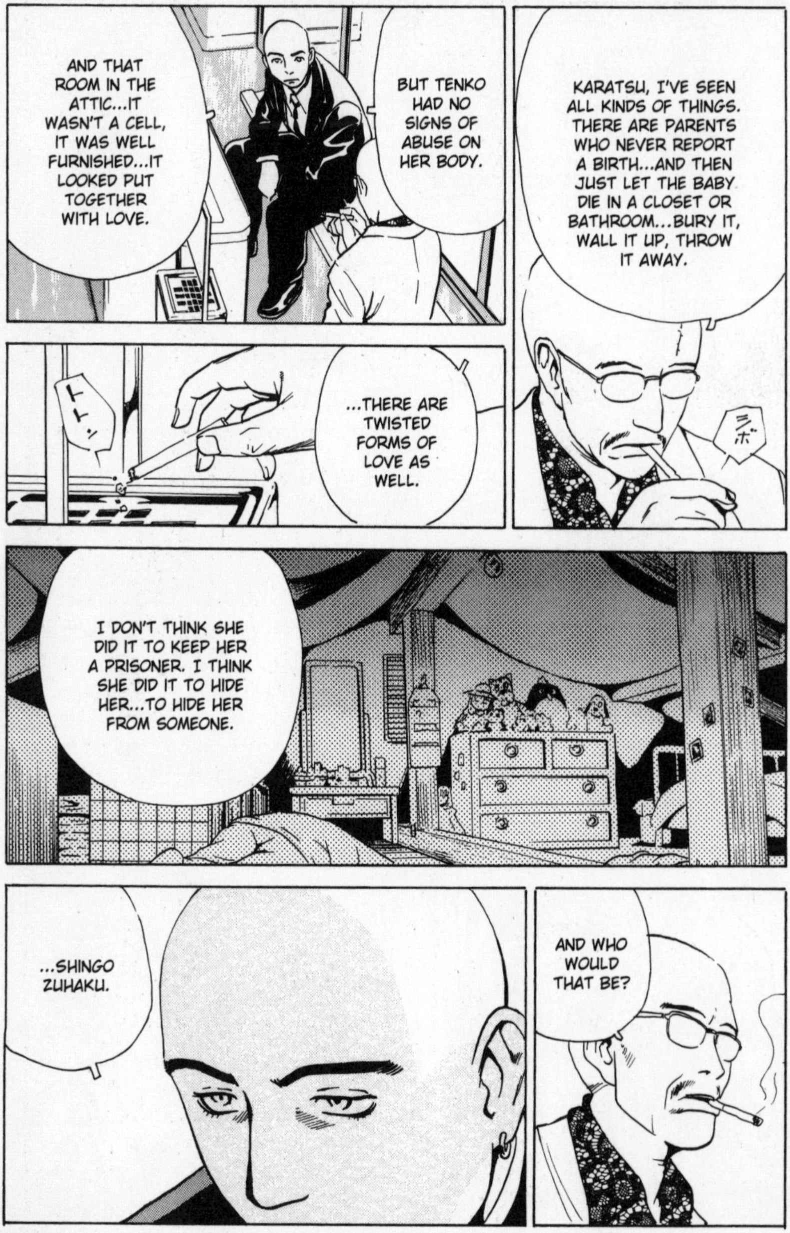
KARATSU, I'VE SEEN ALL KINDS OF THINGS. THERE ARE PARENTS WHO NEVER REPORT A BIRTH...AND THEN JUST LET THE BABY DIE IN A CLOSET OR BATHROOM...BURY IT, WALL IT UP, THROW IT AWAY.
BUT TENKO HAD NO SIGNS OF ABUSE ON HER BODY.
AND THAT ROOM IN THE ATTIC...IT WASN'T A CELL, IT WAS WELL FURNISHED...IT LOOKED PUT TOGETHER WITH LOVE.
...THERE ARE TWISTED FORMS OF LOVE AS WELL.
トトッ
I DON'T THINK SHE DID IT TO KEEP HER A PRISONER. I THINK SHE DID IT TO HIDE HER...TO HIDE HER FROM SOMEONE.
AND WHO WOULD THAT BE?
...SHINGO ZUHAKU.

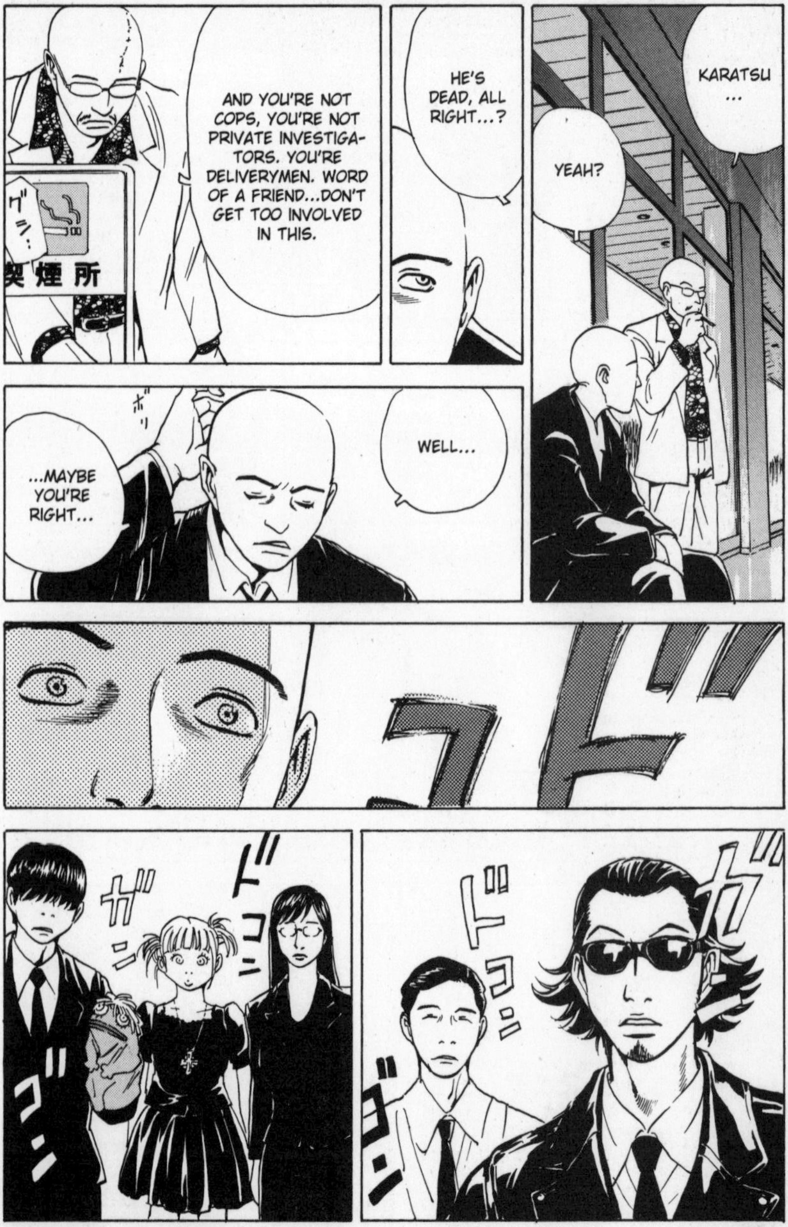
KARATSU ...
YEAH?
HE'S DEAD, ALL RIGHT...?
AND YOU'RE NOT COPS, YOU'RE NOT PRIVATE INVESTIGATORS. YOU'RE DELIVERYMEN. WORD OF A FRIEND...DON'T GET TOO INVOLVED IN THIS.
WELL...
...MAYBE YOU'RE RIGHT...
ドン

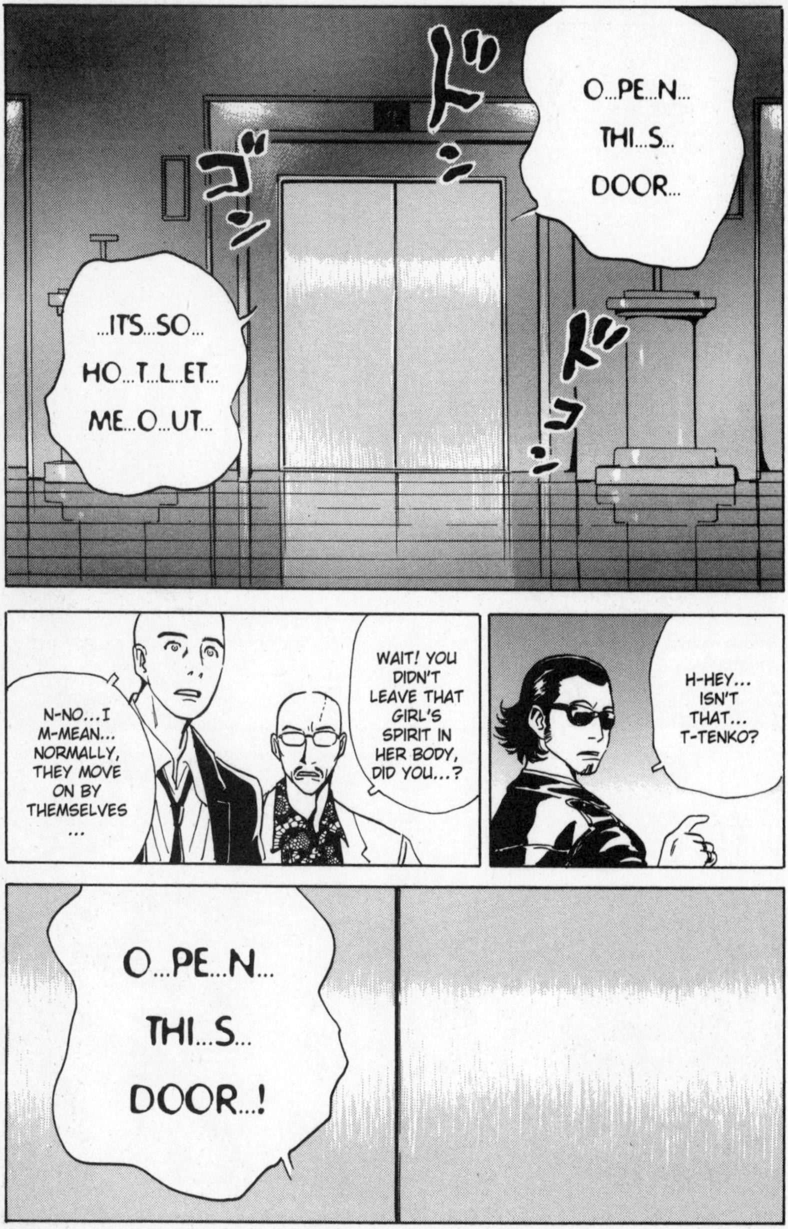
O...PE...N... THI...S... DOOR...
ドン
ゴン
...ITS...SO... HO...T...L...ET... ME...O...UT...
ドン
H-HEY... ISN'T THAT... T-TENKO?
WAIT! YOU DIDN'T LEAVE THAT GIRL'S SPIRIT IN HER BODY, DID YOU...?
N-NO...I M-MEAN... NORMALLY, THEY MOVE ON BY THEMSELVES ...
O...PE...N... THI...S... DOOR...!

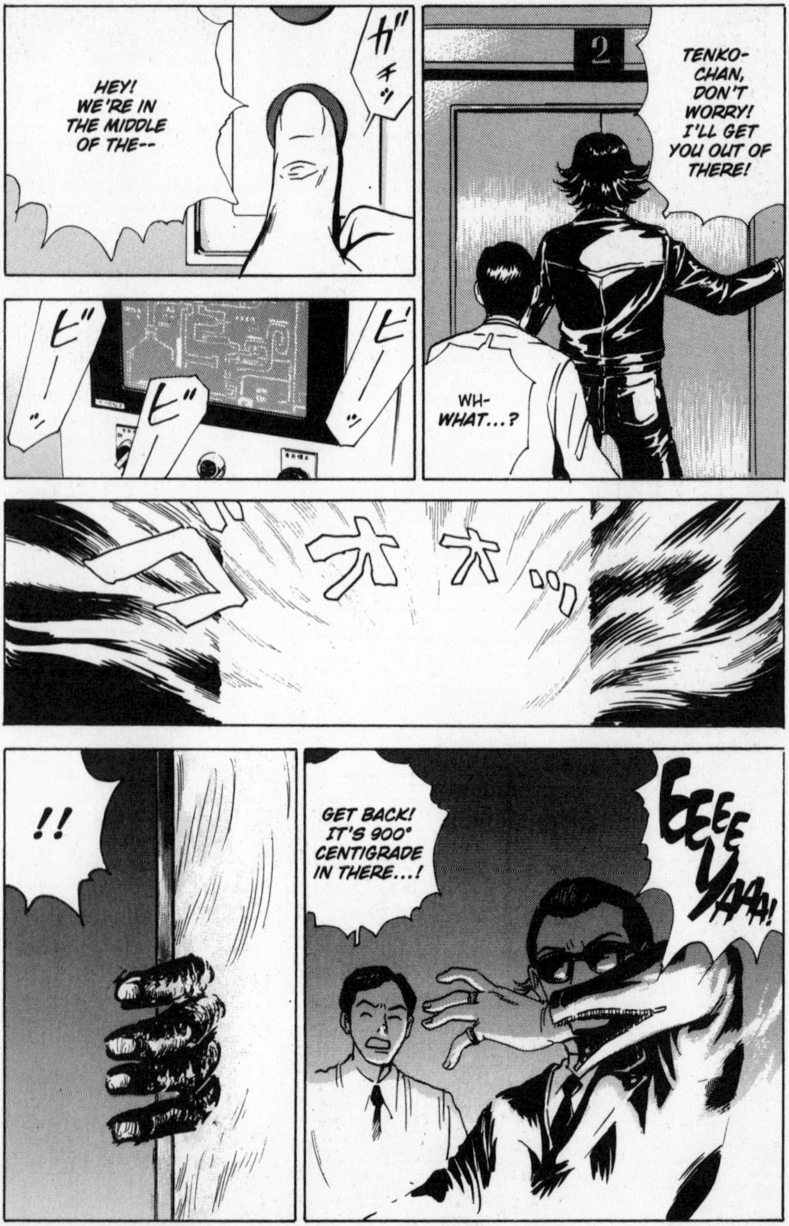

TENKO-CHAN, DON'T WORRY! I'LL GET YOU OUT OF THERE!
WH-WHAT...?
ガチッ
HEY! WE'RE IN THE MIDDLE OF THE--
ビーッ
ビッ
ビーッ
オオッ
EEEEYAAA!
GET BACK! IT'S 900° CENTIGRADE IN THERE...!
!!

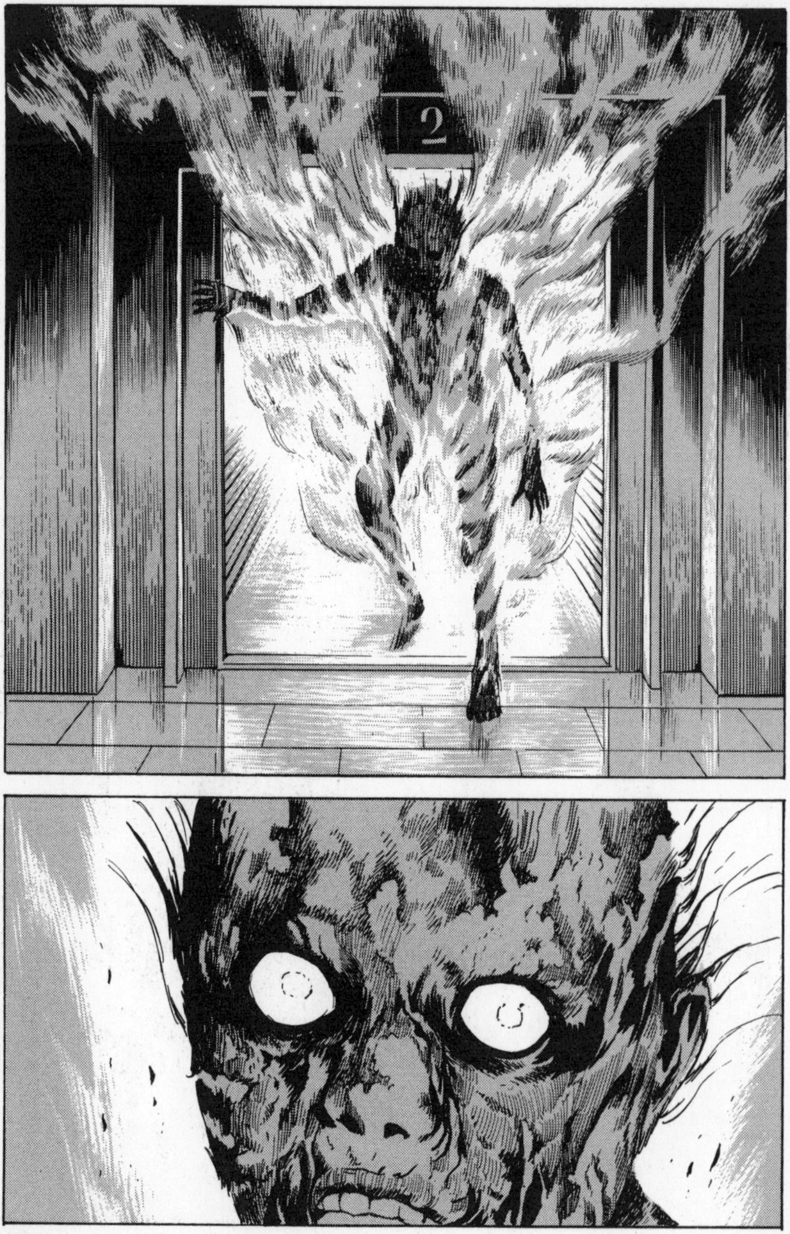
2

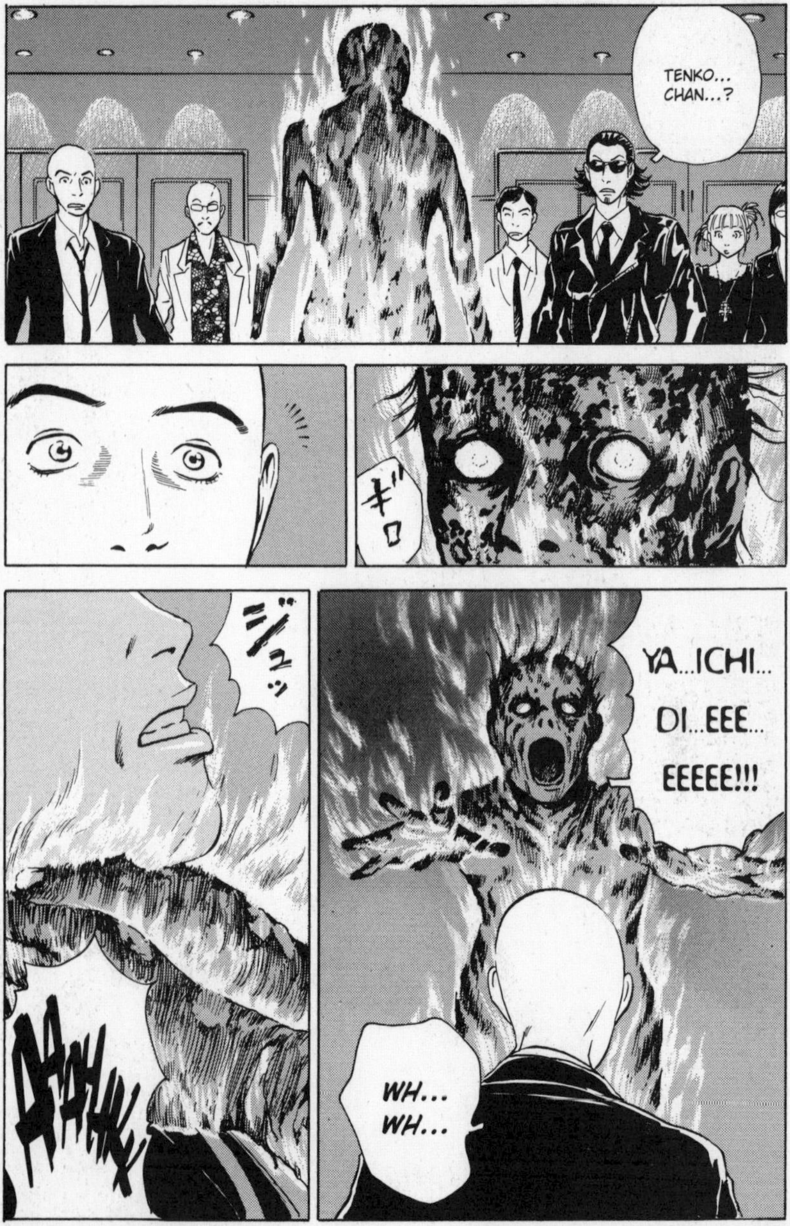
TENKO... CHAN...?
ギロ
YA...ICHI... DI...EEE... EEEEE!!!
WH... WH...
ジュッ

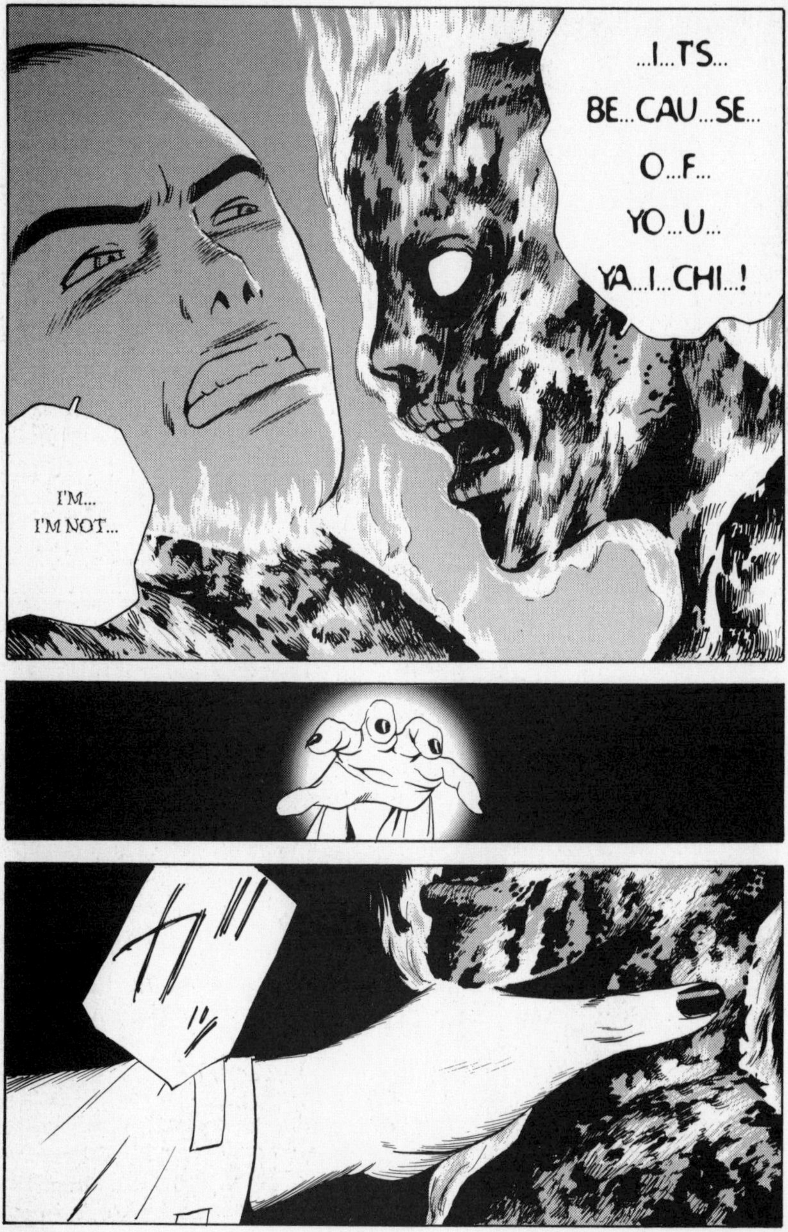
...I...T'S... BE...CAU...SE... O...F... YO...U... YA...I...CHI...!
I'M... I'M NOT...

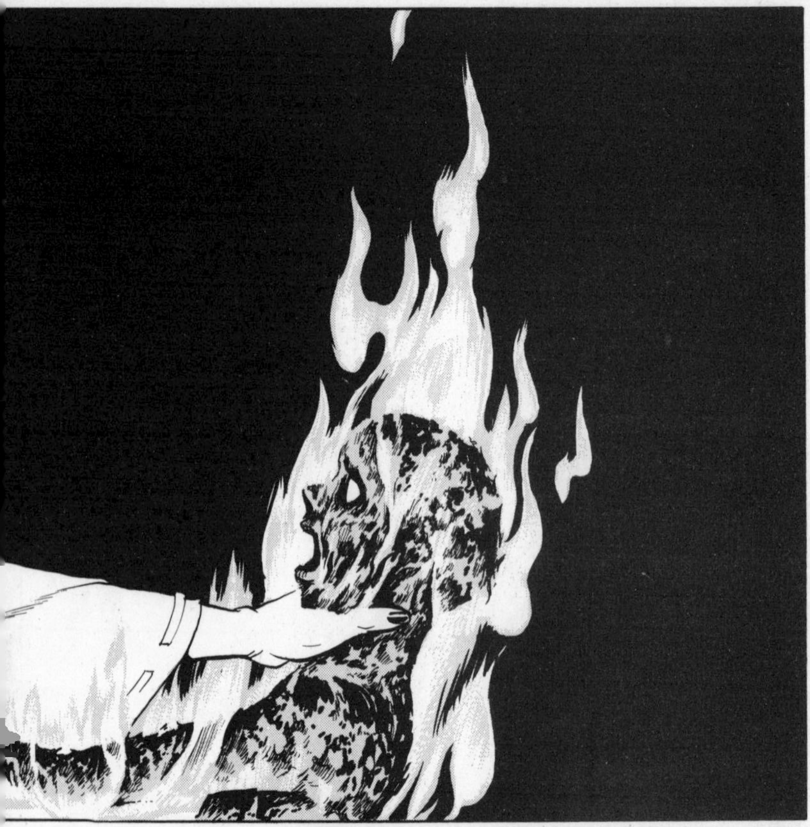
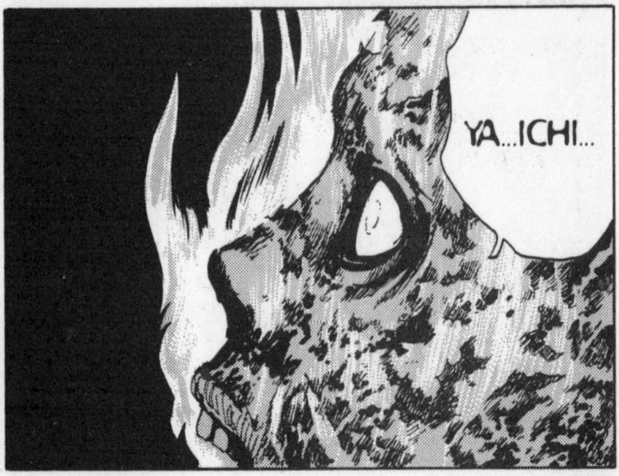
YA...ICHI...
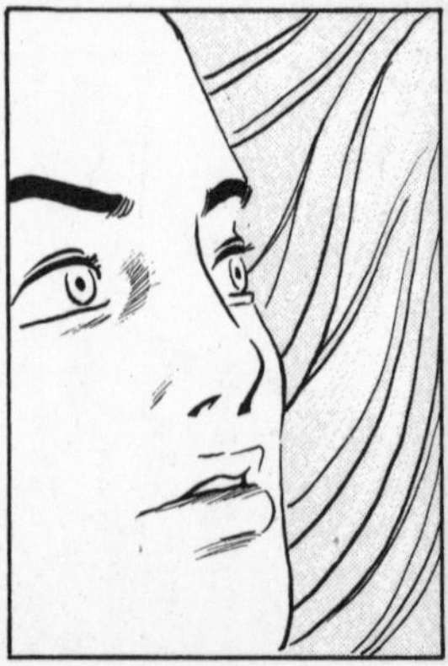

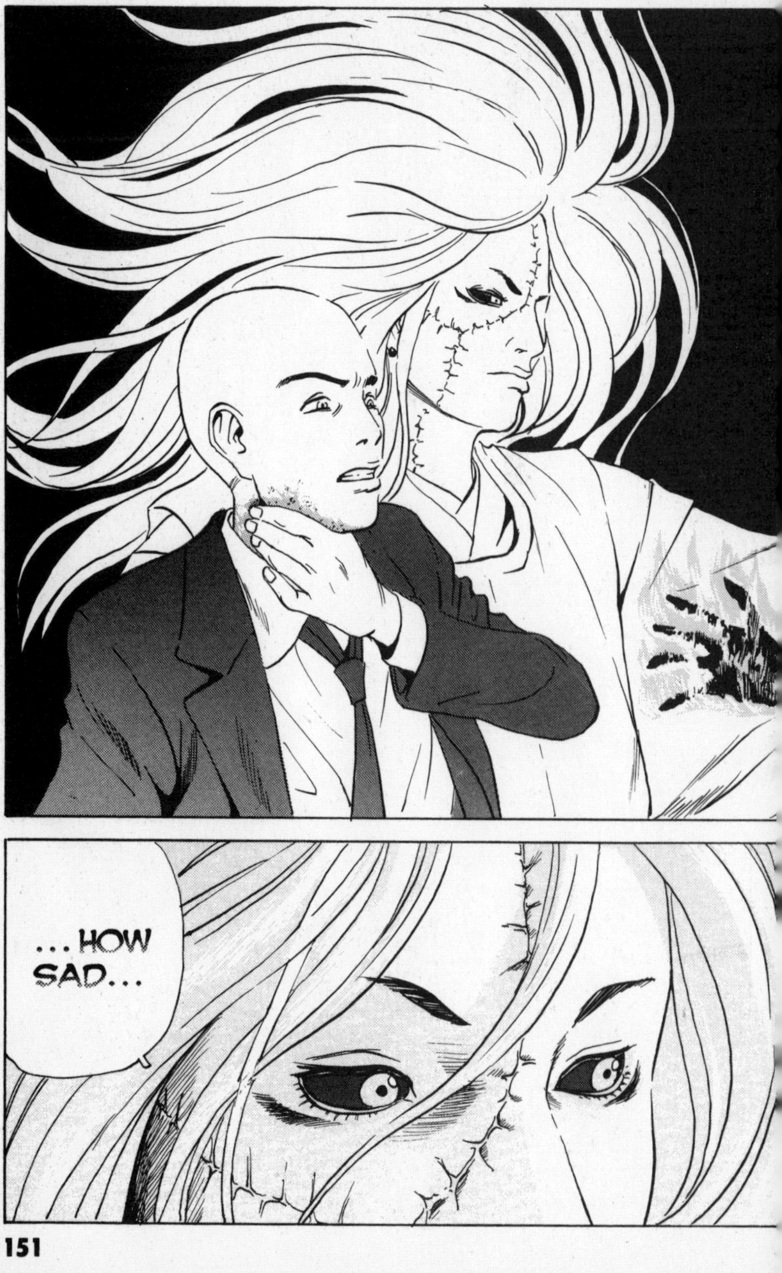
...HOW
SAD...

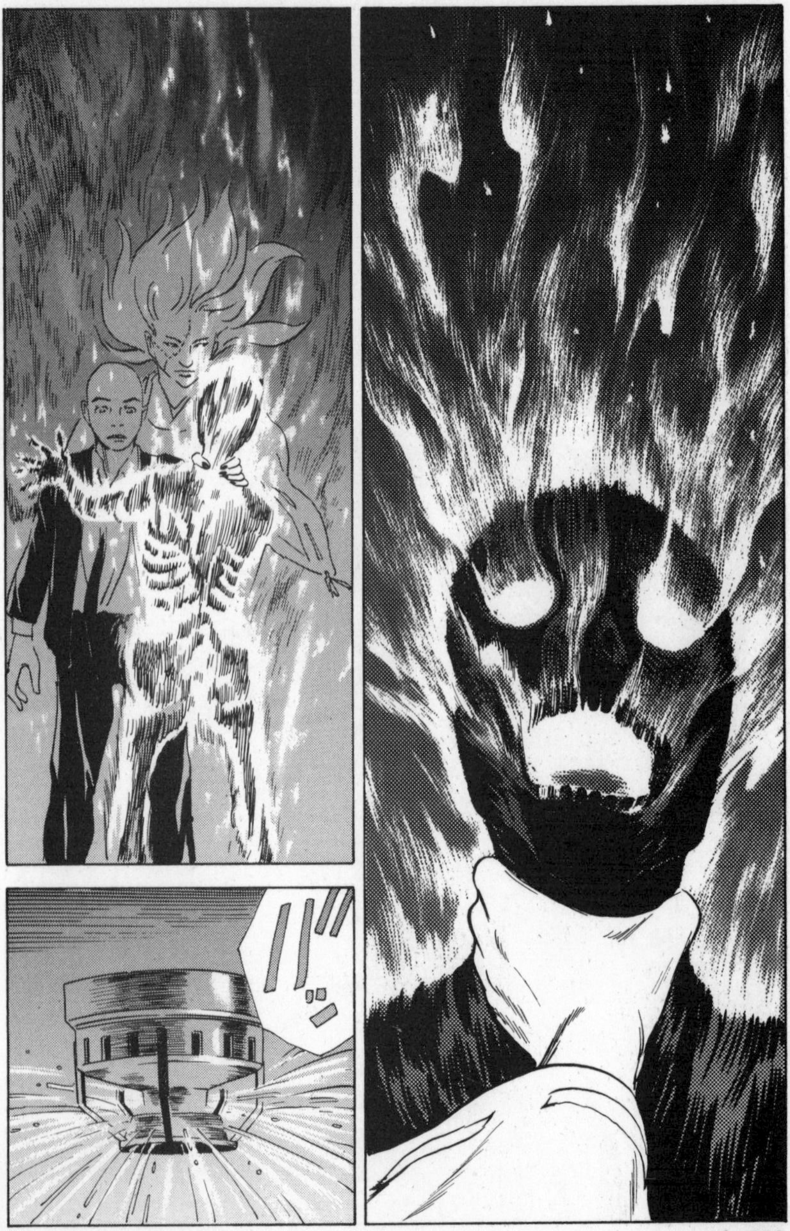

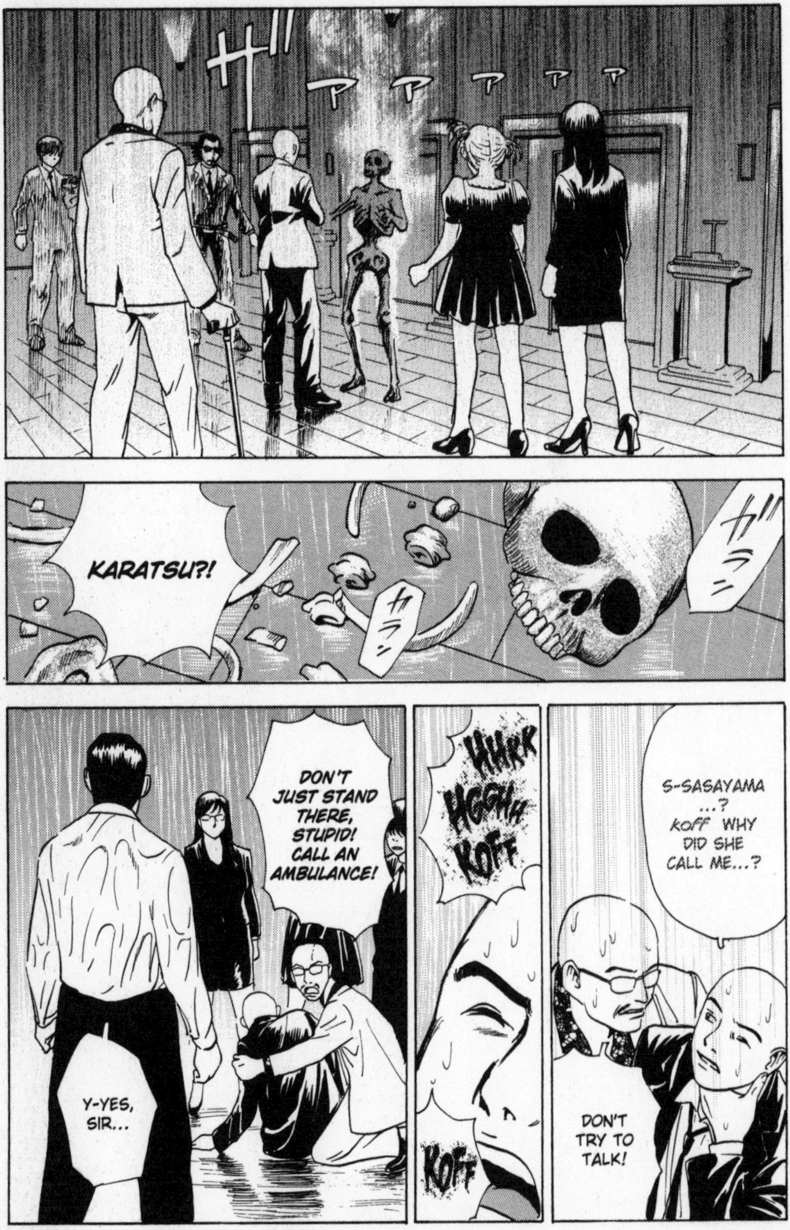
KARATSU?!
S-SASAYAMA ...? koff WHY DID SHE CALL ME...?
DON'T TRY TO TALK!
HHRK HGGHH KOFF
KOFF
DON'T JUST STAND THERE, STUPID! CALL AN AMBULANCE!
Y-YES, SIR...

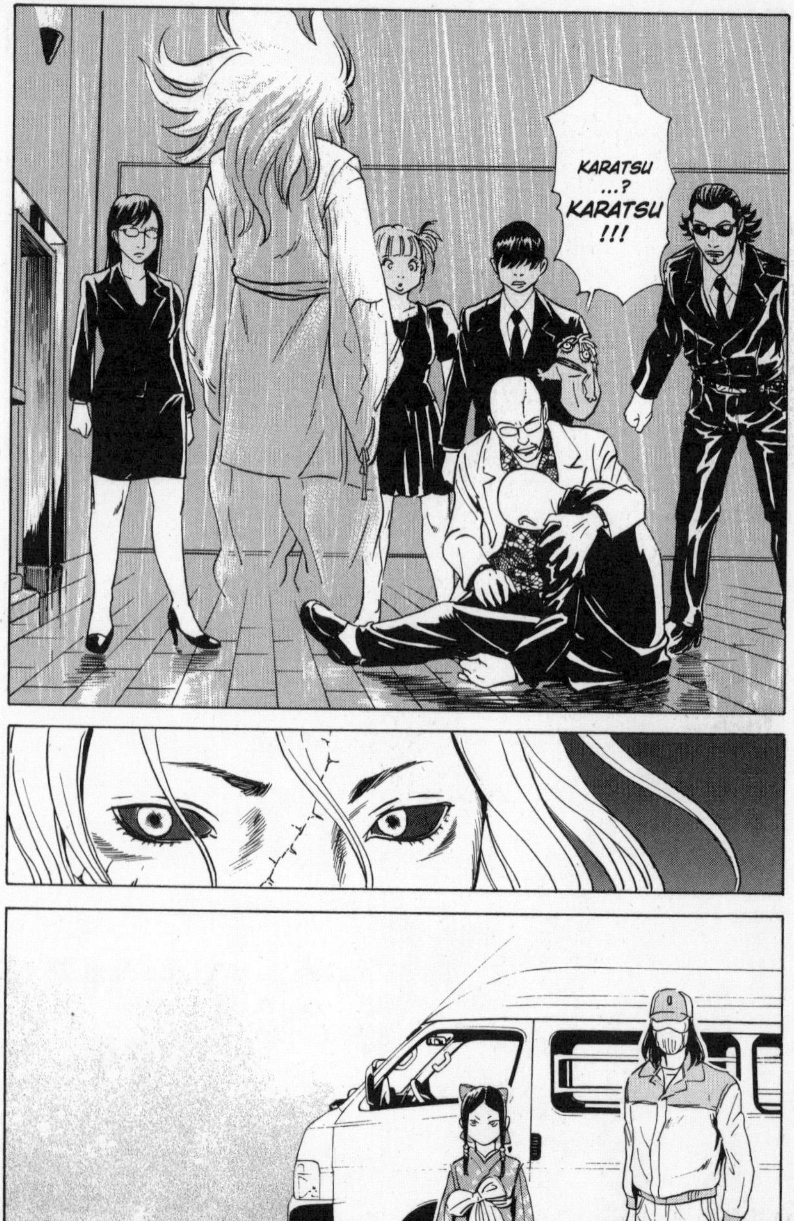
KARATSU ...? KARATSU !!!

4th delivery: for whose good—the end

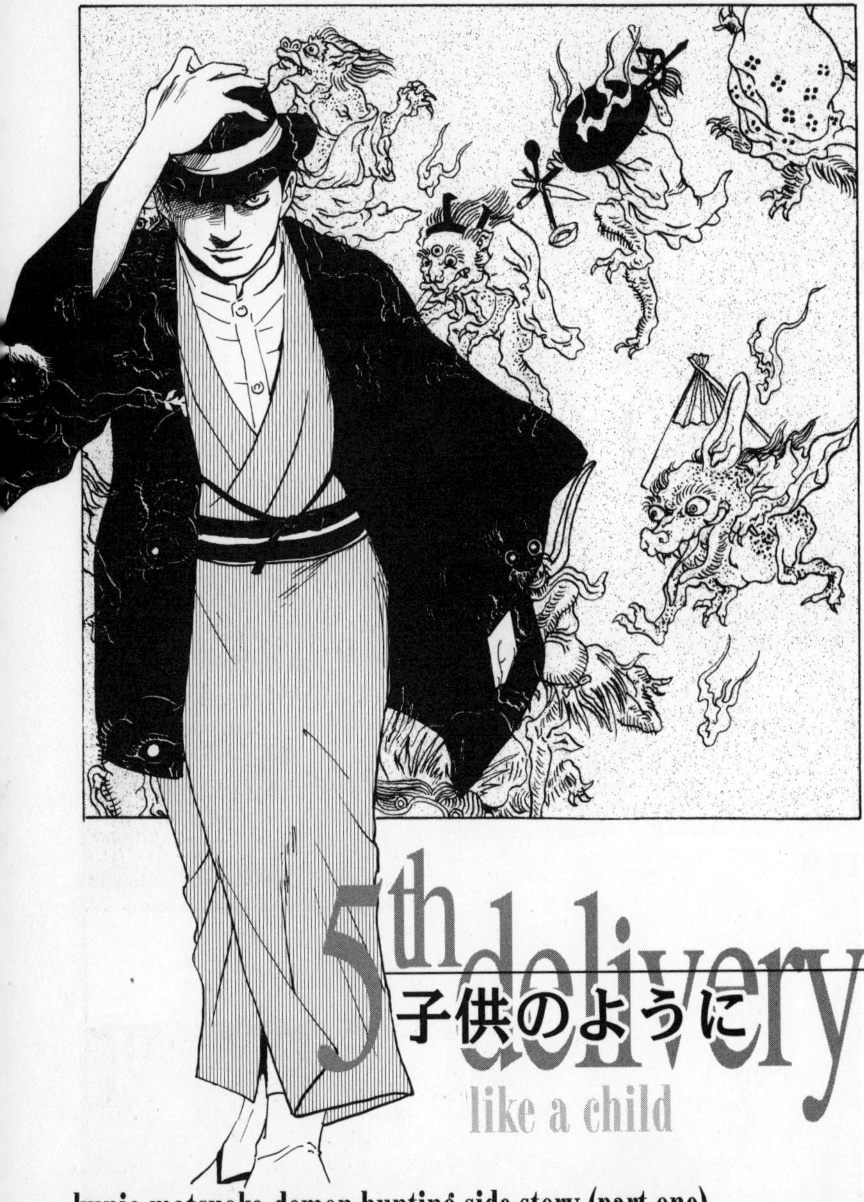

5th delivery

子供のように

like a child

kunio matsuoka demon hunting side story (part one)

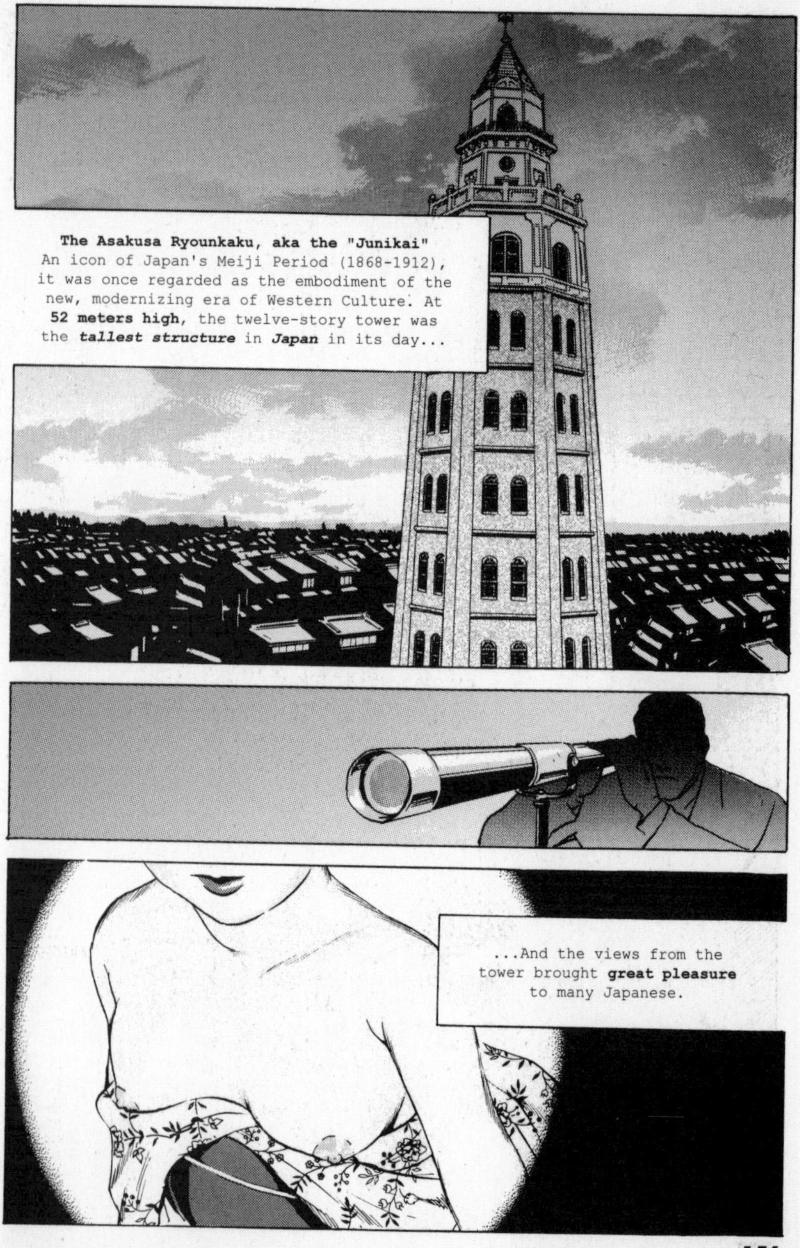
The Asakusa Ryounkaku, aka the "Junikai"
An icon of Japan's Meiji Period (1868-1912), it was once regarded as the embodiment of the new, modernizing era of Western Culture. At 52 meters high, the twelve-story tower was the tallest structure in Japan in its day...
...And the views from the tower brought great pleasure to many Japanese.

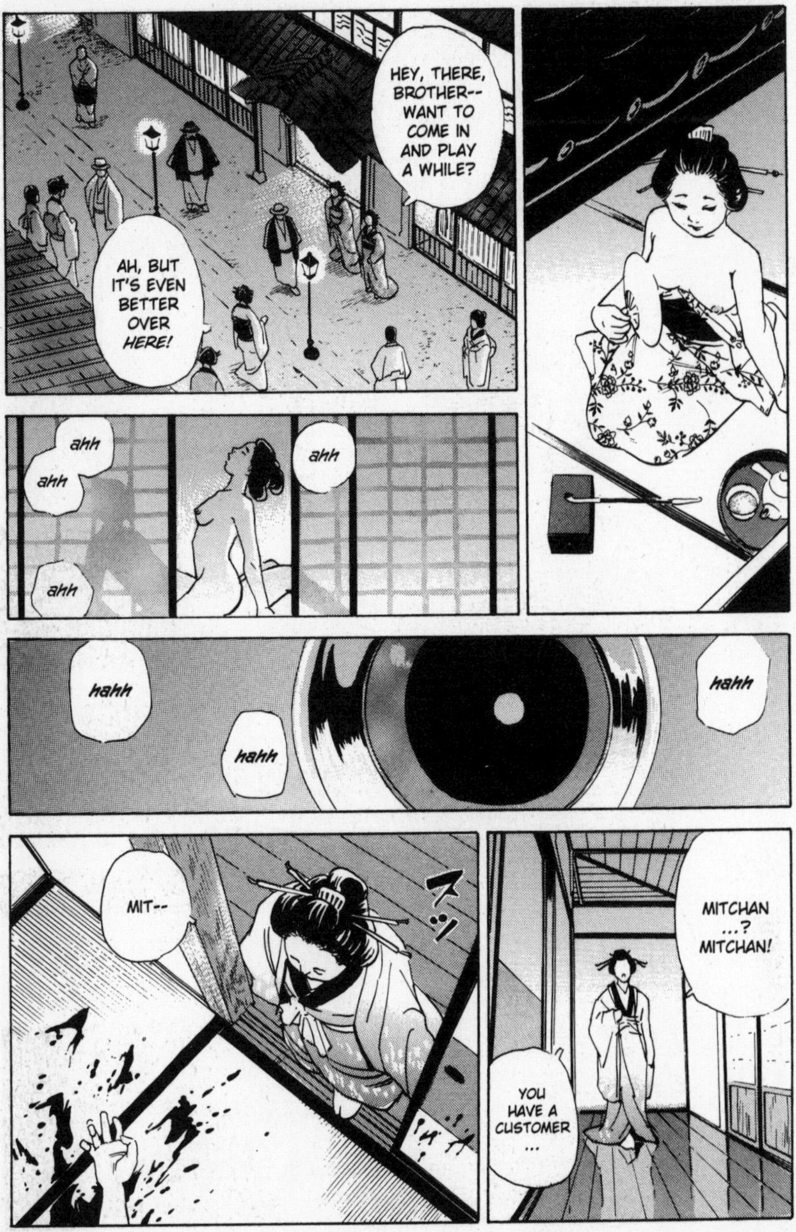
HEY, THERE, BROTHER--WANT TO COME IN AND PLAY A WHILE?
AH, BUT IT'S EVEN BETTER OVER *HERE!*
ahh
ahh
ahh
ahh
hahh
hahh
hahh
MITCHAN ...? MITCHAN!
YOU HAVE A CUSTOMER ...
スッ
MIT--

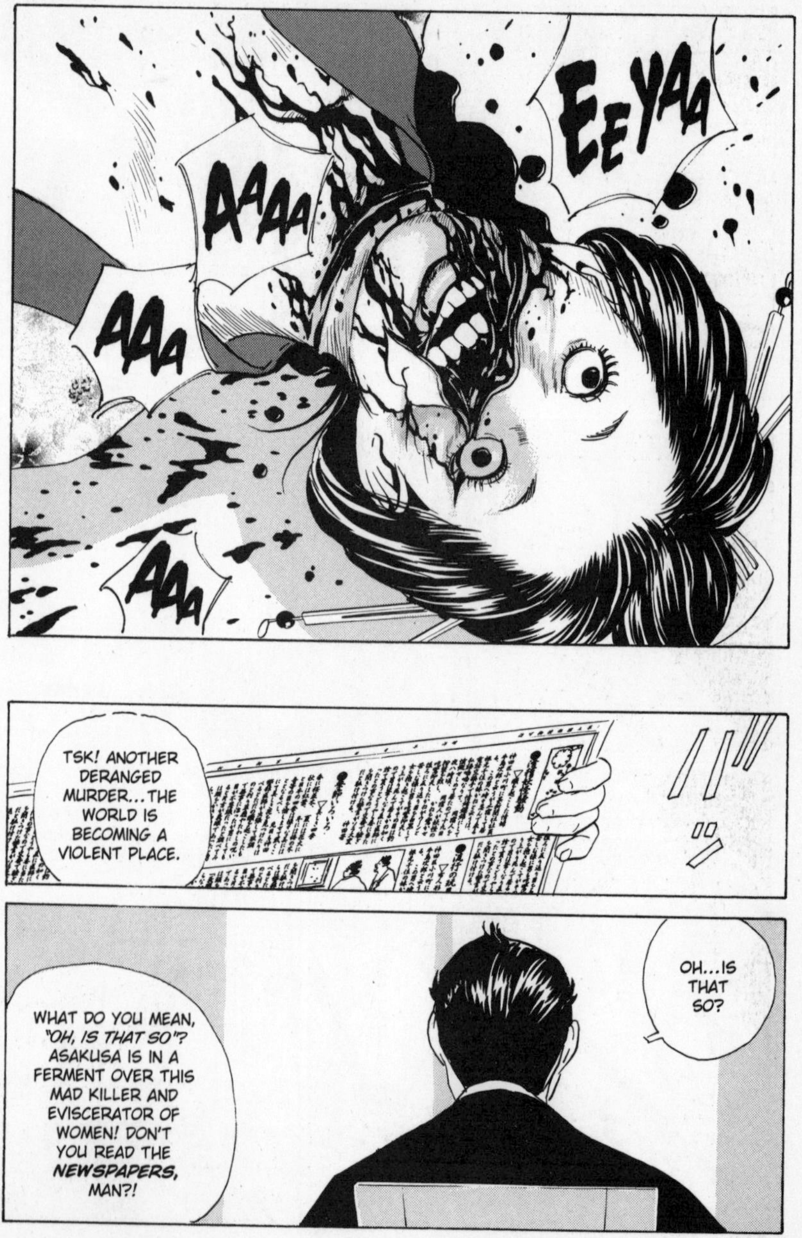
EEYAAA
AAAAA
AAA
AAA
TSK! ANOTHER DERANGED MURDER... THE WORLD IS BECOMING A VIOLENT PLACE.
OH... IS THAT SO?
WHAT DO YOU MEAN, *"OH, IS THAT SO"*? ASAKUSA IS IN A FERMENT OVER THIS MAD KILLER AND EVISCERATOR OF WOMEN! DON'T YOU READ THE ***NEWSPAPERS***, MAN?!

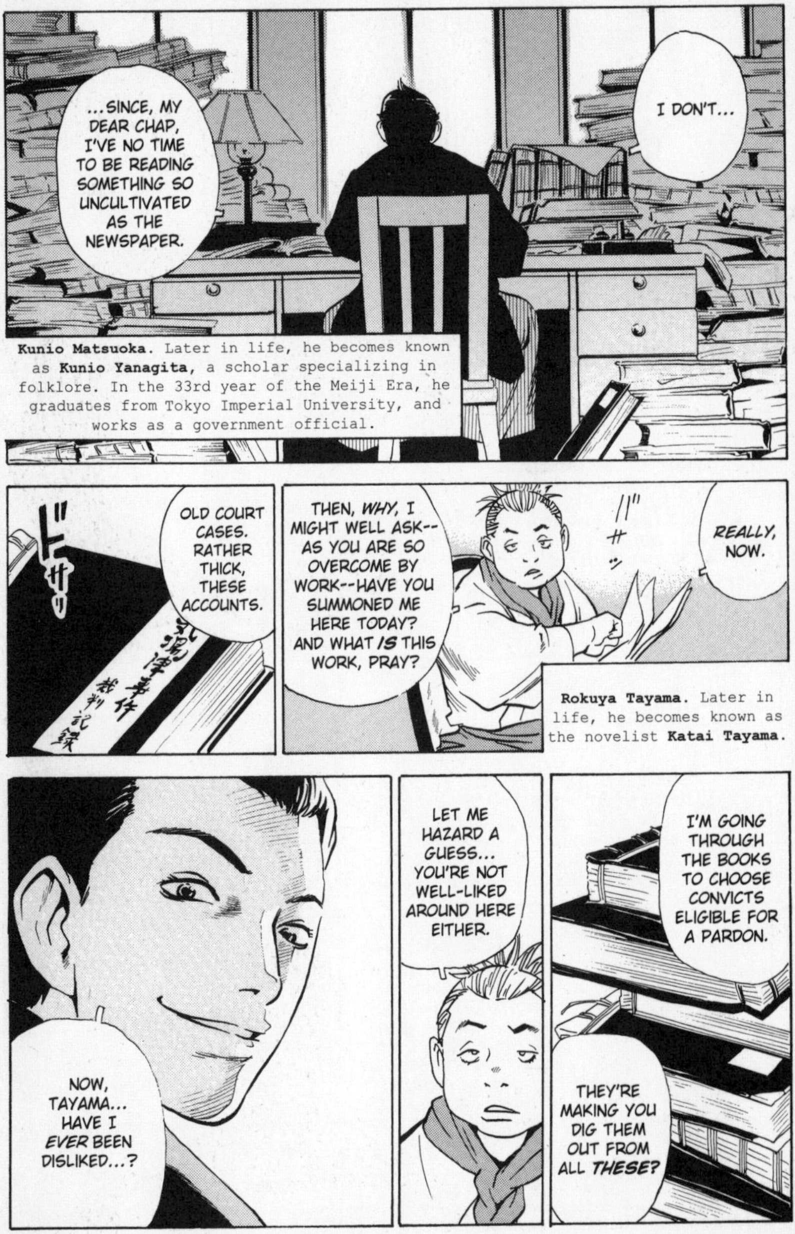
I DON'T...
...SINCE, MY DEAR CHAP, I'VE NO TIME TO BE READING SOMETHING SO UNCULTIVATED AS THE NEWSPAPER.
Kunio Matsuoka. Later in life, he becomes known as **Kunio Yanagita,** a scholar specializing in folklore. In the 33rd year of the Meiji Era, he graduates from Tokyo Imperial University, and works as a government official.
REALLY, NOW.
バサッ
Rokuya Tayama. Later in life, he becomes known as the novelist **Katai Tayama.**
THEN, *WHY*, I MIGHT WELL ASK--AS YOU ARE SO OVERCOME BY WORK--HAVE YOU SUMMONED ME HERE TODAY? AND WHAT *IS* THIS WORK, PRAY?
OLD COURT CASES. RATHER THICK, THESE ACCOUNTS.
ドサッ
I'M GOING THROUGH THE BOOKS TO CHOOSE CONVICTS ELIGIBLE FOR A PARDON.
THEY'RE MAKING YOU DIG THEM OUT FROM ALL *THESE*?
LET ME HAZARD A GUESS... YOU'RE NOT WELL-LIKED AROUND HERE EITHER.
NOW, TAYAMA... HAVE I *EVER* BEEN DISLIKED...?

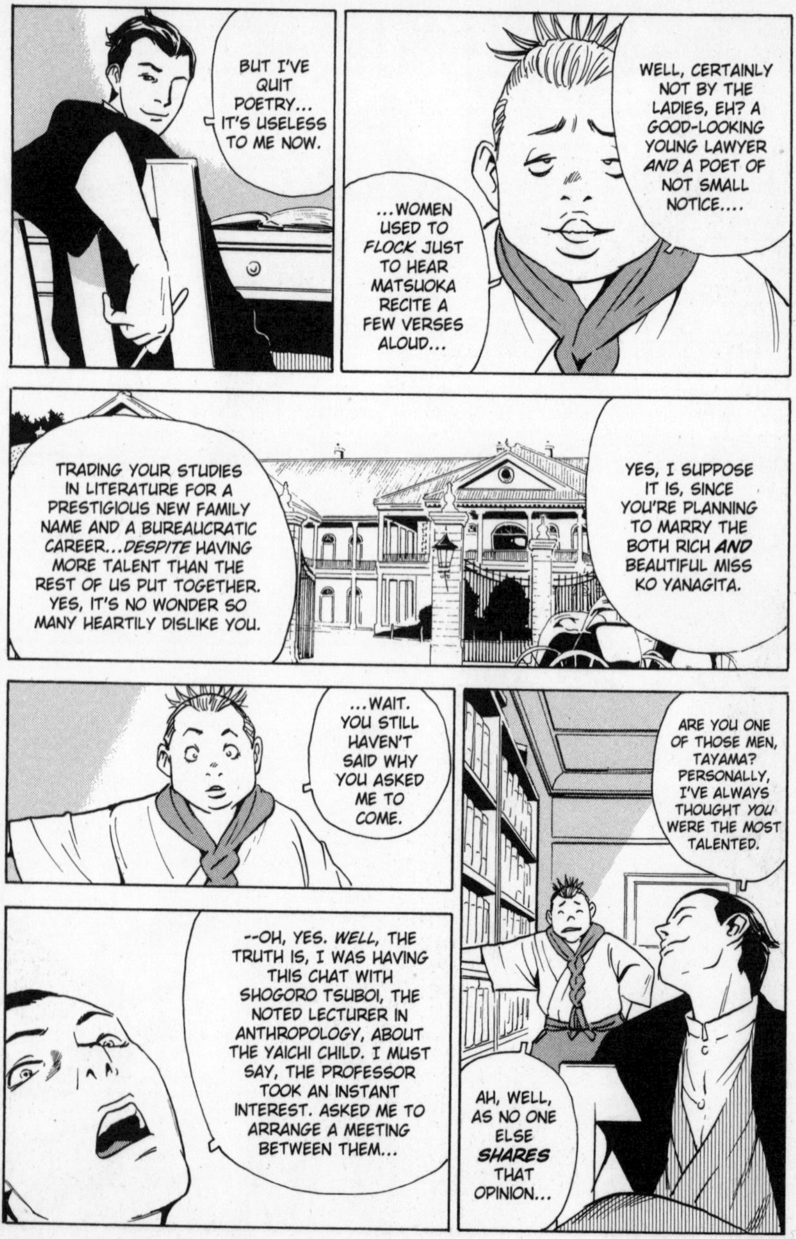
WELL, CERTAINLY NOT BY THE LADIES, EH? A GOOD-LOOKING YOUNG LAWYER *AND* A POET OF NOT SMALL NOTICE....
...WOMEN USED TO *FLOCK* JUST TO HEAR MATSUOKA RECITE A FEW VERSES ALOUD...
BUT I'VE QUIT POETRY... IT'S USELESS TO ME NOW.
YES, I SUPPOSE IT IS, SINCE YOU'RE PLANNING TO MARRY THE BOTH RICH ***AND*** BEAUTIFUL MISS KO YANAGITA.
TRADING YOUR STUDIES IN LITERATURE FOR A PRESTIGIOUS NEW FAMILY NAME AND A BUREAUCRATIC CAREER...*DESPITE* HAVING MORE TALENT THAN THE REST OF US PUT TOGETHER. YES, IT'S NO WONDER SO MANY HEARTILY DISLIKE YOU.
ARE YOU ONE OF THOSE MEN, TAYAMA? PERSONALLY, I'VE ALWAYS THOUGHT *YOU* WERE THE MOST TALENTED.
AH, WELL, AS NO ONE ELSE ***SHARES*** THAT OPINION...
...WAIT. YOU STILL HAVEN'T SAID WHY YOU ASKED ME TO COME.
--OH, YES. *WELL*, THE TRUTH IS, I WAS HAVING THIS CHAT WITH SHOGORO TSUBOI, THE NOTED LECTURER IN ANTHROPOLOGY, ABOUT THE YAICHI CHILD. I MUST SAY, THE PROFESSOR TOOK AN INSTANT INTEREST. ASKED ME TO ARRANGE A MEETING BETWEEN THEM...

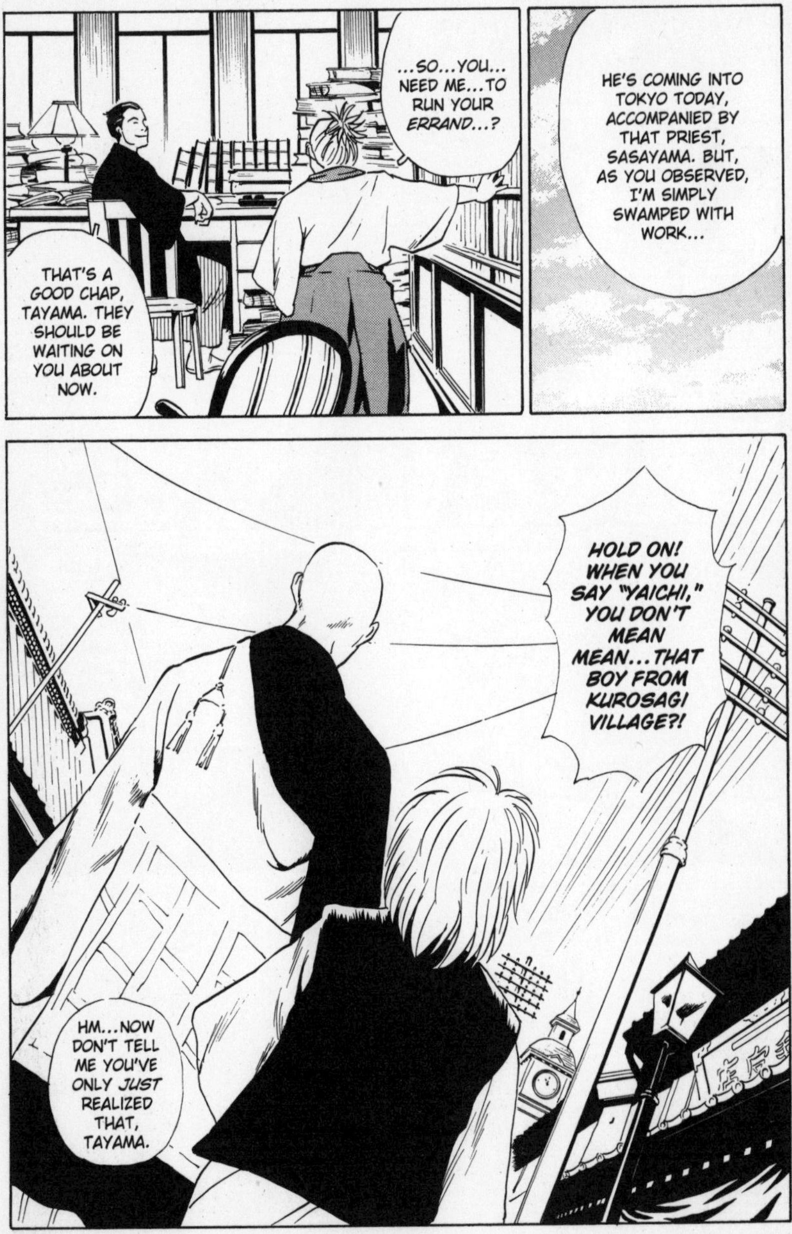
HE'S COMING INTO TOKYO TODAY, ACCOMPANIED BY THAT PRIEST, SASAYAMA. BUT, AS YOU OBSERVED, I'M SIMPLY SWAMPED WITH WORK...
...SO...YOU... NEED ME...TO RUN YOUR *ERRAND*...?
THAT'S A GOOD CHAP, TAYAMA. THEY SHOULD BE WAITING ON YOU ABOUT NOW.
HOLD ON! WHEN YOU SAY "YAICHI," YOU DON'T MEAN MEAN...THAT BOY FROM KUROSAGI VILLAGE?!
HM...NOW DON'T TELL ME YOU'VE ONLY *JUST* REALIZED THAT, TAYAMA.

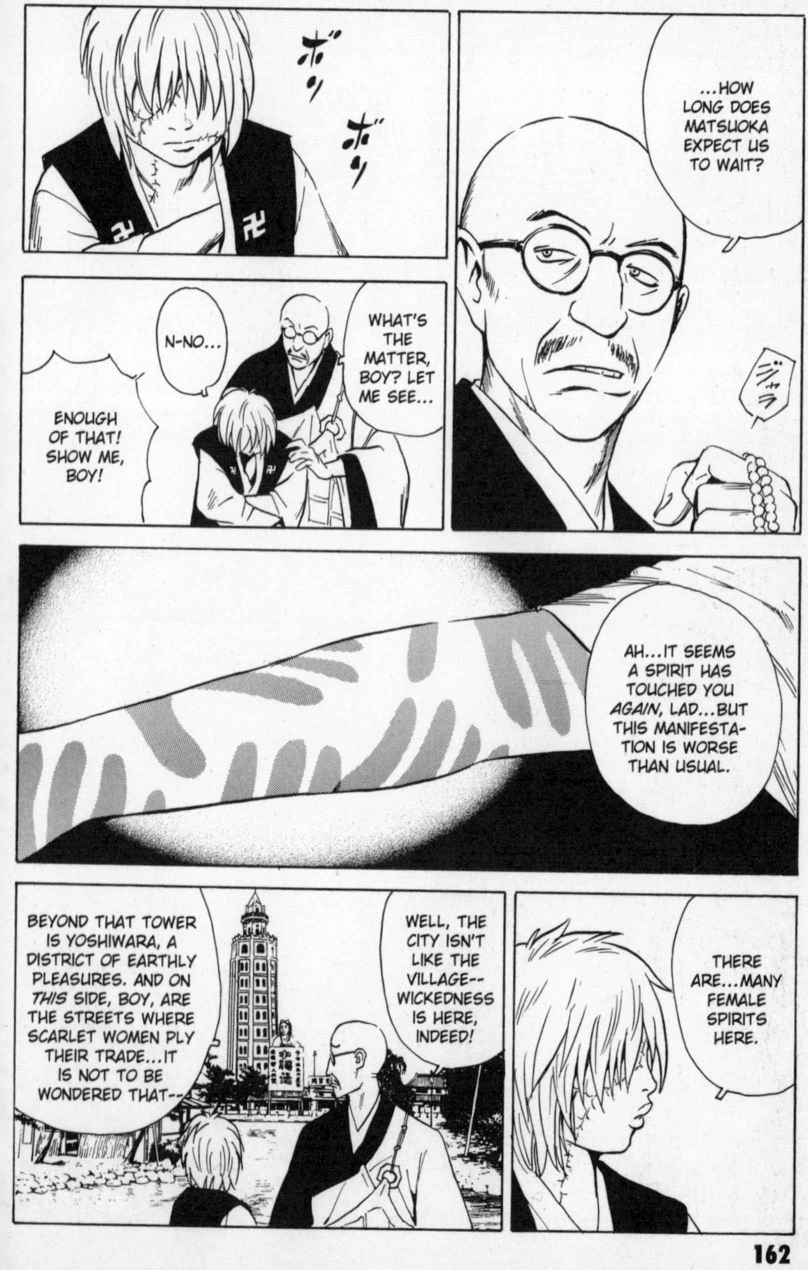
...HOW LONG DOES MATSUOKA EXPECT US TO WAIT?
ジャラ
ボツ
ボツ
WHAT'S THE MATTER, BOY? LET ME SEE...
N-NO...
ENOUGH OF THAT! SHOW ME, BOY!
AH...IT SEEMS A SPIRIT HAS TOUCHED YOU *AGAIN*, LAD...BUT THIS MANIFESTATION IS WORSE THAN USUAL.
THERE ARE...MANY FEMALE SPIRITS HERE.
WELL, THE CITY ISN'T LIKE THE VILLAGE--WICKEDNESS IS HERE, INDEED!
BEYOND THAT TOWER IS YOSHIWARA, A DISTRICT OF EARTHLY PLEASURES. AND ON *THIS* SIDE, BOY, ARE THE STREETS WHERE SCARLET WOMEN PLY THEIR TRADE...IT IS NOT TO BE WONDERED THAT--

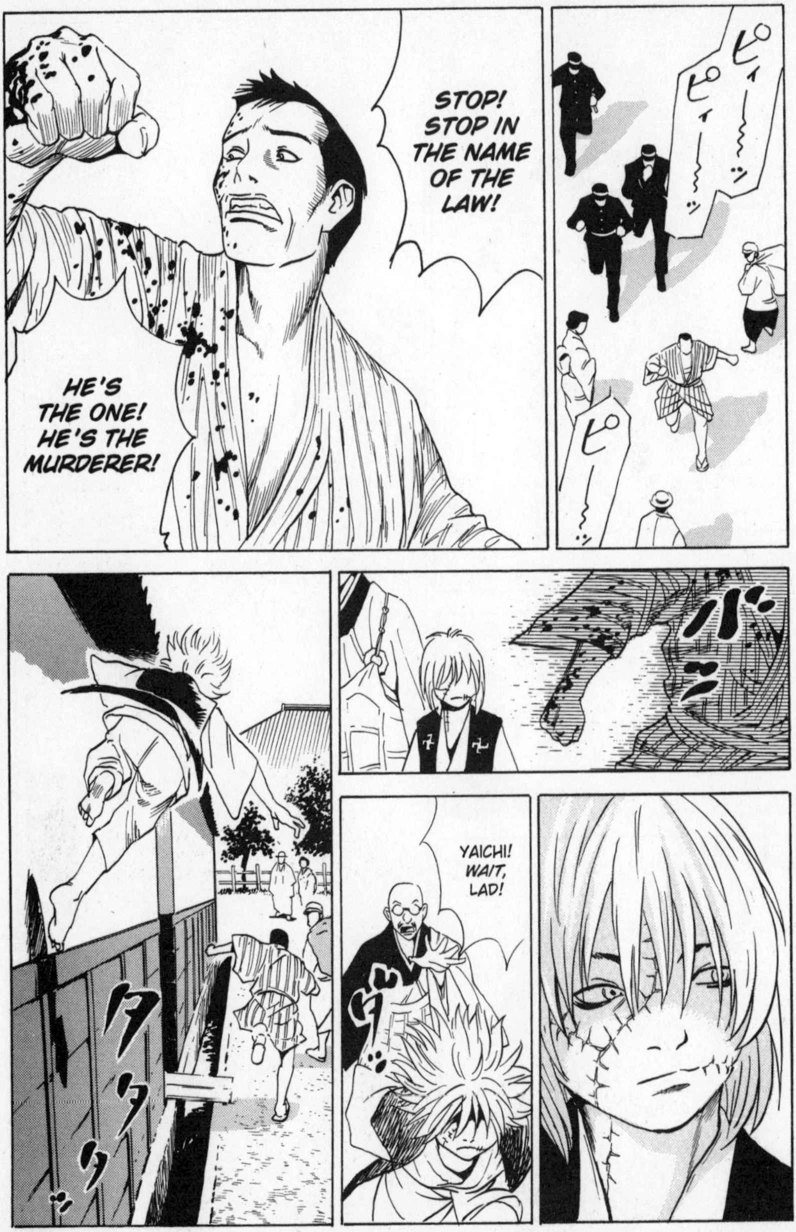
STOP! STOP IN THE NAME OF THE LAW!
HE'S THE ONE! HE'S THE MURDERER!
YAICHI! WAIT, LAD!

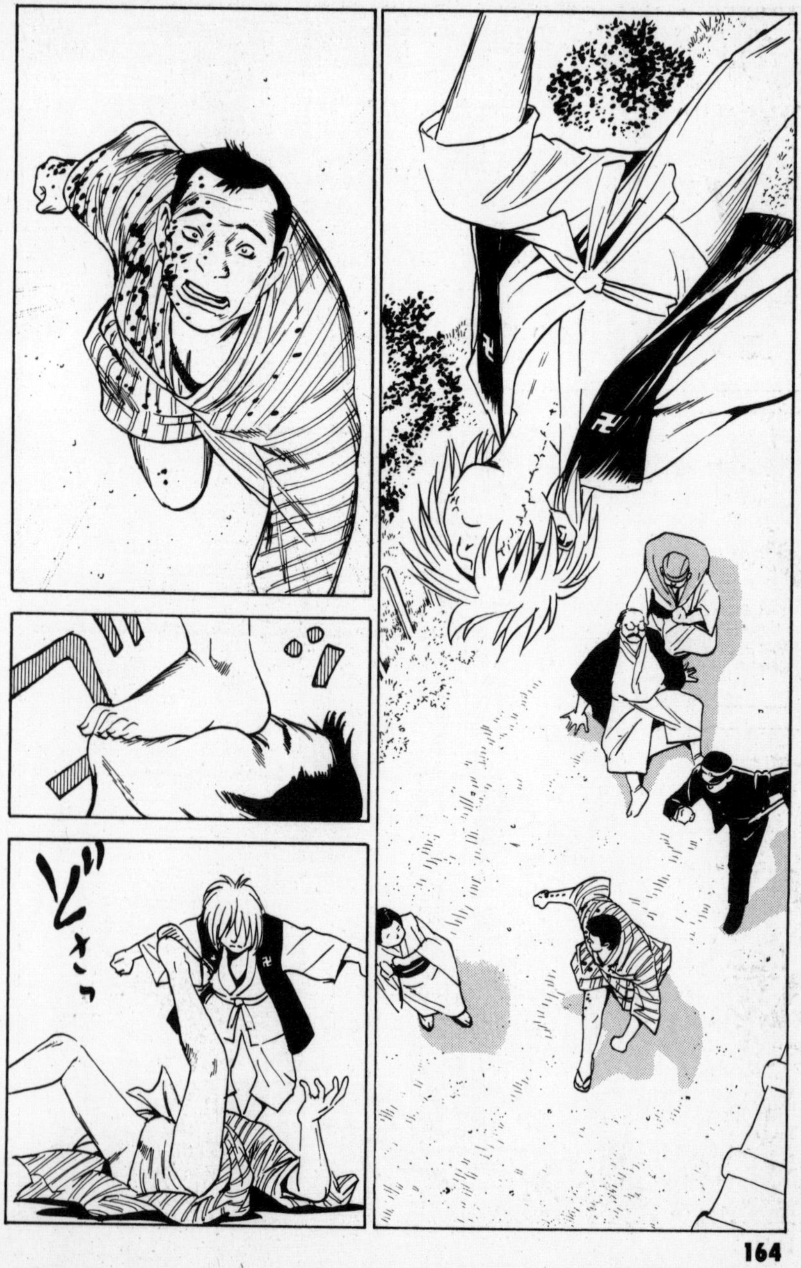
どさっ

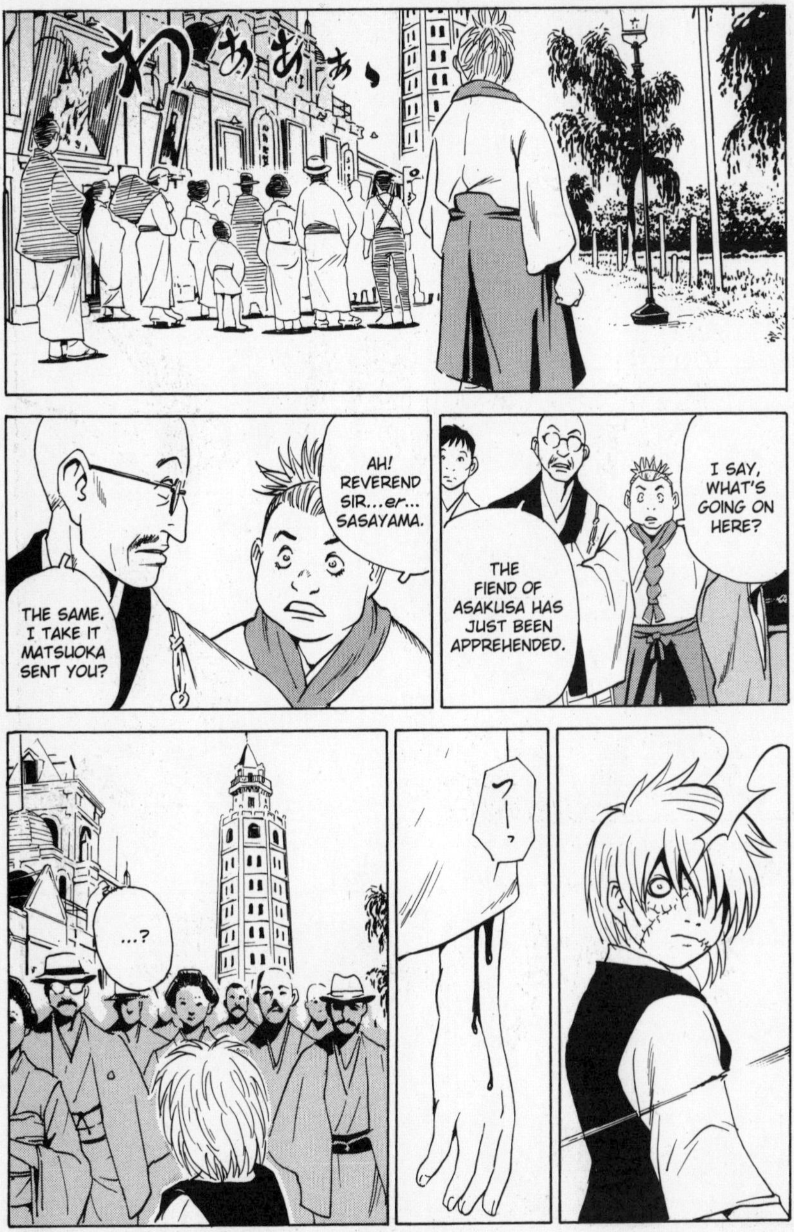
わあああ
I SAY, WHAT'S GOING ON HERE?
THE FIEND OF ASAKUSA HAS JUST BEEN APPREHENDED.
AH! REVEREND SIR...er... SASAYAMA.
THE SAME. I TAKE IT MATSUOKA SENT YOU?
?!
...?

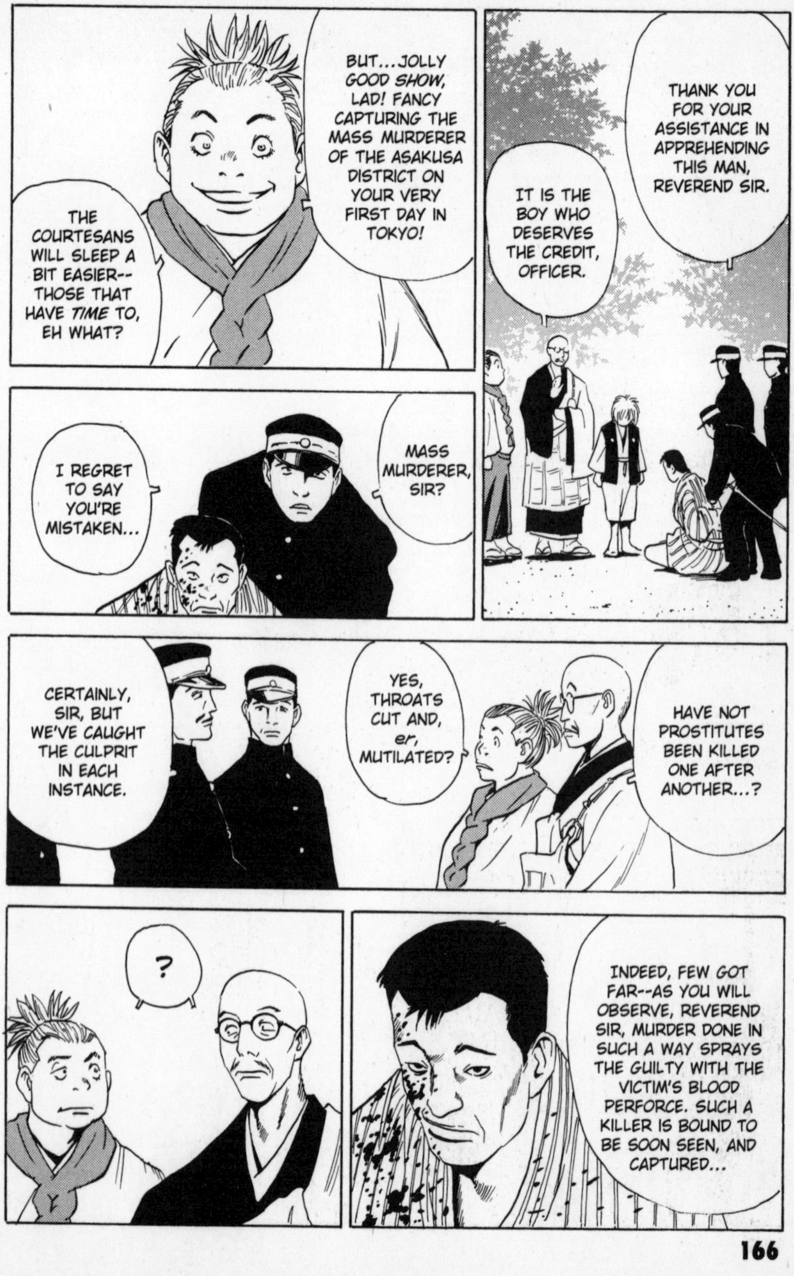
THANK YOU FOR YOUR ASSISTANCE IN APPREHENDING THIS MAN, REVEREND SIR.
IT IS THE BOY WHO DESERVES THE CREDIT, OFFICER.
BUT...JOLLY GOOD *SHOW*, LAD! FANCY CAPTURING THE MASS MURDERER OF THE ASAKUSA DISTRICT ON YOUR VERY FIRST DAY IN TOKYO!
THE COURTESANS WILL SLEEP A BIT EASIER--THOSE THAT HAVE *TIME* TO, EH WHAT?
MASS MURDERER, SIR?
I REGRET TO SAY YOU'RE MISTAKEN...
HAVE NOT PROSTITUTES BEEN KILLED ONE AFTER ANOTHER...?
YES, THROATS CUT AND, *er*, MUTILATED?
CERTAINLY, SIR, BUT WE'VE CAUGHT THE CULPRIT IN EACH INSTANCE.
INDEED, FEW GOT FAR--AS YOU WILL OBSERVE, REVEREND SIR, MURDER DONE IN SUCH A WAY SPRAYS THE GUILTY WITH THE VICTIM'S BLOOD PERFORCE. SUCH A KILLER IS BOUND TO BE SOON SEEN, AND CAPTURED...
?

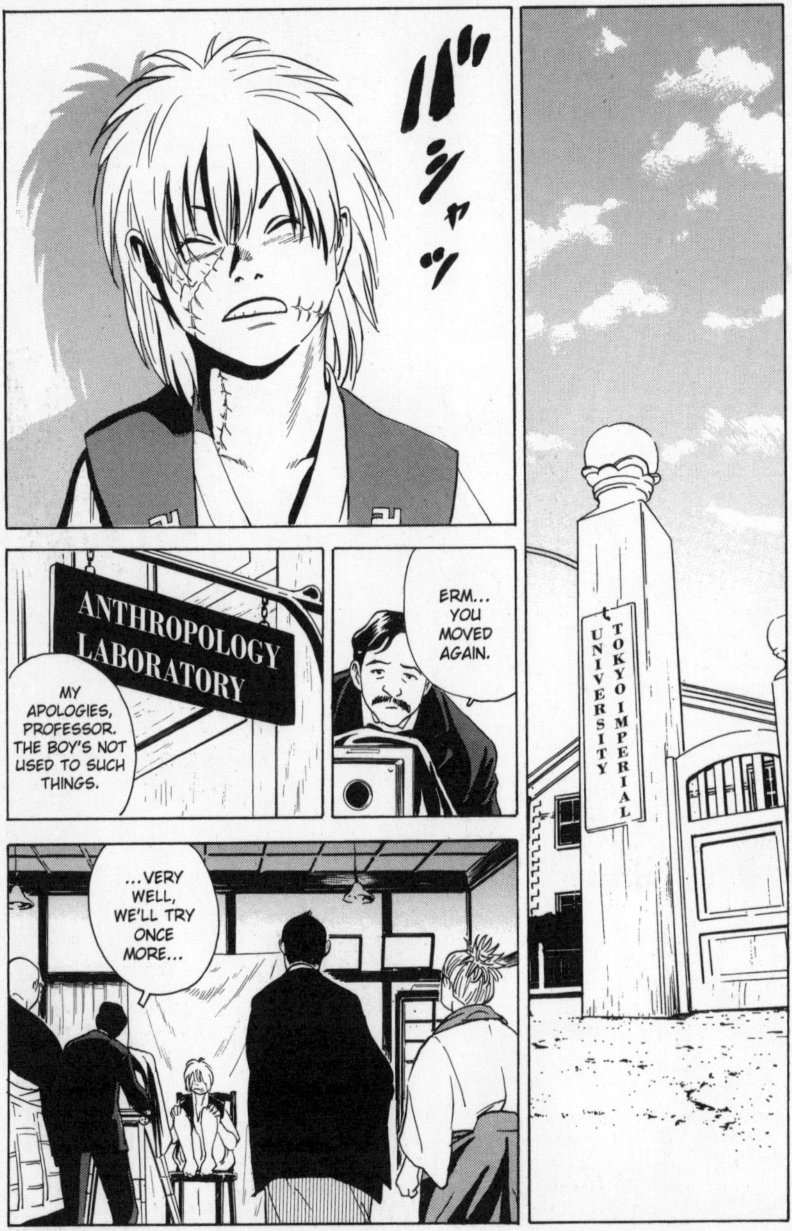
TOKYO IMPERIAL UNIVERSITY
バシャッ
ERM... YOU MOVED AGAIN.
ANTHROPOLOGY LABORATORY
MY APOLOGIES, PROFESSOR. THE BOY'S NOT USED TO SUCH THINGS.
...VERY WELL, WE'LL TRY ONCE MORE...

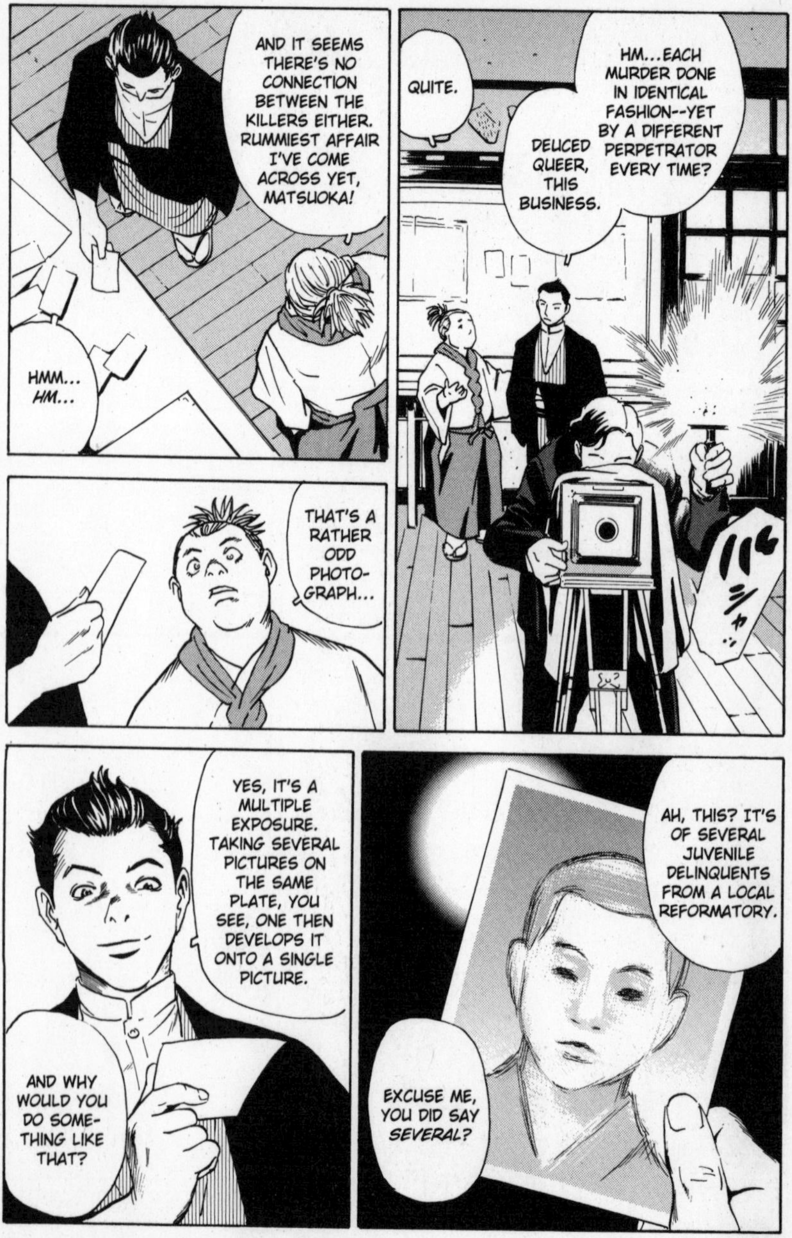
HM...EACH MURDER DONE IN IDENTICAL FASHION--YET BY A DIFFERENT PERPETRATOR EVERY TIME?
DEUCED QUEER, THIS BUSINESS.
QUITE.
パシャッ
AND IT SEEMS THERE'S NO CONNECTION BETWEEN THE KILLERS EITHER. RUMMIEST AFFAIR I'VE COME ACROSS YET, MATSUOKA!
HMM... HM...
THAT'S A RATHER ODD PHOTOGRAPH...
AH, THIS? IT'S OF SEVERAL JUVENILE DELINQUENTS FROM A LOCAL REFORMATORY.
EXCUSE ME, YOU DID SAY *SEVERAL*?
YES, IT'S A MULTIPLE EXPOSURE. TAKING SEVERAL PICTURES ON THE SAME PLATE, YOU SEE, ONE THEN DEVELOPS IT ONTO A SINGLE PICTURE.
AND WHY WOULD YOU DO SOMETHING LIKE THAT?

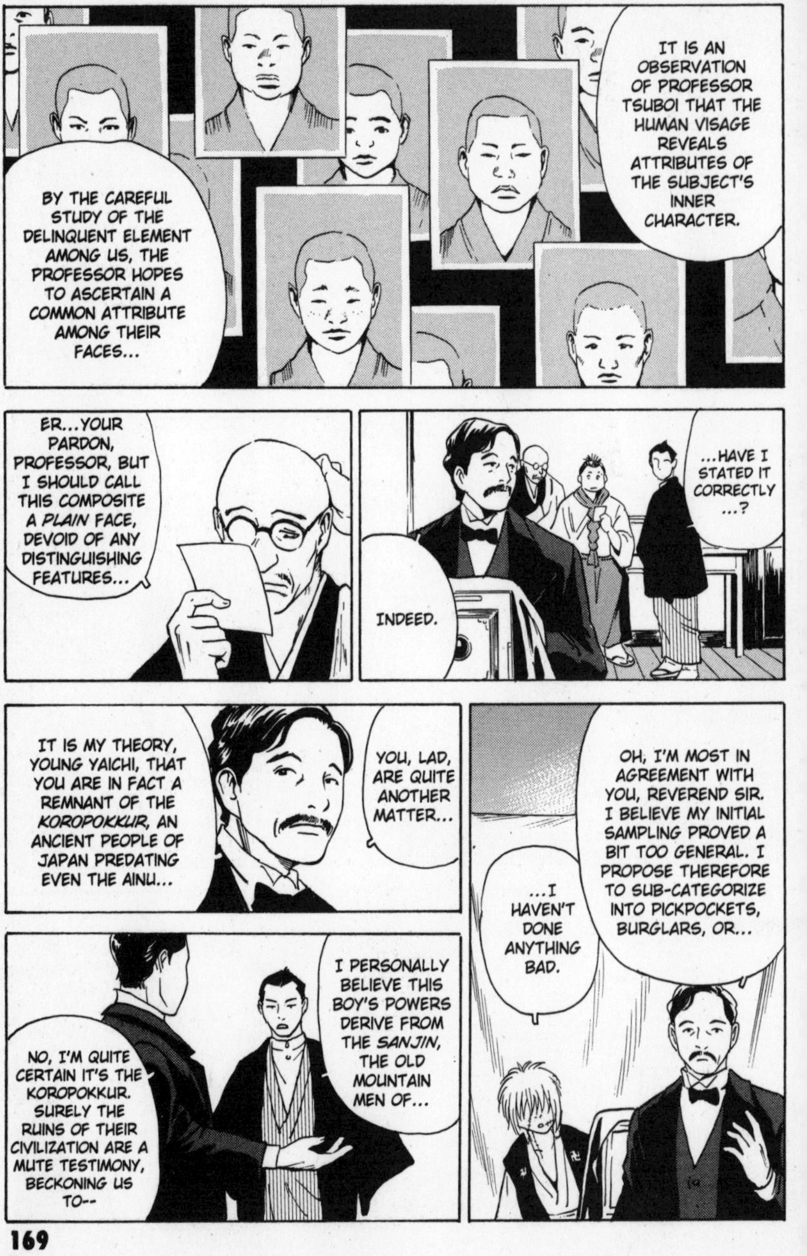
IT IS AN OBSERVATION OF PROFESSOR TSUBOI THAT THE HUMAN VISAGE REVEALS ATTRIBUTES OF THE SUBJECT'S INNER CHARACTER.
BY THE CAREFUL STUDY OF THE DELINQUENT ELEMENT AMONG US, THE PROFESSOR HOPES TO ASCERTAIN A COMMON ATTRIBUTE AMONG THEIR FACES...
...HAVE I STATED IT CORRECTLY ...?
INDEED.
ER...YOUR PARDON, PROFESSOR, BUT I SHOULD CALL THIS COMPOSITE A *PLAIN* FACE, DEVOID OF ANY DISTINGUISHING FEATURES...
OH, I'M MOST IN AGREEMENT WITH YOU, REVEREND SIR. I BELIEVE MY INITIAL SAMPLING PROVED A BIT TOO GENERAL. I PROPOSE THEREFORE TO SUB-CATEGORIZE INTO PICKPOCKETS, BURGLARS, OR...
...I HAVEN'T DONE ANYTHING BAD.
YOU, LAD, ARE QUITE ANOTHER MATTER...
IT IS MY THEORY, YOUNG YAICHI, THAT YOU ARE IN FACT A REMNANT OF THE *KOROPOKKUR*, AN ANCIENT PEOPLE OF JAPAN PREDATING EVEN THE AINU...
I PERSONALLY BELIEVE THIS BOY'S POWERS DERIVE FROM THE *SANJIN*, THE OLD MOUNTAIN MEN OF...
NO, I'M QUITE CERTAIN IT'S THE KOROPOKKUR. SURELY THE RUINS OF THEIR CIVILIZATION ARE A MUTE TESTIMONY, BECKONING US TO--

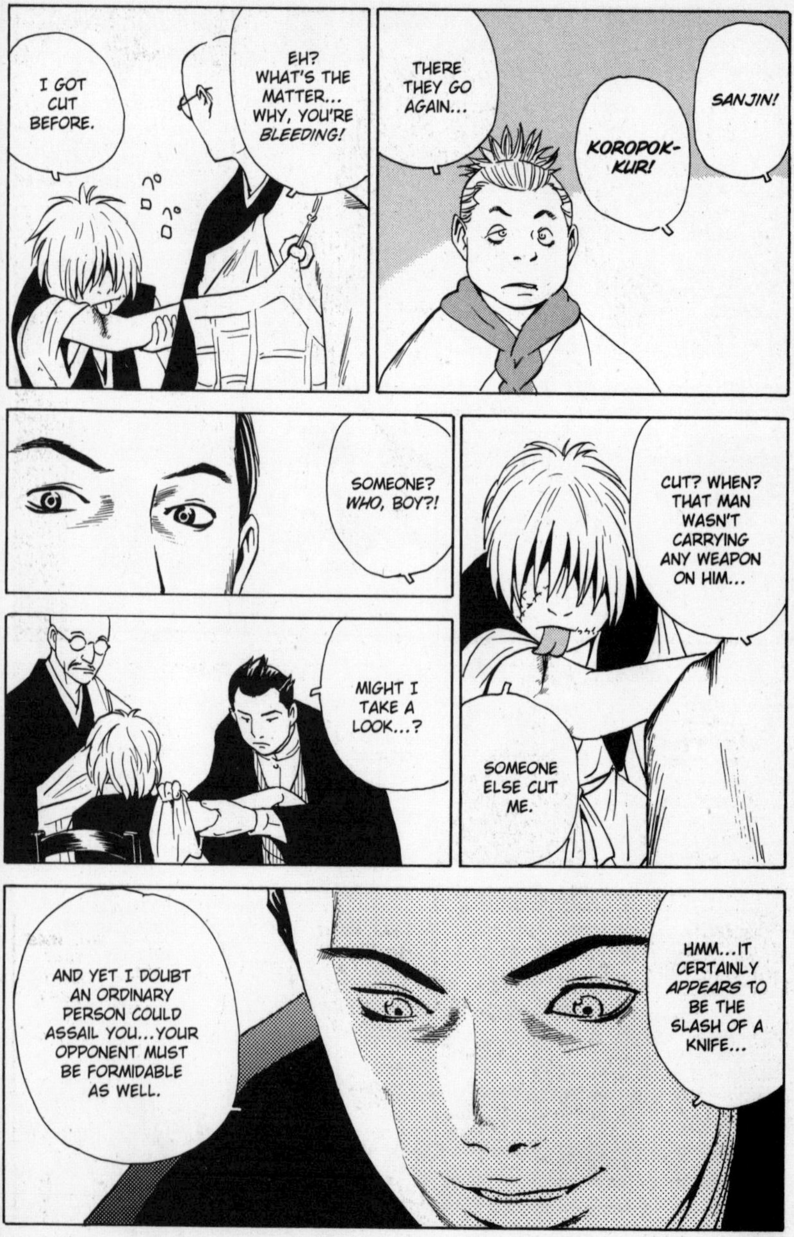
SANJIN!
KOROPOK-KUR!
THERE THEY GO AGAIN...
EH? WHAT'S THE MATTER... WHY, YOU'RE *BLEEDING!*
I GOT CUT BEFORE.
CUT? WHEN? THAT MAN WASN'T CARRYING ANY WEAPON ON HIM...
SOMEONE ELSE CUT ME.
SOMEONE? *WHO,* BOY?!
MIGHT I TAKE A LOOK...?
HMM...IT CERTAINLY *APPEARS* TO BE THE SLASH OF A KNIFE...
AND YET I DOUBT AN ORDINARY PERSON COULD ASSAIL YOU...YOUR OPPONENT MUST BE FORMIDABLE AS WELL.

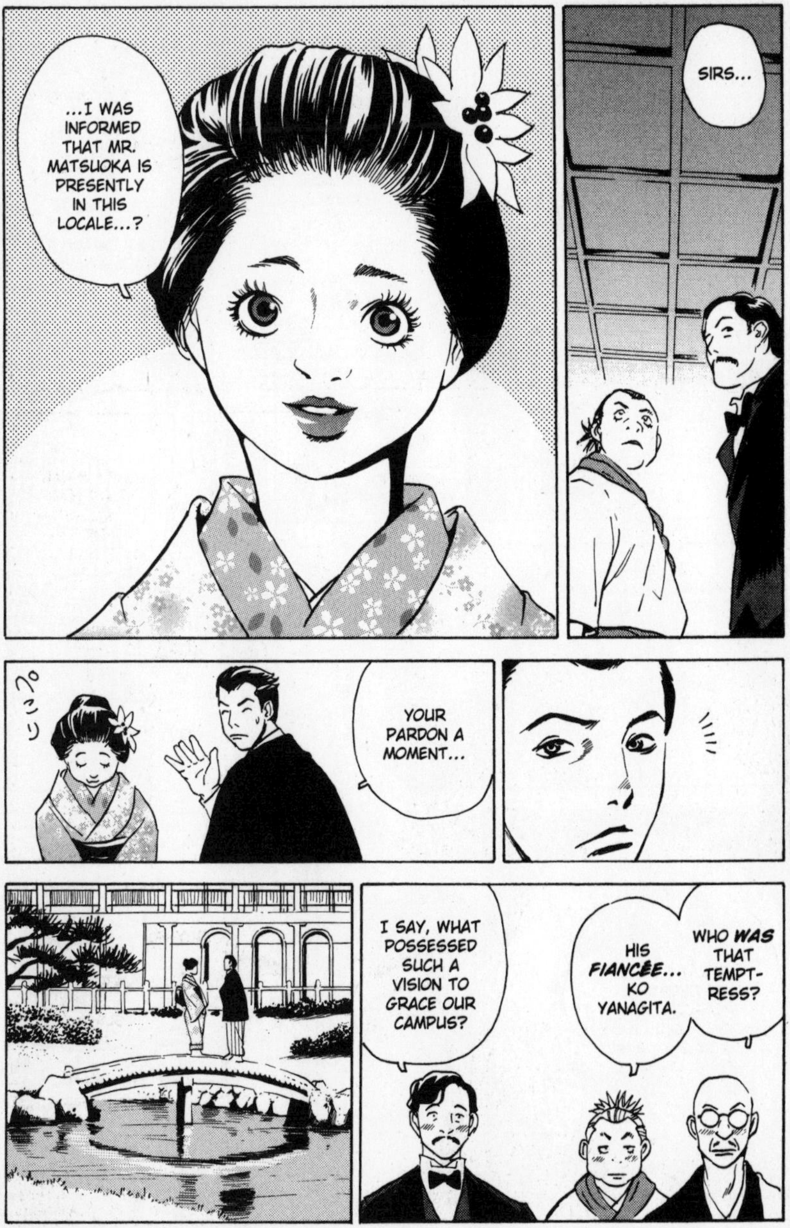
SIRS...
...I WAS INFORMED THAT MR. MATSUOKA IS PRESENTLY IN THIS LOCALE...?
YOUR PARDON A MOMENT...
WHO *WAS* THAT TEMPT-RESS?
HIS *FIANCÉE*... KO YANAGITA.
I SAY, WHAT POSSESSED SUCH A VISION TO GRACE OUR CAMPUS?

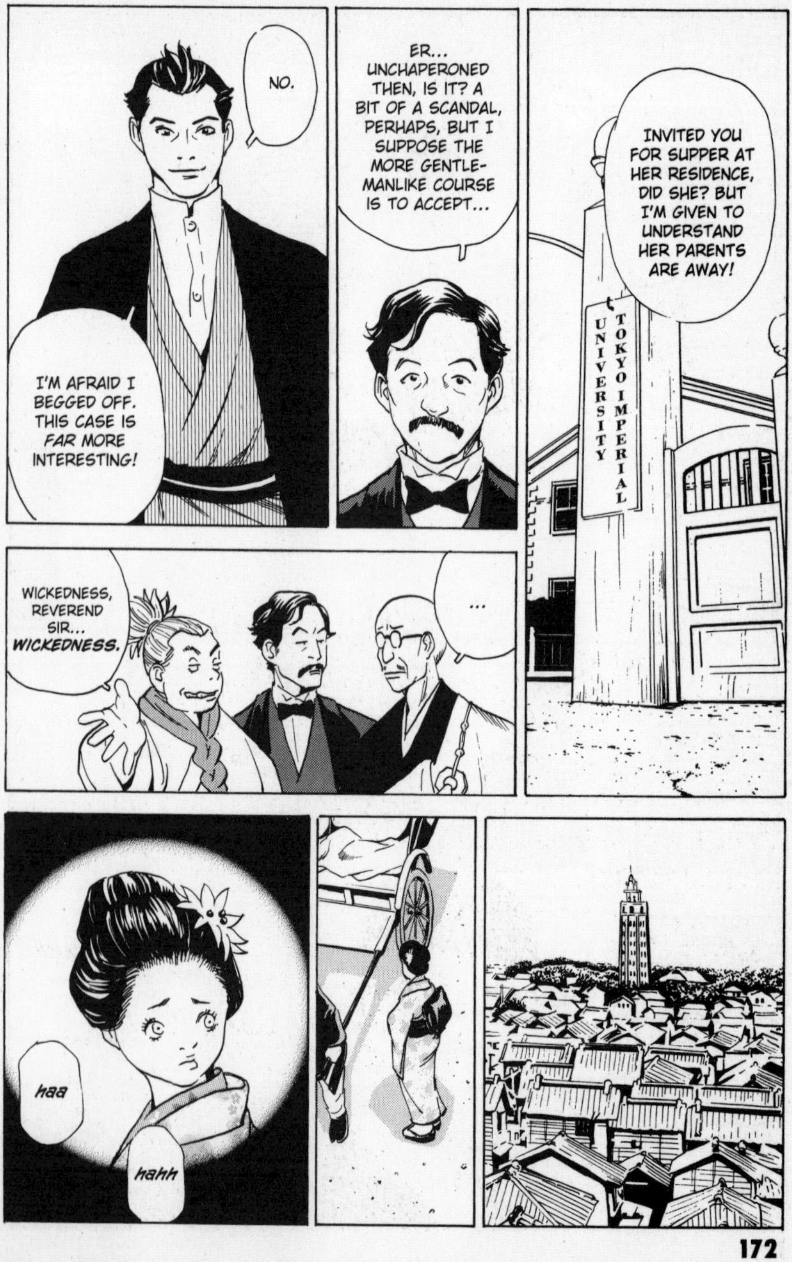

INVITED YOU FOR SUPPER AT HER RESIDENCE, DID SHE? BUT I'M GIVEN TO UNDERSTAND HER PARENTS ARE AWAY!
TOKYO IMPERIAL UNIVERSITY
ER... UNCHAPERONED THEN, IS IT? A BIT OF A SCANDAL, PERHAPS, BUT I SUPPOSE THE MORE GENTLE-MANLIKE COURSE IS TO ACCEPT...
NO.
I'M AFRAID I BEGGED OFF. THIS CASE IS *FAR MORE* INTERESTING!
...
WICKEDNESS, REVEREND SIR... **WICKEDNESS.**
haa
hahh

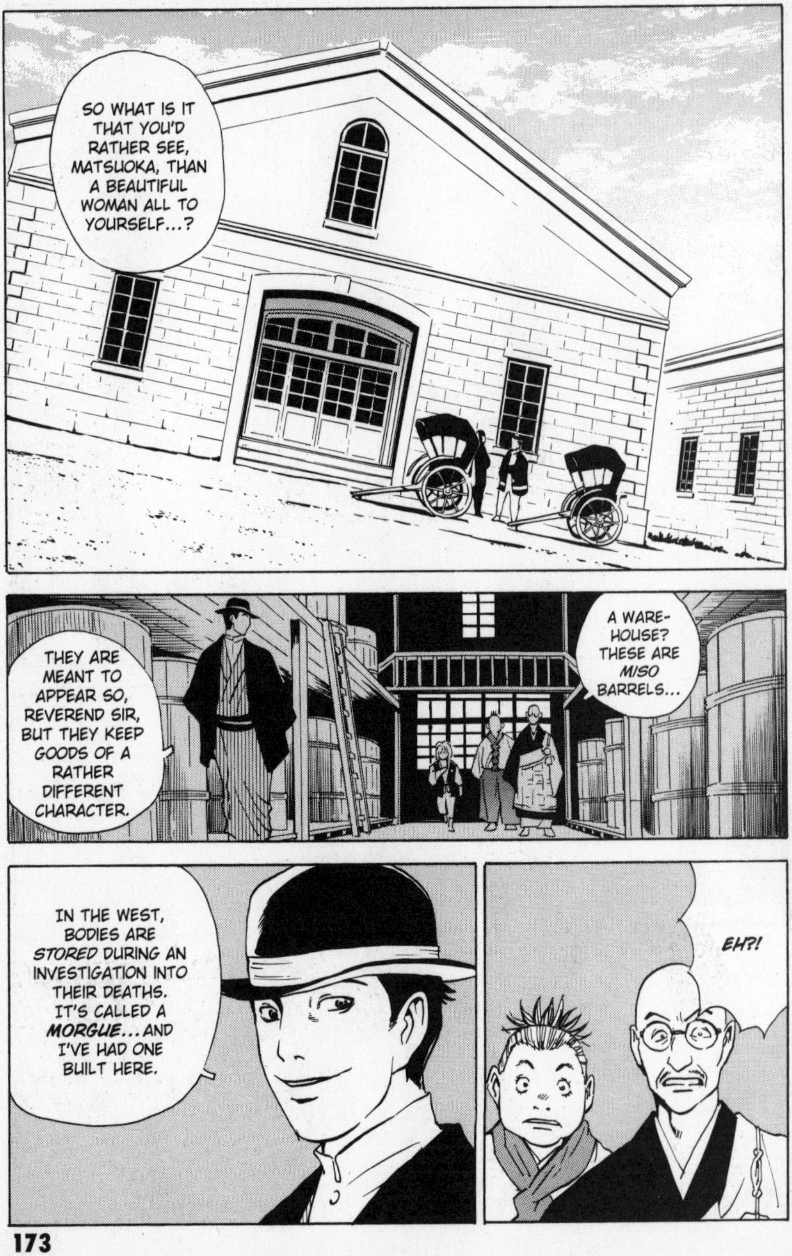
SO WHAT IS IT THAT YOU'D RATHER SEE, MATSUOKA, THAN A BEAUTIFUL WOMAN ALL TO YOURSELF...?
A WARE-HOUSE? THESE ARE *MISO* BARRELS...
THEY ARE MEANT TO APPEAR SO, REVEREND SIR, BUT THEY KEEP GOODS OF A RATHER DIFFERENT CHARACTER.
EH?!
IN THE WEST, BODIES ARE *STORED* DURING AN INVESTIGATION INTO THEIR DEATHS. IT'S CALLED A ***MORGUE...*** AND I'VE HAD ONE BUILT HERE.

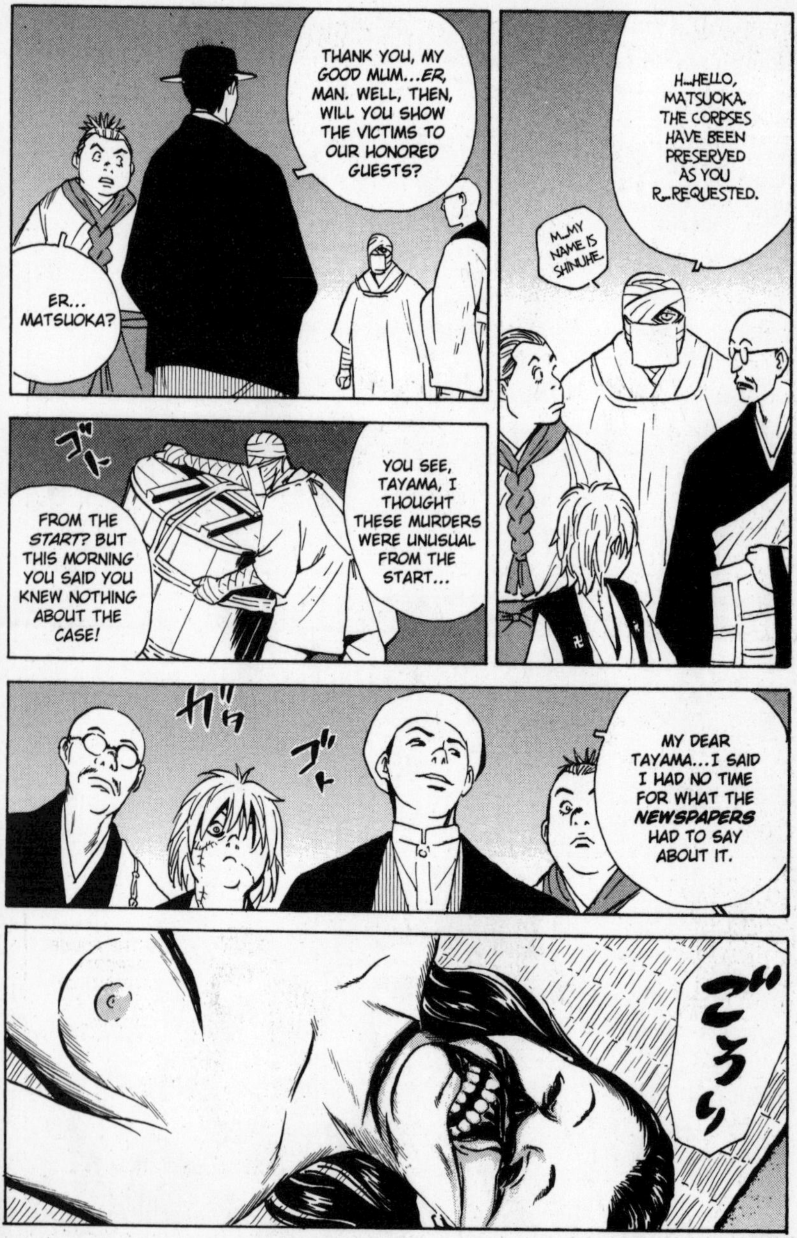
H...HELLO, MATSUOKA. THE CORPSES HAVE BEEN PRESERVED AS YOU R...REQUESTED.
M...MY NAME IS SHINUHE.
THANK YOU, MY GOOD MUM...*ER*, MAN. WELL, THEN, WILL YOU SHOW THE VICTIMS TO OUR HONORED GUESTS?
ER... MATSUOKA?
YOU SEE, TAYAMA, I THOUGHT THESE MURDERS WERE UNUSUAL FROM THE START...
FROM THE *START?* BUT THIS MORNING YOU SAID YOU KNEW NOTHING ABOUT THE CASE!
MY DEAR TAYAMA...I SAID I HAD NO TIME FOR WHAT THE ***NEWSPAPERS*** HAD TO SAY ABOUT IT.

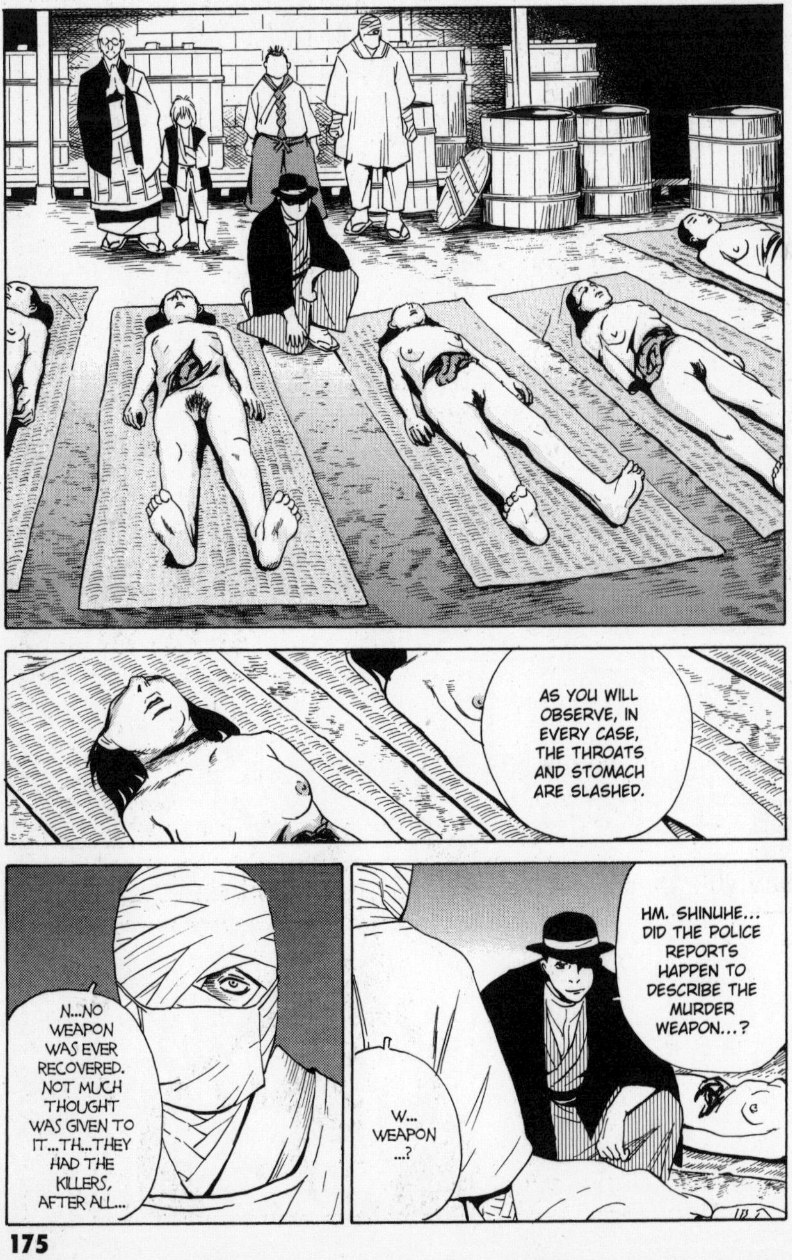
AS YOU WILL OBSERVE, IN EVERY CASE, THE THROATS AND STOMACH ARE SLASHED.
HM. SHINUHE... DID THE POLICE REPORTS HAPPEN TO DESCRIBE THE MURDER WEAPON...?
W... WEAPON ...?
N...NO WEAPON WAS EVER RECOVERED. NOT MUCH THOUGHT WAS GIVEN TO IT...TH...THEY HAD THE KILLERS, AFTER ALL...

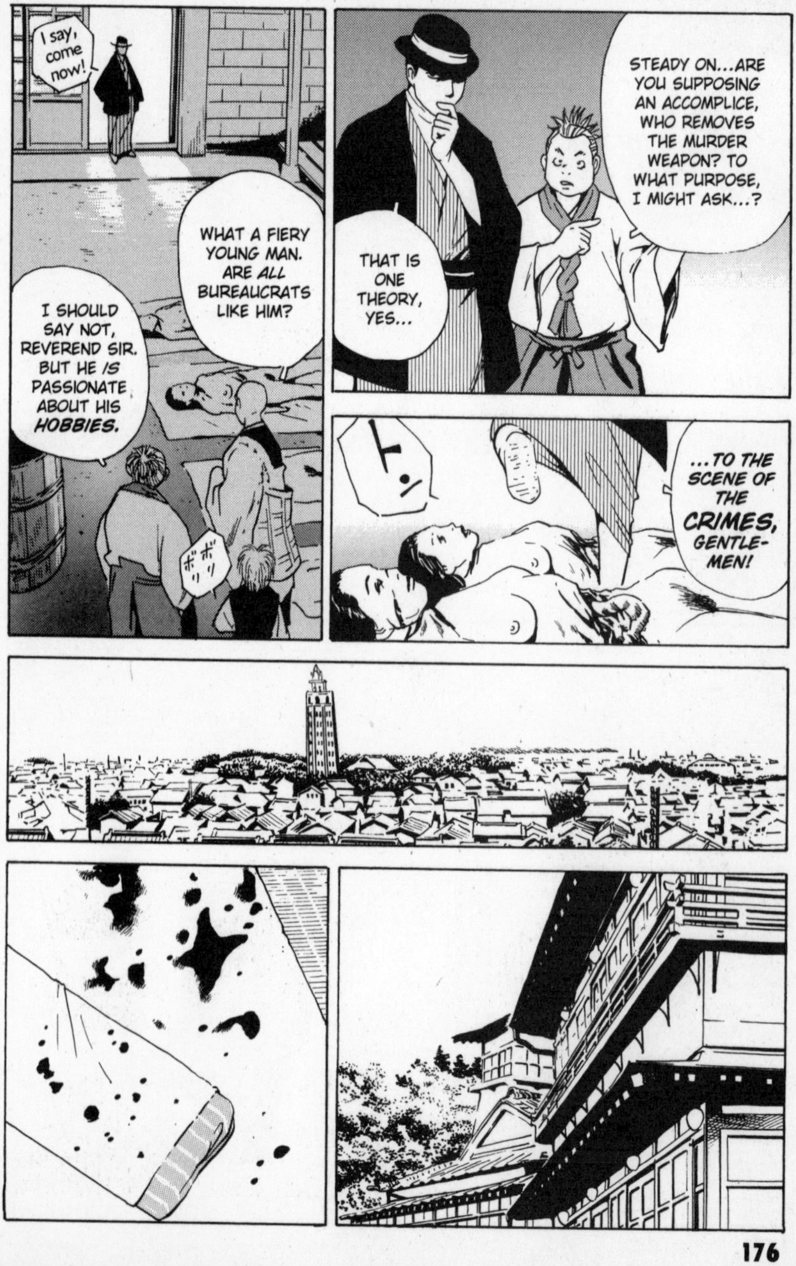

STEADY ON...ARE YOU SUPPOSING AN ACCOMPLICE, WHO REMOVES THE MURDER WEAPON? TO WHAT PURPOSE, I MIGHT ASK...?
THAT IS ONE THEORY, YES...
トン
...TO THE SCENE OF THE CRIMES, GENTLEMEN!
I say, come now!
WHAT A FIERY YOUNG MAN. ARE *ALL* BUREAUCRATS LIKE HIM?
I SHOULD SAY NOT, REVEREND SIR. BUT HE *IS* PASSIONATE ABOUT HIS **HOBBIES.**

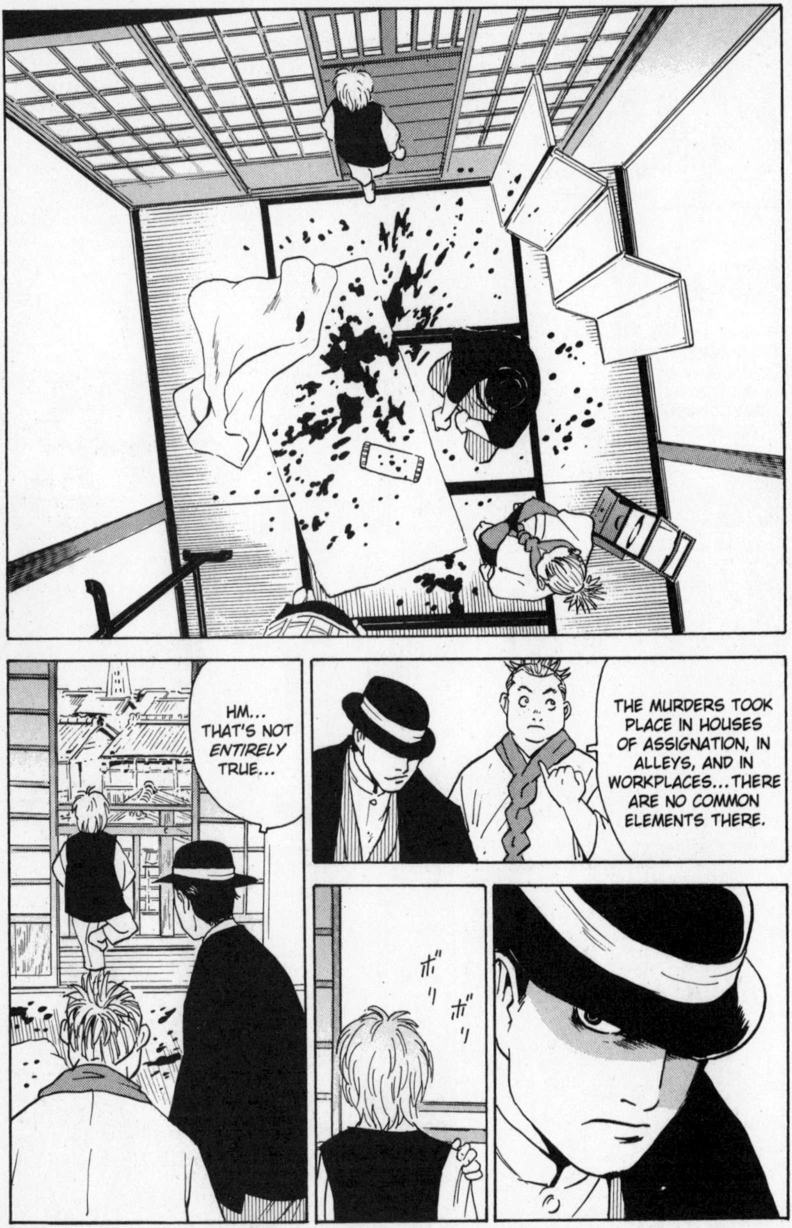
THE MURDERS TOOK PLACE IN HOUSES OF ASSIGNATION, IN ALLEYS, AND IN WORKPLACES...THERE ARE NO COMMON ELEMENTS THERE.
ボリ ボリ
HM... THAT'S NOT *ENTIRELY* TRUE...

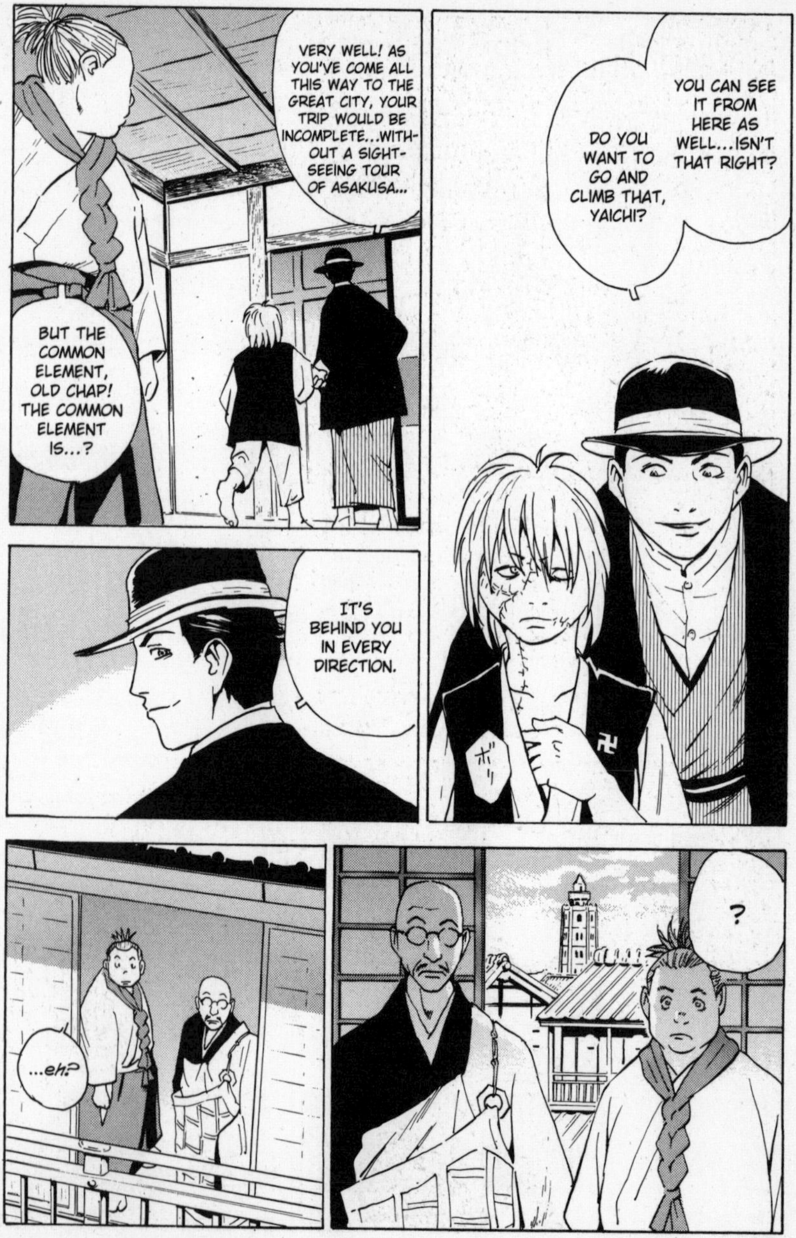
YOU CAN SEE IT FROM HERE AS WELL...ISN'T THAT RIGHT?
DO YOU WANT TO GO AND CLIMB THAT, YAICHI?
ボリ
VERY WELL! AS YOU'VE COME ALL THIS WAY TO THE GREAT CITY, YOUR TRIP WOULD BE INCOMPLETE...WITHOUT A SIGHT-SEEING TOUR OF ASAKUSA...
BUT THE COMMON ELEMENT, OLD CHAP! THE COMMON ELEMENT IS...?
IT'S BEHIND YOU IN EVERY DIRECTION.
?
...eh?

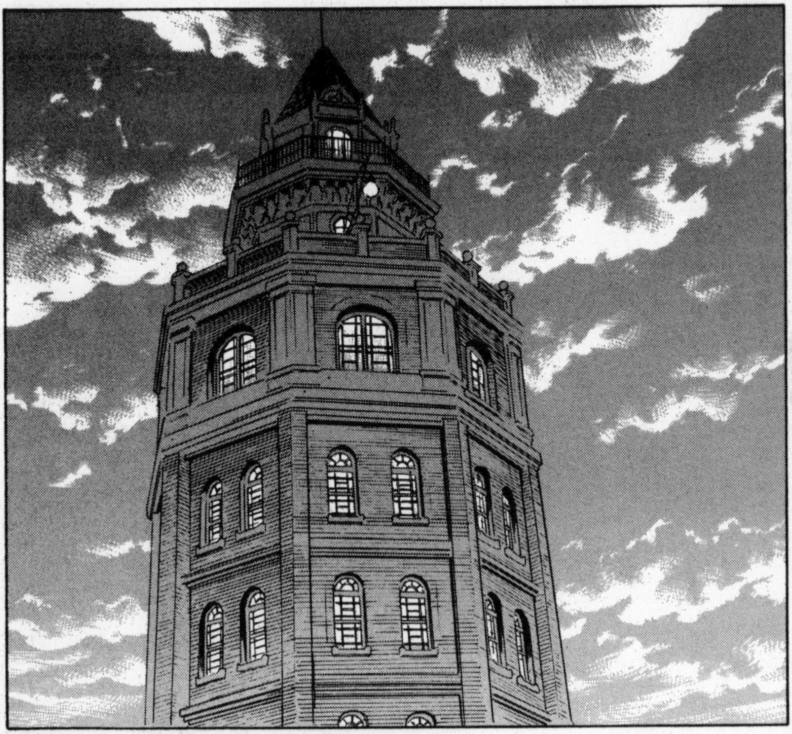

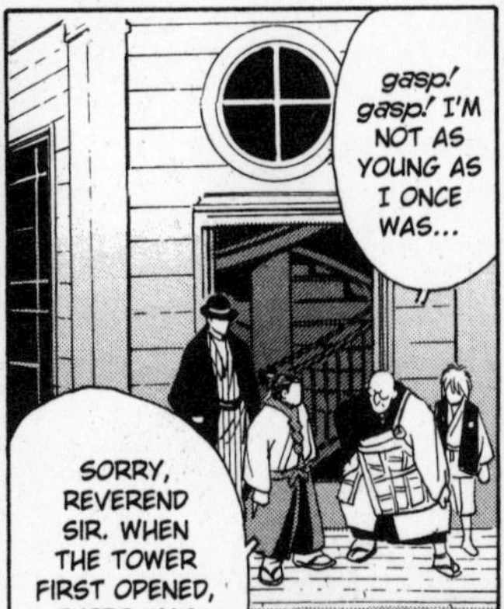
gasp! gasp! I'M NOT AS YOUNG AS I ONCE WAS...
SORRY, REVEREND SIR. WHEN THE TOWER FIRST OPENED, THERE WAS AN ELEVATOR, BUT...

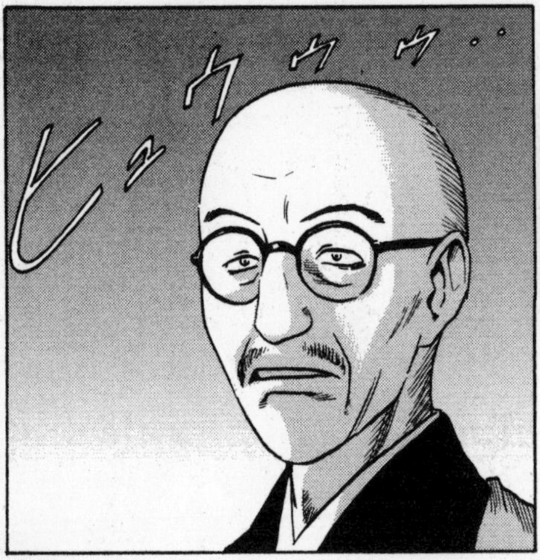
ヒュウゥゥ‥

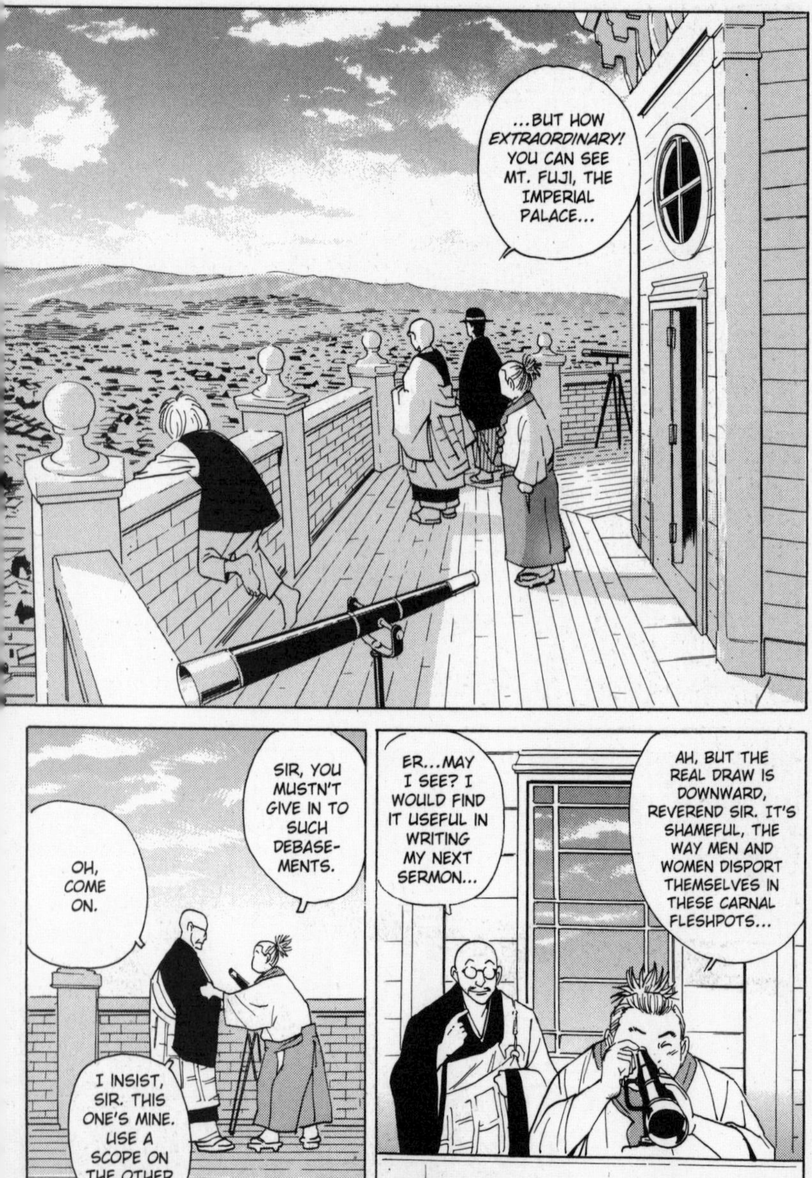
...BUT HOW *EXTRAORDINARY!* YOU CAN SEE MT. FUJI, THE IMPERIAL PALACE...
AH, BUT THE REAL DRAW IS DOWNWARD, REVEREND SIR. IT'S SHAMEFUL, THE WAY MEN AND WOMEN DISPORT THEMSELVES IN THESE CARNAL FLESHPOTS...
ER...MAY I SEE? I WOULD FIND IT USEFUL IN WRITING MY NEXT SERMON...
SIR, YOU MUSTN'T GIVE IN TO SUCH DEBASE-MENTS.
OH, COME ON.
I INSIST, SIR. THIS ONE'S MINE. USE A SCOPE ON THE OTHER SIDE.

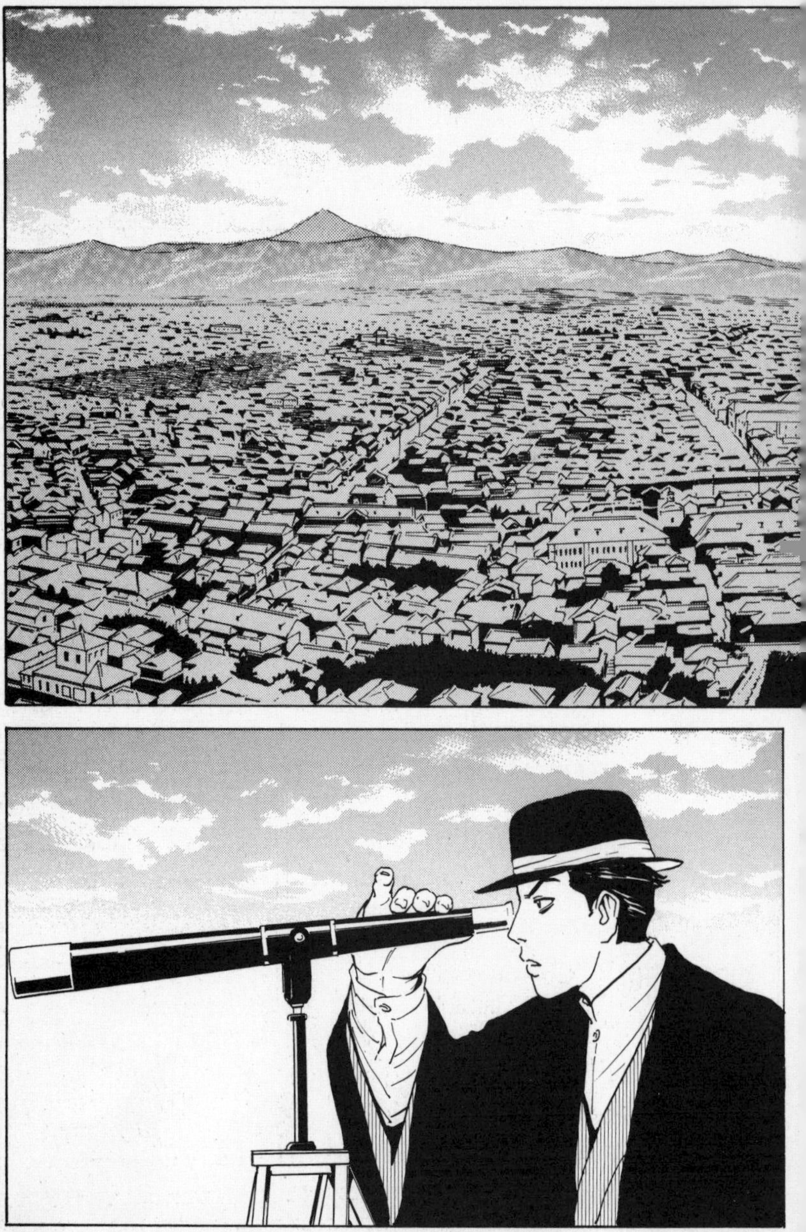

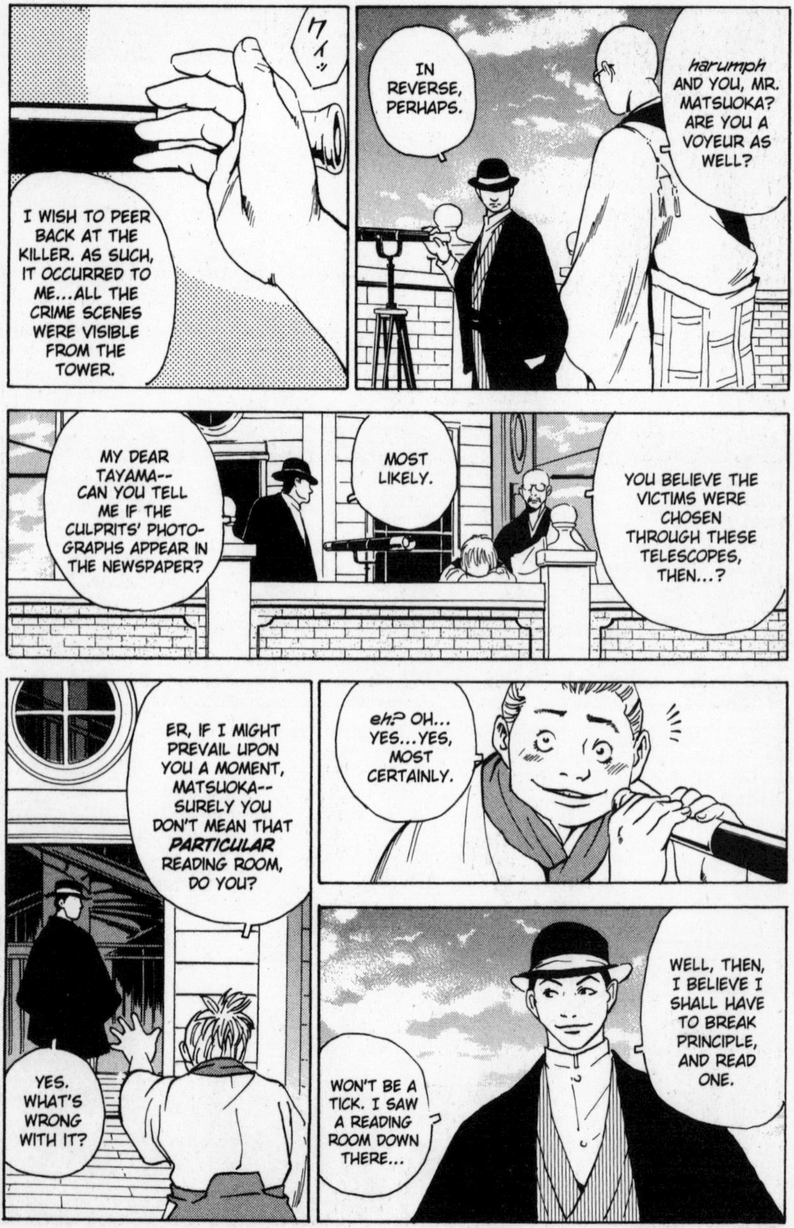
harumph AND YOU, MR. MATSUOKA? ARE YOU A VOYEUR AS WELL?
IN REVERSE, PERHAPS.
I WISH TO PEER BACK AT THE KILLER. AS SUCH, IT OCCURRED TO ME...ALL THE CRIME SCENES WERE VISIBLE FROM THE TOWER.
YOU BELIEVE THE VICTIMS WERE CHOSEN THROUGH THESE TELESCOPES, THEN...?
MOST LIKELY.
MY DEAR TAYAMA-- CAN YOU TELL ME IF THE CULPRITS' PHOTOGRAPHS APPEAR IN THE NEWSPAPER?
eh? OH... YES...YES, MOST CERTAINLY.
WELL, THEN, I BELIEVE I SHALL HAVE TO BREAK PRINCIPLE, AND READ ONE.
WON'T BE A TICK. I SAW A READING ROOM DOWN THERE...
ER, IF I MIGHT PREVAIL UPON YOU A MOMENT, MATSUOKA-- SURELY YOU DON'T MEAN THAT PARTICULAR READING ROOM, DO YOU?
YES. WHAT'S WRONG WITH IT?

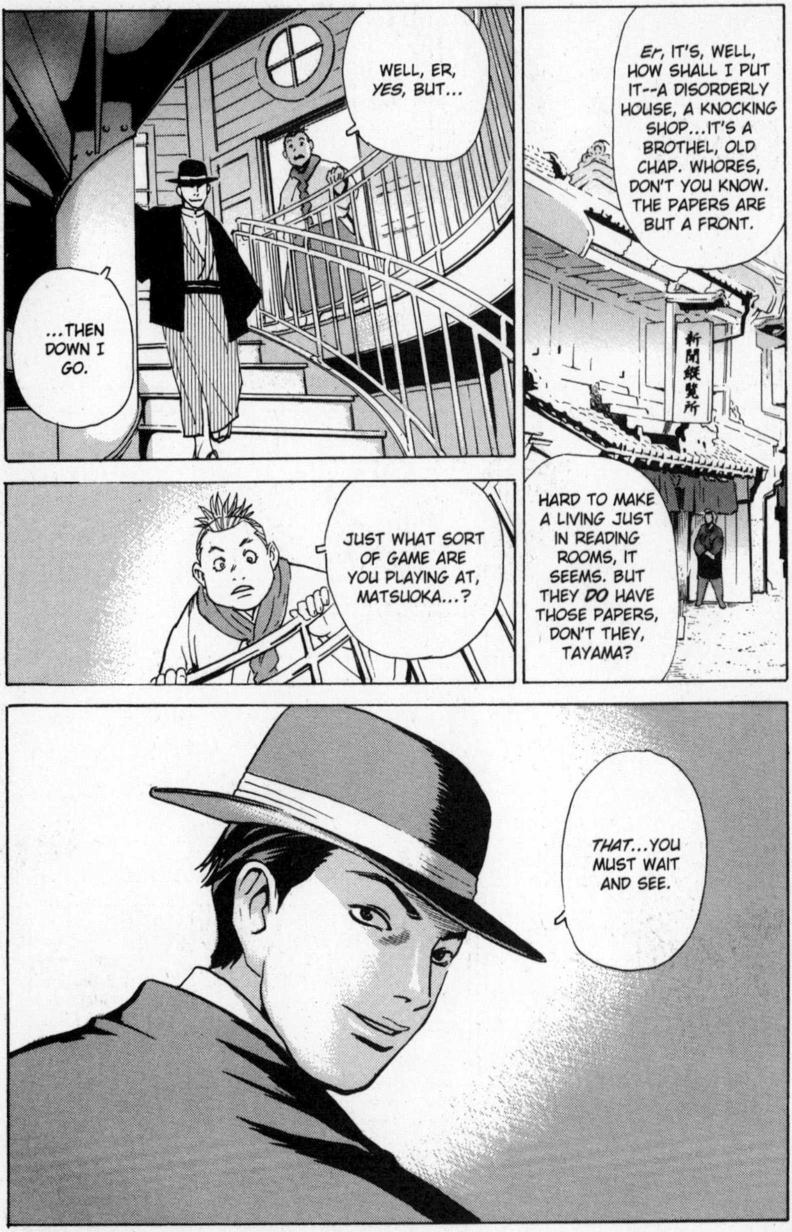

Er, IT'S, WELL, HOW SHALL I PUT IT--A DISORDERLY HOUSE, A KNOCKING SHOP...IT'S A BROTHEL, OLD CHAP. WHORES, DON'T YOU KNOW. THE PAPERS ARE BUT A FRONT.
新聞縦覧所
HARD TO MAKE A LIVING JUST IN READING ROOMS, IT SEEMS. BUT THEY *DO* HAVE THOSE PAPERS, DON'T THEY, TAYAMA?
WELL, ER, *YES*, BUT...
...THEN DOWN I GO.
JUST WHAT SORT OF GAME ARE YOU PLAYING AT, MATSUOKA...?
THAT...YOU MUST WAIT AND SEE.

5th delivery: like a child • kunio matsuoka demon hunting side story (part one)—the end

6th delivery

too long a spring

永すぎた春

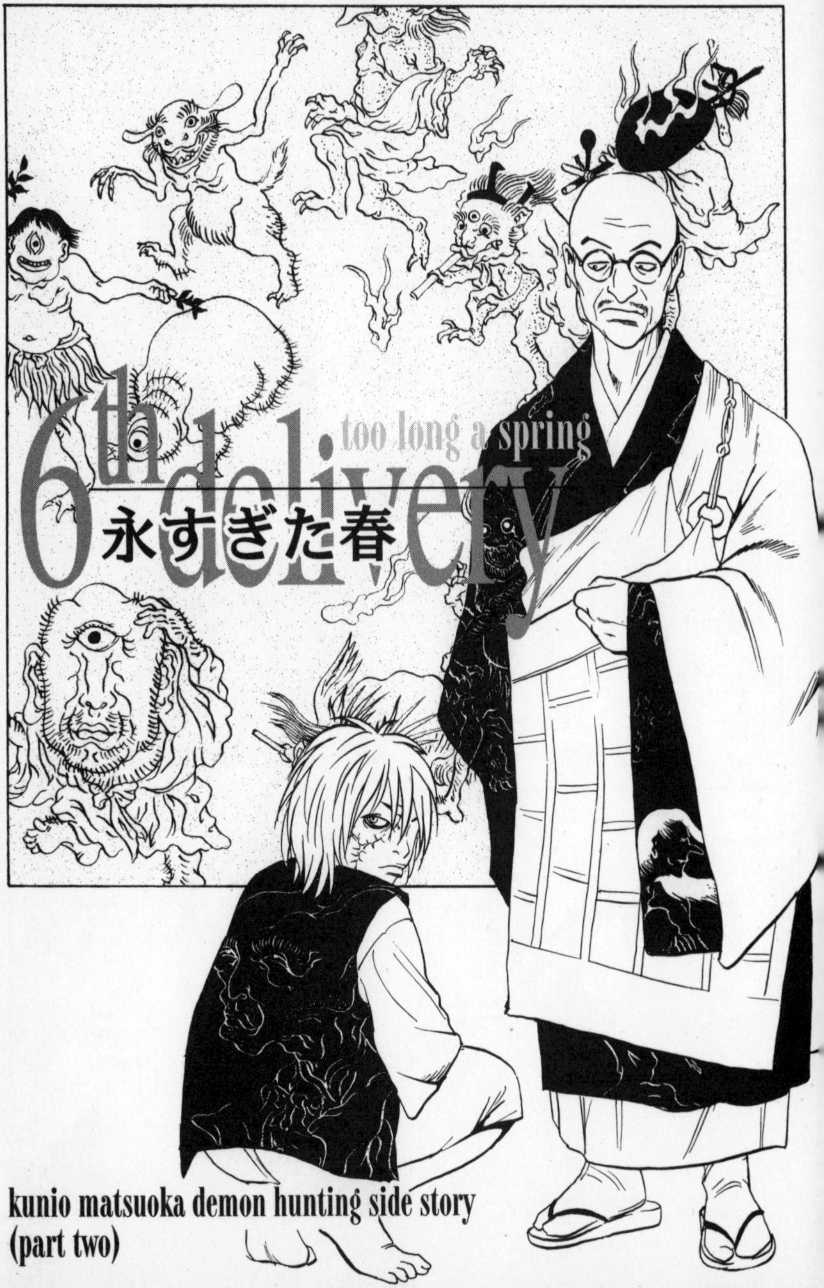

kunio matsuoka demon hunting side story (part two)

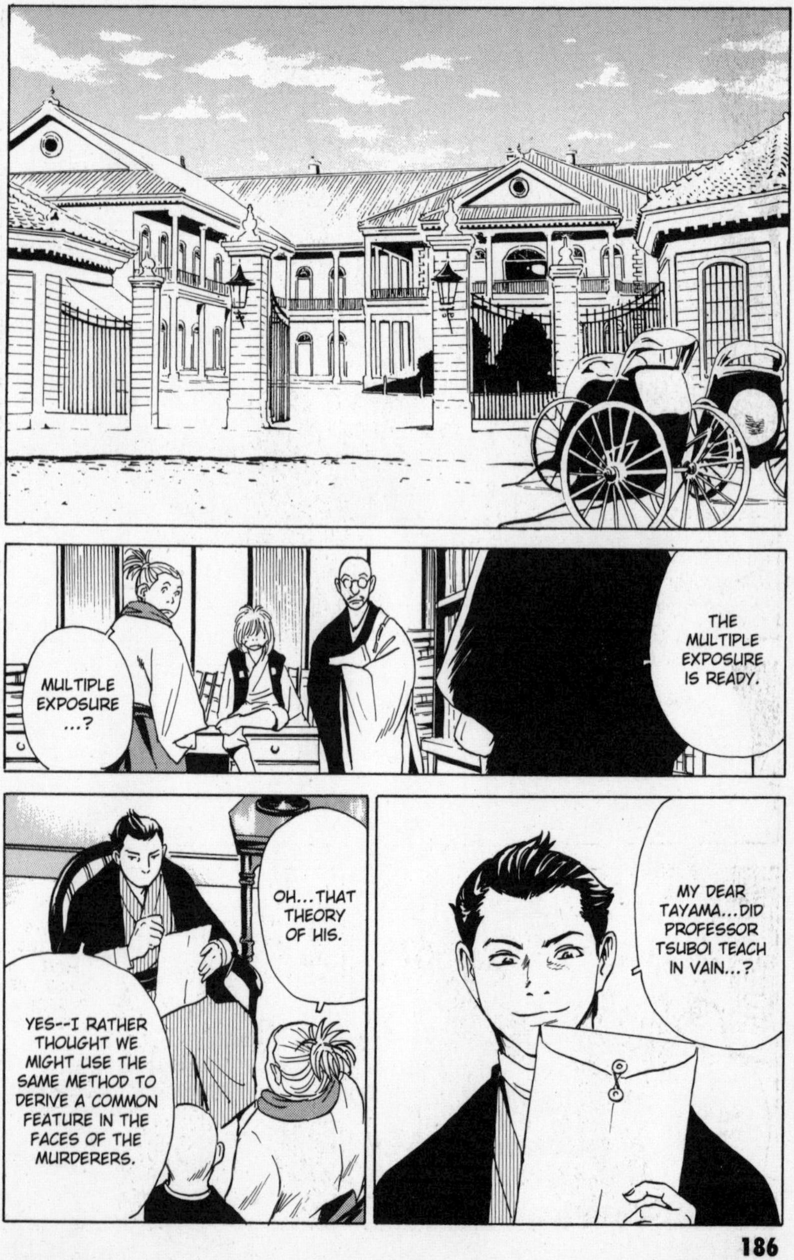
THE MULTIPLE EXPOSURE IS READY.
MULTIPLE EXPOSURE ...?
MY DEAR TAYAMA...DID PROFESSOR TSUBOI TEACH IN VAIN...?
OH...THAT THEORY OF HIS.
YES--I RATHER THOUGHT WE MIGHT USE THE SAME METHOD TO DERIVE A COMMON FEATURE IN THE FACES OF THE MURDERERS.

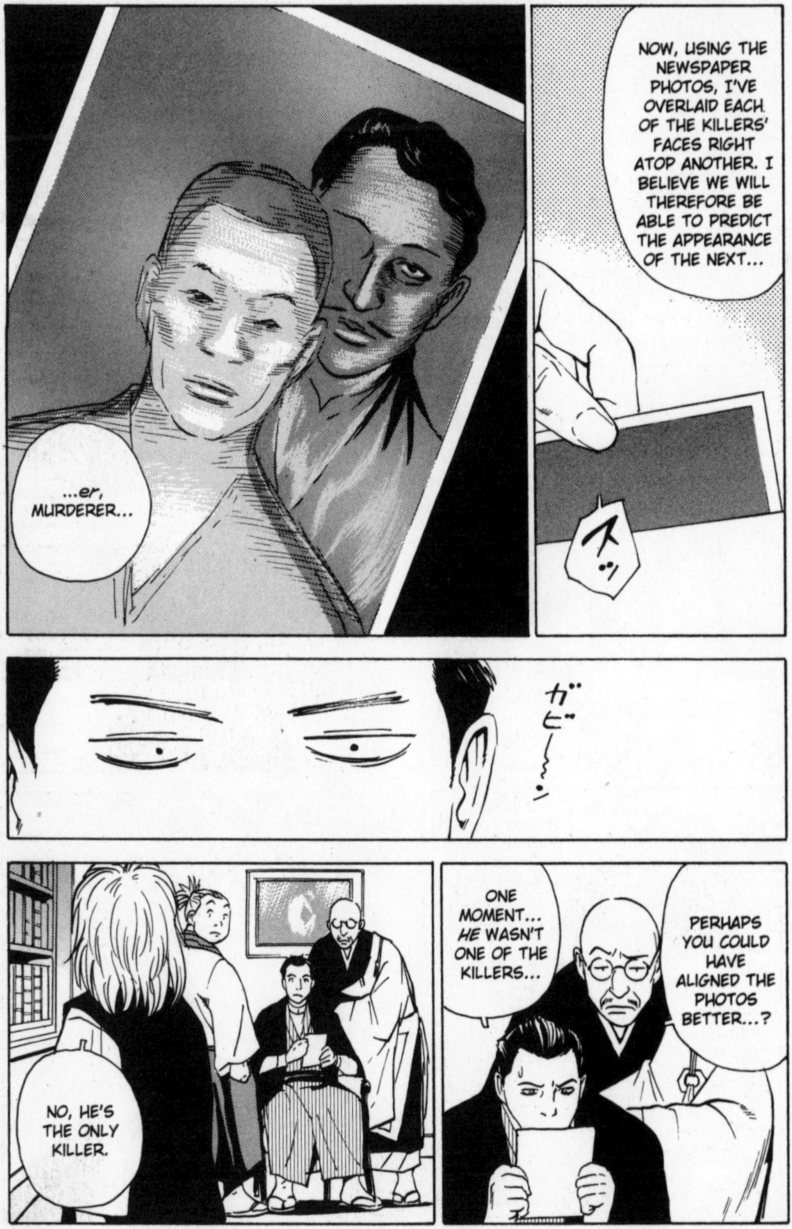
NOW, USING THE NEWSPAPER PHOTOS, I'VE OVERLAID EACH OF THE KILLERS' FACES RIGHT ATOP ANOTHER. I BELIEVE WE WILL THEREFORE BE ABLE TO PREDICT THE APPEARANCE OF THE NEXT...
スッ
...er, MURDERER...
ガビ〜ん
PERHAPS YOU COULD HAVE ALIGNED THE PHOTOS BETTER...?
ONE MOMENT... *HE* WASN'T ONE OF THE KILLERS...
NO, HE'S THE ONLY KILLER.

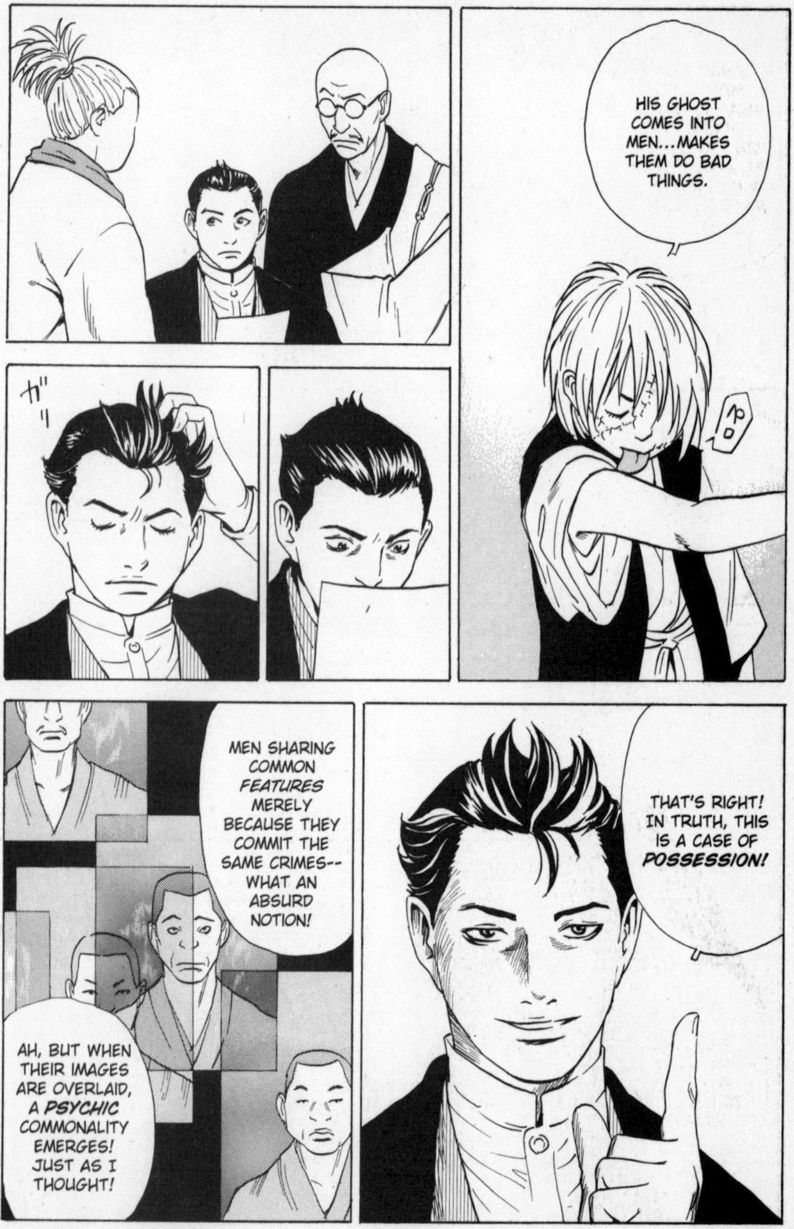
HIS GHOST COMES INTO MEN...MAKES THEM DO BAD THINGS.
ペロ
ガリ
THAT'S RIGHT! IN TRUTH, THIS IS A CASE OF ***POSSESSION!***
MEN SHARING COMMON *FEATURES* MERELY BECAUSE THEY COMMIT THE SAME CRIMES--WHAT AN ABSURD NOTION!
AH, BUT WHEN THEIR IMAGES ARE OVERLAID, A ***PSYCHIC*** COMMONALITY EMERGES! JUST AS I THOUGHT!

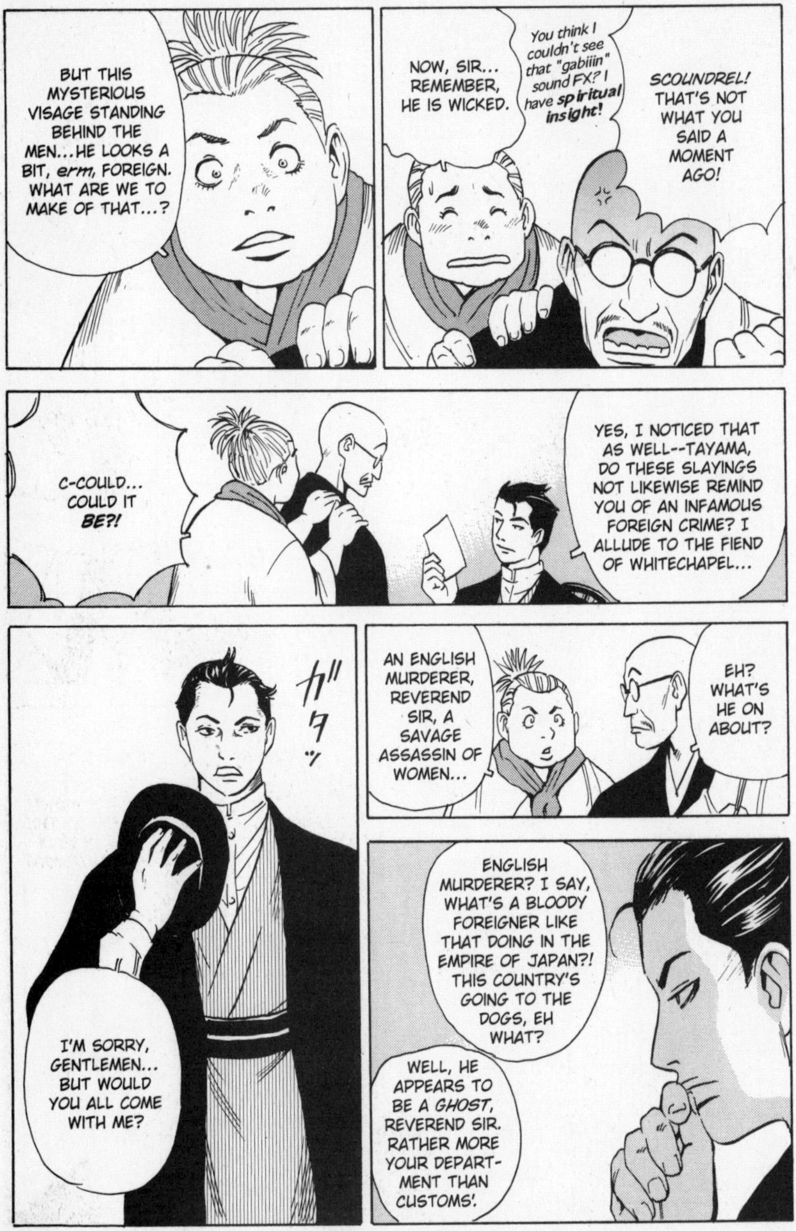
NOW, SIR... REMEMBER, HE IS WICKED.
You think I couldn't see that "gabiiin" sound FX? I have **spiritual insight!**
SCOUNDREL! THAT'S NOT WHAT YOU SAID A MOMENT AGO!
BUT THIS MYSTERIOUS VISAGE STANDING BEHIND THE MEN...HE LOOKS A BIT, *erm*, FOREIGN. WHAT ARE WE TO MAKE OF THAT...?
YES, I NOTICED THAT AS WELL--TAYAMA, DO THESE SLAYINGS NOT LIKEWISE REMIND YOU OF AN INFAMOUS FOREIGN CRIME? I ALLUDE TO THE FIEND OF WHITECHAPEL...
C-COULD... COULD IT *BE?!*
EH? WHAT'S HE ON ABOUT?
AN ENGLISH MURDERER, REVEREND SIR, A SAVAGE ASSASSIN OF WOMEN...
ENGLISH MURDERER? I SAY, WHAT'S A BLOODY FOREIGNER LIKE THAT DOING IN THE EMPIRE OF JAPAN?! THIS COUNTRY'S GOING TO THE DOGS, EH WHAT?
WELL, HE APPEARS TO BE A *GHOST*, REVEREND SIR. RATHER MORE YOUR DEPART-MENT THAN CUSTOMS.
ガタッ
I'M SORRY, GENTLEMEN... BUT WOULD YOU ALL COME WITH ME?

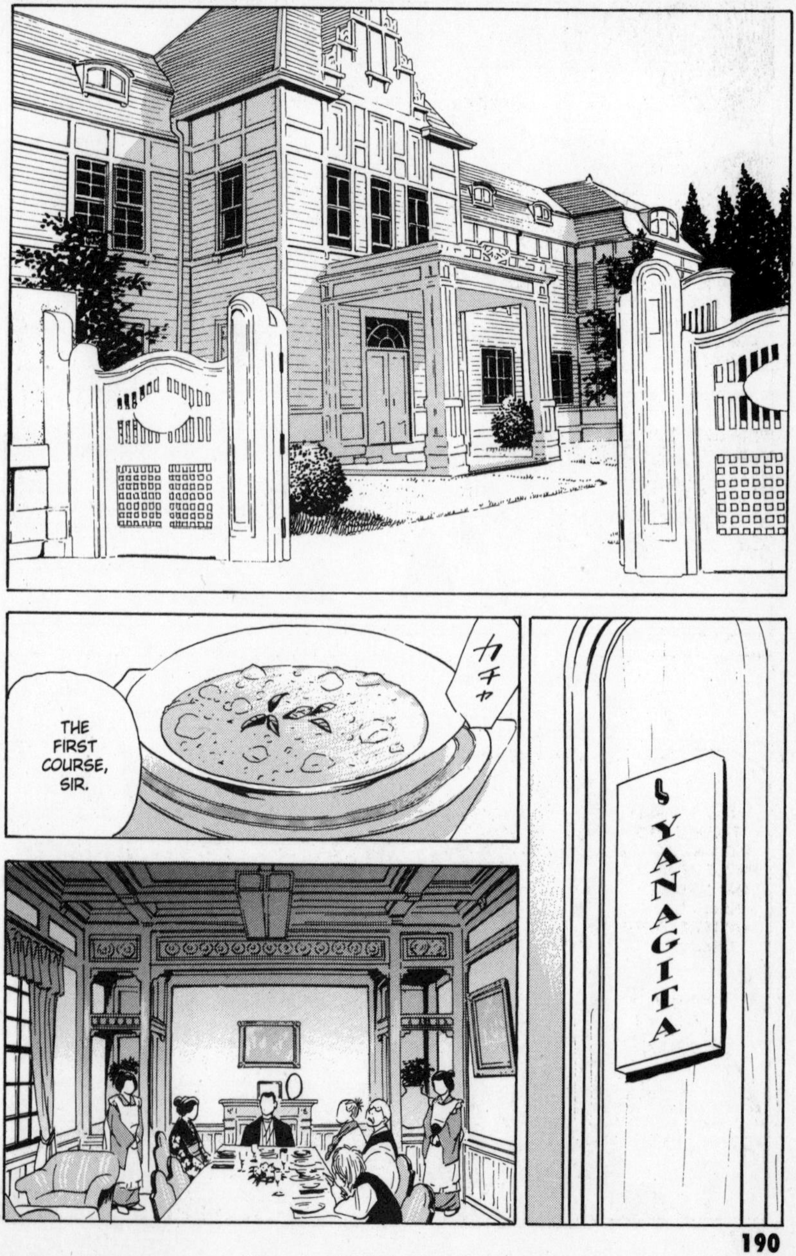
YANAGITA
カチャ
THE FIRST COURSE, SIR.

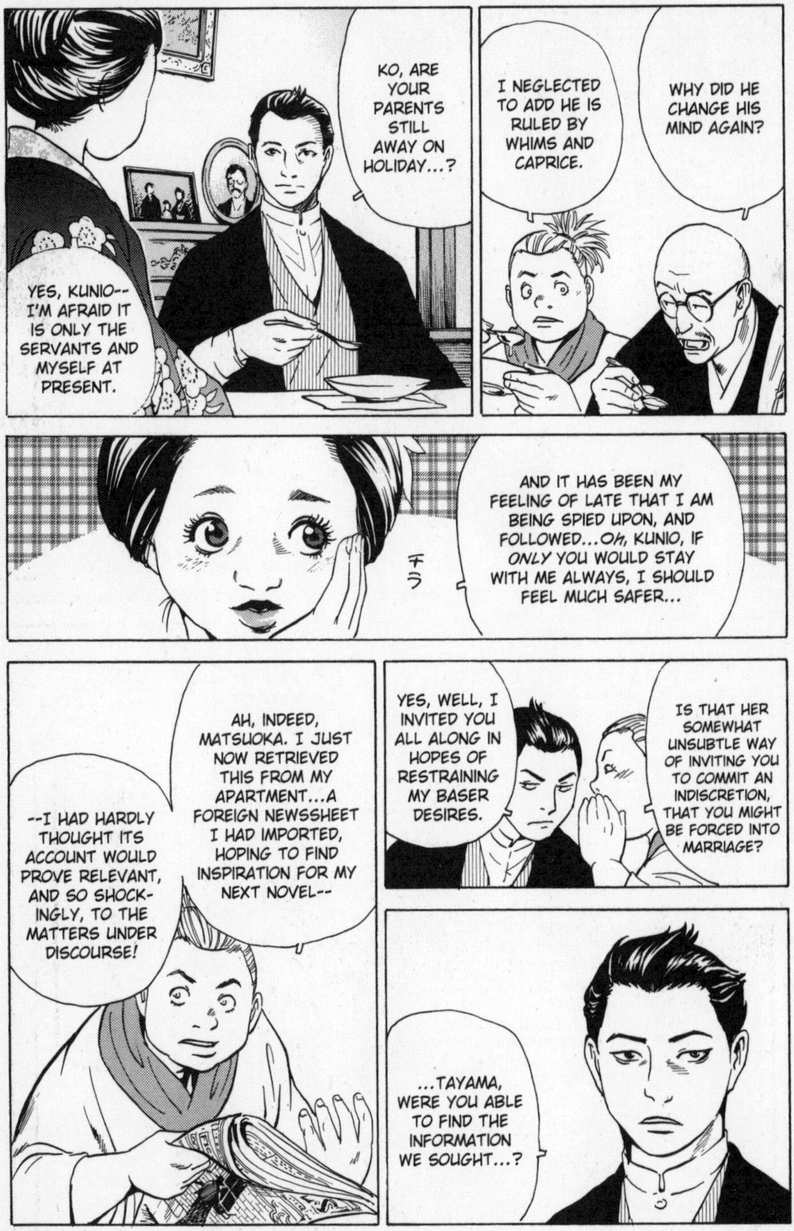
WHY DID HE CHANGE HIS MIND AGAIN?
I NEGLECTED TO ADD HE IS RULED BY WHIMS AND CAPRICE.
KO, ARE YOUR PARENTS STILL AWAY ON HOLIDAY...?
YES, KUNIO-- I'M AFRAID IT IS ONLY THE SERVANTS AND MYSELF AT PRESENT.
AND IT HAS BEEN MY FEELING OF LATE THAT I AM BEING SPIED UPON, AND FOLLOWED...*OH*, KUNIO, IF *ONLY* YOU WOULD STAY WITH ME ALWAYS, I SHOULD FEEL MUCH SAFER...
チラ
IS THAT HER SOMEWHAT UNSUBTLE WAY OF INVITING YOU TO COMMIT AN INDISCRETION, THAT YOU MIGHT BE FORCED INTO MARRIAGE?
YES, WELL, I INVITED YOU ALL ALONG IN HOPES OF RESTRAINING MY BASER DESIRES.
...TAYAMA, WERE YOU ABLE TO FIND THE INFORMATION WE SOUGHT...?
AH, INDEED, MATSUOKA. I JUST NOW RETRIEVED THIS FROM MY APARTMENT...A FOREIGN NEWSSHEET I HAD IMPORTED, HOPING TO FIND INSPIRATION FOR MY NEXT NOVEL--
--I HAD HARDLY THOUGHT ITS ACCOUNT WOULD PROVE RELEVANT, AND SO SHOCKINGLY, TO THE MATTERS UNDER DISCOURSE!

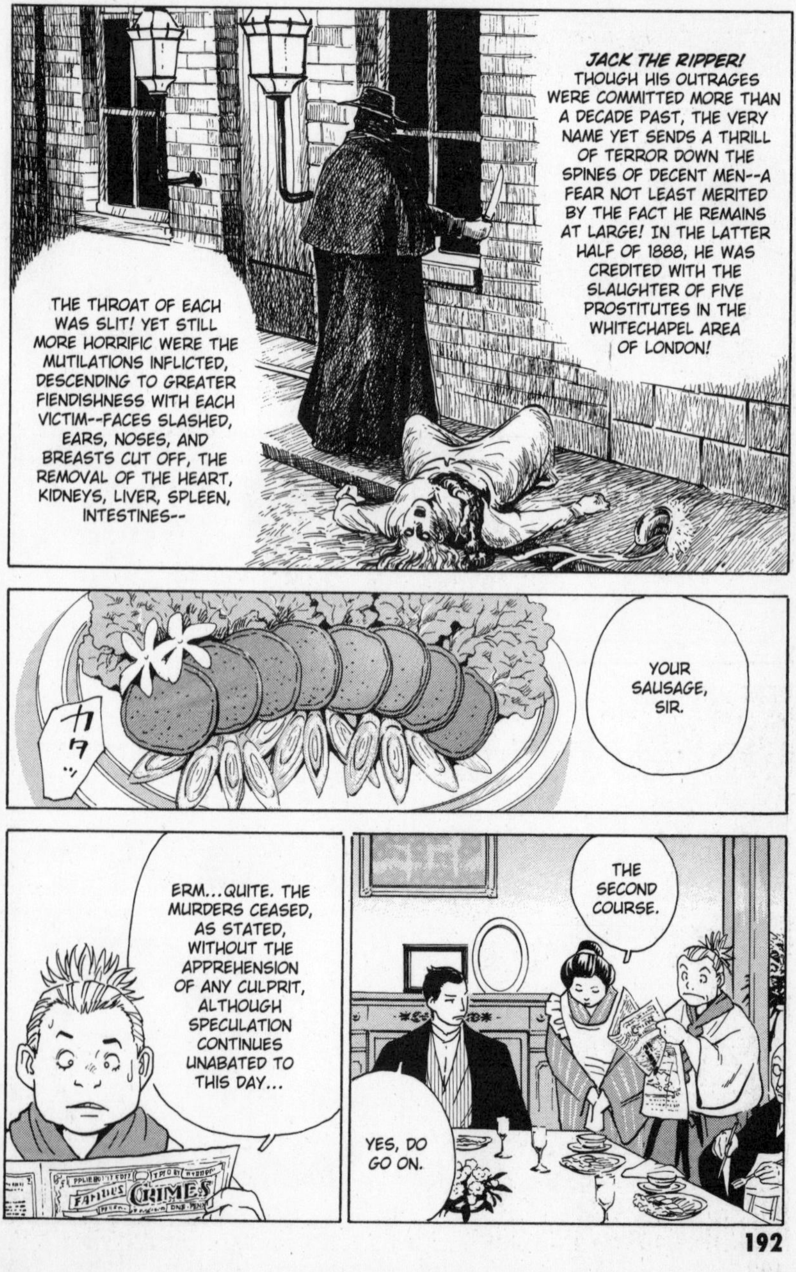
JACK THE RIPPER! THOUGH HIS OUTRAGES WERE COMMITTED MORE THAN A DECADE PAST, THE VERY NAME YET SENDS A THRILL OF TERROR DOWN THE SPINES OF DECENT MEN--A FEAR NOT LEAST MERITED BY THE FACT HE REMAINS AT LARGE! IN THE LATTER HALF OF 1888, HE WAS CREDITED WITH THE SLAUGHTER OF FIVE PROSTITUTES IN THE WHITECHAPEL AREA OF LONDON!
THE THROAT OF EACH WAS SLIT! YET STILL MORE HORRIFIC WERE THE MUTILATIONS INFLICTED, DESCENDING TO GREATER FIENDISHNESS WITH EACH VICTIM--FACES SLASHED, EARS, NOSES, AND BREASTS CUT OFF, THE REMOVAL OF THE HEART, KIDNEYS, LIVER, SPLEEN, INTESTINES--
YOUR SAUSAGE, SIR.
カタッ
THE SECOND COURSE.
YES, DO GO ON.
ERM...QUITE. THE MURDERS CEASED, AS STATED, WITHOUT THE APPREHENSION OF ANY CULPRIT, ALTHOUGH SPECULATION CONTINUES UNABATED TO THIS DAY...
FAMOUS CRIMES

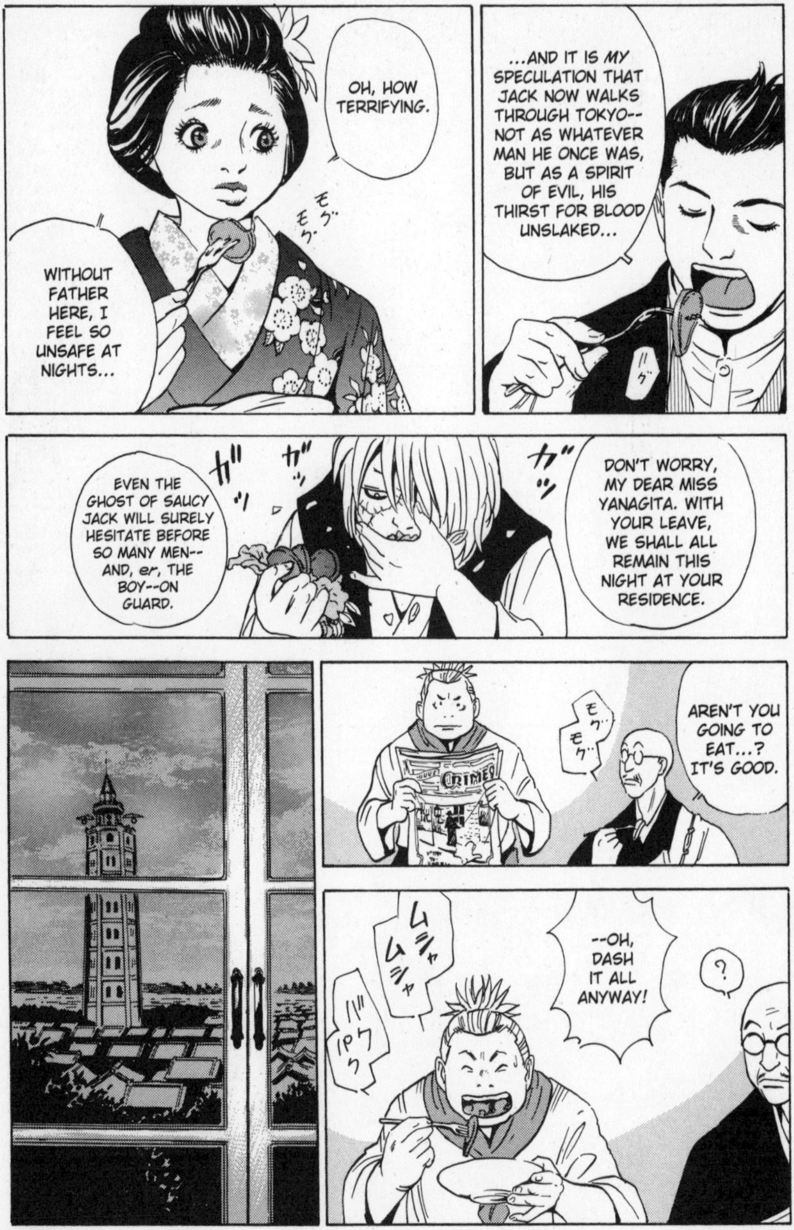
...AND IT IS MY SPECULATION THAT JACK NOW WALKS THROUGH TOKYO--NOT AS WHATEVER MAN HE ONCE WAS, BUT AS A SPIRIT OF EVIL, HIS THIRST FOR BLOOD UNSLAKED...
OH, HOW TERRIFYING.
モグモグ
WITHOUT FATHER HERE, I FEEL SO UNSAFE AT NIGHTS...
ガツ
DON'T WORRY, MY DEAR MISS YANAGITA. WITH YOUR LEAVE, WE SHALL ALL REMAIN THIS NIGHT AT YOUR RESIDENCE.
ガツ
ガツ
EVEN THE GHOST OF SAUCY JACK WILL SURELY HESITATE BEFORE SO MANY MEN--AND, er, THE BOY--ON GUARD.
AREN'T YOU GOING TO EAT...? IT'S GOOD.
モグ.. モグ..
CRIMES
?
--OH, DASH IT ALL ANYWAY!
ムシャムシャ

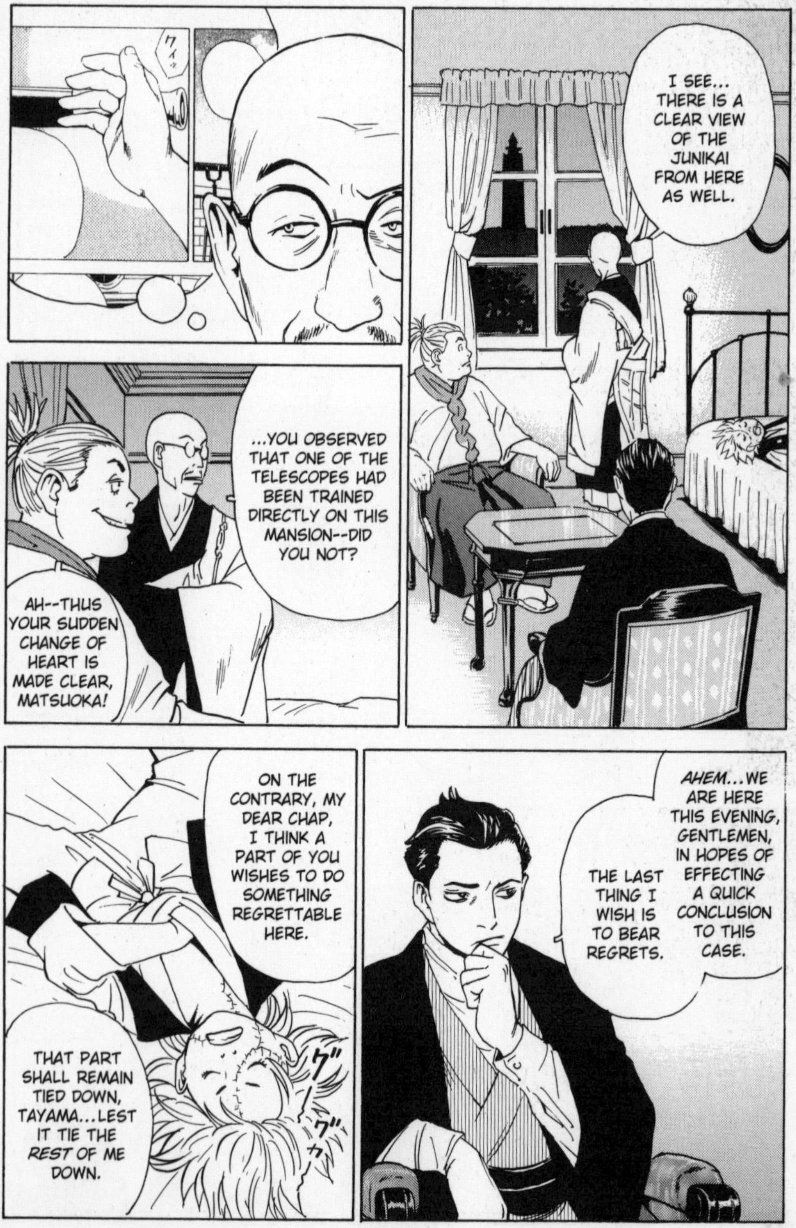
I SEE... THERE IS A CLEAR VIEW OF THE JUNIKAI FROM HERE AS WELL.
...YOU OBSERVED THAT ONE OF THE TELESCOPES HAD BEEN TRAINED DIRECTLY ON THIS MANSION--DID YOU NOT?
AH--THUS YOUR SUDDEN CHANGE OF HEART IS MADE CLEAR, MATSUOKA!
AHEM...WE ARE HERE THIS EVENING, GENTLEMEN, IN HOPES OF EFFECTING A QUICK CONCLUSION TO THIS CASE.
THE LAST THING I WISH IS TO BEAR REGRETS.
ON THE CONTRARY, MY DEAR CHAP, I THINK A PART OF YOU WISHES TO DO SOMETHING REGRETTABLE HERE.
THAT PART SHALL REMAIN TIED DOWN, TAYAMA...LEST IT TIE THE *REST* OF ME DOWN.

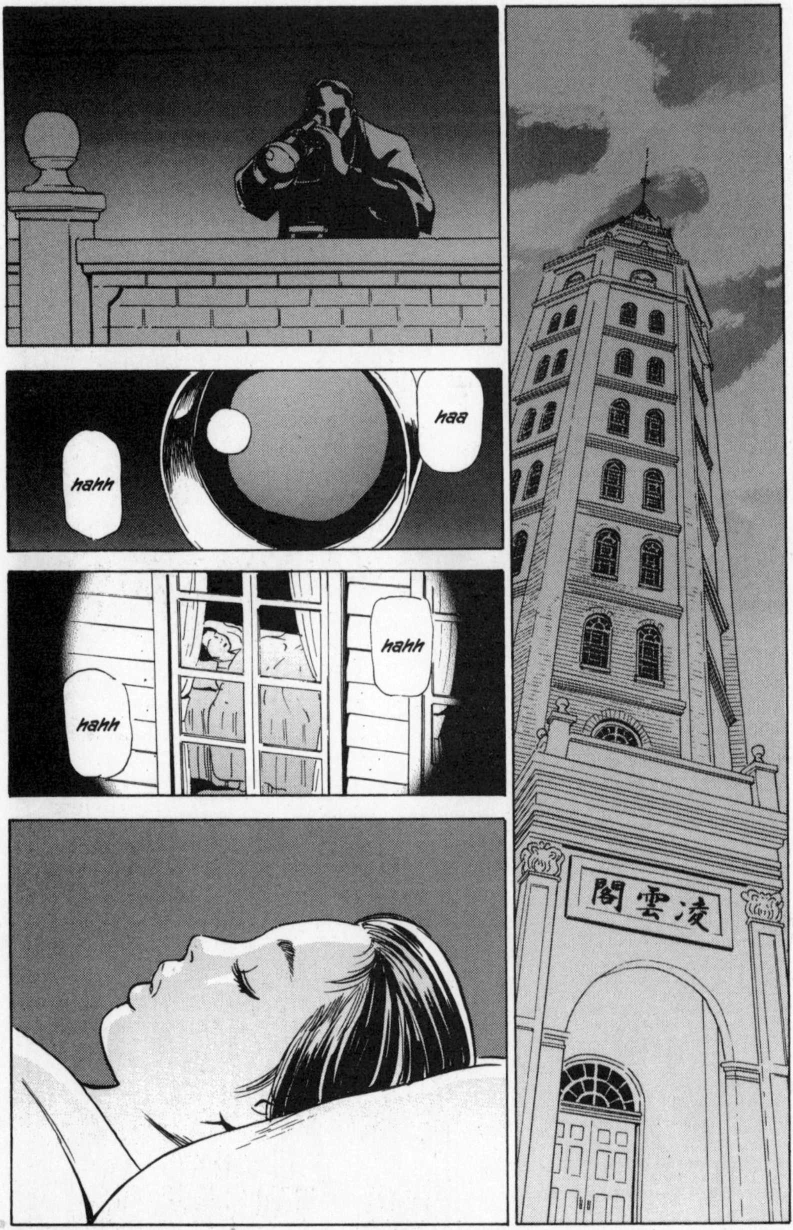
凌雲閣
haa
hahh
hahh
hahh

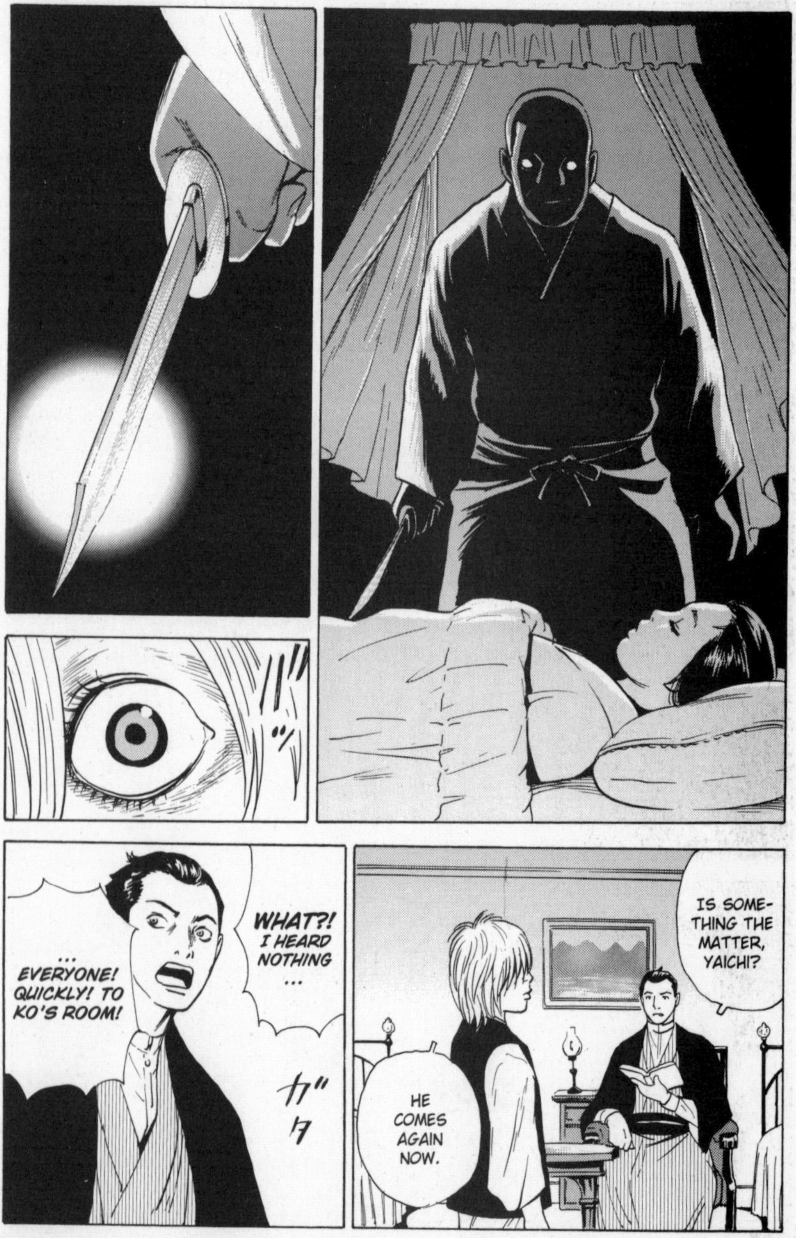
ッ
IS SOME-THING THE MATTER, YAICHI?
HE COMES AGAIN NOW.
WHAT?! I HEARD NOTHING ...
... EVERYONE! QUICKLY! TO KO'S ROOM!
ガタ

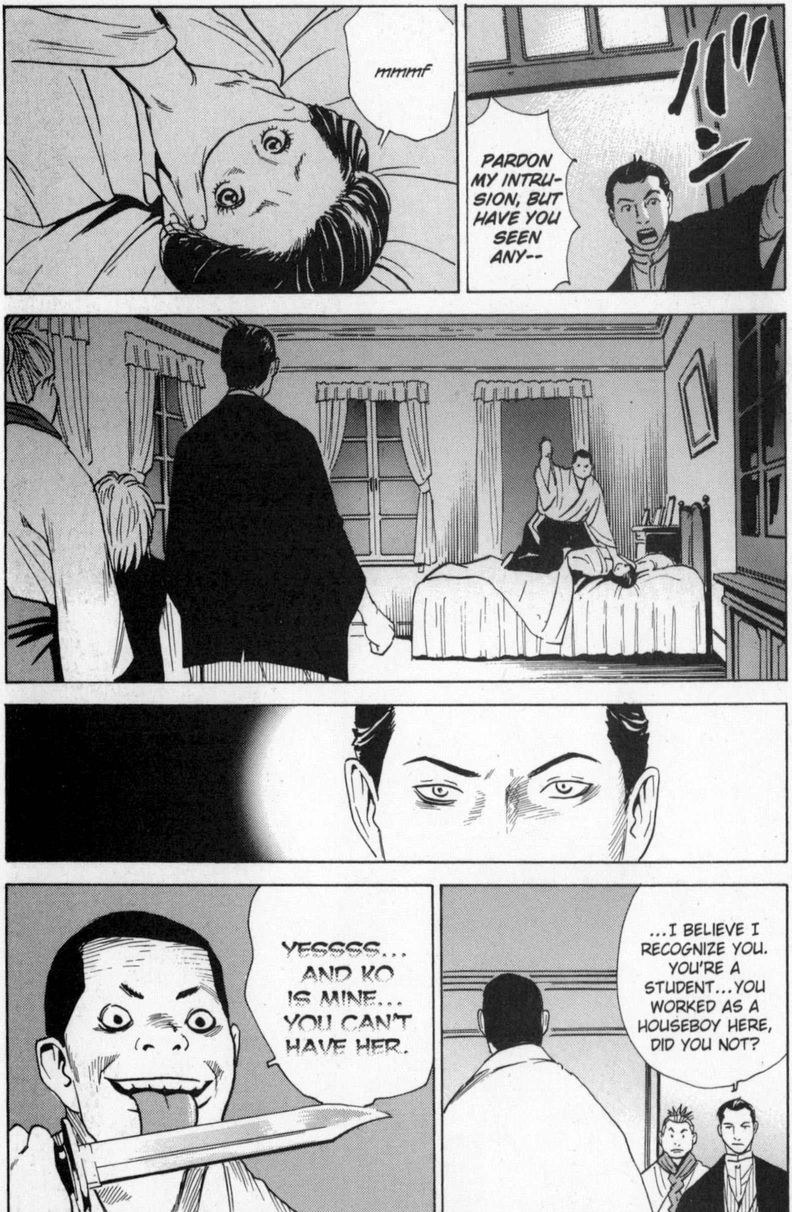
PARDON MY INTRU-SION, BUT HAVE YOU SEEN ANY--
mmmf
...I BELIEVE I RECOGNIZE YOU. YOU'RE A STUDENT...YOU WORKED AS A HOUSEBOY HERE, DID YOU NOT?
YESSSS... AND KO IS MINE... YOU CAN'T HAVE HER.

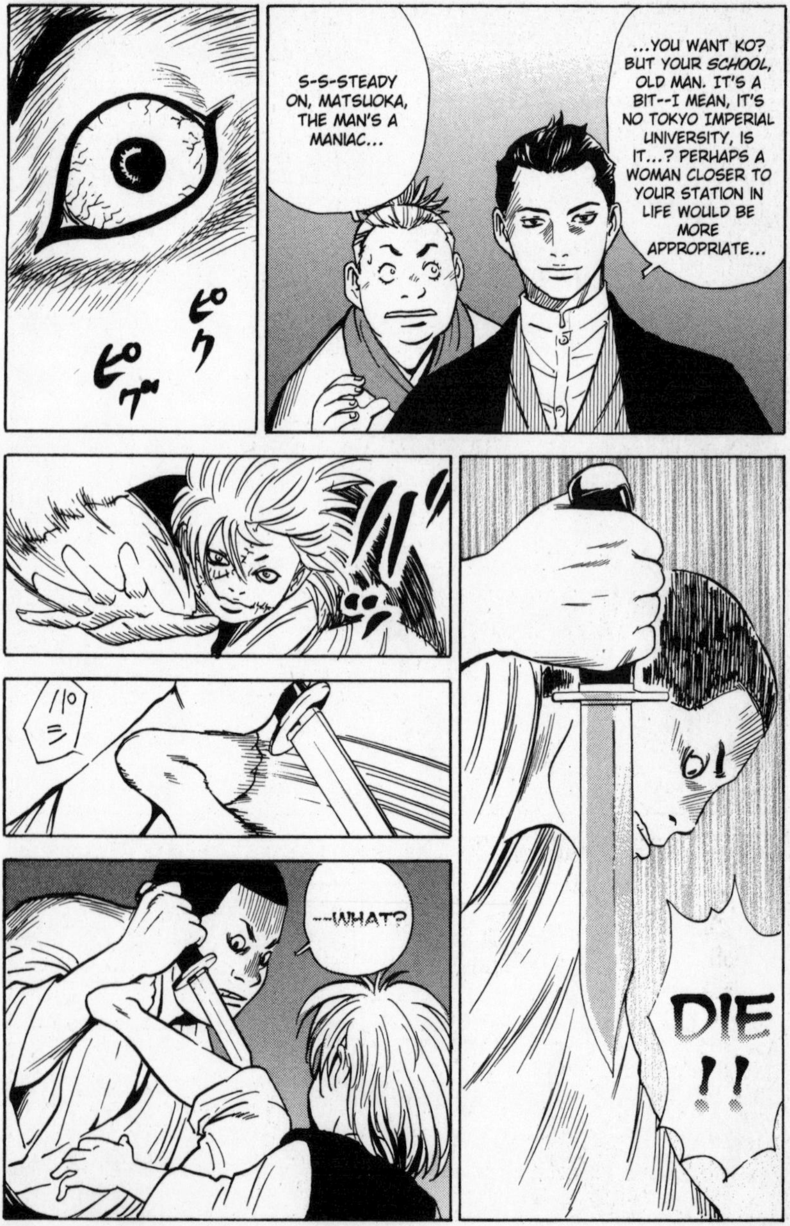
...YOU WANT KO? BUT YOUR *SCHOOL*, OLD MAN. IT'S A BIT--I MEAN, IT'S NO TOKYO IMPERIAL UNIVERSITY, IS IT...? PERHAPS A WOMAN CLOSER TO YOUR STATION IN LIFE WOULD BE MORE APPROPRIATE...
S-S-STEADY ON, MATSUOKA, THE MAN'S A MANIAC...
ピク
DIE!!
パシ
--WHAT?

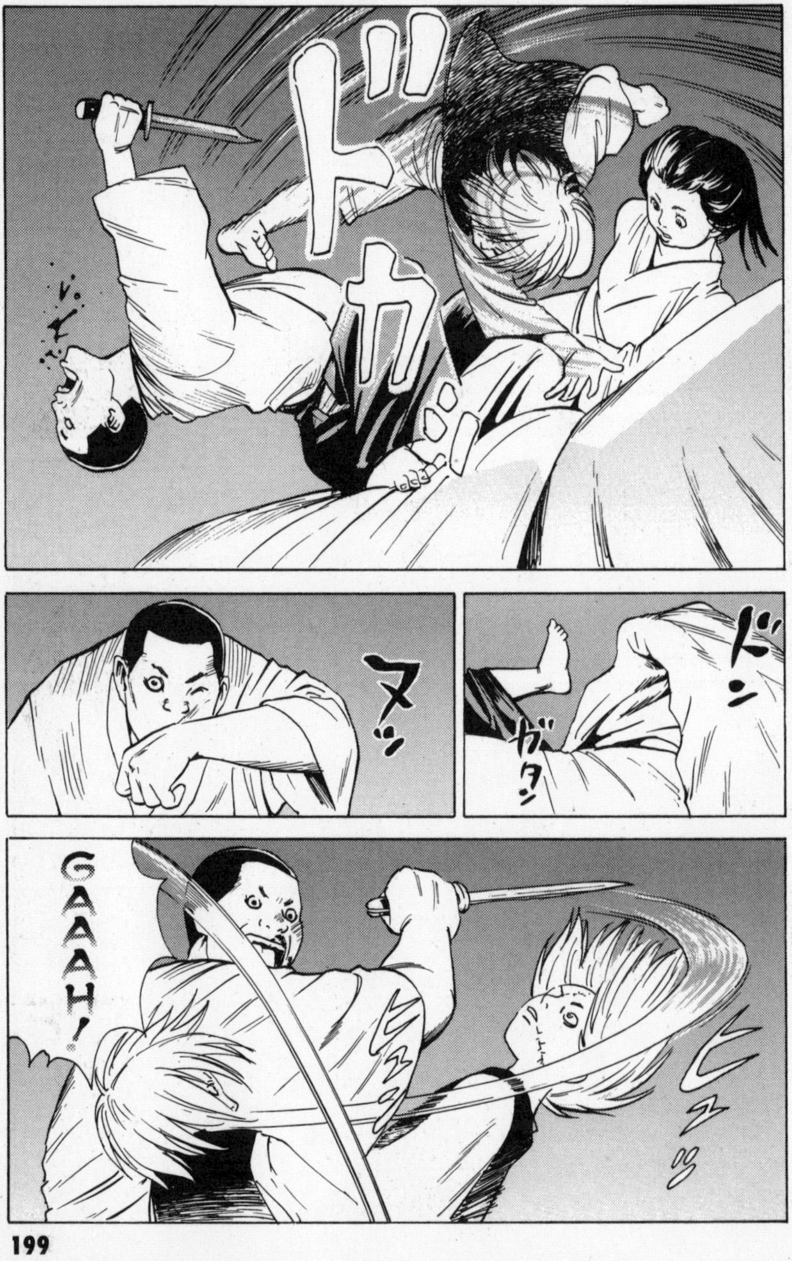
ドカッ
ドン
ガタン
ヌッ
GAAAH!

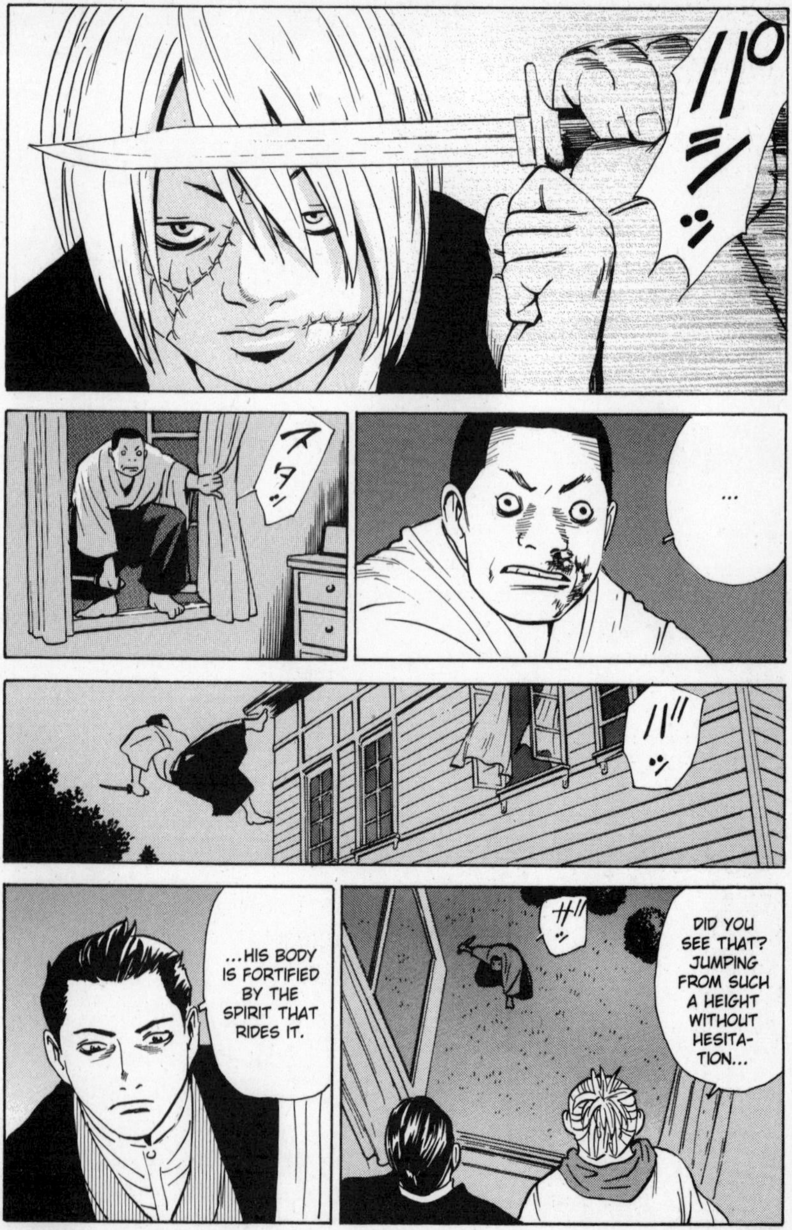

パシッ
...
スタッ
バッ
DID YOU SEE THAT? JUMPING FROM SUCH A HEIGHT WITHOUT HESITATION...
ザッ
...HIS BODY IS FORTIFIED BY THE SPIRIT THAT RIDES IT.

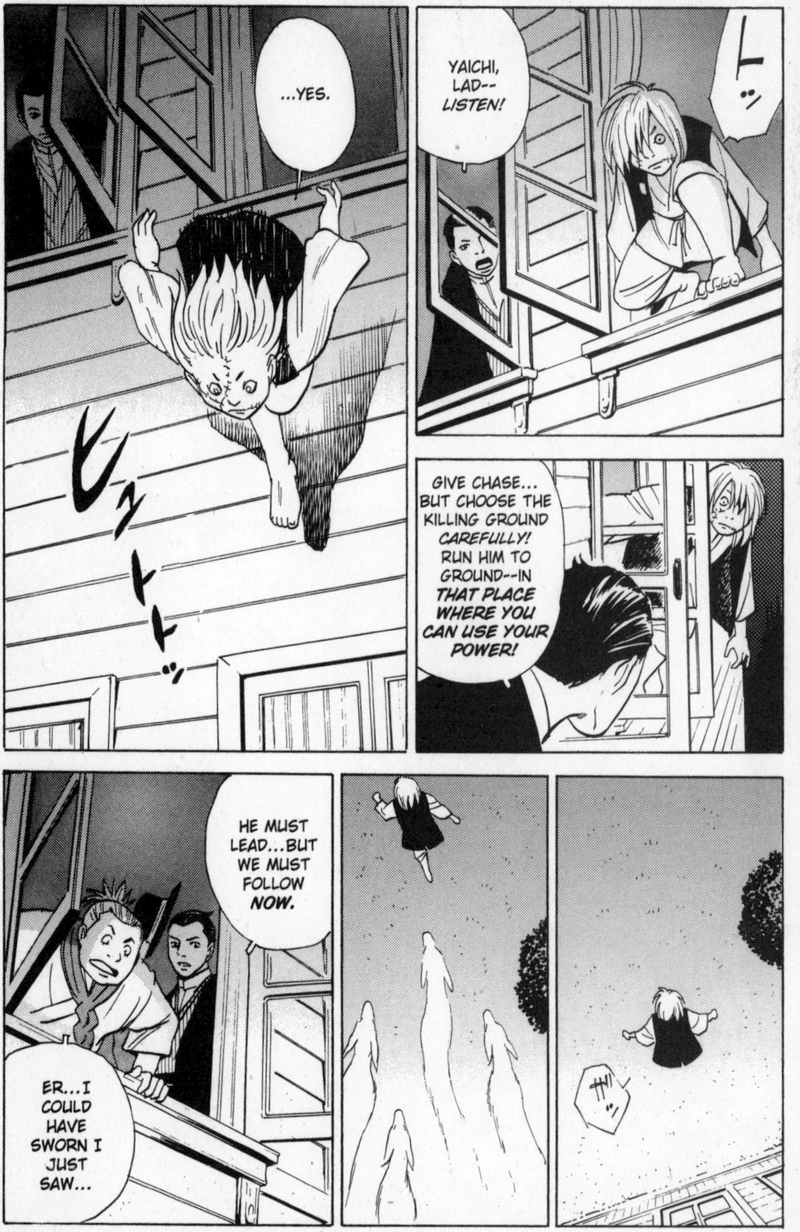
YAICHI, LAD-- LISTEN!
GIVE CHASE... BUT CHOOSE THE KILLING GROUND CAREFULLY! RUN HIM TO GROUND--IN THAT PLACE WHERE YOU CAN USE YOUR POWER!
...YES.
HE MUST LEAD...BUT WE MUST FOLLOW NOW.
ER...I COULD HAVE SWORN I JUST SAW...

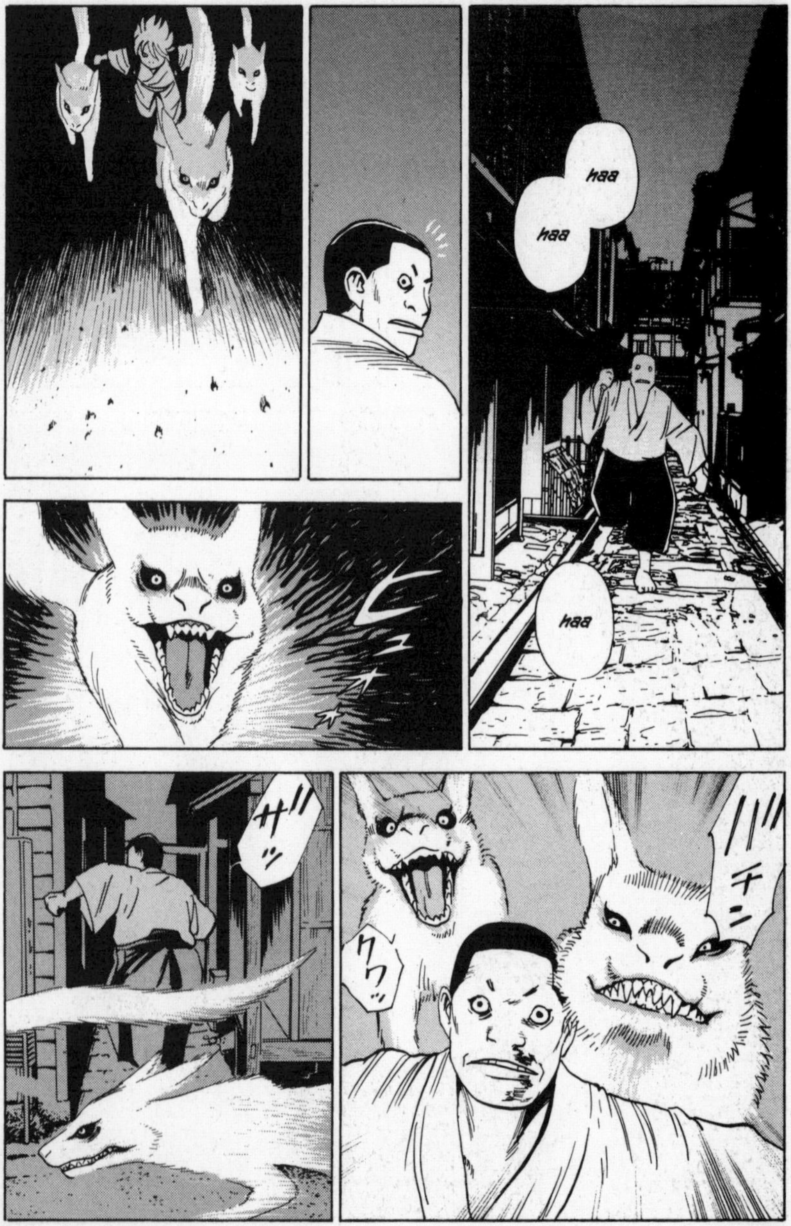
haa
haa
haa
ザッ
クワッ

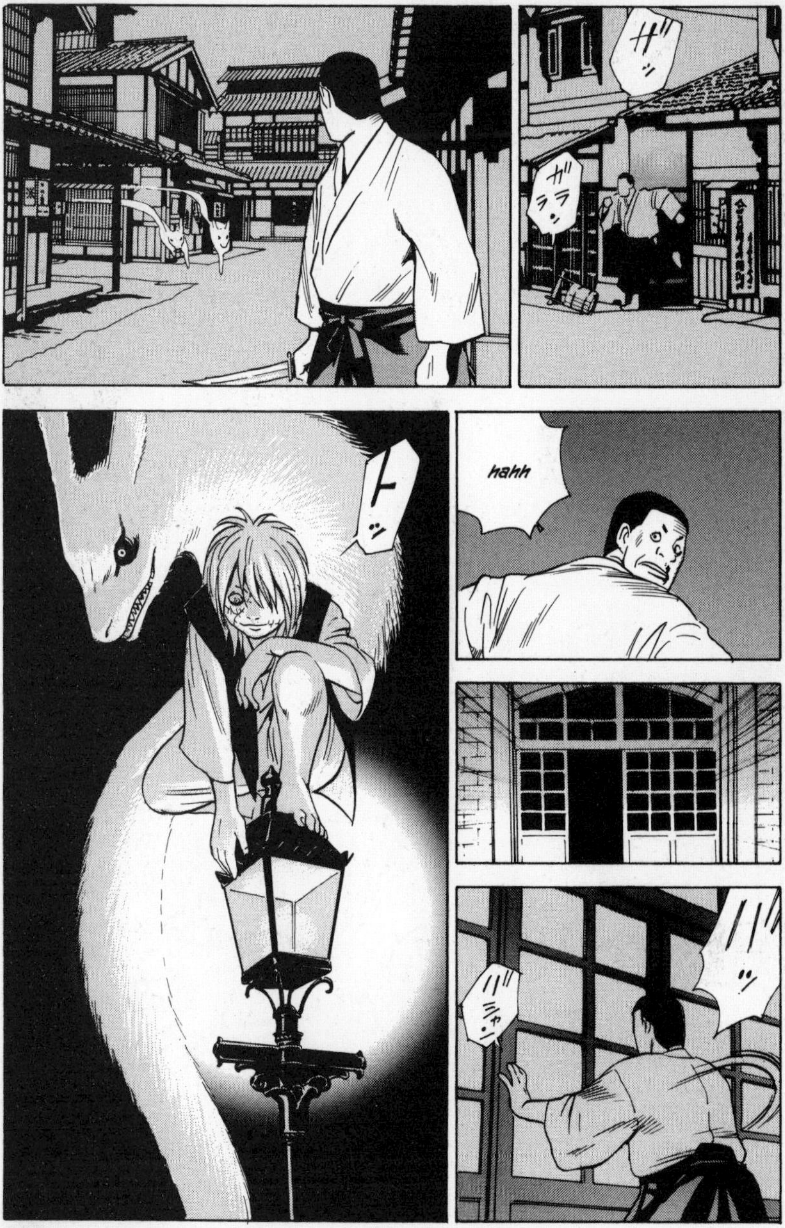
ザッ
ガララッ
hahh
トッ

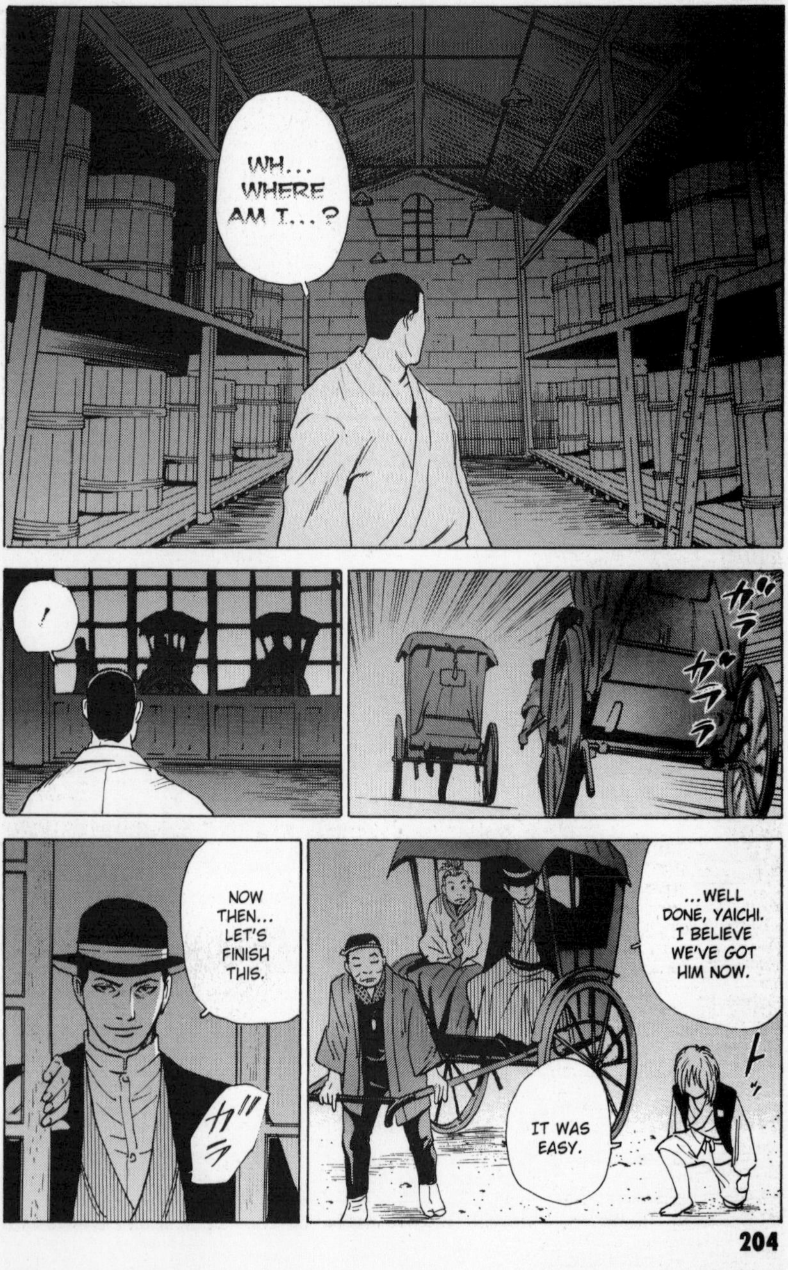
WH... WHERE AM I...?
ガラ ガララ
!
...WELL DONE, YAICHI. I BELIEVE WE'VE GOT HIM NOW.
ト
IT WAS EASY.
NOW THEN... LET'S FINISH THIS.
ガラ

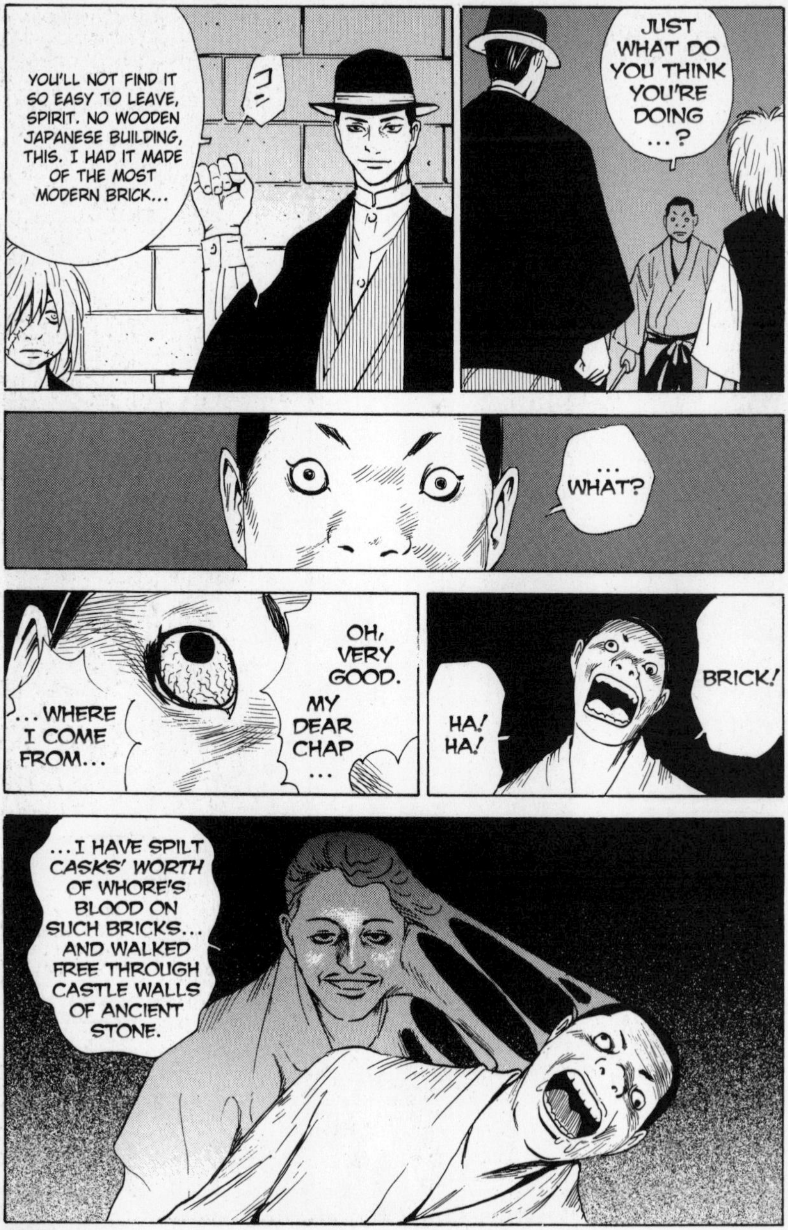
JUST WHAT DO YOU THINK YOU'RE DOING ...?
YOU'LL NOT FIND IT SO EASY TO LEAVE, SPIRIT. NO WOODEN JAPANESE BUILDING, THIS. I HAD IT MADE OF THE MOST MODERN BRICK...
... WHAT?
BRICK!
HA! HA!
OH, VERY GOOD.
MY DEAR CHAP ...
... WHERE I COME FROM...
... I HAVE SPILT *CASKS' WORTH* OF WHORE'S BLOOD ON SUCH BRICKS... AND WALKED FREE THROUGH CASTLE WALLS OF ANCIENT STONE.

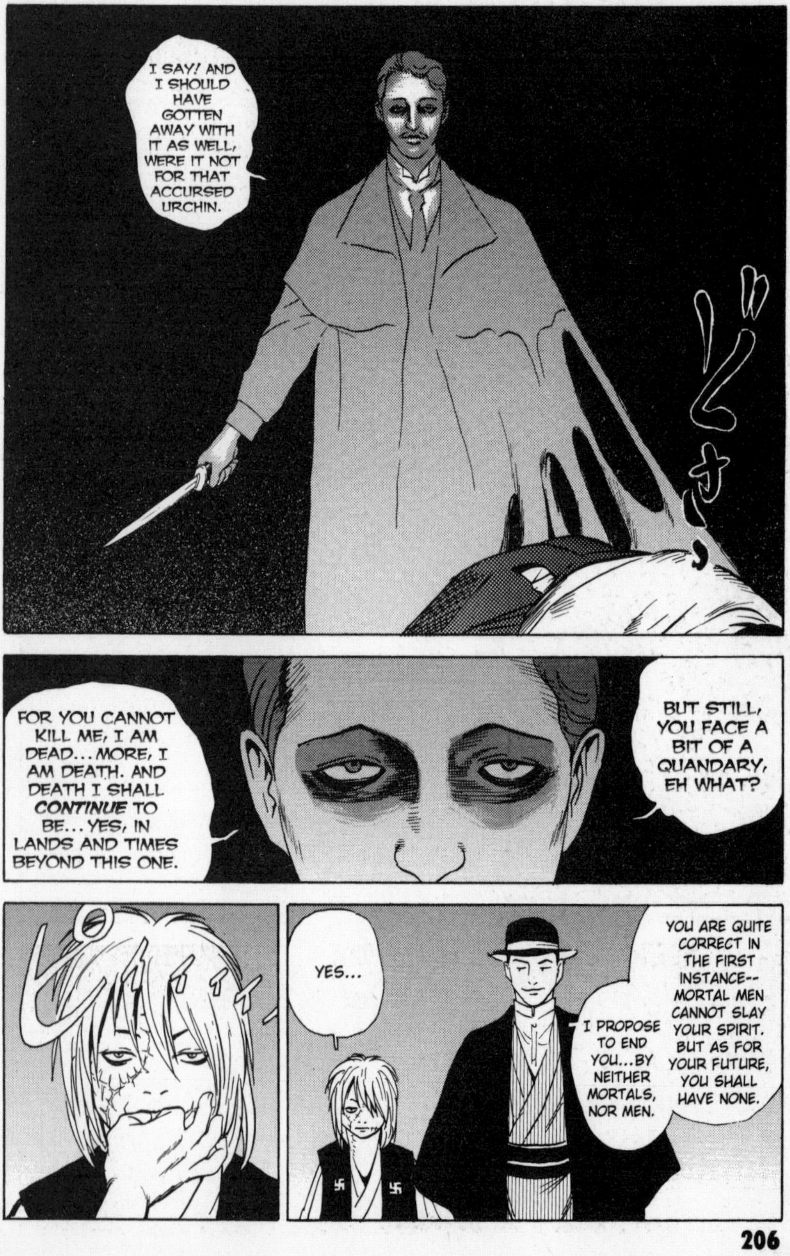
I SAY! AND I SHOULD HAVE GOTTEN AWAY WITH IT AS WELL, WERE IT NOT FOR THAT ACCURSED URCHIN.
BUT STILL, YOU FACE A BIT OF A QUANDARY, EH WHAT?
FOR YOU CANNOT KILL ME, I AM DEAD... MORE, I AM DEATH. AND DEATH I SHALL *CONTINUE* TO BE... YES, IN LANDS AND TIMES BEYOND THIS ONE.
YOU ARE QUITE CORRECT IN THE FIRST INSTANCE-- MORTAL MEN CANNOT SLAY YOUR SPIRIT. BUT AS FOR YOUR FUTURE, YOU SHALL HAVE NONE.
I PROPOSE TO END YOU... BY NEITHER MORTALS, NOR MEN.
YES...

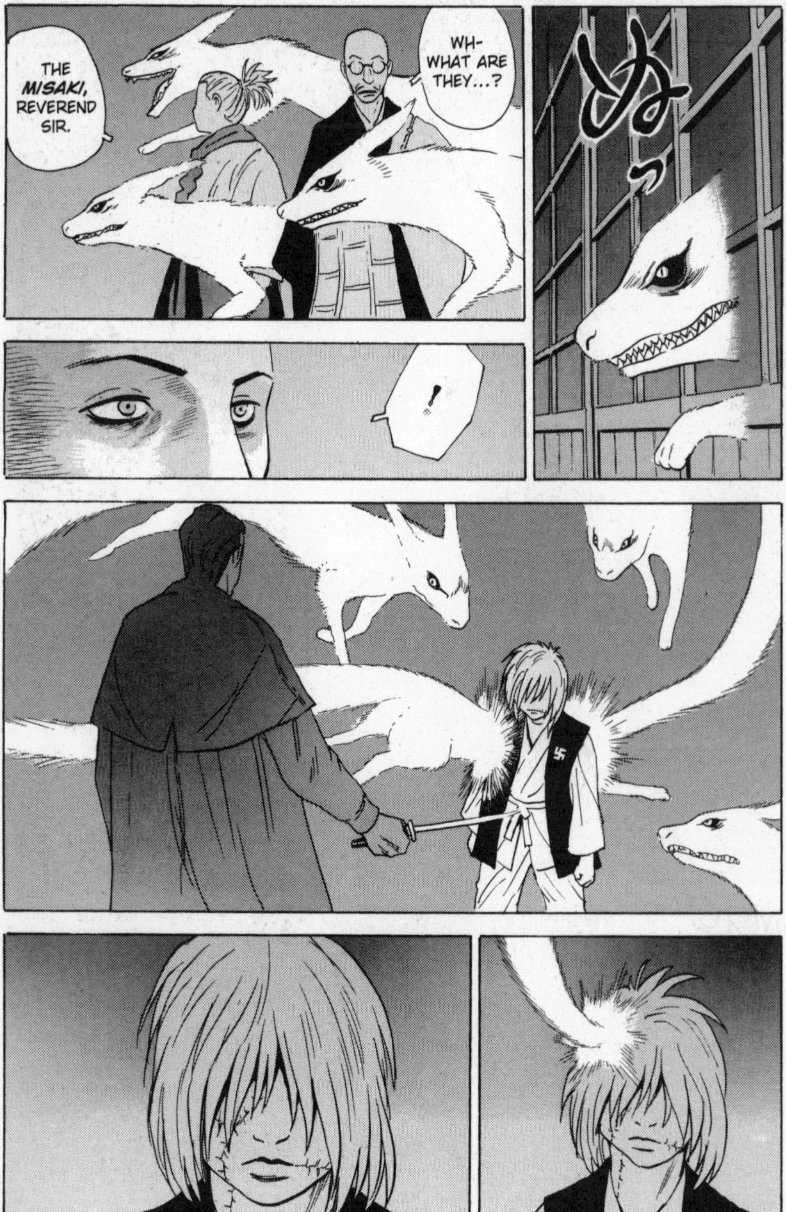
ぬっ
WH- WHAT ARE THEY...?
THE *MISAKI,* REVEREND SIR.
!

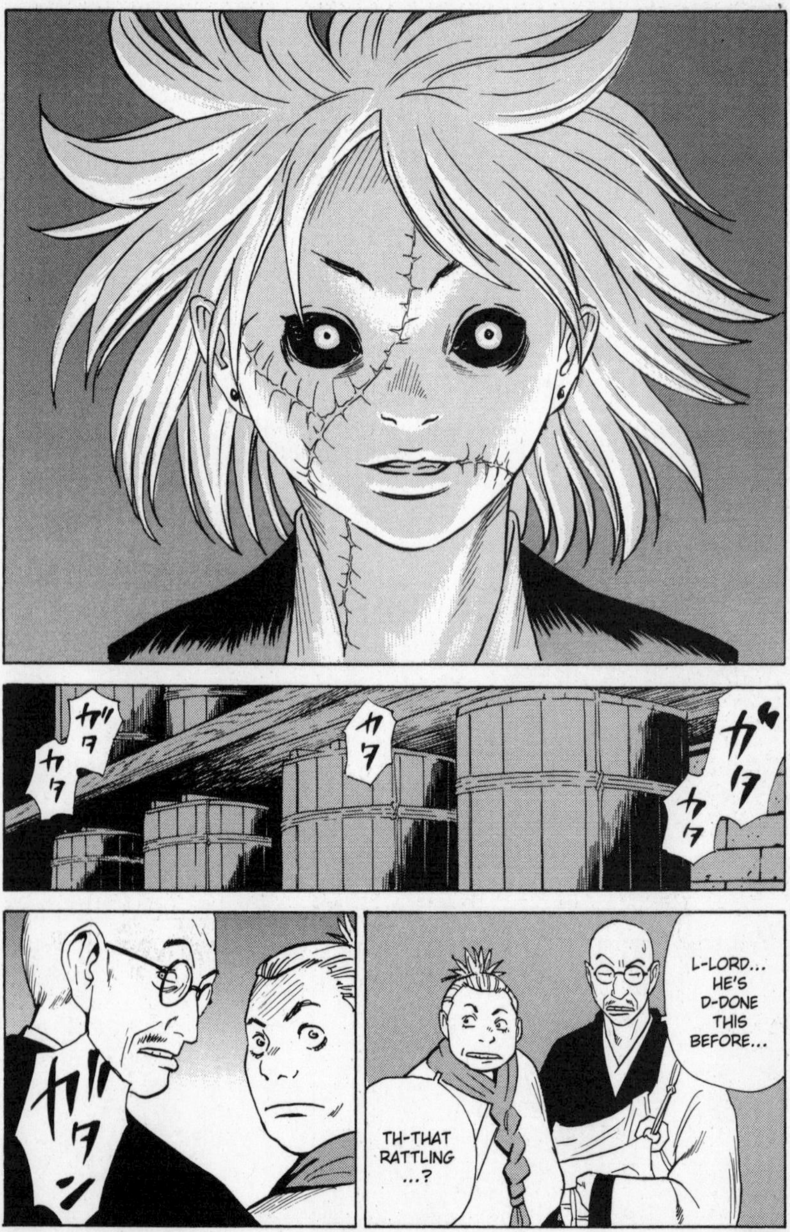
ガタ
カタ
カタ
ガタ
カタ
L-LORD... HE'S D-DONE THIS BEFORE...
TH-THAT RATTLING ...?
ガタン

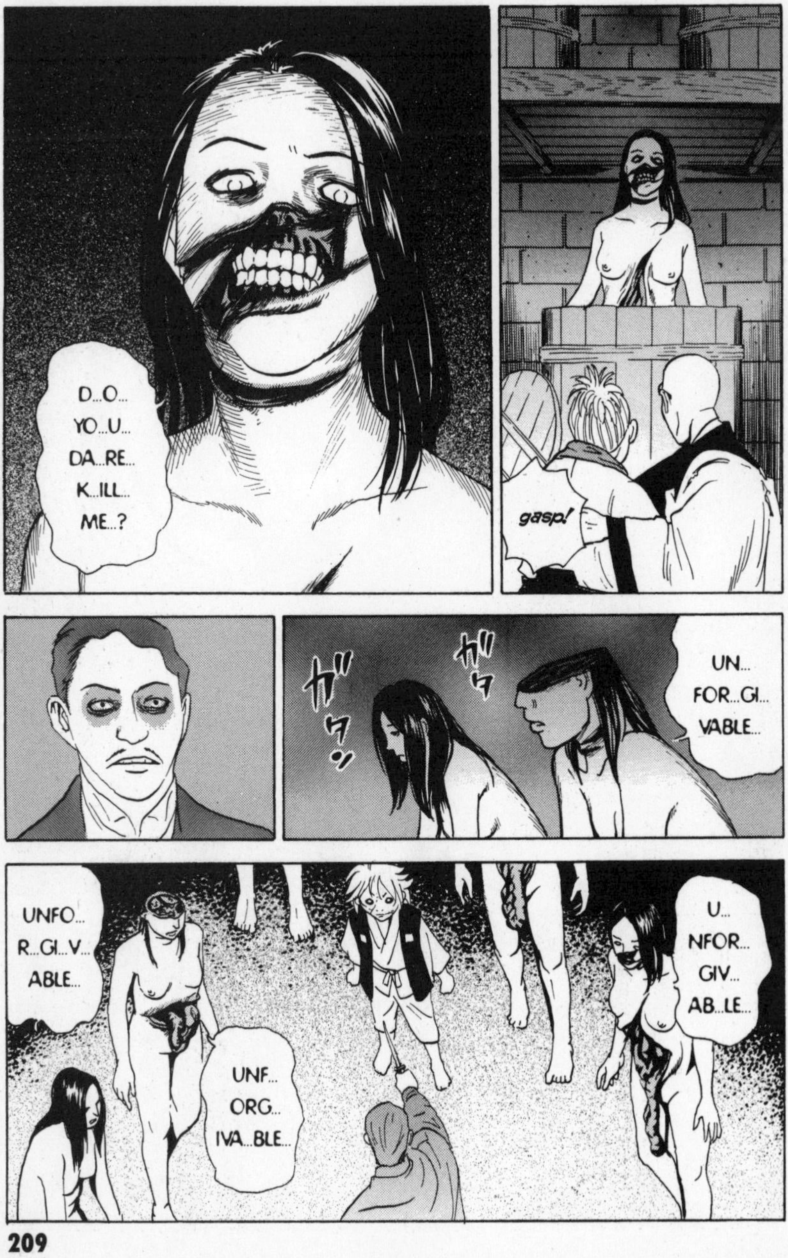
gasp!
D...O... YO...U... DA...RE... K...ILL... ME...?
ガタ
ガタッ
UN... FOR...GI... VABLE...
U... NFOR... GIV... AB...LE...
UNFO... R...GI...V... ABLE...
UNF... ORG... IVA...BLE...

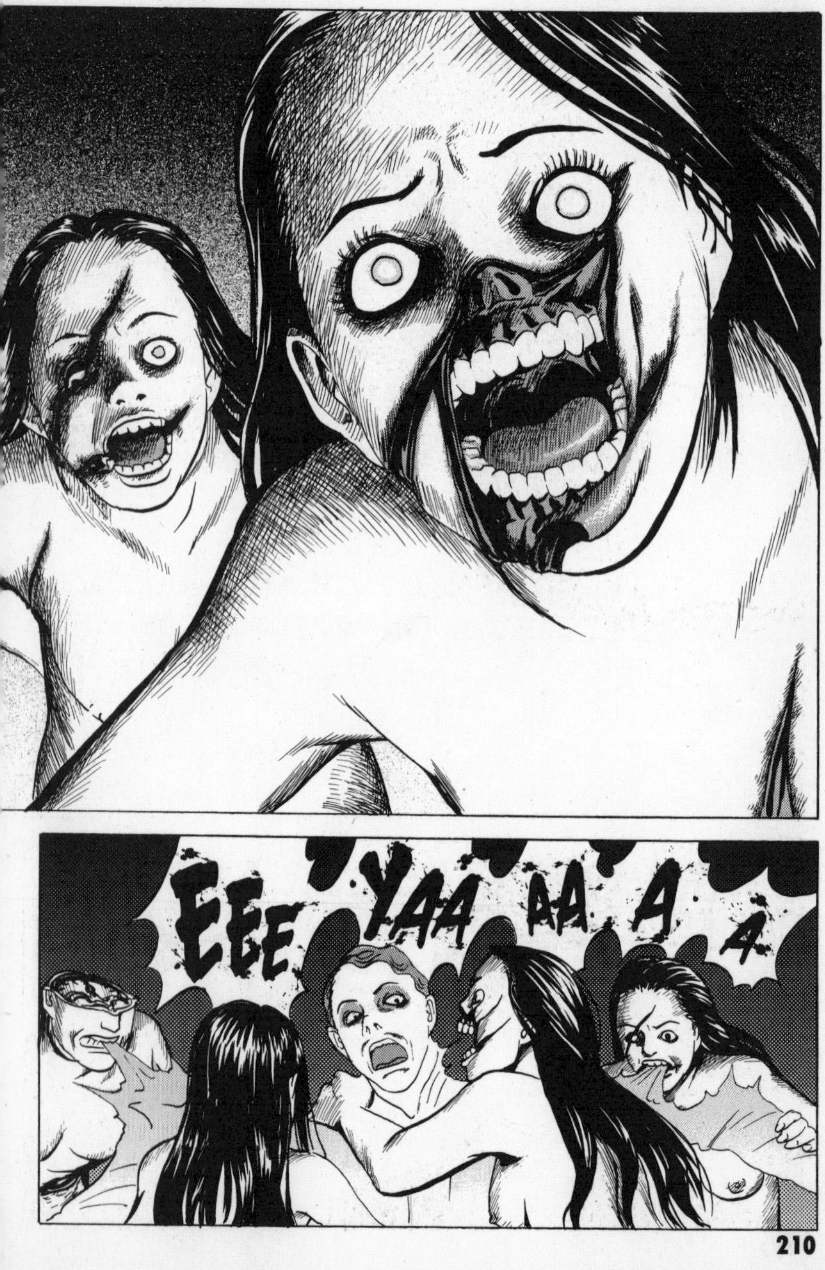
EEEYAAAAAAA

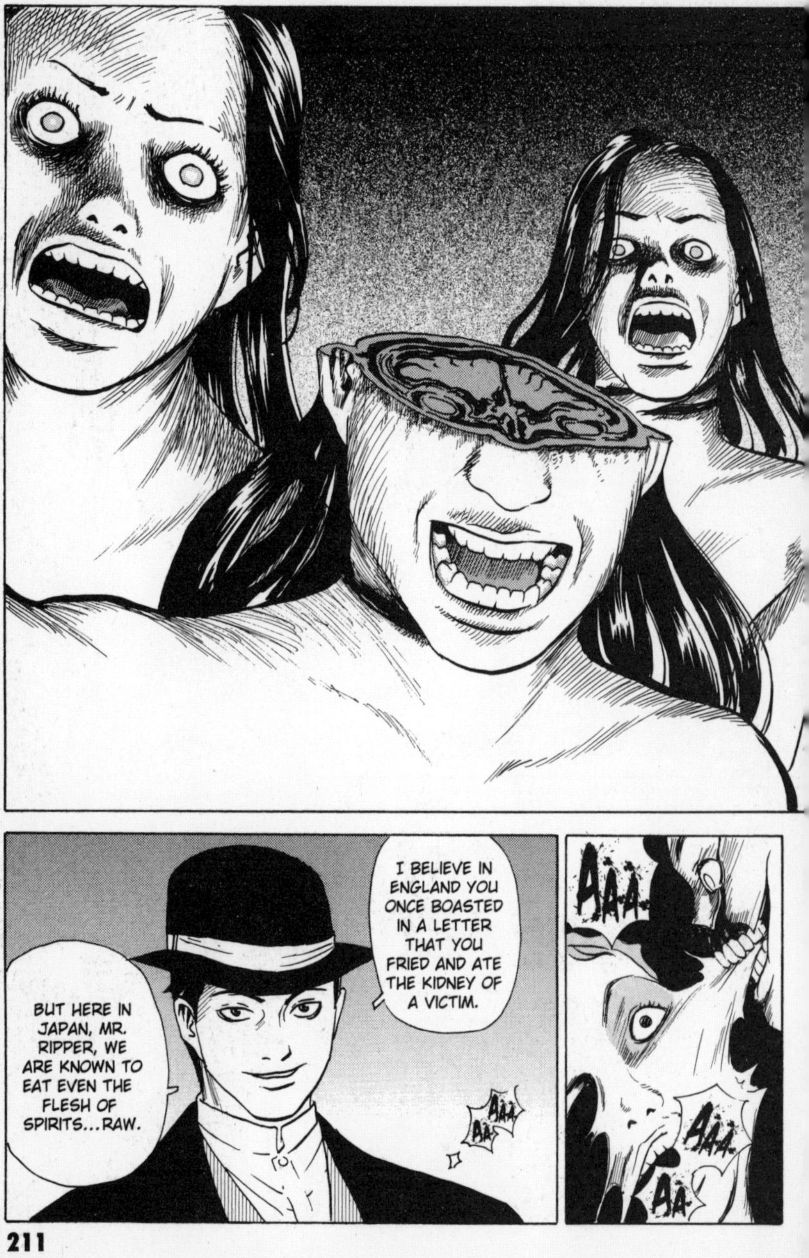
AAA
AAA
AA
I BELIEVE IN ENGLAND YOU ONCE BOASTED IN A LETTER THAT YOU FRIED AND ATE THE KIDNEY OF A VICTIM.
BUT HERE IN JAPAN, MR. RIPPER, WE ARE KNOWN TO EAT EVEN THE FLESH OF SPIRITS...RAW.
AAA
AA

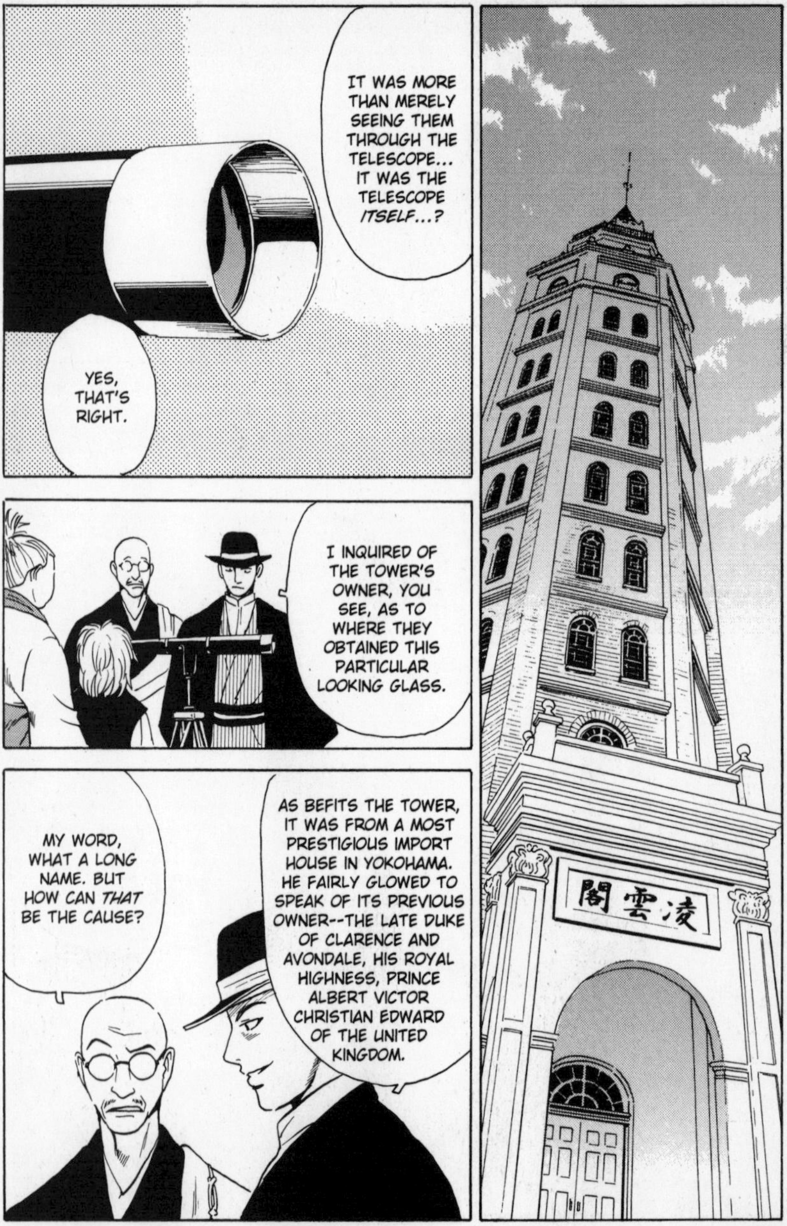
凌雲閣
IT WAS MORE THAN MERELY SEEING THEM THROUGH THE TELESCOPE... IT WAS THE TELESCOPE *ITSELF*...?
YES, THAT'S RIGHT.
I INQUIRED OF THE TOWER'S OWNER, YOU SEE, AS TO WHERE THEY OBTAINED THIS PARTICULAR LOOKING GLASS.
AS BEFITS THE TOWER, IT WAS FROM A MOST PRESTIGIOUS IMPORT HOUSE IN YOKOHAMA. HE FAIRLY GLOWED TO SPEAK OF ITS PREVIOUS OWNER--THE LATE DUKE OF CLARENCE AND AVONDALE, HIS ROYAL HIGHNESS, PRINCE ALBERT VICTOR CHRISTIAN EDWARD OF THE UNITED KINGDOM.
MY WORD, WHAT A LONG NAME. BUT HOW CAN *THAT* BE THE CAUSE?

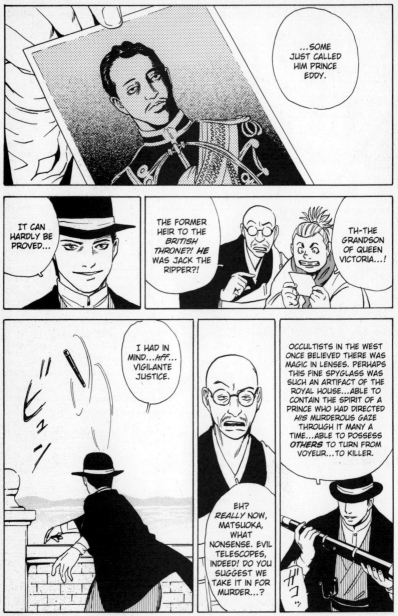

...SOME JUST CALLED HIM PRINCE EDDY.
TH-THE GRANDSON OF QUEEN VICTORIA...!
THE FORMER HEIR TO THE *BRITISH THRONE?!* ***HE*** WAS JACK THE RIPPER?!
IT CAN HARDLY BE PROVED...
OCCULTISTS IN THE WEST ONCE BELIEVED THERE WAS MAGIC IN LENSES. PERHAPS THIS FINE SPYGLASS WAS SUCH AN ARTIFACT OF THE ROYAL HOUSE...ABLE TO CONTAIN THE SPIRIT OF A PRINCE WHO HAD DIRECTED *HIS* MURDEROUS GAZE THROUGH IT MANY A TIME...ABLE TO POSSESS ***OTHERS*** TO TURN FROM VOYEUR...TO KILLER.
EH? *REALLY* NOW, MATSUOKA, WHAT NONSENSE. EVIL TELESCOPES, INDEED! DO YOU SUGGEST WE TAKE IT IN FOR MURDER...?
I HAD IN MIND...*hff*... VIGILANTE JUSTICE.

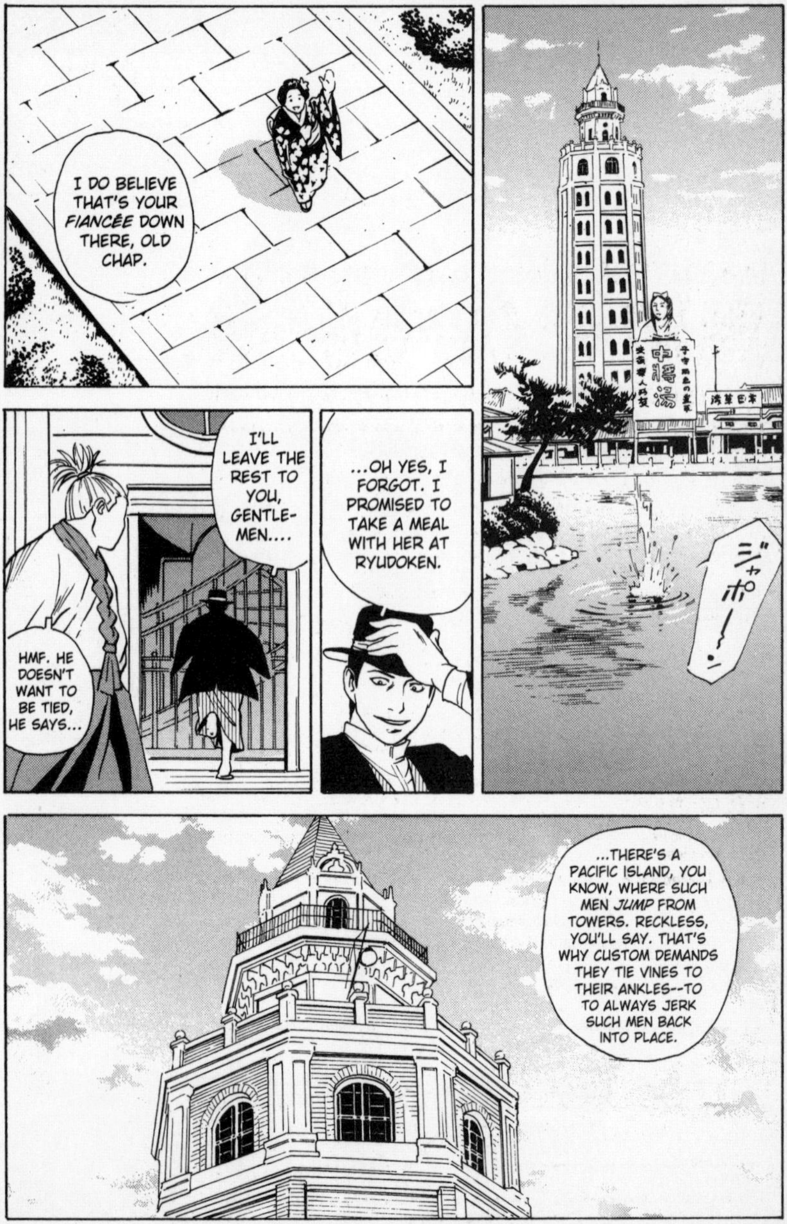
ジャポー～ン
I DO BELIEVE THAT'S YOUR *FIANCÉE* DOWN THERE, OLD CHAP.
...OH YES, I FORGOT. I PROMISED TO TAKE A MEAL WITH HER AT RYUDOKEN.
I'LL LEAVE THE REST TO YOU, GENTLEMEN....
HMF. HE DOESN'T WANT TO BE TIED, HE SAYS...
...THERE'S A PACIFIC ISLAND, YOU KNOW, WHERE SUCH MEN *JUMP* FROM TOWERS. RECKLESS, YOU'LL SAY. THAT'S WHY CUSTOM DEMANDS THEY TIE VINES TO THEIR ANKLES--TO TO ALWAYS JERK SUCH MEN BACK INTO PLACE.

6th delivery: too long a spring • kunio matsuoka demon hunting side story (part two)—the end
continued in the *kurosagi corpse delivery service* vol. 7

the KUROSAGI corpse delivery service

黒鷺死体宅配便

eiji otsuka 大塚英志 housui yamazaki 山崎峰水

---

designer **HEIDI WHITCOMB**
editorial assistant **RACHEL MILLER**
art director **LIA RIBACCHI**
publisher **MIKE RICHARDSON**

English-language version
produced by Dark Horse Comics

THE KUROSAGI CORPSE DELIVERY SERVICE VOL. 6
© EIJI OTSUKA OFFICE 2007, © HOUSUI YAMAZAKI 2007. First published in
Japan in 2007 by KADOKAWA SHOTEN Publishing Co., Ltd., Tokyo. English
translation rights arranged with KADOKAWA SHOTEN Publishing Co., Ltd., Tokyo,
through TOHAN CORPORATION, Tokyo. This English language edition ©2008 by
Dark Horse Comics, Inc. All other material ©2008 by Dark Horse Comics, Inc. All
rights reserved. No portion of this publication may be reproduced or transmitted,
in any form or by any means, without the express written permission of the copyright
holders. Names, characters, places, and incidents featured in this publication
are either the product of the author's imagination or are used fictitiously. Any
resemblance to actual persons (living or dead), events, institutions, or locales,
without satiric intent, is coincidental. Dark Horse Manga™ is a trademark of Dark
Horse Comics, Inc. All rights reserved.

Published by
Dark Horse Manga
A division of Dark Horse Comics, Inc.
10956 SE Main Street
Milwaukie, OR 97222
www.darkhorse.com

To find a comics shop in your area,
call the Comic Shop Locator Service
toll-free at 1-888-266-4226

First edition: February 2008
ISBN 978-1-59307-892-8

---

1 3 5 7 9 10 8 6 4 2

PRINTED IN CANADA

DISJECTA MEMBRA

SOUND FX GLOSSARY AND NOTES ON *KUROSAGI* VOL. 6 BY TOSHIFUMI YOSHIDA
introduction and additional comments by the editor

TO INCREASE YOUR ENJOYMENT of the distinctive Japanese visual style of *Kurosagi*, we've included a guide to the sound effects (or "FX") used in this manga. It is suggested the reader not constantly consult this glossary as they read through, but regard it as supplemental information, in the manner of footnotes. If you want to imagine it being read aloud by Osaka, after the manner of her lecture to Sakaki on hemorrhoids in episode five, please go right ahead. In either Yuki Matsuoka or Kira Vincent-Davis's voice—I like them both.

Japanese, like English, did not independently invent its own writing system, but instead borrowed and modified the system used by then-dominant cultural power in their part of the world. We still call the letters we use to write English today the "Roman" alphabet, for the simple reason that about 1600 years ago the earliest English speakers, living on the frontier of the Roman Empire, began to use the same letters the Romans used for their Latin language to write out English.

Around that very same time, on the other side of the planet, Japan, like England, was another example of an island civilization lying across the sea from a great empire, in this case, that of China. Likewise the Japanese borrowed from the Chinese writing system, which then as now consists of thousands of complex symbols—today in China officially referred to in the Roman alphabet as hanzi, but which the Japanese pronounce as *kanji*. For example, all the Japanese characters you see on the front cover of *The Kurosagi Corpse Delivery Service*—the seven which make up the original title and the four each which make up the creators' names—are examples of kanji. Of course, all of them were hanzi first—although the Japanese did also invent some original kanji of their own, just as new hanzi have been created over the centuries as Chinese evolved.

Note that whereas of course both "kanji" and "hanzi" are themselves examples of writing foreign words in Roman letters, "kanji" gives English-speakers a fairly good idea of how the Japanese word is really pronounced—*khan-gee*—whereas "hanzi" does not—in Mandarin Chinese it sounds something like *n-tsuh*. The reason is fairly simple: whereas the most commonly used method of writing Japanese in Roman letters, called the Hepburn system, was developed by a native English speaker, the most commonly used method of writing Chinese in Roman letters, called the *Pinyin* system, was developed by native Mandarin speakers. In fact Pinyin was developed to help teach Mandarin pronunciation to speakers of other Chinese dialects; unlike Hepburn, it was not intended as a learning tool for English-speakers *per se*, and hence has no particular obligation to "make sense" to English speakers or, indeed, users of the many other languages spelled with the Roman alphabet.

Whereas the various dialects of Chinese are written entirely in hanzi, it is impractical to render the Japanese language entirely in them. To compare once more, English is a notoriously difficult language in which to spell properly, and this is in part because it uses an alphabet designed for another language, Latin, whose sounds are different (this is, of course, putting aside the fact the sounds of both languages experienced change over time). The challenges the Japanese faced in using the Chinese writing system for their own language were even greater, for whereas spoken English and Latin are at least from a common language family, spoken Japanese is unrelated to any of the various dialects of spoken Chinese. The complicated writing system Japanese evolved represents an adjustment to these great differences.

When the Japanese borrowed hanzi to become kanji, what they were getting was a way to write out (remember, they already had ways to *say*) their vocabulary. Nouns, verbs, many adjectives, the names of places and people—that's what kanji are used for, the fundamental data of the written language. The practical use and processing of that "data"—its grammar and pronunciation—is another matter entirely. Because spoken Japanese neither sounds nor functions like Chinese, the first workaround tried was a system called *manyogana*, where individual kanji were picked to represent certain syllables in Japanese. A similar method is still used in Chinese today to spell out foreign names; companies and individuals often try to choose hanzi for this purpose that have an auspicious, or at least not insulting meaning. As you will also observe in *Kurosagi* and elsewhere,

the meaning behind the characters that make up a personal name are an important literary element of Japanese as well.

The commentary in *Katsuya Terada's The Monkey King* (also available from Dark Horse, and also translated by Toshifumi Yoshida) notes the importance that not only Chinese, but Indian culture had on Japan at this time in history—particularly, through Buddhism. Just as in Western history at this time, religious communities in Asia were associated with learning, as priests and monks were more likely to be literate than other groups in society. It is believed the Northeast Indian *Siddham* script studied by Kukai (died 835 AD), founder of the Shingon sect of Japanese Buddhism, inspired him to create the solution for writing Japanese still used today. Kukai is credited with the idea of taking the manyogana and making shorthand versions of them—which are now known simply as *kana*. The improvement in efficiency was dramatic: a kanji, used previously to represent a sound, that might have taken a dozen strokes to draw, was now reduced to three or four.

Unlike the original kanji they were based on, the new kana had *only* a sound meaning. And unlike the thousands of kanji, there are only 46 kana, which can be used to spell out any word in the Japanese language, including the many ordinarily written with kanji (Japanese keyboards work on this principle). The same set of 46 kana is written two different ways depending on their intended use: cursive style, *hiragana*, and block style, *katakana*. Naturally, sound FX in manga are almost always written out using kana.

Kana works somewhat differently than the Roman alphabet. For example, while there are separate kana for each of the five vowels (the Japanese order is not A-E-I-O-U as in English, but A-I-U-E-O), there are, except for "n," no separate kana for consonants (the middle "n" in the word *ninja* illustrates this exception). Instead, kana work by grouping together consonants with vowels: for example, there are five kana for sounds starting with "k," depending on which vowel follows it—in Japanese vowel order, they go KA, KI, KU, KE, KO. The next set of kana begins with "s" sounds, so SA, SHI, SU, SE, SO, and so on. You will observe this kind of consonant-vowel pattern in the FX listings for *Kurosagi* Vol. 6 below.

Katakana are almost always the kind that get used for manga sound FX, but on occasion (often when the sound is one associated with a person's body) hiragana are used instead. In *Kurosagi* Vol. 6 you can see an example on 165.1, with the WAAAA cry of the crowd, which in hiragana style is written わあああ. Note its more cursive appearance compared to the other FX. If it had been written in katakana style, it would look like ワアアア. A different usage of hiragana as FX is seen in 207.1's ぬっ, NU which as an example of *gitaigo* (see below) is the figurative "sound" of menace.

To see how to use this glossary, take an example from page 208: "208.4 FX: GATAN—sound of a coffin lid coming off." 208.4 means the FX is the one on page 208, in panel 4. GATAN is the sound these kana—ガタン—literally stand for. After the dash comes an explanation of what the sound represents (in some cases, it will be less obvious than others). Note that in cases where there are two or more different sounds in a single panel, an extra number is used to differentiate them from right to left; or, in cases where right and left are less clear, in clockwise order.

The use of kana in these FX also illustrates another aspect of written Japanese—its flexible reading order. For example, the way you're reading the pages and panels of this book in general: going from right-to-left, and from top to bottom—is similar to the order in which Japanese is also written in most forms of print: books, magazines, and newspapers. However, many of the FX in *Kurosagi* (and manga in general) read left-to-right. This kind of flexibility is also to be found on Japanese web pages, which usually also read left-to-right. In other words, Japanese doesn't simply read "the other way" from English; the Japanese themselves are used to reading it in several different directions.

As might be expected, some FX "sound" short, and others "sound" long. Manga represent this in different ways. One of many instances of "short sounds" in *Kurosagi* Vol. 6 is to be found in the example from 207.1 given above: NU. Note the small っ mark it has at the end—notice again that this is the hiragana "tsu," and you will far more often see it in its katakana form, ツ. Both forms ordinarily represent the sound "tsu," but its half-size use at the end of FX like this means the sound is the kind which stops or cuts off suddenly; that's why the sound is written as NU and not NUTSU—you don't "pronounce" the TSU in such cases. Note the small "tsu" has another occasional use *inside*, rather than at the end, of a particular FX, where it indicates a doubling of the consonant sound that follows it.

There are three different ways you may see "long sounds" (where a vowel sound is extended) written out as FX. One is with an ellipsis, as in 20.4's BURORORO. Another is with an extended line, as in 187.3's GABIIIN. Still another is by simply repeating a vowel several times, as in 146.4's GOOO. You will note that 137.4's GAAAA has a "tsu" at its end, suggesting an elongated sound that's suddenly cut off; the methods may be combined within a single FX. As a visual element in manga, FX are an art rather than a science, and are used in a less rigorous fashion than kana are in standard written Japanese.

The explanation of what the sound represents may sometimes be surprising; but every culture "hears" sounds differently. Note that manga FX do not even necessarily represent literal sounds; for example the previously mentioned 187.3 FX: GABIIIN, which represents the figurative "sound" of being shocked or aghast. Such "mimetic" words, which represent an imagined sound, or even a state of mind, are called *gitaigo* in Japanese. Like the onomatopoeic *giseigo* (the words used to represent literal sounds—i.e., most FX in this glossary are classed as giseigo), they are also used in colloquial speech and writing. A Japanese, for example, might say that something bounced by saying PURIN, or talk about eating by saying MUGU MUGU. It's something like describing chatter in English by saying "yadda yadda yadda" instead.

One important last note: all these spelled-out kana vowels should be pronounced as they are in Japanese: "A" as *ah*, "I" as *eee*, "U" as *ooh*, "E" as *eh*, and "O" as *oh*.

2 This may be the first volume of *The Kurosagi Corpse Delivery Service* in which a common theme does not link the chapter titles (of course, it's also the first one with "side stories," or *gaiden* as they're known in Japan— stories outside the regular continuity). The translator, despite extensive searching, was unable to find a song title link to 1st and 2nd Delivery; 3rd Delivery, however, matches a song by the early-70s Japanese band Carol (whose lead singer Eikichi Yazawa later had a very successful solo career), whereas 4th Delivery matches a song by the folk combo Akai Tori ("Red Bird") and 5th Delivery, a song by The Boom (www.five-d.co.jp/boom/). 6th Delivery's title is shared with that of a relatively obscure 1956 Yukio Mishima short story (in the original Japanese, *Nagasugita Haru*), described by Gwenn Boardman Petersen in *The Moon in the Water* as the story of a couple's "adventures" during a long engagement.

7.2 **FX/balloon: PIRORI**—PSP beeping

7.5 Junichiro Koizumi—who was in his final months as Prime Minister when this story first ran in July of 2006—had proposed the privatization of the Postal Service, a measure that became fully implemented as of April of 2007 when it became the Japan Post Company. This story touches on actual issues that arose in the lead-up to the privatization. Ramming home the gag with a mallet, the mailman appearing later in the story is named "Juntaro Koizumi," and his dog itself is named "Junichiro."

8.1 It may seem hard to believe that *any* country has a lower voter turnout than the United States (my sister saw a T-shirt of President Bush grinning and flashing a peace sign, saying "Bet you wish you'd voted, hippie"), but apparently Japan has achieved this dubious distinction. *The Wide* is a variety talk show hosted by Hitoshi Kusano on Nippon TV.

8.4 Side mirrors on cars in America traditionally bear the disclaimer that "objects in mirror are closer than they appear," but look closely and you'll note (as is often the case on cars intended for the Japanese domestic market) these mirrors are halfway down the front of the car instead, allowing for objects glimpsed to be seen at their actual distance. Pan Am, however, stopped flying to Japan in 1985 (not long before the once-great airline itself became defunct in 1991), so this is definitely based on an old photo. To be fair, Carlos Ezquerra did the same thing in *A Man Called Kev.*

9.1 **FX: BATA DOTA**—the sound of Numata chasing Yata around the room

12.4 This, as far as I've noticed, is the first time *Kurosagi* has broken the fourth wall—although, as you will see, it's also the first of several firsts that appear in this volume.

14.3 **FX/balloon: GUN**—tugging Yata's arm to make it point

15.2 **FX/balloon: YURA YURA**— pendulum starting to swing slowly

15.4 **FX/balloon: ZA ZA ZA**—running off sound

18.4 **FX/balloon: DO DO DO**— running dog sound

18.5 **FX/balloon: NU**—sound of a dog pushing by

18.6 **FX/balloon: WAN WAN WAN WAAAN**—dog barking

19.1 **FX: PIKU**—twitch

19.3 The Japan Post Company does in fact have a shipping service called YouPack—the "you" is written in hiragana, whereas the "pack" is in katakana. But in this story, it's *YuuPack,* where "pack" is spelled the same, but the first part is written with the kanji for "ghost," pronounced Yuu (the same one as in the manga *Yu Yu Hakusho,* although the English transliteration of that title uses only one "u"). Note that above the front bumper of the van in 20.1, you can see the logo of the real YouPack service.

20.3 **FX: BAN**—slamming car door sound

20.4 **FX: BURORORO**—car engine sound

22.5 The original joke in Japanese worked like this: Juntaro spoke of the "rules and regulations"— *yuubin yakkan*—but *yakkan* is what they used to call a "ten-dollar word" (currently 1,134.56 yen, and falling) so Kuro mistakes it for *yuubin yakan*—*yakan* being a metal kettle, like the one always being employed in *Ranma 1/2.*

And Toshi translated that, too, so he should know.

23.1 **FX/balloon: KOTO**—putting tea cup down

23.4 **FX/balloon: KUWAA**—dog yawning

25.1 There's nothing particularly outlandish about the idea; among other things, the Japanese Post Office used to be one of the largest savings banks in the world, as its conservative image led millions to entrust their money to it. These assets are now in the privatized Japan Post Bank.

26.1 **FX/balloon: ZAPU**—pulling wet washcloth out of the water

26.3 Notice Kereellis is wearing a towel to cool his little felt head. In the original Japanese, he joked that Numata had turned out to be an *ichi nichi shochoo*, a "one-day director," a common Japanese publicity stunt where a celebrity will be named a (honorary) police chief or fire marshal for a day.

26.4 **FX: BASHA BASHA**—running in water sound

26.5 **FX: PITA**—stopping sound

29.1 **FX: DON**—putting body down

29.2 This, of course, is a reference to the infamous scene in Vol. 1 of Eiji Otsuka's *MPD-Psycho*, and the first indication (later reinforced by the flashback at the beginning of this volume's "4th Delivery") that the Sasayama in each manga is the same person—although how the hapless, full-haired, four-limbed Sasayama of *MPD-Psycho* became

the worldly bald peg leg of *Kurosagi* must be a story in of itself. Or maybe it isn't the first—I missed the reference in vol. 4's 180.1. For your convenience, Dark Horse also publishes *MPD-Psycho*, so we'll see how things unravel. My guess is, with a great deal of blood.

30.4 **FX: PATAN**—closing lid

31.1 **FX: MOMI MOMI**—hands squeezing together in anticipation of getting paid

31.5 **FX: PI**—hanging up

31.6 **FX: BA**—handing over money

34.2 **FX: SU**—putting hand on body

35.5 **FX/balloon: PIKU**—twitch

35.6 **FX/balloon: VWOOO**—growling

36.1 **FX/balloon: WAN WAN WAN**—barking

37.3 **FX: BISHI**—pulling rope taut between hands

37.6 **FX/balloons: WAN WAN WAN WAWAN WAN**—barking

39.1 **FX/balloon: KUWOON**—whimpering sound

39.3 **FX/balloon: WAN WAN WAN**—barking

39.4 **FX/balloons: WAN WAN WAN**—barking

39.5 **FX/balloon: WAN**—bark

39.6 **FX/balloons: HA HA HA**—dog panting

45.2.1 **FX/balloon: GO**—heads hitting each other

45.2.2 **FX/balloon: GURI**—rubbing face in maggots

45.5 **FX/balloon: SHUBO**—sound of lighter being lit

46.2 **FX/balloon: KON KON**—knock knock

46.4 **FX/balloon: ZA**—footstep

46.5 **FX/balloon: KACHIRI**—unlocking door

47.1 **FX:DOGASHA**—door being kicked in

47.2 **FX: KARAN KACHA PAKI**—clinking and breaking glass sounds

48.3 **FX/balloon: PI**—starting to rip tape off

48.4 **FX/balloon: BIII**—sound of tape being ripped off

49.1 **FX/balloon: KASA**—sound of cardboard being moved

49.2 **FX/balloons: GASA GASA GOSO**—sound of a box being opened

49.3 **FX: BARI BARI BARI**—sound of ripping cardboard

50.3 **FX/balloon: POTATA**—blood droplets on floor

50.4 **FX/balloon; UNI KUNYA UNI**—sound of maggots squirming in the blood

51.1 **FX/balloon: DORORI**—blood oozing out of nose and mouth

52-53.1 **FX/balloons: KA KOTSU KO**—footsteps

52-53.4 **FX/balloon: KA**—footstep

54.2 **FX/balloon: HARA**—piece of paper falling from hand

54.3 **FX/balloon: PASA**—paper landing on corpse

55.1 **FX/balloon: DOSARI**—body dropping onto corpse

56.5 **FX/balloon: SA**—flipping the notice over

57.1 For those playing the home version of our game, note the Kadokawa reference.

57.3 **FX: FWAN FWAN FWAN**—police sirens

59.4 In the original Japanese, Karatsu also refers to her power to make the dead speak as being that of *kuchiyose*—literally, "to call forth a mouth."

63.2 **FX/balloon: JARA**—rattling keys

63.3 **FX/balloon: GACHA**—door opening

63.4 **FX: VUVUVU VUVUVU**—buzzing flies

66.4 **FX/balloon: BURORORO**—car engine sound

67.3 **FX/balloon: BAN**—closing car door

67.4 **FX/balloon: PAPAA**—car horn

67.5 **FX/balloon: KI**—braking sound

69.4 *Shirosagi* means "White Heron," just as *Kurosagi* means "Black Heron, and although some of the early publicity materials for Vol. 6 used "White Heron," the editor eventually decided to give the Japanese rather than the translation in the book itself, so that it's rendered in a consistent manner with *Kurosagi*. Note that just like Kurosagi, Shirosagi leaves the "corpse" out of the name painted on their van (as seen on 67.6); just as Kurosagi's vehicle says "Kurosagi Delivery

Service," Shirosagi's vehicle says only "Shirosagi Cleaning Service." *Unlike* Kurosagi, however, they do include the "Corpse" on their business card itself—perhaps because theirs is a legitimately recognized sort of business, although, as noted later in the story, a still unusual one in Japan. Besides "Ichiro Suzuki"'s patently phony name, the neighborhood of "Nantoka-machi" they're supposedly based in is a homophone in Japanese for "some town or other."

72.3   **FX/balloon: KORON**—ice clinking in glass

72.4   **FX: MOGU MOGU**—chewing noodles

73.3   If you look closely (and it is the editor's job to do so), you can notice what appears to be two eyeballs among the bloody mash on the wall. No wonder Yata paused in mid-noodle.

73.4   The sound effect of Yata vomiting is lifted directly from Garth Ennis and Steve Dillon's run on *The Punisher*. You know that saying, "death with dignity." Well, Ennis and Dillon are masters of death with *indignity*; people tend to perish with goofy expressions in their work: bug-eyed, cross-eyed, or—an apparent favorite—with their lower jaw shot away, which somehow almost always seems to engender a look of confusion and disbelief on the remainder of the face, not to mention humorous attempts to get a few last comprehensible words out. Now, it may seem rather callous to laugh at

such portrayals, but of course, the larger truth to remember is that you shouldn't put people in that position by killing them in the first place.

75.4   **FX: BA**—moving face up close

78.1   **FX/balloon: KARA**—opening sliding window

80.4   These aren't sutras *per se* (actual sutras being hundreds or thousands of characters long), but rather excerpts from a sutra, written as a lucky charm, something like a single Bible verse.

82.4   The word for "ceiling" in Japanese is *tenjo*, so Makino is being her usual supportive self by taking the first character in *tenjo*, and substituting *jo* for *ko*, a typical ending for girls' names in Japan.

82.5   **FX/balloon: BATAAN**—slamming door

83.3   **FX: DOKA DOKA**—stomping off

83.4   **FX/balloon: YURA YURA**—sound of the pendulum swinging

84.5   **FX: GU**—grasping shoulders

86.5   Sasaki is possibly making up the phrase *Tanin-mitsunyu-shojo*, although the Edogawa Rampo reference is to an actual story (it was the pen name of Taro Hirai; he chose it as a tribute to *Edgar Allen Poe*, spelling it with a string of kanji that sounded like Poe's name). Rampo's stories of mystery and the macabre have remained an enduring influence on Japanese pop culture; "The Attic-Stroller," first published in 1925, is being re-printed in English (under the name "The Stalker in the Attic") as part of the forthcoming *The Edogawa Rampo Reader* from Kurodahan Press, which deserves to be bought just for the awesome cover photo of the old man himself, brandishing a gat. Check it out at http://www.kurodahan.com/e/catalog/titles/j0020.html.

89.3 **FX: HYUN HYUN HYUN HYUN**—sound of pendulum swinging

89.6 **FX/balloons: GON GOTO**—sound of tapping at ceiling with a bat

90.1.1 **FX: BAKAN**—ceiling tile falling off

90.1.2 **FX/balloon: BURAAN**—sound of body dangling

91.4 **FX/balloon: GATA**—sound of a Karatsu climbing up closet

91.5 **FX/balloon: KATAN**—sound of a wooden tile being moved

99.2 Actor and director Werner Herzog (after seeing his turn in *Julien Donkey-Boy*, I wished for him to play the live-action Gendo: "I vant you to be a vinnah, not a quittah!") made the story of Kaspar Hauser into a 1974 film with the irresistible title *Jeder für sich und Gott gegen alle* (*Every Man for Himself and God Against All*).

100.1 **FX: SU**—placing hand on shoulder

100.5 **FX: KATA KATA KATA KATA**—small rattling sound

101.1 **FX: GATA GATA GATA GATAN**—body really shaking

101.2 **FX: BAN BATAN**—feet banging on table

101.3 **FX: GUGUGU**—chin lifting upward as head arches back

102.1 **FX: BA**—taking hand away

102.2 **FX: KAKUN**—head relaxing

105.4 **FX: PASA**—sound of hair falling/body being placed into chair

106.3 **FX: SA**—hiding behind Sasayama

107.2 As is more typical in Japanese society, the characters in *Kurosagi* are usually addressed, and address each other, by their last names—but just as a reminder, the full names of the members of The Kurosagi Corpse Delivery Service are Kuro Karatsu, Ao (short for Aosagi) Sasaki, Makoto Numata, Keiko Makino, and Yuji Yata.

108.2 **FX/balloon: SA**—putting hand on corpse

108.4 **FX: KATA GTA GATA PIKU**—shaking and twitching

110.2 **FX/balloon: KOKU**—nod

110.4 **FX/balloon: KU**—hand twitching

110.5 **FX: FURU FURU**—hand quivering

110.6 **FX/balloon: TO**—finger pointing to chest

111.1 **FX: SUKU**—standing up

112.4 EMDR, strange as it may appear, is a real and reasonably well-studied (though not on corpses) therapy technique, first developed in 1987 by an American psychologist named Francine Shapiro. The efficacy of EMDR has been demonstrated; however, the theory behind why it works (as explained by Dr. Kayama) is somewhat more speculative, but itself may suggest some very intriguing insights into cognitive science. The official website of the EMDR Institute is at http://www.emdr.com/index.htm.

113.2 **FX/balloon: KOKU**—nod

113.4 **FX: KATA KATA KATA**—body beginning to shake

113.5 **FX: GAKU GATAN GATAN**—body really shaking violently

113.6 **FX: KATA GATA GAKUN KATA**—body shaking

114.1 **FX: GAKU GATA GATA**—shaking

114.2 **FX/balloon: BA**—eyes snapping open

114.4 **FX: SUU**—finger moving slowly

114.5 **FX: GATA KATA GATA**—shaking

114.6 **FX: KAKU GATA KAKU**—shaking a little less

115.2 **FX: KATA KATA KATA**—small shakes

116.5 **FX/balloon: GACHA**—door unlocking

117.1 **FX/balloon: KIIII**—door closing slowly

117.2 **FX/balloon: KI**—creaking to a stop

117.3.1 **FX/balloon: BAN**—door slamming shut

117.3.2 **FX/balloon: GACHA**—door locking

118.1 **FX/balloon: SU**—taking out syringe

118.2.1 **FX: DOTA BATA**—sound of struggling feet

118.2.2 **FX/balloon: PASA**—cap falling onto floor

118.3 **FX: GA**—grabbing head

118.4 **FX: PU**—sound of needle piercing skin

118.7 **FX/balloon: DOSA**—body hitting floor

121.2 **FX/balloon: PASA**—putting down photo

124.2 **FX/balloon: SU**—picking up photo

128.2 In this flashback, you see Sasayama much as he appears in the manga *MPD-Psycho*, although if, as he says, this was his first case, it presumably takes place before the events of *MPD*.

130.1 **FX: PAAAAN**—echoing gunshot

135.3 In a Japanese cremation, unlike a typical American one, the remaining fragments of bone are not ground up after the burning of the body; rather, there is a ritual, usually performed by the family of the deceased, of using chopsticks to pick up the fragments and place them in the burial urn. The translator notes this is why it's considered uncouth to ever pass someone food using your chopsticks; he once got bawled out by his grandmother for doing it at the dinner table.

136.2.1 **FX/balloon: BURORORO**—car engine sound

136.2.2 **FX/balloon: KI**—car braking

136.3.1 **FX/balloon: KO**—footstep

136.3.2 **FX/balloon: GO**—heavier sounding footstep. The translator notes that since both "GO" and the previous "KO" seem to belong to Zuhaku (the rattling "KARA"

below is the as-yet unnamed girl's sandal), and since "GO" suggests a heavier sound to him than "KO," he wonders whether there's a subtle suggestion here of a prosthetic foot, or some other element to explain the uneven tread—although it may also simply be a variation.

136.3.3 FX/balloon: KARA—sound of a wooden sandal

137.1 FX/balloon: CHIRA—sound of the girl peering up at the sensor

137.3 FX/balloon: PA—door sensor reacting

137.4 FX/balloon: GAAAA—sound of sliding door opening

137.5 FX/balloons: KATSUUN KATSUUN—echoing footsteps

137.6 FX/balloon: KACHA—door opening

137.7 FX/balloon: GARARA—sound of the body being slid out

138.2 FX/balloon: SU—putting hand out

140.4 FX/balloon: PATAN—closing coffin

141.1 FX/balloon: WIIII—motorized cart sound

141.2 FX/balloon: GOTON—sound of coffin being moved into crematory

141.3 FX/balloon: KACHI—click of a switch

141.4 FX/balloon: WIIIII—sound of fireproof door closing

141.5 FX: GAKOOON—sound of door shutting tight

142.3 FX: KWOOOO—sound of flames beyond the doors

143.1 FX/balloon: SHIBO—lighter igniting

143.3 FX/balloon: TOTO—tapping ashes

144.3 FX/balloon: GUSHI—stubbing out cigarette

144.4 FX: PORI—scratching head

144.5 FX: DOKO—sound of banging on metal doors

144.6 FX: GAN DOKON GON—more banging

144.7 FX: DOKON GAN GON—more banging

145.1 FX: DOKON DON GON—banging sounds

146.2 FX/balloon: GACHA—hitting button

146.3 FX/balloons: VIII VIII VIII—alarm sounds

146.4 FX: GOOO—sound of flames coming out

148.2 FX/balloon: GIRO—glare

148.5 FX/balloon: JYU—sound of skin sizzling

149.3 FX/balloon: GA—grabbing throat sound

152.3 FX/balloon: BA—sprinklers coming on

153.1 FX: ZAAAA—sound of falling water

153.2.1 FX/balloon: GARAN—sound of skull hitting floor

153.2.2 FX/balloon: KARAN—sound of bones hitting floor

155.1 Here we have another first for *Kurosagi*—a side story. I talked to fellow editors Philip Simon and Rob Simpson about what the American comics equivalent of the concept "side story" was, and I wasn't sure there was an exact one. *Solo, stand-alone, flashback, one-shot,* or even *imaginary story* all touch on it, but don't quite meet the mark. Basically, in manga, a side story, or *gaiden*, is a story that is outside the continuity of the main or ongoing storyline, yet evidently connected to it, although it is often left to the reader to figure out exactly how the connection works. It could focus on minor characters, entirely new characters, or even the main characters in a different context. From an LDS point of view, for example, 3 Nephi is a New Testament *gaiden*.

156.1 The Junikai, an icon of the Meiji period, survived it only by eleven years; it was destroyed by the Great Kanto Earthquake of September 1,1923, which left nearly two million homeless and 100,000 dead in the Tokyo era (and thus Tokyo has been destroyed twice within living memory: once by the earthquake, and again by the firebombing raids of 1945).

157.6 FX: SU—opening sliding door

158.2 FX: BA—opening up newspaper

159.1 As anyone who saw *Evangelion* knows, Japan has the custom where young men occasionally take their wife's name upon marriage (often, because the wife has no male siblings, and the bride's father wishes the family name to be carried on through this "adopted" son-in-law). As will be seen in this story, this is what happened eventually to Kunio Matsuoka, who later married into the Yanagita family. Faithful *Kurosagi* readers will also realize this is the same "Kunio Yanagita" whose account of the legend of Dendera Field was central to Vol. 1's 2nd Delivery, "Lonely People." Eiji Otsuka is clearly a fan, so much so that he drafts Matsuoka and Katai Tayama (below) into this Holmes-and-Watson role.

159.2 FX: BASA—closing paper. Katai Tayama would write his most famous story only a few years after the "events" of this manga; 1907's *Futon* (available in English in the 1981 edition *The Quilt and Other Stories* from the University of Tokyo and the Columbia University Press. The title was rendered as "The Quilt," apparently because in 1981, *futon* was not yet accepted as a loan-word in English. Even two years later in *Valley Girl*, Michelle Meyrink would tell Nicolas Cage, "It's like, *sushi*, don't you know"?). Phyllis Lyons, writing in *Monumenta Nipponica*, says of Tayama that "the sheer 'honesty' of his depictions of the dumb, animal misery lodged in the breasts of ordinary men, and thinking men as well, struck a responsive chord in his fellow writers and readers of the day, and gave Katai the professional reputation that had long eluded him."

159.3 FX: DOSA—dropping a thick record book

162.1 **FX/balloon: JARA**—sound of rosary beads moving. We see here the third version of Sasayama in just this volume alone, although presumably this is an ancestor. Despite being in some ways the most worldly and grounded of *Kurosagi's* main cast, Otsuka delights in suggesting odd things about Sasayama, including his near look-alike cousin in Vol. 4.

162.2 **FX: BORI BORI**—scratching sound

163.1.1 **FX/balloons: PIIII PIIII**—police whistles

163.1.2 **FX/balloon: PIIII**—police whistle

163.3 **FX: BA**—sound of the man running by

163.5 **FX: DA**—running off sound

163.6 **FX: TATATA**—running along wall sound

164.1 In the unlikely event you don't read *Blade of the Immortal*, a word about the symbols Yaichi bears on his vest: they are the *manji*, the same counterclockwise version of the swastika borne by *Blade's* eponymous hero, and an ancient symbol of good fortune in Buddhism. It is the clockwise version that the Nazi party made infamous, but as Kenneth Hite points out in *GURPS: Weird War II* (a 144-page, well-researched sourcebook that should be your one-stop shop for everything strange but semi-plausible about the occult, espionage, and mad science aspects of the Second World War) the idea that swastikas going one direction are associated with good, and the other, with evil, is a myth—ones going both ways have been used by various human cultures (including the Greeks and the Navajo). Of course, before you now go bearing one proudly through town, armed with your fresh *Disjecta Membra* knowledge, don't forget a little common sense is always called for.

164.3 **FX: GO**—foot to the face sound

164.4 **FX: DOSA**—sound of man falling down

165.1 **FX: WAAAA**—impressed crowd noise

165.5 **FX/balloon: TSUUU**—sound of blood running down arm

167.2 **FX: BASHA**—sound of a camera flash

168.1 **FX/balloon: BASHA**—camera flash

170.1 This was an famed academic debate, although in RL, as the kids say these days, Professor Tsuboi (1868-1913) had it with Yoshikiyo Koganei (1858-1944), a professor of anatomy at the medical school of Tokyo Imperial University, and the argument was not over some urchin's powers, but as to the ethnic identity of Japan's stone-age people. Actually, there were other differences as well, but, unusually for *Disjecta Membra*, we're not going to get into it.

170.2 **FX: PERO PERO**—licking wound

171.4 **FX: PEKORI**—bowing sound

174.1 Hmm—perhaps Shinhue really *is* a revived Egyptian mummy,

Limey—they're wearin' bloomers in America these days."

193.1 FX/balloon: HAGU—biting into sausage

193.2 FX: MOGU MOGU—chewing sounds

193.3 FX: GA GA GA—munching sound

193.4 FX/balloons: MOGU MOGU—chewing sounds

193.5.1 FX/balloons: MUSHA MUSHA—eating sounds

193.5.2 FX/balloons: BAKU AKU—more eating sounds

194.2 Flashback FX: KUI—moving telescope sound from 182.2

194.5 FX: GUU GUU—snoring

196.3 FX: BA—Yaichi's eyes snapping open

196.5 FX: GATA—getting up from chair

197.1 FX: BAN—door banging open

197.5 The practice of students in Tokyo working as houseboys for local families in exchange for room and board was known as *shosei*, and was common during the Meiji and Taisho eras. It is also, of course, a practice seen among the contemporaneous protagonists ("contemporaneous protagonists" is battling it out with *Monumenta Nipponica* for the most pretentious phrase this volume—there's still time to vote) of Stonebridge Press's (Jamie WHASSUP) much-recommended *The Four Immigrants Manga: A Japanese Experience in San Francisco, 1904-1924*. Translated by Frederik Schodt (perhaps the only person *capable* of translating

Shirow's *Ghost in the Shell*—go thing he does it), *The Four Immigrants Manga* was originally a sort of 1930s doujinshi that circulated only among creator Yoshitaka "Henry" Kiyama and his friends, giving an account of the ups and downs of Japanese immigrant life in early-20th century America. Japanese houseboys were considered a status symbol in many prosperous white American households, although one of the eponymous *Four Immigrants* does note to himself (while peeling potatoes) that even though he's educated, he's making more money as a houseboy in America than he could expect in a white-collar job back in Japan.

198.2 FX: PIKU PIGU—eyes twitching in anger

198.4 FX: BA—jumping sound

198.5 FX/balloon: PASHI—foot stopping arm

199.1 FX: DOKA—kicking sound

199.2 FX: DON GATAN—sound of falling on the floor then falling over

199.3 FX: NU—sound of the killer standing

199.4 FX: HYUN HYUN—sound of the knife swishing through the air

200.1 FX/balloon: PASHI—blocking sound

200.3 FX/balloon: SUTA—landing on windowsill

200.4 FX/balloon: BA—jumping sound

200.5 FX/balloon: ZA—landing sound

201.1 FX/balloon: TO—landing on ledge sound

and not just a burn victim who happens to be an expert on ancient Egyptian burial practices.

174.3 **FX: GOTO**—coffin being moved

174.4 **FX: GAKU GOTO**—coffins being moved

174.5 **FX/balloon: GORORI**—sound of the body rolling over

176.2 **FX/balloon: TON**—hopping over body sound

177.2 For "houses of assignation," Tayama used the archaic word (it was explained even in the original Japanese) *ageya*, meaning a house you would rent temporarily to arrange a visit by a prostitute. The French used to call these *maisons de passe*; it seems to have been one of the endless dodges (see also p. 183) used in human societies to conceal or skirt the issues of ho'in.

177.4 **FX: BORI BORI**—scratching sound

178.1 **FX/balloon: BORI**—scratching sound

179.3 **FX: HYUUU**—sound of wind

182.2 **FX/balloon: KUI**—moving telescope

187.1 **FX: SU**—taking out photo from an envelope

187.3 **FX: GABIIIN**—shocked / aghast sound

188.4 **FX: GARI**—scratching head

189.1 Another unusual example of fourth-wall breaking in *Kurosagi* Vol. 6; usually, characters don't deign to notice the sound FX.

189.6 **FX: GATA**—getting up out of chair

190.3 **FX/balloon: KACHA**—sound of clinking silverware

191.3 **FX: CHIRA**—peering over sound

192.2 **FX: KATA**—a plate being put down. The maid used the old-fashioned *chozume* for sausage, which means literally "stuffed intestine"—although, of course, that is traditionally how sausages are made.

192.4 The paper Tamiya has been reading from appears to be a copy of Vol. 1 of *Famous Crimes: Past and Present*, an illustrated broadsheet released in 1903—hence suggesting a possible date for the events of this chapter of the manga, as it is the latest datable event mentioned within the story itself. *Famous Crimes* was edited by Harry Furniss, who is said to have also done illustrations for the famous Victorian magazine *Puck* (whose Meiji-era Japanese imitator *Tokyo Puck* was featured in Frederik Schodt's indispensable history *Manga! Manga!*). Vol. 1 of *Famous Crimes*, a special on Jack the Ripper, was reprinted in a facsimile edition in 1999 by Dave Froggatt (all four volumes of the series were more recently reprinted by Thomas Schachner), and it's quite possible that Eiji Otsuka, an author himself known for his interest in serial killers, laid ink- (if not blood) stained hands on a copy. As for Furniss, a final otaku irony is that he is said to have later emigrated to America and worked on pioneering animated films for Thomas Edison. "What'd you say that was called again, fella? *Gothic Lolita*? I don't know about all them petticoats,

201.3 FX: **HYUTOTO**—jumping and running down side of house

201.4 FX/balloon: **ZA**—landing sound

202.4 FX: **HYUWOOO**—sound of an incoming lunge

202.5.1 FX/balloon: **BACHIN**—sound of jaws snapping

202.5.2 FX/balloon: **KUWA**—sound of jaws opening wide

202.6 FX/balloon: **ZA**—footsteps running into alley

203.1.1 FX/balloon: **ZA**—footstep

203.1.2 FX/balloon: **GARARAN**—sound of a bucket being kicked over

203.5.1 FX/balloon: **BA**—sound of killer quickly turning around

203.5.2 FX/balloon: **BASHAN**—sound of door being shut (wooden door with windows that rattle a bit)

203.6 FX/balloon: **TO**—landing sound

204.2 FX: **GARA GARARA**—sound of wooden wheels on a rickshaw rolling

204.4 FX: **TO**—landing sound

204.5 FX/balloon: **GARA**—sound of door being slid open

205.2 FX/balloon: **KO**—knocking on brick

206.1 FX: **DOSA**—sound of the young man falling down

206.4 FX: **PIIIII**—whistling sound

207.1 FX: **NU**—spirit coming through wall

207.2 The *Misaki* are said to be spirits that manifest as a precursor to a god or other higher spiritual power entering the human world. They often take the form of a fox or *yatagarasu*, a kind of crow or raven, which are themselves the totemic forms of certain Japanese gods.

208.2.1 FX/balloons: **GATA KATA**—sound of rattling coming from the coffin

208.2.2 FX/balloon: **KATA**—sound of rattling coming from the coffin

208.2.3 FX/balloons: **GATA KATA**—sound of rattling coming from the coffin

208.4 FX/balloon: **GATAN**—sound of a coffin lid coming off

209.3 FX: **GATA GATAN**—sound of more coffins opening

213.1 Though Price Albert Victor (the genital piercing of fame is sometimes said to be named for him, although more often for his grandfather, Victoria's Prince Consort) has been associated with the Jack the Ripper murders in folklore since the 1960s, and perhaps most famously in comics through Alan Moore and Eddie Campbell's *From Hell*, the idea is long on theories and short on evidence. Albert Victor, a.k.a., "Prince Eddy" died in 1892, so any guest appearance he might make in this story would have to be as a spirit. Interestingly, however, he apparently *did* visit Meiji Japan during his naval service in 1881. In his *The Japanese Tattoo and Britain During the Meiji Period* (Cambridge University Library) Noboru Koyama suggests that Prince Eddy (as well as other noble Royal Navy officers, including the future King George V) received traditional tattoos there; Admiral Lord Charles Beresford wrote of "the astonishment of Japanese officials and nobles" at this, for "in Japan none save the common people is tattooed."

213.4 FX/balloon: GAKO—taking telescope off of the stand

213.6 FX: BYUN—throwing sound

214.1 FX/balloon: JAPOOON—splash

214.3 Ryudoken is a famous French restaurant in the Roppongi district of Tokyo, over a century old. It played an important part in the cultural life of prewar Japan, being known as the literary canteen of the so-called "naturalist" novelists, including Doppo Kunikida (whose *River Mist and Other Stories* is available in English from Kodansha) Toson Shimazaki (his ground-breaking *Broken Commandment* is translated by the University of Tokyo Press), as well as Kunio Yanaigta and Katai Tayama themselves. Ryudoken also gained political notoriety as the meeting place of the radical Kodoha faction of the Imperial Japanese Army, a clique led by junior officers that advocated a return to the traditional values of pre-Westernized Japan, purged of foreign ideas. Their famous attempted coup of February 26–29, 1936 (still known as the *Ni-Niroku jiken*, or "2/26 Incident" in Japan) failed, but in retrospect, Kodoha's decision to make a French restaurant the hangout of their cause seems to suggest a certain lack of ideological rigor. You can still hatch plots of your own at Ryukoden, located at 1-14-3 Nishi-Azabu, Minato-ku, Tokyo 106-0031, tel 03-3408-5839. Reservations recommended.

214.5 The custom Tayama alludes to here is from Pentecost Island (what are the odds the word "Pentecost" would show up twice in the same manga?), today part of the South Pacific nation of Vanuatu—it is said that this centuries-old practice of "land diving," also known as the Nagol ceremony, is what would later inspired the origins of modern bungee jumping in the late 1970s. The tourism board of Vanuatu describes it in some detail at www.vanuatutourism.com/vanuatu/cms/en/islands/pentecost_maewo.html

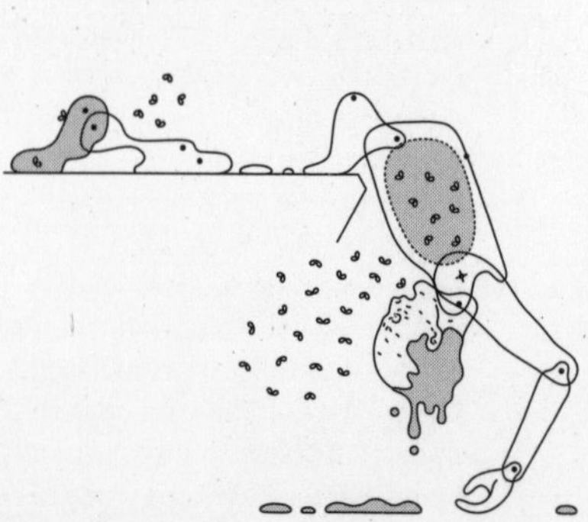